The Promise of Memory

SUNY series in Contemporary Continental Philosophy

Dennis J. Schmidt, editor

THE PROMISE
OF MEMORY

History and Politics in
Marx, Benjamin, and Derrida

MATTHIAS FRITSCH

STATE UNIVERSITY OF NEW YORK PRESS

Published by
STATE UNIVERSITY OF NEW YORK PRESS
ALBANY

For information, address
State University of New York Press
194 Washington Avenue, Suite 305, Albany, NY 12210-2384

Production, Laurie Searl
Marketing, Anne M. Valentine

Library of Congress Cataloging-in-Publication Data

Fritsch, Matthias.
   The promise of memory : history and politics in Marx, Benjamin, and
Derrida / Matthias Fritsch.
      p. cm. — (SUNY series in contemporary continental philosophy)
   Includes bibliographical references and index.
   ISBN 0-7914-6549-7 (hardcover : alk. paper) — ISBN 0-7914-6550-0
   (pbk. : alk. paper)
    1. Marx, Karl, 1818–1883. 2. History—Philosophy. 3. Political
science—Philosophy. 4. Benjamin, Walter, 1892–1940. 5. Derrida,
Jacques. I. Title. II. Series.

JC233.M299F758 2005
335.4'119—dc22
                                                          2004029610

10   9   8   7   6   5   4   3   2   1

Contents

Acknowledgments

Perhaps we expect an author's gratitude from a book on memory in particular, although the gratitude would have to be inseparable from the promises it carries from those who helped it leave an imprint visible at least for a time. Since the list of helpers necessarily ends, without ending, in the sea of the nameless, naming names is not an unproblematic gesture; I will have to assume its violence, even if it exceeds me. Rudi Morawietz first introduced me, in the no-man's land of rural apoliticism, to philosophy in general, and the burning pages of Benjamin's "Theses" in particular. Günter Schulte inoculated madness into those trying to read Stirner, Marx, and Nietzsche. John Caputo's erudition and clarity proved to be invaluable. Discussions with Dennis Schmidt created an atmosphere in which ideas proliferated and grew into arguments. I would also like to thank the Social Sciences and Humanities Research Council of Canada and the Fonds québécois de la recherche sur la société et la culture for financial assistance at some points in the development and execution of this project. Most of all, those who built today's riches, fought for an educational system allowing people with little means to study, and those who wrote about such struggles, need to be acknowledged as having generated the bulk of this book. Maybe epigone is not such a bad title to bear, even on Sundays.

Abbreviations

References to the frequently used French texts cite the page number of the English translation first, followed by the original. Occasionally, translations have been modified. All translations from Benjamin's works are my own, though I may have consulted English translations when they exist.

I–VII   Walter Benjamin, *Gesammelte Schriften*. References give the volume number followed by the page number.

CV   Walter Benjamin, "On the Critique of Violence" In *One-Way Street and Other Writings*. Translated by E. Jephcott, Kingsley Shorter. London: Verso, 1979.

"Thesis"   Walter Benjamin, "Über den Begriff der Geschichte," I 691–I 704. English translation: "Theses on the Philosophy of History" in: *Illuminations. Essays and Reflections*. Translated by H. Zohn. New York: Schocken, 1968.

AF   Jacques Derrida, *Archive Fever. A Freudian Impression*. Translated by E. Prenowitz. Chicago: University of Chicago Press, 1996. (*Mal d'Archive*. Paris: Galilée, 1995.)

FL   Jacques Derrida, "Force of Law: The 'mystical foundation of authority,'" *Cardozo Law Review* 11:5–6 (1990). The French original is on the facing pages.

Points   Jacques Derrida, *Points . . . Interviews, 1974–94*, ed. E. Weber. Translated by P. Kamuf et al. Stanford: Stanford University Press, 1995. (*Points de suspension. Entretiens*. Paris: Galilée, 1992.)

OG   Jacques Derrida, *Of Grammatology*. Translated by G. Spivak. Baltimore: Johns Hopkins University Press, 1976. (*De la grammatologie*. Paris: Minuit, 1967.)

SM   Jacques Derrida, *Specters of Marx*. Translated by P. Kamuf. New York: Routledge, 1994. (*Spectres de Marx*. Paris: Éditions Galilée, 1993.)

WD   Jacques Derrida, *Writing and Difference*. Translated by A. Bass. Chicago: University of Chicago Press, 1978. (*L'écriture et la différence*. Paris: Éditions du Seuil, 1967.)

Capital   Karl Marx, *Capital, Volume One*. Translated by Ben Fowkes. New York: Vintage Books, 1977.

Exordium

───────────────────────

Among the many prosopopeitic voices, the voices of stones and of the dead, the poetry of Paul Celan has bequeathed two words to us. There is the word that might reach us through the scars of time, by way of groping fingers and through haunting darkness. Then there is the word of the shepherd, a former Spanish revolutionary. The first is a word of suffering, put to sleep by time, unrecognized by those who do not see, a word that tries to awake, a word that wishes to shine, against the odds:

Engführung

[. . .]
Der Ort, wo sie lagen, er hat
einen Namen—er hat
keinen. Sie lagen nicht dort. Etwas
lag zwischen ihnen. Sie sahn nicht hindurch.
Sahn nicht, nein, redeten von Worten. Keines
erwachte, der
Schlaf kam über sie.
*

[. . .]
Jahre.
Jahre, Jahre, ein Finger
tastet hinab und hinan, tastet
umher:
Nahtstellen, fühlbar, hier
klafft es weit auseinander, hier
wuchs es wieder zusammen—wer
deckte es zu?
*

       Deckte es
          zu—wer?
Kam, kam.
Kam ein Wort, kam,

The Straitening

[. . .]
The place where they lay, it has
a name—it has
none. They did not lie there. Something
lay between them. They did not see
through it. Did not see, no, spoke of
words. None awoke,
sleep came over them.
*

[. . .]
Years.
Years, years, a finger
feels down and up, feels
around:
seams, palpable, here
it is split wide open, here
it grew together again—who
covered it up?
*

       Covered it
          up—who?
Came, came.
Came a word, came,

kam durch die Nacht,	came through the night,
wollt leuchten, wollt leuchten.	wanted to shine, wanted to shine.
Asche.	Ash.
Asche, Asche.	Ash, ash.
[. . .]	[. . .][1]

One might suggest here that the word that wishes to shine names the word of suffering opening up another history, speaking, with Levinas, against the history of the appropriation of the works of the dead and for the dead themselves, trying to recall those forgotten by time, calling us to responsibly inherit by responding to the dead.[2] One might also argue, with Derrida, that the ashes reveal that "no one bears witness for the witness," as Celan's *"Aschenglorie"* has it, revealing an affinity between a date, a proper name, and ashes. As repetition and as memory, time relentlessly reduces the name of the dead to ashes, exposing every date to the wound inscribed within it, adding a second holocaust, at every hour, to the Holocaust that is "the hell of our memory."[3] And yet the question resonates: "Who covered it up?" Who—not what—covered up the scars that memory tries to retrace, like a finger groping along the seams of time through which the word must pass? Remaining ambiguous, hovering between time itself and the irresponsible inheritor, between ineluctable finitude and redressable occlusion, the cover-up indicates the night through which the word must shine while it burns to ashes.

The other word grows out of the constellation of dates in order to invent a new calendar, against the forgetful calendar that, in suggesting the identity of all time with the objective time of nature, with what Benjamin calls homogenous and empty time, suppresses the singularity of what is dated in it.[4] This constellation configures 'in one' what is otherwise separated, thus "blasting out of the continuum of history" a past "filled with the presence of 'now,'" actualizing that which concerns the present most of all, but lies buried under the canons of cultural history.[5]

In Eins	*In One*
Dreizehnter Feber. Im Herzmund	Thirteenth of February. Shibboleth
erwachtes Schibboleth. Mit dir,	roused in the heart's mouth. With you,
Peuple	Peuple
de Paris. *No pasaràn.*	de Paris. *No pasaràn.*
Schäfchen zur Linken: er, Abadias,	Little sheep to the left: he, Abadias,
der Greis aus Huesca, kam mit den Hunden	the old man from Huesca, came with
über das Feld, im Exil,	his dogs over the field, in exile
stand weiß wie eine Wolke	white hung a cloud
menschlichen Adels, er sprach	of human nobility, into our hands
uns das Wort in die Hand, das wir brauchten, es war	he spoke the word that we needed, it
Hirten-Spanisch, darin,	was shepherd-Spanish, and in it

im Eislicht des Kreuzers 'Aurora':
die Bruderhand, winkend mit der
von den wortgroßn Augen
genommenen Binde—Petropolis, der
Unvergessenen Wanderstadt lag
auch dir toskanisch zu Herzen.

Friede den Hütten!

in icelight of the cruiser 'Aurora':
the brotherly hand, waving with
the blindfold removed from
word-wide eyes—Petropolis, the
roving city of those unforgotten,
was Tuscanly close to your heart also.

Peace to the Cottages![6]

This word is also one of memory, but this time of a revolutionary memory, recalling resistance to oppression as a promise of peace. It is the word that we need, that concerns us most of all, for, by it, the past intends and addresses the present. Its regional dialect does not prevent it from indicating universal human nobility. It speaks in many tongues, and the old age of the revolutionary does not detract from its power. Rather, its saturation with a political memory of action opens eyes, frees for a memory of the unforgotten, and aims at the elimination of war. It acts as a shibboleth, granting passage to those who reach out with the brotherly hand. In moving from mouth to hand, the promissory word of the past incites to action in the present.

The following work wonders about the relationship between these two words of memory. How does the word of the revolutionary promise, a memory geared toward the future, relate to the word of suffering that resists being covered up, and that wonders who covered up the scars of the past? The argument unfolded in the following pages is that only in conjunction, intermingling the word of a memory of suffering and the word of the promise, can they form what Celan has called a counterword (*Gegenwort*). This counterword is a word of resistance; it speaks of a memory of suffering that is also a memory of the future. It is the "word that does not bow down before the 'do-nothings' and 'show-horses' of history, it is an act of freedom. It is a step."[7]

Introduction

How can one at all remember the final, non-revisable loss of the victims of the historical process to whom one owes oneself, and still be happy, still find one's identity?
—Helmut Peukert, *Science, Action, and Fundamental Theology*, 209 (translation modified)

It has often been remarked that the events of the twentieth century in particular, and, we might add, of Western modernity in general, force its inheritors to reconsider the structure and content of a 'tradition' that they might still feel compelled to recognize as 'theirs,' even if its 'ownership,' and the limits of the community it implies, is part of what is in question. These events—from two world wars to Vietnam, from the Holocaust to the Gulag—ask us to question the basic assumptions guiding our lives that we inherited from a past whose continued relevance and moral worth have become problematic due to the violent victimizations that they brought about. Neoliberal triumphalism responds with the counting and comparing of the victims of fascism and communism, while its own, in the past and in the present, are deemed unworthy by its increasingly centralized media conglomerates that try to write history as it happens.[1] The calculation of victims takes place in an age that is marked by an increasing acceleration of technological 'progress' and change, and thus by a rise of calculative rationality as well as a rapid outmoding and forgetting of times that count as contemporary. Some have characterized these accelerated times as being marked by an increasing repression of death, even an incapacity to mourn for the dead in general, and the victims of political violence in particular.[2]

Nonetheless, current political and cultural discourses cannot avoid a less calculative response to this situation. While many countries faced with the long aftermath of direct and indirect Western colonialism, from Argentina to

South Africa, set up the now-famous Truth and Reconciliation Commissions,[3] the most economically developed countries, while generally averse to such commissions about their own past, witness a variety of seemingly disparate debates about the significance of assuming a memory of the victims of past historical and political violence. To name but the most contemporary and mediatized debates, we might refer to the now well-known historian's debate of the 1980s in Germany and the discussions about the gigantic Holocaust Memorial in reunified Berlin; the political debates about the legacy of Stalinism that are particularly prevalent in Russia, but also in France and Italy with their strong Communist Parties; the political and legal questions currently resurfacing in the United States and Canada about affirmative action and the justification of privileging in certain contexts the descendants of the victims of past slavery, dispossession, genocide, and sexist exclusion. What these debates have in common is that they revolve around the issues of the manner in which historical atrocities can be remembered, given their due, and what promises they imply for the future.

The discussions in and around TRCs, memorials, and histories' victims, then, attempt to connect the memory of past violence with a promise for a just future. Regarding affirmative action, for instance, it has occasionally been observed that this largely compensatory practice is Janus-faced, that is, forward- and backward-looking at the same time.[4] It is directed toward the 'rectification' of past injustice as well as toward the building of a more tolerant and egalitarian future. Hence, even if we, perhaps naively, believe in an ultimately final compensation or rectification of past loss and suffering, the attempt to account for it in the present takes place in view of a better and less violent future to which we promise our efforts to remember. In this way, as I will try to elaborate, the issue of memory is always linked to the question of a future promise, or perhaps even a utopia, in the broadest sense of this word, despite the fact that our times appear to have liberated themselves from the great historical narratives that project themselves onto a goal in the future.

Without a more sustained reflection on the relation between memory and promise, however, the debates in question remain faced with the danger of favoring one at the expense of the other. If the memory of victimization is brought to the foreground without clear recourse to a promise of change, the insistence on violence and irretrievable loss may slip into a melancholic occlusion of the promise inherent in all useless suffering. Moreover, a peculiarly late-modern culture of victimhood witnesses all parties vying for the desired status of a victim in an endless battle that tends to hamper both the mutual understanding that is necessary for the formation of collective agency and the concentrated political action of agents less willing to rest content with the receiving end of welfare measures. Perhaps even more disastrously, such memory can easily lend itself to the oblivion, or even justification, of violence inflicted on others—in the past as well as in the present and the future. According to the faulty reasoning that petrifies a victim's identity, victims and their descendents are incapable of themselves becoming perpetrators.

On the other hand, promises of justice without reflective links to memory may also lead to the justification of violent means claimed to be necessary on the way to an end that alone is seen as just. The problem here is particularly pernicious if it is bolstered by two views intimately connected to the self-understanding of Western modernity: the idea of the progressive unfolding of history toward a just end, especially if the claimed progress assigns tasks to agents who thus know themselves to be in agreement with the meaning of history, and the equally illusory dream of wiping the slate clean, cutting one's losses, and beginning all over again.[5] While the idea of progress, in its self-righteousness similar to the cultivation of supposed victimhood, neglects real regress, the *tabula-rasa* approach not only abandons the hopes of the past and victimizes the dead a second time, but forgets its own historicity and, with it, perhaps its finitude. Reflection on politically viable interpenetrations of memories and promises is thus very much in demand.

If the legacy of Marxism appears a particularly promising starting point for this reflection—thus justifying the fact that I will single it out as a springboard for developing the promise of memory—it is not only because Marxism is implicated in the unleashing of the totalitarian violence the last century had to witness. Less controversially than, say, Western capitalism, institutions that professed to adhere to a kind of Marxism allowed that unleashing to happen precisely in the name of a promise for emancipation and liberation. Efforts to uncover this violence culminated in the publication of the *Livre Noir du Communisme* in which, among others, former partisans settle devastating accounts with the history of communism, figuring the number of its victims around eighty million.[6] If one does not wish to prematurely sign the death certificate issued for Marx's promise, the need to reformulate it in light of a memory of violence recommends itself: to maintain it, the promise must be articulated with a memory of especially the victims of its own attempt to institutionalize itself. Such articulation may begin with an inquiry into the possibility of the promise to lead to totalitarian violence. Speaking summarily, the emancipatory promise needs to be divested of its tie to a logic of history that guarantees its victorious fulfillment by which, as the verdict of History, it can justify suffering in the past and in the present. Correspondingly, the understanding of memory is to be definalized, such that the suffering of the past cannot be thought to be overcome or redeemed once and for all.

On the other hand, the Marxist promise is, of course, itself heir to the Enlightenment to which Western capitalist democracy owes its roots as well. This might suffice to dispel the simple acknowledgment of the Marxist failure in favor of a neoliberal alternative by default. At the same time, and despite appearances, a look at Marx with questions of memory in mind reveals that he already attempted to link memories of historical atrocities with the idea of the classless society. Thus, uncovering and criticizing the sort of link between memory and promise that Marx proposes, and doing so to prevent atrocious outcomes in the name of justice, expands the focus on the victims of institutionalized Marxism to include the victims of what we might term the instituting violence of capitalism. The memory of this violence is, today more than ever, equally necessary to maintain the Enlightenment promise of justice in general and Marx's version in particular. For one of the greatest challenges for the promise of democratic equality is the very real lack of motivation on the part of the less well-off, especially in the most developed countries. In an age increasingly characterized by the prevalence of instrumental over moral and political rationality, this lack must to a large extent be explained by the partial overlap of strategic interests between owners or managers of productive assets and those they hire to amortize the value of these assets—an overlap that results in part from an absence of radically different political economies, which in turn is connected to the weakness of motivated action aiming at such different arrangements. As is well known, under the partly ideological and normative banner of globalization, the latter today threatens democratic nations and citizens with capital flight, thus exploiting what Adam Przeworski, following Gramsci, calls the "material basis of consent."[7] In this context, it is crucial to recall the violence in history that brought about the 'consent,' and that what Marx called the "silent compulsion of economic relations" (*Capital* 899)—the highly ambiguous 'freedom' to sell one's labor power in the absence of other modes of access to productive assets—could only be able to secure consent once more directly physical and state-organized forms of violence had done their job. Here, an often overlooked form of motivation directly connected to historical memory can complement, in crucial ways, normative or strategic motives for political action, and help build communities of resistance.[8]

As these reflections indicate, the political inheritance of Marx and Marxism today requires a reelaboration not only of the understanding of the promise for emancipation, but also of the political import of memory. For this reason, the present work will investigate in what way the promise and memory can be conjoined in a single constellation. In this constellation, the promise must include a memory of loss and suffering, while such memory will be seen to be invested with a promise that renders it both interminable and allows it to further contribute to political changes in the present: *a memory of the promise as well as a promise of memory.* The resulting reformulated promise thus cannot be seen to surpass or overcome its own troubled history, but needs to revise the temporality that merely opposes the future to the past, that plays off a utopia, or any future ideal, to the remembrance of the past.

In attempting this constellation of a promise and its inheritance, I will draw on a number of texts by Jacques Derrida, including *Specters of Marx*

(1993), which stands out as an engaged philosophical response to the inheritance of Marxism after 1989. But I will also enlist Walter Benjamin's significant but recondite rewriting of Marx's promise in the 1920s and 1930s, in the wake of the Russian Revolution and the rise of fascism in Western Europe, and in the context of his broader philosophical and historiographical investigations into the political legacy of the nineteenth century. The interweaving of the texts and proposals of these authors will occur gradually in the course of the entire work. In the remainder of this introduction, I will present a brief synopsis of the main argument.

In the interest of holding on to a political promise of a just future while articulating it with a memory of injustice and historical violence, the first chapter investigates Benjamin's reading of Marx. I begin with Marx's account of the relation between the memory of violence and the promise of liberation. Contrary to superficial readings and some later Marxists, I show that Marx is very well aware of the political significance of such memory, especially in regard to the non-economic violence that was required to set modern capitalism on its path. The reading of Marx advanced here vindicates Benjamin's positive yet selective appropriation of Marx in this regard against those who accuse him of serious misunderstandings. However, Benjamin criticizes the way in which Marx connects the memory of violence with the promise for a classless society. If the connection is made by way of a teleo-logic of history that accounts for both the violence of the past and the necessity of liberation, the promised future is viewed as, in some sense, redeeming and possibly justifying the violence that is to be remembered. It is in this context that Benjamin rejects 'communist goals' and demonstrates the ultimately quietist consequences of reading history in terms of allegedly scientific laws and a final, redemptive goal. Benjamin accuses orthodox Marxism, beginning with certain texts by Marx himself, of conceiving the victims of yesterday as the rightful victors of tomorrow. A logic of certain victory has overtaken and absorbed the indignation at suffering and oppression, a logic that is willing to trade off a memory of the oppressed in favor of the speculative appropriation of the victims' alienated works in and for the future, in the form of technological advances and the creation of a universalized humanity. Rather than the promise of certain victory, it is the memory of past victimization, and the uncovering of the 'barbarism' at the heart of the material and cultural richness of a tradition, that are essential to motivate resistance in the present. This resistance seizes the political chances of the day, rather than postponing them to an indefinite future. Accordingly, as I show toward the end of chapter one, Benjamin outlines two tasks required for the reception of what he calls the messianic claim of the oppressed of history. The first concerns a materialist method of reading history that I will deal with in chapter four, and the second, addressed in chapter three, concerns a concept of political action that resists established power in the present. Resistance and materialist historiography must go hand in hand for Benjamin, as the latter helps motivate the former, which in turn resists, along with oppressive relations in the present, dominant discourses of history that occlude a memory of victimization.

However, Benjamin largely lacks the conceptual temporal account he needs to maintain a connection between memory and promise, past and future, while refusing Marx's teleological one. This account is to link futural openness, the general interpretability of the past and the constructedness of stories of continuous progress, and memorial retrieval in and through the discontinuity of time. Apart from some general obscurities, this lack becomes clear in the reemergence of an opposition between images of 'enslaved ancestors' and 'liberated grandchildren,' and is connected to his apparent rejection of Kantian regulative ideas (or 'realistic utopias') in general as quietist, not just those whose goal is promised on the basis of an allegedly scientific teleology. In part to remedy these defects, chapter two turns to Derrida's account of the promise of memory in terms of the quasi-transcendental law of repetition. What I will call the promise of repetition establishes an intimate connection between, on the one hand, a thinking of the promise to an open future—as the promise *that* there is a future rather than of *what* the future will bring—and the not only political, but also (quasi-) transcendental necessity of memory, on the other. For Derrida rethinks the nature of the promise in general as not one speech act among others, but as a promise that opens up the past and the present to an interminable repetition from the future. Insofar as memory is a kind of repetition, it is thereby exposed by the promise to an unforeseeable future, a future whose unpredictably changing contexts turn repetition into a productive 'iteration' in difference. I will unfold the thinking of this ineluctable and quasi-transcendental promise in order to demonstrate its productivity for the conjoining of memory and the promise in general, and the reformulation of the Marxist promise of history in particular. In regard to the latter, we will see that an emancipatory discourse that promises itself to the future cannot conceive of the future and its alterity as a radical liberation from the past or as the fulfillment of the essential mission or telos of history. Rather than projecting the revolution as a radical break with the past, a break that involves a relinquishing of the dead, this discourse needs to restructure its prophetic promise so as to make room for memory.

In the last section of chapter two, I show that Derrida's account of the relation of history to the future is not antiutopian, as it does not reject the projection of political goals altogether. It is better understood as what we might call postutopian, in that it reveals the necessity of projecting horizons of the future which, however, are never final. His is a more complex concept of the future that allows for both projected horizons of writing history or stipulating political goals, and a more radical, empty future 'to come' that constitutes at once the possibility of memory and the impossibility of final accounts of history. The Derridian account of the promise-memory nexus

thus effectively complements Benjamin's mere gesture at a temporality linking an open future and memory without a reemerging opposition between
future and past. It also does not disallow utopian projections, but renders
them eminently contestable. At the same time, against the quietist conclusions Benjamin feared in the Kantian Marxism of his day, the future to come
also signals the ethical and political urgency of interrupting attempted
progress toward stipulated goals.

Having discussed Benjamin's political import of memory and Derrida's
conceptual link between memory and the future, I then seek to integrate the
two in chapter three by revisiting Benjamin's "Critique of Violence" and Derrida's reading thereof. However, before the issues raised in the first two chapters can be interwoven in this way, I attempt to demonstrate the coherence
of the early Benjamin's reflections on violence and power with his later texts
on history. The connection between early and late Benjamin will help
explain what the "Theses" mean by the historical continuity of power relations and the history of victors, as well as its 'messianic standstill' brought
about by way of political action as well as in historiography. Concerning the
former, Benjamin proposes a decidedly non-instrumental mode of political
action, which he describes in terms of Sorel's proletarian strike. It exposes the
violence embedded in politico-legal institutions of the 'victors' who tend to
write history in terms of progress, teleology, and final goals, thereby muffling
the resistance that both reveals the violence subtending history and that is to
be conditioned and motivated by it. Only a non-instrumental, and hence
nonviolent, resistance to the capitalist state, as a representative of class
power, can be both responsive to and liberate a memory of victims. Since this
non-instrumental action proceeds from the need of power to continually re-
institute itself according to what Benjamin calls a 'law of oscillation,' receiving and assuming the messianic call of history's 'oppressed' is made possible
by the finitude of power itself. Only the transience of all power, its inherent
weakness and exposition to change, allows for a concept of action that breaks
through inherited power relations and thus frees us for a memory of victims.

Derrida and Benjamin will be seen to agree that the finitude of power
contributes what Benjamin calls a 'weak messianic force' to the struggle
against oppression in the present and for a memory of victims. However, Derrida's reconsideration of power, law, and justice complicates in significant ways
Benjamin's theory of a non-instrumental, nonviolent, and memorial political
action. If Derrida's 'law of repetition' is seen to operate as Benjamin's 'law of
oscillation' at the heart of all power, there can be no messianic realm free of
state power, law, and violence. Since we must resist the temptation to oppose
the messianic in a binary fashion to a political power that Benjamin sees as
conducting a violent politics, we cannot see law and power as being interrupted or even overturned from without, as Benjamin ambiguously suggests.
Consequently, we also cannot single out a subject (such as the proletariat) that

would be uniquely situated to respond to past victimization and to receive the messianic claim of past generations upon the present one. The promise of repetition, opening the past as well as power and law to an indeterminate ('messianic') future, also returns the constitution of such a subject to the ever renewed work of repetition, thus disallowing a clear dividing line between the dominant and the dominated, between violence and nonviolence, and between memory and forgetting. Derrida's concept of the differential promise of repetition points us to the necessity of a democratic negotiation of questions regarding the identification of victors and oppressed.

In fact, we will see Derrida argue that the messianic promise not only opens up the past for its inheritance and remembrance, but that it also institutes an 'originary violence' at the heart of all action and an originary forgetting at the heart of all memory. This is what Derrida names the double bind of all inheritance: Memory also effaces that which preserves itself only by way of memory. In the fourth and last chapter, I discuss the implications of this double bind and this originary violence for Benjamin's messianic claim of the dead. Contrasting Benjamin and Derrida on the question of the relationship between memory and responsibility, we will see that the latter resituates the messianic call as arising not with the dead or even with identifiable victims (of capitalist modernity, say), but with this originary violence itself. Accordingly, I first show that Benjamin's proposals for reading dominant history against the grain and for constructing a counterhistorical montage of history's trash demonstrate that Benjamin seeks the claim of the dead, as a call to responsibility, in inherited cultures and traditions, rather than, like Levinas, beyond visible history altogether. I then ask how the attempt to render legible the double violence of history—at the level of *res gestae* and the occlusions at the level of *rerum gestarum memoria*—may be reconciled with an emphasis on the inevitable violence of all memory as well as of all calls to responsibility.

Derrida thinks an anterior otherness that is installed in responsible subjects as the (continually withdrawing) origin of ethical and political responsibility insofar as it opens up the subject of responsibility in the first place. He claims that a 'nonpositive' affirmation of human finitude as anterior alterity, as the pre-cedence of language and inheritance, is the condition of all responsible politics, and can be said to elaborate Benjamin's thought of the messianic claim of the dead on the living. However, Derrida's notion of responsibility names only the originary opening up of every subject to otherness, and thus indicates the condition of possibility of moral and political concepts of responsibility. Hence, I will argue that Derrida's suggestion—according to which his account of our responsibility in the face of a history of violence is close to Benjamin's messianic claim of past generations—overlooks that, for Benjamin, this claim is first and foremost linked to the oppressed of a particular history and a particular cultural transmission of that history, such that the claim is muffled or drowned out by it, rather than originating with the dead in general, and being muffled, merely or primarily, by finitude and its originary violence as such. Accordingly, Derrida's notion of responsibility cannot do without Benjamin's more concrete account of a politically responsible relation to the violence of capitalist modernity, as exposed in chapter one. For Derrida's argument, I will show, entails that there is no otherness 'as such'; rather, spectral anteriority can only be thought within a particular context and a specific history of violence. If Derrida's affirmation of an originary injunction is to be more than a traditionalist affirmation of the inherited canons and dominant hegemonic discourses of the past, it must affirm what is excluded and forgotten by the canons that tend to hide the voice of suffering. Thus, the affirmation of an originary otherness must be transformed, with Benjamin, into the exposure of the specific and unnecessary 'barbarism' that allows those canons to legitimate themselves in the first place.

I will argue, then, for a productive oscillation between Derrida's insistence on the 'unreadability of violence' and Benjamin's demand that violence be made legible. For capitalist modernity and its social relations of production, this must mean, above all, a memory of the expropriation and displacement that made capital formation possible: While there can be no democracy without the future to come that keeps its projections contestable, there can also be no genuine democracy without the attempt to address the severe constraints the history of capital-formation continues to place on the equal right to free participation. Given that the memory of capitalist democracy is suffused with a promise, the political community it might establish is one that fosters a sense of identity through the permanent deferral of the completion of that identity, through a mode of action and praxis that keeps it up for discussion. Interpreting the world will thus be seen, perhaps more against Engels than against Marx,[9] as an integral part of changing it.

ONE

Benjamin's Reading of Marx

THE EVENTS MARKED by the year 1989 can largely be seen as severing a certain political messianism from its institutionalization. Thereby, they provide the opportunity to reopen the inheritance of Marx's text with the intention of salvaging and reformulating its promise for a future, a promise that had been overshadowed and appropriated by totalitarian systems. It is not the case, of course, that Marx's promise for a classless society could only be reinterpreted after its institutionalization in the Soviet Union had been overcome. On the contrary, such reinterpretations constitute the multifarious history of Marxisms. However, the breakdown of the Soviet Union, and the waning of institutionalized Marxism elsewhere, provide a perhaps privileged starting point, and even an obligation, to reinterpret the promise. On the other hand, this privilege comes with an additional burden. Especially after 1989—and the opening of Soviet archives, revealing more clearly than before Soviet atrocities, beginning with Lenin—any reinterpretation of the Marxist promise of social justice can no longer afford to ignore the violence committed in the name of its institutional realization. One way of broaching this reinterpretation, then, consists in the attempt to ask about the relation between the promise of a classless society and the memory of such violence in history, with the intention of seeking a closer integration between them.

Among the previous, pre-1989 rewritings of this promise there is arguably none that concerns itself more intensely with the relationship between the promise of a liberated future and the memory of the violence that explains the need for such a promise—a violence that attends both the failure to fulfill the promise and the claim to have instituted it—than Walter Benjamin's. Thus, this chapter will investigate Benjamin's relationship to Marx. My main concern will be the unfolding of Benjamin's argument that this promise for liberation, even for its own sake, has to be related in a non-instrumental manner to a particular attention given to precisely the victims of political and economic violence in the past. On pain of losing its emancipatory impulse, the promise may not view itself as surpassing or overcoming that history. Benjamin's work on the Paris Arcades (the *Passagenwerk*) in particular asked these questions of the inheritance of Marx, under very different political conditions, to be sure, but in a way that, nonetheless, merits closer analysis today.

Given these reasons for rereading Benjamin on Marx, however, the reader who consults the rapidly expanding secondary literature on the former's oeuvre will be surprised to find that little of substance has been written about his relation to Marx. The student movement of the 1960s, especially in Germany, might be said to have rediscovered Benjamin for political theory and action, reopening the texts that his friend Adorno had made available in the 1950s, after a period of near-total neglect by the broader public. Although the discussions that followed were dominated by the question of the opposition between Marxist materialism and theological messianism, scholarly investigations into Benjamin's complicated relationship to Marx's texts are rare. No doubt the unavailability of the *Passagenwerk*, published only in the 1980s with certain manuscripts still outstanding, contributed to this lack of research, since that left scholars with only the sparse comments on Marx in the "Theses on the Concept of History" and the essays on Baudelaire and Eduard Fuchs. Particularly earlier essays—like the 1921 "On the Critique of Violence," which the third chapter will take to be crucial to an understanding of the "Theses"—were mostly neglected or bypassed as precisely belonging to the early, "theological" Benjamin. It is, however, perhaps this very opposition between Marxism and theology, materialism and messianism, that disallows a proper assessment even of Marx himself: It brushes aside the way in which Marx—despite his claim that the critique of political economy begins after the critique of (Christian) religion—is reworking and renegotiating a tradition of messianic and eschatological thought, as Karl Löwith was perhaps the first to systematically argue—and cast in a negative light.[1] One of the merits of Derrida's *Specters of Marx* is, as we will see, that it excavates and reformulates this messianic thought in the Marxist tradition after 1989. By insisting on the idea of unconditional responsibility that messianic thought harbors, Derrida attempts—against the scientific, structural interpretation of Althusser, for example—to interpret the liberation of the messianic aspects in Marxism from their institutionalization as a chance for political philosophy and political responsibility. Benjamin also recalls Marx to this tradition of messianic thought—for Benjamin, an eclectic and mostly kabalistic tradition, mediated by his friend Gershom Scholem—while still affirming Marx's 'secularization' of the messianic idea, as we will see.

However, insofar as these efforts of Benjamin were recognized in the secondary literature, this affirmation was, and often is, discredited or viewed as attempts at the impossible. This explains the list of commentators who do not tire to point out how incompatible (and therefore impractical) Benjamin's historical materialism—a word Benjamin makes his own during the 1930s—is with Marx and Marxism, rather than motivating a rereading of the latter.[2] In this sense, the year 1989 presents a genuine opportunity that calls for a reassessment, perhaps revealing Benjamin as the *contretemps* he theorized in his historical reflections: as an event waiting for its sudden reappearance and unlocking by another, discontinuously related event.

Although the last twenty years witnessed a shift of accents in Benjamin scholarship, in particular in Germany and the United States, but increasingly also in France and Italy, they did not decisively return Benjamin to Marx. The massive intrusion of 'postmodern' theory in critical theory as a whole led to a renewed interest in Benjamin's literary achievements and his esoteric philosophizing that most often presents itself in the guise of literary readings (the German *Trauerspiel* of the seventeenth century, the interpretations of Goethe, Baudelaire, etc.). Deconstructive readings of Benjamin now abound, especially after de Man and Derrida themselves engaged his writings.[3] From the standpoint of Benjamin scholarship, it must seem ironic that the publication of Benjamin's most political and historical writings in the 1980s is accompanied by an increased awareness of his linguistic sensibilities and figural strategies centering on the theory and technique of presentation (*Darstellung*). Given these sensibilities and these emphases, Benjamin's often indirect, notoriously recondite and allusive styles of writing, but also his theoretical and philosophical attempts to define language and politics, among other things, are meeting with greater attention. While this has led to a general reopening of his texts to the point of infatuated canonization, these tendencies have not only relegated the question of Benjamin and Marx to a secondary position, but seem to have forgotten it altogether. In the sea of secondary literature, only very few refer to this question, as if language and materialism, literature and politics, theology and Marxism, were once again in irreconcilable opposition. It is as if the downfall of communism now allowed us to welcome the literary and theological side of Benjamin, whereas he precisely tried to rework the opposition between political action and literary and theological interpretation.[4] A further tendency of this new wave of secondary literature is to appropriate Benjamin for postmodern theory, attended by the familiar resistance on the part of some Marxists, such that Benjamin—more precisely, interpretations of Benjamin—became one of the key figures in the (now somewhat stale) debate between 'modernity' and 'postmodernity.'[5] I will here try to avoid these oppositional tendencies in order to reopen the question and interweaving of politics, language, memory and historiographical presentation.

For these reasons, I will begin with an analysis of Benjamin's critique of Marx and the role that the concept of the messianic plays in it. Perhaps it is not surprising that a confrontation over this concept is triggered by the issue of violence in history, for the messianic has lent expression to a more than understandable dissatisfaction in the face of the irretrievability of loss, an irretrievability that appears to affect the self-righteousness of concepts of justice. It is often overlooked that Marx, especially in *Capital*, devoted considerable resources to recount victimization in the past, and to point out the importance of its memory in political and economic contexts. In the first section, I analyze the way in which Marx construes the relationship between a memory of the victims of capitalism's beginnings and the promise for liberation from it, a relationship most often governed by the idea of immanent laws of progress. In section two, I argue that Benjamin revises the question of history in order to direct it away from the alleged laws of historical development, focusing instead on the ever new 'construction' of the past in the present. (This construction, or Benjamin's theory of the 'constellation' of the past and the present, will receive fuller treatment in chapter four.) Benjamin's resistance to the idea of progress and the notion of linear time will then allow us to inquire into his claims for a non-instrumental, nonprogressivistic relationship to the future, a future to which Benjamin wishes to restore what he calls a messianic face. I will argue here that Benjamin attempts to retain the 'secularized' theologico-political imperative he sees embodied in 'communist' political action (which Benjamin seeks to divorce from 'communist goals'), but that this imperative, if given its full weight, requires the abandoning of a Marxist sacralization of history by way of the theory of progress. (The conception of this non-instrumental political action, and its problematic ambiguities, will be more fully elaborated in chapter three by way of a reading of the early essay "On the Critique of Violence" and its Derridian interpretation in "The Force of Law.") Benjamin's reformulation of Marx's promise for the future will then be seen to uncover heretofore buried aspects and 'energies' of the past, but also to place the present under the claim of the victims of history.

A word of caution about the interpretation of Marx in this and the next two chapters is in order. The reading of Marx advanced here is a reading that is willing to emphasize teleological tendencies and economic determinism but does, on the whole, not seek out other tendencies—with the exception of uncovering the extent to which Marx was concerned with a memory of injustice. This reading does not claim to be the only possible one. Different texts as well as different layers of Marx's writings might, with good justification, be mobilized. Nonetheless, the reading presented is a legitimate one, especially if one keeps in mind its purpose in the present context. First, what is needed is the relevant background to Benjamin's (and, later, Derrida's) critique of the contemporary Marxism of the Second International, and also of Marx himself. Second, and more important, for the sake of grasping the significance of Benjamin's and Derrida's objections, it is necessary to understand how the institutionalization of Marx's promise could lead to the totalitarian violence now associated with it, despite the difficulty of tracing a continuous line from Marx to Stalin. As noted, any attempt to inherit Marx's promise today must take account of this violence. I believe it is worthwhile to read Marx differently, for example, as undermining a Leninist or Kautskian appropriation, but such a reading, especially if it wishes to join a memory of injustice to a promise of justice, may not be oblivious to those layers of Marx that permitted such an appropriation.

REMEMBERING THE INSTITUTING
VIOLENCE OF CAPITALISM

Let us proceed to the argument that Marx already connected a sense of loss and anger at past victimization to his promise for the future, but that, in the end, a certain teleo-logic of history comes to dominate the thinking of the relation of the past to the future in his writing. While analyzing the suffering of the oppressed in the past as well as in the present, Marx views the final materialization of his promise for the classless society as following the very same logic that brought about the suffering, such that the promise would in some sense justify the suffering and surpass a mournful memory of those victims. This account provides the background against which we should read Benjamin's explicit and largely overlooked critique of Marx. This critique hints at a way to inherit the promise that neither opposes it to memory nor justifies past suffering. Indeed, Benjamin will be seen to argue that a focused assumption of loss and suffering in the past is necessary to the inheritance of past promises, but also necessary to guard against the belief in a simple fulfillment of the promise. For Benjamin, this inheritance requires a radical rejection of a politics of 'endism,' one that directs itself to the goals or the ends of history or of politics. Rather, Benjamin tries to conceptualize a theory of political action that derives its efficacy and motivation not from its political goals, but from a political imperative, which, while interrupting the linear time of progressive history, at the same time finds its sustenance in a memory of violence and suffering. For Benjamin, as I will elaborate in greater detail in chapter three, a concept of emancipatory action that is motivated by the promise of the past but does not neglect this memory, indeed requires a refusal of every instrumental or utilitarian logic that uses its goal to justify the means, and which relies on the future in order to sacrifice or surpass the past. While Benjamin's critique of Marx's progressive logic of history denies the conception of a future as a utopian goal, this critique reveals, in various ways, the crucial impact on emancipatory struggles of a memory of promises that is also a memory of loss. (In the third chapter, I will ask about the possibility and desirability of denying political goals altogether.)

Benjamin encountered Marx's writing at a time when its reception was still dominated by the Second International (1889–1914), a loose federation of parties and trade unions whose doctrine and influence was largely embodied and dominated by German Social Democracy, the most important party during the Weimar Republic. Benjamin is especially critical of the Social Democratic neo-Kantian, Bernsteinian interpretation of Marxism. As we will see, Benjamin argues that on this goal-fixated and ultimately quietist view, the promised classless society becomes a regulative ideal and the struggle for it an "infinite task" without urgency (I 1232). By contrast to the dismissive treatment of Social Democracy, he usually approaches Marx's texts more carefully and affirmatively. In the *Passagenwerk*, his unfinished account of the history of the nineteenth century as crucial to an understanding of modernity, Benjamin is mostly interested in Marx, and in particular in the "Eighteenth Brumaire" (the text that we will see Derrida privilege for an access to Marx's account of 'active forgetting'), insofar as it itself belongs to the object of the study, that is, as a privileged source for his historical 'commentary.' Consequently, one hopes in vain to find there a detailed philosophical, sociopolitical, and methodological confrontation with Marx. Nonetheless, as I will show, in particular in his notes to the "Theses on the Concept of History," Benjamin is quite explicit about his critique of Marx's concept of history as preparing the way for the later errors of quietism—in contrast to the "Theses" themselves, which largely and boldly attribute to Marx a more unorthodox view of history (cf. I 701). This practice of commentary, of allusive, unorthodox reading, and out-of-context citation, resulting in an apparent ambivalence of Benjamin's relation to Marx, may easily lead to confusion among commentators.[6]

As noted, the interpretive inheritance of Marx's promise today requires, at the very least, that we remember the violence that its institutionalization inflicted upon it. Therefore, before tackling Benjamin's reading of Marx more directly, we need to take note of that dimension of Marx's text that, already for Benjamin in the 1930s, allowed the self-proclaimed successors of Marx to implicate his name in a totalitarian interpretation whose "technocratic features"—as displayed, for instance, in the Social Democratic concept of labor—Benjamin views as akin to fascism (Thesis XI). Marx's philosophy of history is by no means devoid of performative elements—and Derrida, as we will see, underlines this performativity as much as possible. Many of its constative assurances regarding the law-governed unfolding of history can also be viewed as a performative call to action and a scientific support to its promises. Nonetheless, the view that Marx claimed to have discovered the laws of history's dialectical movement is not without support in his texts. The motor of history would be the dialectic of the forces and relations of production and the concomitant class wars. Once capitalism has attained its more or less 'natural' limit in the utter impoverishment of the majority, this dialectic can (or even will) lead to a democratic revolution ending the period of class wars, what Marx famously calls the "prehistory of humanity."[7] Since the class struggle between the bourgeoisie and the proletariat is governed by the (largely unconsciously operating) laws of historical necessity, politics plays a role in the struggle only insofar as economic interests are represented in it.

The task of the proletariat is to recognize these laws as the 'content' of the historical process, that is, to consciously appropriate the historical opportunity provided by the economic movement of history. Marx, following but also revising the tradition of the *Aufklärung* with its emphasis on the 'availability' of history to human action, recognizes history as the history of the one who (for the first time) 'makes' it, albeit in the context of inherited circumstances.[8] Marx can, in a gesture characteristically wavering between the constative and performative mode, designate a historical subject that can and should consciously appropriate the historical process. The proletariat has arrived (or ought to arrive) at itself as the 'content' of that process and thus is no longer in need of world-historical reminiscences for the motivation of revolutionary struggles. According to Marx, such memories occurred to bourgeois revolutionaries in the moment of action to deceive themselves and the oppressed people about the limited nature of the revolutions that merely aimed at substituting one form of domination for another. In the 1848 Paris revolution, for example—a revolution that, as we will see, sent Marx into mourning for the loss of a promised but missed opportunity—the past appears as merely the tradition of dead generations, a tradition that is cited precisely when the task would have been to cut through this tradition in order to "create something that does not yet exist."[9] Marx's response to his mourning is revealing: instead of placing his hope in memory, he opposes memory to the future and famously argues that

> the social revolution of the nineteenth century cannot draw its poetry from the past but only from the future. It cannot begin with itself before it has stripped off all superstition in regard to the past. Earlier revolutions required world-historical recollections in order to drug themselves concerning their content. In order to arrive at its content, the revolution of the nineteenth century must let the dead bury their dead.[10]

Marx thus distinguishes between bourgeois revolutions, which did not accomplish the historical self-creation of humanity, and the proletarian revolution that can accomplish this task only by parting with the past 'cheerfully' in order to fulfill its project. In the famous 1843 letter to Ruge, Marx had claimed that through a 'reform of consciousness' "[i]t will transpire that it is not a matter of drawing a great dividing line between past and future, but of carrying out the thoughts of the past. And finally, it will transpire that mankind begins no *new* work, but consciously accomplishes its old work."[11] According to this historical dialectic, therefore, Marx does not argue for a new beginning of history by wiping clean the slate of "the tradition of the dead generations [that] weighs like a nightmare on the minds of the living."[12]

Instead, he divides the problematic collective singular of 'the past' up into the nightmarish dream and its latent meaning striving for its release: Fulfilling the past's project, what Marx calls a 'world-historical task,' precisely requires abandoning the dream- and ghostlike form which that which 'is' no longer tends to assume. It is this abandonment that is supposed to make possible what Jacques Rancière, in his recent analysis of this logic of fulfillment, has called "the collective identity of the dreaming cogito," attained at the cost of the "delegitimation of speech positions" and at the expense of the "multiplicity of little narratives."[13]

Thus, at different stages of his career, Marx argues for a 'cheerful' separation from a past seen as superstitiously hampering historical development. Of course, this active forgetting in favor of the self-presence of the subject of history is, for Marx, only possible insofar as this subject knows itself to be in harmony with the structural processes underlying history, its laws being rendered accessible by Marx's scientific analyses of historical modes of production. Before turning to Benjamin's critique of this unifying teleology, I want to turn to two texts by Marx in which the issue of the relationship between politico-historical violence and an adequate response to it in the present is at least operative, if not explicitly governing the discourse. For it would be a mistake—one that would be at a loss to explain Benjamin's affirmative gestures to Marx in this regard—to think that an insight into the importance of the memory of historical violence and oppression is absent from Marx's discourse altogether, as Derrida's focus, in *Specters of Marx*, on the "Eighteenth Brumaire" might lead one to believe. In a brief discussion of, mostly, a part of *Capital*, serving as an indispensable backdrop to Benjamin's critique of Marx, my argument will be that Marx's promise is already suffused with a memory of those who were oppressed and brushed aside by the historical genesis and forward march of capitalism. Nonetheless, the promise for the classless society, demanding the 'expropriation of the expropriators,' follows the logic of a history of violence, thus overcoming or redeeming the mournful memory for which it nonetheless calls. Today, after the outbreak of totalitarian violence in the twentieth century, including the atrocities committed in the name of Marx, we largely tend to see this heeding of the call for memory as indispensable. Benjamin was perhaps the first to point out this necessity, especially for Marxist emancipatory struggles. He therefore criticizes precisely a unifying teleology in Marx.

Before Marx's disillusionment, in 1852, with an impending proletarian revolution, he had concerned himself in a newspaper article with the memory of the 'victims' (*Opfer*)—a word he, but not Benjamin, is willing to use, at least in minor texts[14]—of the 1848 June insurrection in Paris. Marx makes a distinction here between the proletarian victims and the bourgeois victims of the battles in the streets of Paris, thus perhaps anticipating Benjamin's famous distinction between a history of victors and of the oppressed.[15] "One will ask us whether we have no tears, no sigh, no word for the victims who died before the anger of the people," Marx writes.[16] The French state will, he says, honor the victims of the bourgeoisie and take care of the relatives of the deceased, but the task of the remembrance of the proletarian victims, almost as martyrs, Marx assigns to the democratic press:

> But the plebeians, torn by hunger, reviled [geschmäht] by the press, aban-
> doned by the doctors, cursed by the respectable thieves [Honetten] as fire-
> brands and galley slaves, their women and children plunged into even more
> boundless misery, their best survivors deported overseas—to wind the laurel
> around their threatening gloomy heads, that is the *privilege*, that is the right
> of the *democratic press*.[17]

To bind the laurel wreath, sign of victory, around the dead victims of eman-
cipatory struggles: This is how Marx envisions the work of mourning of those who continue the struggle. Taking over the struggle from those who can con-
tinue it no longer is perhaps the best way to both remember them and to assume their promise for emancipation. It is, however, the transformation of this memory of the dead into the promise of victory that, as we will see, seems problematic from Benjamin's perspective.

This transformation is confirmed by Part Eight of *Capital I*, entitled "So-
called Primitive Accumulation," in which Marx presents the historico-polit-
ical violence and the "bloody legislation against the expropriated since the end of the 15th century" on which capitalism, viewed as a historical period, is based. Marx argues there that the "process that creates the capital-rela-
tion [. . .] cannot be something other than the process of division between the worker and the condition of labor" (*Capital* 874). The origin of capital—
understood as a *social* relation rather than reified as mere assets that, without living labor, would lack their conditions of realization and amortization—
thus lies in the twofold creation of these conditions by turning the social means of subsistence and production into capital, and by turning the immediate producers into wage-laborers without ownership of capital. Taking 'cap-
ital' to mean any asset that can generate an income for its owner, as bourgeois political economy does, forgets, according to Marx, that inanimate objects do not generate wealth and interest by themselves but require labor power as a social relation. This is, at bottom, what Marx means by 'capital fetishism.' It marks an attitude to capital that blocks any memory of the violent process that created capital in the first place. In a certain sense, then, the critique of fetishism—which Derrida, as we will see, rejects as an exorcist ghost hunt—
precisely tries to free us for this memory, for the specters of the victims that Marx sees crushed by bourgeois ideology. (We will return to the relationship between fetishism and memory in chapter four.)

The process that creates capital as a social relation thus requires the separation of laborers from the means of production and subsistence. Europe's

serf population had to be removed from the land, common land had to be enclosed, and, in the United States (where originally there were neither serfs nor immigrants without land), Native American and, later, African slaves had to fulfill the need of labor power.[18] Thus, focusing mostly on England, Marx presents the process of the violent creation of a 'free market' as having slavery as its precondition, and as expropriating the agricultural population from common land, thereby robbing them of their means of subsistence and forcing them to work in the cities without adequate wages, many of them left to starve as the victims of the birth of capitalism. The tone of Marx's writing of history here is well captured by the conclusion to his account of capital accumulation in the United States: "A great deal of capital, which appears today in the United States without any birth-certificate, was yesterday, in England, the capitalized blood of children."[19] Marx mourns the 'victims' of history not only by writing about them in a 'scientific' work, thus countering an at times deliberate forgetting of which Marx accuses the bourgeois theoreticians of political economy (who resort to Christian theology for this active forgetting; cf. *Capital* 873). But furthermore, throughout *Capital* and in this chapter in particular, Marx's tone also reveals moral indignation in showing that today's riches are built on the back of past suffering, especially that of serfs, slaves, and wage-laborers. Marx prefaces his account by pointing out that the violent victimization that was necessary for the creation of capitalism remains a stain of violence inherent in capitalism: "And this history, the history of their expropriation, is inscribed in the annals of mankind in inextinguishable letters of blood and fire" (*Capital* 875).[20] At one point Marx's outrage overwhelms his historical account to such an extent that he is willing to let go, for a moment, of the writing of history in terms of its economic laws of development: "We leave on one side here the purely economic driving forces behind the agricultural revolution. We deal only with the violent means employed" (*Capital* 883). With a view to these passages, it perhaps becomes more apparent why Ernst Bloch called Marx's theory a "political economy (*Nationalökonomie*) from propheticism in despair."[21]

It is, however, again instructive to observe Marx's response to this indignation at the violent victimization of farmers and would-be proletarians, as the prophetic side takes over from the despair. After the brief suspension of the laws of history in the previous passage—a suspension, as I will argue, that alone allows a memory of loss—Marx returns to write history in the teleological framework enabling him to discover a latent meaning in the suffering he recounts. Marx finds comfort in the belief in the process's necessity to overcome the "universal mediocrity" of feudal society in favor of the "further socialization of labor" (*Capital* 928). After having exposed the violent means by which feudalism was destroyed—an exposition that forces Marx to admit, in a variation on the famous formula from the *Contribution to the Critique of Political Economy*, that it is not only new forces of production, but also "new passions" that drive history forward[22]—Marx now argues that this violence was necessary for history to progress. It is a violence that will now allow a proletarian revolution. The same necessity that gave rise to capitalism will lead to the proletarian revolution, which thus sublimates the (in its extremity, unnecessary) violence of the past Marx so meticulously recounts: one expropriation following another, that is, following the "immanent laws of capitalist production itself" that, "with the inexorability of a natural process, [begets] its own negation" (*Capital* 929). These laws allow Marx to call for their practical execution, wavering between the constative and the performative mode: "What is now to be expropriated is not the self-employed worker, but the capitalist who exploits a large number of workers" (*Capital* 928).[23]

Thus, toward the end of Part Eight, Marx transforms the commemorative outrage directing his pen into the apparent certainty of the proletariat's victory, thus performatively calling on workers to derive a sense of the 'world-historical task' from this history of victimization. Insofar as its victory would follow the logic of history striving for fulfillment in the 'social revolution of the nineteenth century,' Marx surreptitiously attaches a latent meaning to past victimhood: "It is the bad side that produces the movement which makes history," as he wrote elsewhere.[24] In the most general terms, it is thus Marx's faith in progress, and his elevation of the memory of victims to a place in this line of socioeconomic development, that can be seen to evade the fuller implications of such memory for the promise of emancipation, even when it takes note of the importance of memory. While he attempts to connect a sense of loss to the promise of the past for a better future, that promise, in giving meaning to the loss by connecting it to a logic of victory, ultimately dissipates it. As we will see, Benjamin tries to disentangle the promise of a classless society from the historical dialectic, to let us as its heirs experience its call. Benjamin inherits from Marx the outrage about the 'inextinguishable' horrors that are associated with the origins and development of capitalism, but he disavows the promise of progress into which Marx transformed this outrage. Both Marx and Benjamin attempt to conceive a memory of past injustice that acts as a motivation for emancipatory struggles, but in Marx, this memory is joined to the promise of progress and victory.

THE PRIMACY OF POLITICS OVER HISTORY

Before we turn to Benjamin's critique of Marx, let us be clear about the historical and political consequences in the history of Marxism of Marx's emphasis (whether performative or constative) on historical necessity and what came to be known as economic determinism. For Benjamin's relation to Marx is situated within these consequences and unintelligible without reference to them. I have already remarked that Benjamin encountered Marxism mostly in the form of the German Social Democrats, and he often—in unorthodox formulations that in turn cannot be equated or reconciled with the 'classical' Marxist theory—defended Marx against this party's interpretations, premised on the growing disjuncture between classical Marxism and the political practice of Social Democracy. But Benjamin also traveled to Moscow in the late 1920s and returned to Berlin disappointed at the "class" and "caste state" (IV 334) of Marxism–Leninism. What then is the connection between Marx's theory and the failure of its promise, a failure much more obvious to us after 1989 than perhaps in the 1920s and 1930s? Why is Benjamin reacting against, as we will elaborate in a moment, the Marxist emphasis on the underlying laws of history and the notion of progress, and what is the connection of the latter theme with his insistence on a memory of history's oppressed?

There can be no doubt that both in Lenin and in the primary theorists of Social Democracy—Kautsky and Bernstein—the role of economic determinism had the gravest consequences for the conception of working-class politics. In fact, Benjamin's famous "Theses on the Concept of History" may, to some extent, be seen as a response to the Nazi–Soviet Non-Aggression pact of 1939, in that Benjamin blames the politics of Social Democracy for allowing the German fascists to rise to power (Theses VIII, X, XI, XII, XIII).[25] This background give the "Theses" their dramatic and urgent appeal, and it allows one to surmise that the primary target of the critique of progress is not (or not only) bourgeois historiography, but indeed the Marxism of Social Democracy. Allow me to briefly indicate the historically fateful connection between writing history in terms of its underlying (economic) laws, laws that carry the promise of emancipation, and the totalitarian (rather than liberating) results of Marxist politics. For Benjamin, the promise must be freed from this tie to the progress of productive forces in order to be 'messianized,' as we will see.

If history must be written in terms of the prevalence of the mode of production, which falls into the developing dialectic of the forces and relations of production, then the working class as the primary agent of social change finds its unity and identity, including its political identity of interests, outside of the sphere of politics, in the relations of production alone. The laws of economic development assign a more or less preestablished identity to the proletariat, prior to the moment of politics. In this way, its historical chance to become a politically democratic movement (by articulating the demands of the working classes with other political actors) is preempted. Due to its privileged place in the mode of production, Marx raised the working class to the status of the 'universal class,' representing the interests of the masses as a whole, of all actors, and ultimately of history itself. Both Lenin and Kautsky had to respond to the crises of Marxism that resulted from the lack of the increasing immiseration of most sectors of society, which would have given some plausibility to the idea of the universal class, representing the future "dissolution of all classes," as Marx put it in the *German Ideology*.[26] But rather than revising the thesis of the ontological centrality of the working class—for example, by theorizing the social relations of the working classes with the peasants, the petty bourgeoisie, the *Lumpenproletariat*, the intellectuals—Lenin transferred this centrality to the political leadership of the working class—the vanguard—which is further endowed with an epistemic privilege: It knows the underlying movement of history.[27] The Communist Party represents the economic interests of the proletariat, and thus of the mode of production as a whole, in a unilateral and transparent fashion. This is the turn to an authoritarian politics that surrendered Marx's commitment to a democratic revolution. In this turn of events, history (i.e., the concept of history founded on the economy) takes precedence over politics, as the 'base' takes precedence over the 'superstructure.' In Kautsky, the reaction to the crisis of Marxism took the less authoritarian form of a strategy of hibernation: Given the empirical fragmentation of the working class, the Party has to recognize and represent, by way of science (as opposed to politics), the future unity of the working class guaranteed by the movement of the economic base. This seemingly radical and orthodox strategy prepares the way for the political quietism of Social Democracy, insofar as the lawful movement of history does not require any political intervention.[28] It is this quietism, this conception of automatic progress, that Benjamin believes has been most harmful to the politics of the working class, and he models his new understanding of history in opposition to it. Accusing the "politicians in whom the opponents of fascism had placed their hopes" of a betrayal of the working classes, Benjamin writes:

> Our consideration proceeds from the insight that the politicians' stubborn faith in progress, their confidence in their 'mass basis,' and, finally, their servile integration in an uncontrollable apparatus have been three aspects of the same thing. It seeks to convey an idea of the high price our accustomed thinking will have to pay for a conception of history that avoids any complicity with the thinking to which these politicians continue to adhere (Thesis X).

We have already seen that Benjamin, in opposition to the idea that conceptions of the future must animate a politics of resistance, goes back to Marx in order to recover a sense of indignation, and thus a motivation for such struggles, from violence in the past. For Benjamin, Eduard Bernstein's neo-Kantian interpretation of Marxism—which emphasizes the autonomy of politics more than Kautsky does—betrays the same spirit of sacrificing present politics for the ultimate progress toward an infinite "ideal" of the classless society (I 1231). When Benjamin thus radically disallows conceptions of the future for emancipatory struggles, citing the Jewish prohibition to investigate the future as support (I 704), we should keep in mind that the future Benjamin rejects is one that, as a form of quietism, makes present action seem less urgent, and justifies suffering in the present and the past by reference to a future ideal connected to a conception of progress.

Before we now turn to a more direct treatment of Benjamin's critique, let me note briefly that Benjamin rejects almost all the features that unite the various responses to the crises of Marxism at the end of the last century and the beginning of the next. As we just saw, he rejects the naive belief that politicians of the working-class parties have the support of, and thus unilaterally represent, the 'masses.' Benjamin thereby opens up the possibility of a gap between the working class and the masses, a gap that questions the conception of the vanguard and allows for the possibility that the Marxist primacy of working-class struggles over the struggles of all other political groups is misdirected (although Benjamin largely holds on to this primacy). Benjamin further rejects the hierarchy of the economic infrastructure over the superstructure and over politics, arguing instead that modern techniques of reproduction and tele-technology (and thus of mass manipulation) allow politics a much more independent and central role than orthodox Marxists are willing to admit (see I 434ff.).[29] As I will elaborate, this also means for Benjamin a conception of the "primacy of politics over history" (V 1057, cf. V 491). In effect, we will see that Benjamin wishes to reconsider the relationship between history and politics altogether.

As this discussion of a few texts has shown, Marx fashions a subject of history that, while turning all its attention to the future, to the 'creation of what does not yet exist,' either abandons a memory of the past in order to know itself to be in agreement with the law or the 'content' of history—as in "The Eighteenth Brumaire of Louis Bonaparte"—or it is called on by Marx to derive a sense of the enormity of its task from loss and victimization in the past—as in Part Eight of *Capital, Volume One*. In the latter case, Marx tries to connect a memory of loss to the promise for a liberated future by relying on the logic of history: the very same laws of development that expropriated peasants, serfs, and slaves should and will lead to the 'expropriation of the expropriated.' The future is thus projected and predetermined as that which, putting an end to all class conflict and exploitation, 'redeems' the violent past by fulfilling its latent promise. The interpretation of history in terms of a lawful development of the productive forces retroactively justifies past violence as necessary for the possibility of fulfilling the promise. In Benjamin's critique of Marx it will be a matter of retaining Marx's promise, but in such a way that the future is not conceived as the aim of history, as an end that fulfills the promise. Therefore, Benjamin opposes to the idea of a memoryless subject incarnating the future—that is, to the very opposition between the past and the future—a suspension of the past in order to save its promises and its possibilities. What has to be elaborated in greater detail is the intrinsic connection between these two gestures, the one that refuses futural goals as *teloi* of history, and the one that 'rescues' memory and inherited promises. Contrary to Marx, Benjamin suggests that the link between loss and the promise cannot be established by the 'laws' of history, and that the meaning Marx attached to the victims of the past on the basis of these laws misses those dimensions of history that let the 'voice' of the oppressed be heard in a register different from what he famously calls the "history of the victors" (Thesis VII).

To be sure, in coining this phrase Benjamin most explicitly turns against an objectivist historicism and a bourgeois "cultural history" that he characterizes as the "booty" [*Beute*] carried along in the "triumphal procession" of the victors (ibid.). Nonetheless, as I will try to show, the elaboration of the suspension of the past—which requires a brief look at Benjamin's critique of historicism, and which leads him to a revision of the question of history—also applies to Marx's view of history's underlying processes. It is this revision that prepared Benjamin for a rejection of the teleological dimensions of Marx's text, dimensions that Benjamin thought had disastrous consequences for revolutionary politics—in particular with regard to the question of memory, a question that Benjamin from the beginning associates with the conception of the future implied in this politics. Thus, I find myself in agreement with those interpreters of Benjamin who view as the primary object of attack, especially of the "Theses," the Enlightenment philosophy of history rather than bourgeois historicism, although Benjamin often strikes at both in a single gesture.[30]

REVISING THE QUESTION OF HISTORY

In what way, then, does Benjamin argue for a revision of the question of history? Benjamin is not primarily interested in what we might call the knowledge of history (and its laws), but in the writing of history.[31] When Benjamin first systematically presented his historical methodology as a critique of epistemology, in the 'epistemo-critical prologue' to his study of the seventeenth-century German *Trauerspiel*, he turned against 'scientific verificationism' and a science that disregards its own language. Benjamin sees language as constitutive of any presentation (*Darstellung*) of phenomena, especially historical and aesthetic ones (I 222, I 207). Against the objectivist method of the German Historical School of the nineteenth century (e.g., Ranke, Treitschke, Meinecke)[32]—which will again constitute one of the central targets of the "Theses"—Benjamin argues for a "revision of the question" concerning history. The revision "can be formulated in the consideration of how the question: How was it actually? can not so much be scientifically answered, but rather can be posed" (I 222). In a Nietzschean vein, Benjamin thus asks from what perspective the historicist-scientific question concerning the reconstruction of the past is legitimate, and what presuppositions must be in place for it to be posed.[33] The revision presupposes that history, or rather histories, while dialectically conditioning the present, constitute themselves in the present of their writing, a presentation that thus cannot be abstracted from the present. The resulting emphasis on the logic of the 'after-the-fact' (*Nachträglichkeit*), on a "construction" of history out of the present (I 702), its dependence on the "focal point (*Fluchtpunkt*) of our own historical experience" (I 1104), can be traced through all of Benjamin's writings.[34] This linguistic-historical approach is not only contrasted with the historicist attempt to reconstruct the past, in Ranke's well-known phrase, 'the way it really was,' but it also places Benjamin in advance, so to speak, in a critical position vis-à-vis a view that fundamentally asks about the underlying processes of history. As we will see, Benjamin in particular rejects the guiding idea of linear time, and the notion of a final exhaustibility of historical objects. Both of these presuppositions, in Benjamin's view, preclude the inheritance of promises from the past, promises that bind the past and the present to the future. As we will also see, however, a closer look at Benjamin's "Theses" reveals that the present in question is in turn deprived of its seemingly superior position over the past by a certain relation to the future, a relation that places the present under the claim of the past. Furthermore, it should be emphasized that Benjamin, from his first encounter with the Historical School, rejects their objectivism—which in Ranke is justified by the claim that all generations are equal "before God"[35]—in the name of a premodern, less unitary, and finalized understanding of our relationship to history, without recommending a return to premodern forms of historiography. The medieval chronicle, which Benjamin defends in Thesis III, stands in his usage not for the mere listing of events without interpretation, but for a multiplicity of layers in relation to the past (VI 97). Already in 1921, Benjamin noted what recent scholarship has taken efforts to demonstrate: that modernity invents the collective singular of history, assured by the historicist, scientific method.[36] In a note entitled "On the Philosophy of History of Late Romanticism and of the Historical School," Benjamin writes:

> The lack of fertility, which attaches itself to this philosophy of history despite its significant thoughts, stems from its characteristically modern features. For it shares with many scientific theories of modernity [*Neuzeit*] the absolutism of method. Since the Middle Ages, the insight into the richness of layers [*Reichtum von Schichten*], in which the world and its best meanings [*Gehalte*] construct themselves, has been lost (VI 95).

Revising the question of history must thus also uncover a multiplicity of histories not to be written in a singular, law-governed totality. This shift of perspective from the laws of history to its writing in the present further allows Benjamin not only to ask about the interests in a perspective that claims to know the *telos* of the historical process to which these laws are oriented, but it also allows him to look for what is worthy of rescue (*Rettung*) in history—

not in that which contributes to its alleged, visible teleology, but in what Benjamin calls the "cracks and jags" (*Schroffen und Zacken*) of a tradition (V 592). In subsequent chapters, I will ask about these interruptions of linear time and narrative history, and their significance for both the writing of history and political resistance. For the moment, let us note that Benjamin's revision concerning the question of history and temporality allows him to ask about the interests, prejudices, and conceptual presuppositions that the present brings to its reading of the past. The revision implies that the present and the past stand in a dialectical relationship to each other in which the one influences and conditions the other. In his own way, then, Benjamin arrives at an insight that has become commonplace since Heidegger's *Sein und Zeit* and Gadamer's *Wahrheit und Methode* in particular: the insight into the dialectical interpenetration, the hermeneutic circle, of the past and the present. Especially Gadamer has shown that—contrary to the older hermeneutic tradition (Schleiermacher and Dilthey in particular), which emphasizes understanding the meaning of texts and historical events in the way the authors and actors understood them—our very historicity results in the impossibility of returning to the perspective of past authors and actors. This impossibility, however, is the very condition of historical understanding, for it consists in relating one's own preconceptions and prejudices to the past in a 'fusion of horizons' (*Horizontverschmelzung*) of past and present.[37]

How does Benjamin arrive at this hermeneutic insight? In his *Passagenwerk*, Benjamin argues that the task of the (Hegelian or Marxist) dialectical method—"to do justice to the concrete historical situation"—is insufficient: "For, to the same degree this method is concerned with doing justice to the concrete historical situation of the *interest* for its historical object" (V 494, Benjamin's emphasis). The dialectical method must also take into account the present historical situation that gives rise to its historical interests, what Gadamer called the 'prejudices' orienting one's view. Gesturing toward his later account of the way in which past elements suggest their own "recognizability," "citability," or "readability" to the present, Benjamin, in a characteristic reversal, describes this interpenetration of the past and the present as the way in which a historical object "preforms" by itself the interest a later time might have in it. This means, according to Benjamin, that the interest, and the historical situation that gives rise to it, "concretizes that [historical] object in itself," thereby bringing it to a "higher concretion" in the now (V 495). Benjamin characterizes this concretion and formation of the object, in the interplay of past and present, as its latent formation, preparing itself for its being read. He then wonders why this process can be seen as a "higher concretion" of the object, as its attaining a "higher degree of actuality" (ibid.). He emphasizes that the rise in concretion cannot be understood under the premises of the "ideology of progress" but must be seen as the inevitable increasing "condensation" (*Verdichtung*) and "integration" of past

reality from the perspective of the present. It is this process of the "dialectical interpenetration and presentation of past contexts" that yields, as we will
see later, Benjamin's much-discussed "dialectical image" (ibid.). As an example, taken from his earlier writings on presentation and condensation, we
might refer to epistolary correspondence as historical "testimony" (VI 95).

Thus, our interest in the past is not simply external to the object, but the
object itself suggests—in a "jolting, intermittent way" (V 495)—its interesting character, its readiness for being read or taken up. Benjamin's account of
the "prefiguration" or "historical index" of the readability of, and interest in,
a historical object should be seen as an attempt to overcome the presupposition of the subject-object model in historical understanding. It is an attempt
to overcome the idea of the imperial purview of the historian over the past,
from above, in control of his or her subject matter and freely choosing the
method, perspective, and the object. Instead, we should accept that, in a way
to be explored, the past—which is always a particular past, a specifically condensed "image"—*claims* us in asking to be read. Benjamin wishes to emphasize that the "true" and singular image of the past, the one that concerns the
singularity of the present most of all (due to its political significance),
requires a "presence of mind" (*Geistesgegenwart*) and is always in danger of
being missed and lost forever:

> The true image of the past flits by. The past can be seized only as an image
> which flashes up at the instant when it can be recognized and is never seen
> again. 'The truth will not run away from us': in the historical outlook of his-
> toricism these words of Gottfried Keller mark the exact point where histor-
> ical materialism cuts through historicism. For every image of the past that is
> not recognized by the present as one of its own concerns threatens to dis-
> appear irretrievably (Thesis V).

For Benjamin, as we will see, the image that is most important to (Marxist)
emancipatory struggles is the condensed image of the "tradition of the
oppressed" (Thesis VIII). It is this image, however, that both a Gadamerian
account of historical understanding and a teleological Marxism are bound
to miss. I will return to Benjamin's critique of orthodox Marxism in a
moment, after briefly contrasting Benjamin's view of historical presentation
with Gadamer's.

The 'epistemological' idea that 'images' of the past, by prefiguring the
interest of later times in them, address themselves to us in the present, is
charged by Benjamin with the ethical and political significance of uncovering oppressed voices in history, and of assuming their promise of being heard,
their 'claim' (*Anspruch*) to be represented in contemporary discourses, especially if that requires a change in the power structures of representation. By
insisting that the past claims us in the present (cf. Thesis II), Benjamin also
turns against the more obvious, Gadamerian emphasis on the way in which

the past, as the classical tradition forming the background horizon of understanding, already predetermines the present. Although both Gadamer's and
Benjamin's view of historical understanding insist on the dialectical interpenetration of past and present, a crucial difference emerges between them.
For Benjamin, the claim that the present and its interpretive procedures is
always already indexed to, and indebted to, its tradition, neglects the fact
that effective history (*Wirkungsgeschichte*) excludes the voices of those
oppressed ones who nonetheless contributed to its emergence. For Benjamin, as we will see, those who were repressed and forgotten during their
lifetime, are crushed a second time by the "triumphal march" of history
(Thesis VII). The many lives who are not represented or acknowledged in
our heritage lead Benjamin to call for a "memory of the nameless" insofar as
the "inventory of culture owes its existence not only to the efforts of the
great geniuses who created it, but to the nameless drudgery of their contemporaries" (I 1241; cf. Thesis VII). It is these "nameless" ones who, according
to a Benjaminian view, are forgotten by Gadamer's classicism, as also by the
"historical objectivism" against which Gadamer writes.[38] If, according to
Gadamer, time is no longer understood as the "yawning gap" but, following
Heidegger, as the "ground of happening, in which the present is rooted,"
then the temporal distance separating the ages (*Zeitenabstand*) is "filled with
the continuity of the emergence and of tradition."[39] Benjamin opposes to
this continuity, which he associates with a conservative "appreciation" or
"apologia" of tradition, the "revolutionary moments of the course of history":
"The appreciation or apologia only gives weight to those elements of a work
that have already generated an after-effect. It misses those points at which
the transmission breaks down and thus misses those jags and cracks which
call a halt to those who wish to move beyond it" (I 658, cf. V 591f.). Benjamin is thus not only interested in the way in which the past and its cultural heritage provide, in a 'continuous' handing down, the horizon of
understanding on the basis of which the present turns to the past, but in
what is left out of consideration by this heritage. We will return to the more
specific question of why, for Benjamin, the 'rescue' of this so very different
claim that a forgotten or 'subaquatic' (*unterseeisch*) past can have on the present, requires a focus on the discontinuities, interruptions, the 'messianic
cessation' and the breakdown of transmission.[40]

As this brief excursus makes clear, Benjamin's preoccupation with the
historicity of historiography, and the relation to the past in general, is motivated by political concerns that do not harmonize with Gadamer's classicism.
This is, if you wish, the epistemological background to Benjamin's political
polemic against "historians who wish to relive an era" by "blotting out everything they know about the later course of history" (Thesis VII). For by denying the dialectical interplay of past and present, and by trying to understand
historical events from the perspective of the actors, Benjamin argues, these

"objective" historians will inevitably side with, or "empathize" (*einfühlen*) with, the victors of history. This is a crucial claim for Benjamin's project insofar as it allows him to associate political resistance to domination in the present with the 'liberation' of the voice and promise of the oppressed in history. This renders it all the more surprising that this claim is largely, and interestingly, uncritically accepted and unexamined in the secondary literature. I will analyze this claim in greater detail in chapters three and four, in the context of a discussion of Benjamin's notion of a discontinuous presentation of history. At the moment, I wish to highlight the fact that this critique of victor history, in its difference from a hermeneutics of effective history, led Benjamin to be critical not only of bourgeois historians, but also of orthodox Marxism and a Marxist conception of progress.

Benjamin rejects the notion of "empathy" not only on the basis of the Marxist doctrine that, as Marx put it in *The German Ideology*, "the ideas of the ruling class are in every epoch the ruling ideas."[41] In that case, the claim would be that bourgeois historians read history in terms of the dominant ideologies and power relations of the present, and thus cannot uncover alternative histories, for instance, histories that take into view the "nameless drudgery" of the contemporaries of "great geniuses" and political victors (I 1241). By neglecting, in the attempt to attain an objective, contextless viewpoint on history, the influence of dominant 'ideologies' on contemporary historical research, historians are all the more subject to their influence, and therefore cannot read history of, or from the perspective of, the oppressed. This critique of bourgeois historicism is in agreement with the Marxist critique of ideology, in particular the ideology of the autarky of culture and cultural history (cf. V 583, II 465ff.).

Benjamin connects this critique with a more radical claim—one that is, at least in a strong version, more difficult to defend, as we will see in chapter two—according to which there is a continuity of the oppressors in history. "All rulers are the heirs of those who were victorious before them. Thus, empathy with the victors benefits, in every case, the present rulers" (Thesis VII; see also I 1241). Not only does a scientific objectivism about historical knowledge uncritically affirm a history of violence, Benjamin suggests, but it also, at the same time, reifies present structures of oppression and domination. A continuous presentation of history thus (perhaps inadvertently) plays into the hands of the history of victors and the continuity of oppression: "The continuum of history is the continuum of the oppressors," Benjamin suggests (I 1236). Even if the ruling classes, and the systems of domination and exploitation, change, they continue oppression and form a victor history. One might still take this view as quite compatible with the Marxist conception of history as the history of class struggles. However, the point for Benjamin is not to deny that there is continuity in history—such continuity can always be found and constructed from out of the 'richness of layers' that make up what we call history. Rather, the point is to resist the identification of this continuity with history in general. For this would endow history, and oppression and domination in history, with a sense of necessity and inevitability. Benjamin finds this conception of the necessary course of history not only in bourgeois historians, but also in the Social Democratic version of Marxism, in Kautsky's orthodox Marxism as well as in Bernstein's revisionist interpretation. It is for this reason that Benjamin undertakes a "critique of automatic progress," in particular a "critique of the theory of progress in Marx [which is] there defined by the unfolding of the forces of production" (I 1239).

BENJAMIN'S CRITIQUE OF MARX'S TELEO-LOGIC

Given Benjamin's revision of the question history, we may begin the presentation of his explicit critique of Marx's promise by asking: What, then, are the specific 'interests' that Marxist orthodoxy might have invested in the teleological construction of the laws of history? I already mentioned the possibility of interpreting Marx's claims about history in performative terms. Underwriting a call to revolutionary action, however, by the scientific insistence that history, by way of the 'inexorable' laws of capitalist development, demands it, might backfire by turning into its opposite. Benjamin's emphasis on the writing of history would in effect suggest that Marx, or at least the Social Democratic Marxists after him, are always in danger of conceiving the proletariat as "moving with the current" of history (Thesis XI). By drawing on economic determinism and the theory of (quasi)automatic progress, the Social Democrats would thus be following the conformist and ultimately quietist logic of the 'history of victors.' Benjamin's term for this quietism is derived from the "theologians of the Middle Ages": it is the doctrine of *acedia*, an "indolence of the heart," which, in its despair, abandons the promises of history and the hopes of its victims (Thesis VII, I 696).[42] As we will see, however, this political quietism is for Benjamin not merely an aberration of the true Marxist doctrine, but is derived from Marx's conception of history itself. When Marx famously argues that the 'fetters' that the relations of production impose upon the forces of production, preventing the latter from moving forward, are also the fetters and chains of the oppressed classes, he suggests that the 'victory' of the proletariat is identical to the logic of history. For, on this view, the development of the productive forces is the decisive factor in the historical evolution toward socialism. The productive forces—primarily, the deployment of labor, technological machinery, and energy resources at the disposal of the capitalist class—condition an increasing gap within the relations of production. The latter lead to the formation of an ever more numerous and increasingly dispossessed proletariat, whose historical mission is defined on the economic (as opposed to political) level: to take control of and collectively manage the highly socialized forces of production, thereby preventing future economic crises (which characterize capitalism in its advanced stage). The class struggle between the bourgeoisie and the proletariat is thus merely the social and political articulation of a dialectical movement of the economic base and its law-governed, progressive development. The rationality of history is, as we have seen, tied to the forces of production, which, however, develop 'behind the backs' of the individual producers, such that history may be said to be governed by its unconscious production. It is this rationality that Benjamin exposes as a logic of the history of victors.

> The conformism which has been part and parcel of Social Democracy from the beginning attaches not only to its political tactics but to its economic views as well. It is one reason for its later breakdown. Nothing has corrupted the German working class so much as the notion that it was moving with the current. It regarded technological developments as the fall of the stream with which it thought it was moving (Thesis XI).

For Benjamin, this means that "historical materialism" as the theory that assigns primacy to the economic 'infrastructure' (which includes technological advances) needs to be revised in such a way that history can no longer be told in terms of a linear development. "Historical materialism strives neither for a homogenous nor for a continuous presentation of history. As the superstructure works back on the infrastructure, it turns out that a homogenous history, say, of economics, exists as little as one of literature or jurisprudence" (V 588). Benjamin could hardly be clearer: If historical materialists have to abandon the primacy of the economy (which is to be replaced by the primacy of politics), then the idea of a continuous, progressive 'development' (a term the *Passagenwerk* always places in quotation marks) of history has to be forsaken, too. Needless to say that with this rejection of the exclusive primacy of the productive forces as the determining factor (of history and of politics), Benjamin proposes a very different 'historical materialism,' one that appropriates the method of 'montage' for its discontinuous presentation of history, rather than relying on the bourgeois or Social Democratic "epic" element of history (cf. V 575, I 1240f.). It is a historical materialism that is distrustful of the teleological promise of the future, and instead seeks to allow "historical correspondences" and political "memory" to motivate and enhance the struggle (I 1236). It is a historical materialism that is aware of the injunction or "claim" the past has on the present (Thesis II), and the "danger" that affects the tradition of the oppressed and "the dead," if the "enemy" does not cease to be victorious (Thesis VI). For Benjamin, this claim or address of the past can only be reciprocated in a political action that does not place its trust in History's final goal. Only a historical materialism suspicious of all 'communist goals,' and sufficiently aware of the precariousness of the struggle, can truly inherit the Marxist promise of emancipation.

Given his effort to 'save' Marx's promise, it should come as no surprise, then, that Benjamin's critique of Marx focuses on the concept of progress and, as we will see, the concept of the revolution. The central issue in this critique, as I am trying to show, is Marx's connection between loss and the promise, a promise that Marx saw as arising with the immanent laws of history driven by the forces of production. Marx's emancipatory promise thus needs to be freed from its tie to the 'forces of production,' including the role of technology in historical 'development'. As will become clearer in Derrida's reading, it is Marx's attempt to speculate on capitalism, and in particular on the technology it brings about, as a good investment that reencloses Marx in the logic of capital, precisely at the moment that he tries to overcome it. (We will see later that Benjamin, too, explicitly criticizes this logic of speculative investment.) A resistance to this logic that amounts to a reformulation of Marx's promise is therefore not only an attempt to break through the dominant, 'victorious' path of history to a dimension in which a memory of the oppressed has a place. Rather, this resistance at the same time breaks with the, at least in the nineteenth century, widespread enthusiasm for technological progress and the processes of modernization—a process Marx almost hymnically celebrated in the *Communist Manifesto*.[43]

When Benjamin, in his 1935 exposé for the Arcades Project, investigates what he calls the utopian 'wish-symbols' the nineteenth century invested primarily in technology, and which he sees as renewing 'ur-historical' images of a Golden Age (*Schlaraffenland*, V 47), he also concerns himself with Marx, who likewise sets his store by the productive forces. Not by chance, then, Benjamin uses Marx's term the "classless society" in order to designate these utopian images in the exposé (V 47). When Benjamin further approvingly suggests that Marx's classless society secularized messianic time (I 1231), what is at stake in this revisitation of a messianic structure upon Marx, as I will elaborate later, is a wresting away of the messianic promise from the primacy of the productive forces and technology.[44] For Benjamin, World War I sufficiently demonstrated the destructive effects of technology, as he showed in particular in his review of the fascist celebration of the 'warrior' in a 1930 collection of articles edited by Ernst Jünger ("Theories of German Fascism," III 238–250).[45]

We have seen that Benjamin inherited from Marx the attempt to join a memory of past violence with the emancipatory promise for change. Further, we noted the former's revision of the question of history so as to take into account its writing in the present rather than focusing on the economic and technological development on whose basis Marx connected memory and promise. In light of these concerns, we will now see that Benjamin's explicit critique of Marx confirms the guiding suspicion that the critique of 'victor-history' is not only leveled against scientific historicism and bourgeois versions of a theory of historical progress, and also not only against the Social

Democratic account of progress, which can be read as an *embourgeoisement* of Marxism. Rather, Marx himself becomes a target of this critique. As indicated, the concept of the messianic promise, as well as its temporality and its secularization in Marx's classless society, play a large role in this critique. The secularization of messianic time, the way Benjamin wishes to understand it, ushers into a rereading of Marx's promise, notably, into a different understanding of the time of historical action and the role of memories in it. Benjamin's critique of Marx, centered on the notion of messianic time, leads to apparent ambiguities of that notion, ambiguities that I hope to resolve. (A fuller and more satisfying account of the messianic, especially as regards the interpretation of its temporality, will have to wait for the second chapter, which treats Derrida's covering of much the same ground as Benjamin's.)

It is in his notes to the "Theses on the Concept of History," rather than in the posthumously published text, that Benjamin's explicit critique of Marx is to be found. Benjamin proposes there that the "classless society" not be viewed as the "goal of progress in history but its often failed and finally accomplished interruption" (I 1231). Benjamin's criticism here thus addresses Marx's conception of the revolution. Contrary to viewing it as the outcome and continuation of the history of victors, that is, as Marx's "locomotive of world history," Benjamin suggests that we see it as the "emergency brake" of the passengers in the train of history (I 1232). In another note, Benjamin succinctly presents his point of intervention in Marx's view of history, an intervention that crucially involves the relationship between the future and the past. After having identified the "class struggle," "progress," and the "classless society" as the "three basic concepts" of Marx's theoretical apparatus for conceptualizing 'history,' Benjamin criticizes how Marx "welds" [*verschweißen*] them together:

> With Marx, the structure of the basic thought presents itself as follows: In the course of historical development, humanity arrives at the classless society through a series of class struggles. But the classless society is not to be conceived as the endpoint [*Endpunkt*] of an historical development. From this erroneous [*irrigen*] conception emerged, among other things, the idea held by his epigones of a 'revolutionary situation' which, as is well known, never wanted to come. To the concept of the classless society, its real messianic face [*echtes messianisches Gesicht*] must be returned, and indeed, in the interest of the revolutionary politics of the proletariat itself (I 1232).

Benjamin thus rejects the teleological conception that, as we saw, allowed Marx to connect the memory of the instituting violence of capitalism with the emancipatory promise. He rejects it here primarily on political grounds: He holds it responsible for the quietism we discussed earlier. Further, this passage indicates that, contrary to a widespread understanding of messianism, Benjamin opposes the 'messianic face' to the idea of an 'end' of history, conceived as a progressive unfolding that moves toward its goal. (We will see in a moment that Benjamin also rejects the idea of a beginning or origin of such a development, an idea that is traditionally tied to teleological or eschatological conceptions.) The messianic face that Benjamin wishes to restore to Marx's promise designates a certain relationship with a future that disallows any closure or totality of 'the' past or history, whose unity and univocity is thus put into question in an effort to recover the 'richness of layers' of which Benjamin had spoken in his early treatment of the Historical School (VI 95). In this context, one should also recall that "Thesis B" affirms the Jewish ban on investigating the future in order to allow remembrance *(Eingedenken)*. It appears, then, that the unknown status of the future, as opposed to its projection as a goal or endpoint, is viewed as the precondition for a memorial relation to the richness of the past, a relation that in turn is claimed to be crucial for revolutionary politics. As the following citations will further demonstrate, the messianic for Benjamin not only refers to a nontelic future, but also to the past, a past that therefore cannot simply be opposed to the future. It is these connections among the messianic promise to an unknown future, the memory of the past, and political action ("revolutionary politics") that stand in need of explication. (Especially the notion of political action indicated here, however, will receive fuller treatment only in chapter three.)

In an adjacent note that I will cite in a moment, Benjamin clarifies what he means by the 'revolutionary situation' that Marx's 'error' prepared and by which the German Social Democrats set their store, deferring political action to the most distant future, either in an economistic or neo-Kantian interpretation of Marxism. If Benjamin here criticizes the basic tenets of Marx regarding history, in the following note, it appears—as in the more familiar "Theses on the Concept of History"—that Benjamin only faults the Social Democratic interpretation of Marx, and not Marx himself, for the assimilation of the Marxist view of history (and its connection with the future) to the historicist idea of progress with its 'empty' linear temporality. As indicated, Benjamin often, already in his early encounter with the question of proletarian politics, tries to have Marx agree with his more, from an orthodox point of view, 'esoteric' conception of history, thereby frustrating commentators on his relationship to Marx.

> Marx secularized the idea of messianic time in the idea of the classless society. And that was good. The misfortune began with Social Democracy elevating this idea to an 'ideal.' Neo-Kantian doctrine defined the ideal as an 'infinite task.' [. . .] Once the classless society was defined as an 'infinite task,' empty and homogenous time transformed itself, so to speak, into an anteroom [*Vorzimmer*] in which one could wait with more or less calm [*Gelassenheit*] for the arrival of the revolutionary situation. In truth, there is no moment that is not accompanied by *its* revolutionary chance—it simply

must be defined as a specific chance, namely as the chance of a wholly new solution in the face of a wholly new task. To the revolutionary thinker, the peculiar revolutionary chance of every historical moment confirms itself from out of the political situation. But it confirms itself no less through the key power [Schlüsselgewalt] of this moment over a very specific chamber [Gemach] of the past that was locked hitherto. Entering this chamber strictly coincides with political action, and it is this entry that offers political action, however annihilating [wie vernichtend immer], to cognition as a messianic one (I 1231).

Instead of the irresponsible and acquiescent politics of deferral advocated by orthodox and neo-Kantian Marxists, Benjamin argues for a seizing of the political chances of every moment, tackling the urgent problems at hand rather than postponing action to the time when substantial political differences will have been overcome by the march of history. It is important to observe that, for Benjamin, this focus on every moment with its political chances allows for a 'messianic' return of specific moments of the past, confirming the association of the messianic with the past rather than with the future alone, thereby necessitating a recasting of historical time altogether. Regarding the messianic, which we will discuss in greater detail, it is further to be noted that Benjamin is fully aware of the theological, prophetic background to Marx that later commentators uncovered. This renders doubtful the view that a melancholic and pessimistic Benjamin turned to theological motifs in order to 'save' or even eschew a leftist agenda in general or a Marxist one in particular that is otherwise alien to them.[46] Furthermore, Benjamin not only recognizes this background, but unmistakably affirms the translation of religious semantic potentials into a materialist view of history in which the messianic dimension is associated with, and discovered in, a this-worldly politics. This also casts doubt on the view that an essentially theological Benjamin only 'flirted' with Marxism for circumstantial reasons. Neither a merely profane Marxism, then—which would neglect the secularization of the messianic dimension, its temporality, insights, and energies—nor an apolitical theology—which might be as quietist as Social Democracy.

MESSIANIC TIME: SEIZING THE MOMENT

The crucial question, of course, is how the messianic dimension is to be understood and made relevant to politics. For Benjamin, we cannot just equate the revolution with Judgment Day and the classless society with the messianic realm, for such an uncritical secularization results in a highly questionable teleology with undesirable political consequences. And yet—in what appears to be a contradictory gesture, another seemingly subjective ambivalence to which we will have occasion to return—the genuinely messianic face must be returned to Marx. In further analyzing the significant passage previously cited—a full elaboration of which must wait until we turn to Benjamin's notion of political action (in chapter three)—let us first of all note that its basic argument against a postponement of action in Marxist goals, and for an insistence on the necessity of political decision in every moment, is in accord with a 1926 letter to Scholem in which Benjamin defends his 'communism.' A brief turn to this letter can thus illuminate our understanding of the earlier passage. Discussing the need "to leave the purely theoretical sphere," and his interest in communist practice, Benjamin argues that the task is not "to decide once and for all, but to decide at every moment. But to *decide*. [. . .] If I one day were to join the Communist Party [. . .] my own conviction would be to proceed radically, never consistently, in the most important matters."[47] What sounds like mere decisionism here is an insistence on the necessity to reconfirm each time one's obligation to act in the profane sphere of politics, without the consistent focus on the goals of communism, goals that might lead to the justification of quietism in the present.[48] Benjamin continues by emphasizing the "mistake [*das Unzutreffende*] of the materialist metaphysic, or, if you will, also of the materialist conception of history," thereby revealing that his misgivings about Marx's 'welding together' of his three basic concepts of history are not just political. However, he insists that if one wishes to "understand the present historical moment as a struggle, one cannot reject the study and praxis of that mechanism whereby things (and relations) and the masses affect one another" (ibid.). A commitment to political action requires the Marxist dialectical analysis of the 'concrete' historical relations and an assessment of the political possibilities of the present with regard to the masses, but it does not involve a wholesale commitment to the communist concept of history. Thus, Benjamin concludes his explanations to Scholem by pointing out that he considers "anarchist methods unserviceable and Communist 'goals' meaningless and non-existent. Which does not detract one iota from the value of Communist action, because it is the corrective of Communist goals" (ibid.).

A genuine concept of political action, which for Benjamin implies an opening of a hitherto locked 'chamber of the past' and thus a certain form of memory, can on this view be turned against the focus on communist goals. Indeed, what makes an action 'messianic' is not, first of all, its relationship to the future classless society, but its opening up of memory. This conception of the messianic does not, however, oppose the past and the future on a conception of linear time that Benjamin explicitly rejects as underlying the theory of progress: "The concept of the historical progress of mankind cannot be sundered from the concept of its progression through a homogenous, empty time" (Thesis XIII). Let us defer (until chapter three) a discussion of the mention, in the long passage previously cited, of a "messianic" annihilation or destruction, which, as the "Theses" tell us, "blasts open" (Thesis XIV) and interrupts the epic continuum of linear history. Instead, I will continue the explication of the passage quoted earlier, drawing mainly on the "Theses."

Benjamin concludes his convoluted reconceptualization of revolutionary political action in that passage by emphasizing that the "classless society is not the end-goal (Endziel) of progress in history but its often failed [and] finally accomplished interruption" (I 1231). In this debate with Marx, then, Benjamin clearly rejects the futural projection of an end to politics, insofar as this end can be used to defer political action to an end, goal, or final point. Such finality in politics seems to Benjamin to compromise the political chances of every moment with its potential and its unique political constellation. Contrary to the Marxist conception of history ushering into the (potential) end of politics, Benjamin here—following his 'revision' of the question of history, as discussed earlier—envisages the primacy of politics over history (V 491; II 300), where history, in the collective singular, refers to a largely law-governed, conceptual structure totalized by its reference to the future. It would be this totalization that first of all allows us to speak of progress. It is thus, for Benjamin, no accident that a certain conception of history, taking its bearings from Marx's concept of progress, ushers into either an orthodox and economistic or a neo-Kantian Marxism after the failure of Marx's predictions and hopes for a proletarian revolution.

In criticizing the goal-directedness of history and the scientific theories of progress that dominate the nineteenth century, Benjamin also turns against the idea of the wholeness of history, as this wholeness is achieved by history's reference to its end goal. As we have seen, this wholeness is expressed in the Marxist tradition as the distinction between different stages of history ('stagism'), the logic of their succession (processes of increasing socialization leading to crises and revolutions), and the goal that gives direction and meaning to the succession of stages. This goal can be seen as 'ending the pre-history of humanity' and, at the same time, as the starting point for another history, or it can be infinitely deferred, such that progress becomes an infinite process. After Benjamin argued that this version of progress neglects the indignation and memory of the struggling masses by turning all its attention to the future (Thesis XII), the following Thesis on the concept of history explicitly criticizes "Social Democratic theory" and its "dogmatic claims" about progress. Benjamin isolates three objectionable aspects of this version of progress. First, in line with his refusal to focus on the productive forces alone, he claims that Social Democratic Marxism confuses advances in human knowledge and technology, which augment the exploitation of nature, with "the progress of mankind itself" (Thesis XIII; cf. Thesis XI). We might say that what Benjamin aims at here is the automatic association of technical progress with moral progress for all human beings, whereas in truth, proponents of the former tend to forget the "retrogression of society" (Thesis XI) as well as the suffering of the past (Thesis XII). In this context, it might seem to be no surprise that it is in the nineteenth century that the ethical theory of utilitarianism rose to prominence, for according to it, a future positive balance of gains and losses justifies past and current injustices. It is this utilitarian justification of past and present injustice by reference to a promised future that Benjamin finds lurking in all theories of progress, despite Marx's criticisms of utilitarianism.

The second controversial aspect applies to the *embourgeoisement* of Marxism in Social Democracy. It is the idea of the boundlessness or interminability of progress "in keeping with the infinite perfectibility of mankind" (Thesis XIII). As noted, Benjamin criticizes the quietist politics of deferral that ultimately plays off the future against the present and the past. Third, Benjamin mentions the idea of automatic progress that, I have argued, he views as originating with Marx's idea that he had discovered the laws of history. He finds all three aspects highly questionable, but argues that we should not overlook what they have in common—namely, the idea of the irreversibility of a linear and empty time. It is the 'continuum of history' that must be resisted first of all by revolutionary struggles, a resistance and a "messianic cessation of happening" that seizes "a revolutionary chance in the fight for the oppressed past" (Thesis XVII). Again, Benjamin associates radical political action with the possibility of retrieving hitherto unknown aspects of that past, aspects that are 'oppressed' by present relations of domination (Thesis VI) as well as by bourgeois and Marxist versions of progress. The 'messianic' refers here to the cessation or interruption of the progressive timeline that makes the retrieval of this past possible. The counterhistoriography and the political action Benjamin has in mind thus have to rely on a different temporality, one in which "the present is not a transition, but in which time stands still" (Thesis XVI).

Before turning to a more detailed investigation of Benjamin's understanding of messianic time, it should be noted that Benjamin does not reject the concept of progress for all domains and in all contexts, as Adorno hastened to emphasize.[49] It is the projection of history onto a goal, its resulting totalization and unification along the lines of scientifically observable laws, that yields the concept of progress to be questioned. Indeed, if freed from its end or goal, and from the concomitant totality of history, progress can have critical functions, for example, by highlighting regressive tendencies in society (V 594). Benjamin writes that the concept of progress loses these critical functions when it designates the automatic and lawful passage "between a legendary beginning and a legendary end of history" (V 596). He continues: "as soon as progress becomes the signature of the course of history *on the whole*, its concept appears in the context of an uncritical hypostatization instead of a critical questioning" (V 598f.; Benjamin's emphasis). These passages should render it questionable to attribute to Benjamin, at least to the later Benjamin, an "archeo-teleological" or an "archeo-eschatological" conception of history, as Derrida does in "The Force of Law" (FL 1015).

Benjamin sees this notion of the totality of progress as deriving in particular from the "saturated bourgeois class" (V 599). However, as soon as the political power this class wields over the dominant conception of history is challenged in the course of the nineteenth century, bourgeois writers such as Hermann Lotze become more reserved. It is with Lotze's *Mikrokosmos* (1864) in mind that Benjamin criticizes the notion of progress in the name of the 'claim' the dead have on the living, so famously mentioned (after a citation from Lotze) as the "*weak* messianic power" in the "Theses." For in a chapter entitled "The Meaning of History," Lotze, whom Benjamin cites often in "Konvolut N" of the *Passagenwerk*, condemns the "unreflected enthusiasm" of those idealist philosophies of history that "count as little the claims [*Ansprüche*] of individual times and of individual humans and overlook their misfortune if only humanity in general progresses" (V 599).[50]

For Benjamin, as previously indicated, the exposure to a non-telic, unknown, and in this sense messianic future allows the present to uncover moments of the past that had previously been buried in the historical and cultural 'richness of layers.' These moments are characterized as an 'oppressed past' (Thesis XVII) that is to be recovered and experienced, a buried history that, with this turn to Lotze's 'claims,' appears to carry both a power or force (*Kraft*) to be inherited and a demand placed upon us, the present generation. The second Thesis suggests that "like every generation that preceded us, we have been given a *weak* messianic force to which the past has a claim [*Anspruch*]" (Thesis II). I will turn to a more detailed interpretation of the "Theses" in light of these ideas in a moment. What I would like to emphasize at present is that with the notion of the 'claim' of the past on the present, the idea of retrieving the richness of historical experience, against historicism and the philosophies of history, acquires distinctly ethical and political import: The "secret agreement" between the past and the present, the past's "expectation" of us (Thesis II), places present generations under an obligation: the obligation to remember the 'oppressed past,' the "toil of the nameless" (Thesis VII) to which we owe so much. Already speaking a language means repeating the dead, and listening to others, Benjamin indicates, means listening to the dead ("Is there not an echo of voices that have now grown silent in the voices to which we lend our ears?" Thesis II). But Benjamin means more. It is this 'more' that allows him to associate the response to the 'address' (*Anspruch*) of the dead with a 'weak messianic force,' with the inheritance of past energies fuelling present struggles, and disrupting inherited power relations.

What is this 'more'? The memory of the dead, for Benjamin, is also a memory of promises. The Thesis under consideration begins with Lotze's insight that present generations generally do not envy future generations.

Benjamin concludes from this that the concept of happiness is constituted not primarily by the hope for future fulfillment, but by past experiences of it, and, above all, by the unfulfilled, missed opportunities of the past. Happiness is sought in the present realization of past possibilities. Claiming this insight for individual experience as well as for the collective or generational level of history, Benjamin then maintains that "in other words, the idea of happiness inseparably carries with it the idea of redemption" (Thesis II). The "Theses" thus confirm what we discovered earlier: Benjamin does not associate the messianic with the future alone, at least not with the future of the present generation, as this is ordinarily understood. The messianic idea of redemption does not, in the first instance, refer to the future of the present, but the future of the past, which, by our response to it, may become 'our' future, a new future indexed by our present in its constellation with the past. But the focus is not on our future, for a turn to it is always in danger of forgetting the future 'in' and 'from' the past. The idea of a future that is not also the future of the past has to be abandoned, and this is why the theological concept of the messianic, with its implication of all generations, including those of the past, is so attractive to Benjamin. The idea of a future that is merely 'our' future, the future of the present generation, is to be "disenchanted," as in the Jewish ban on graven images (Thesis B). This is also why the idea of progress, to which even Marx succumbed, receives, as we saw, Benjamin's gravest strictures for its underlying concept of linear, homogenous, empty time. For linear time views the present as the watershed that divides the past and the future, thus disallowing the idea of a future in, of, or from the past. Linear time abandons the past as lost, as dead and gone. It must be interrupted in a "messianic cessation of happening" (Thesis XVII) and replaced by a concept of time in which the future of the past has a chance to be assumed—in a sense to be specified—by the present.

The messianic concept of redemption, then, does not refer to a plenitude at the end of our future, but captures most fully the sense that "nothing that has ever happened is to be regarded as lost for history" (Thesis III). The past we inherit—and this is certainly true of the history of Marxism and of Marx's text—is saturated with latent promises that arise from missed chances, lost struggles, and failed revolutions. Every moment with its specific political task of resisting oppression has the unique opportunity to discover, inherit, respond to, and, perhaps, fulfill such a promise, assume such hope, resist again the failure. So every political task in the present is also a "revolutionary chance in the struggle for the oppressed past" (Thesis XVII). The greatest "danger" is, once again, the idea, shared by bourgeois historians and Social Democracy, that "'the truth will not run away from us'" (Thesis V). The danger consists in the missing of one's always singular chance of seizing the 'oppressed past' from further occlusion by conformists who, knowingly or not, are complicit with those in power (Thesis VI). As we will discuss in greater detail, resisting the power structures in the present permits the uncovering of past promises. In a curious psychological and experiential twist—whose curiosity may in part explain the 'weakness' of its force—the memory of failures and promises may energize present struggles "nourished by the image of enslaved ancestors" (Thesis XII). Such a constellation, then, allows a transfer of power from the past to the present, from the present to the past: a "*weak* messianic force" (Thesis II). A memory of promises figures the promise of memory.

SECULARIZING MESSIANISM

Before we turn to a more detailed analysis of the promise of memory that, largely in Benjamin's "Theses," emerges out his critique of Marx's teleology, we should return to the question regarding Benjamin's relation to the "secularization" (I 1231) of the messianic idea in Marx. For our analysis so far indicates that Benjamin rejects the theological or eschatological schema under-writing many conceptions of progress (the plan of Providence or the intention of nature or of reason), transferred to the immanence of history. Nonetheless, Benjamin uses the language of Jewish messianism in order to renegotiate the inheritance of the Marxist promise. What then does Benjamin mean by the secularization of the messianic?[51]

We should first remind ourselves that in his notes to the "Theses," Benjamin affirms Marx's 'secularization' of the messianic in no uncertain terms: "In the idea of the classless society, Marx has secularized the idea of messianic time. And that was good" (I 1231). At the same time, however, Benjamin claims, as we have seen, that this secularization has miscarried, with disastrous consequences such as the rise of European fascism and the disempowerment of the working classes. After having criticized Marx's construction of the classless society as the goal and end of history, Benjamin writes: "To the concept of the classless society, its real messianic face [*echtes messianisches Gesicht*] must be returned, and indeed, in the interest of the revolutionary politics of the proletariat itself" (I 1232). So the religious idea of messianic time must be secularized, and its translation into the worldly political, social, and economic realm is to be affirmed. At the same time, this translation must be undertaken in such a way as to preserve 'the true messianic face.' The messianic, then, cannot be understood as referring to an end. This indicates that what is valuable in the theological concept of the messianic is not its eschatology, as the study of last things, or even a teleology, as a latent or visible, progressive or desultory, evolutionary or revolutionary unfolding toward a goal. I argued earlier that, for Benjamin, the idea of the messianic, by contrast, represents, on the one hand, the unknowability and openness of the future, and, on the other, the irruptive retrieval of hitherto buried images of the past. Benjamin largely lacks a conceptual account of the link between futural openness and memorial retrieval, for which we may, then, profitably turn to Derrida's account of the promise of memory in terms of the quasi-transcendental law of repetition. Benjamin does, however, associate messianic time as well as the classless society with 'cessation,' 'standstill,' or 'interruption' in which openness to the future allows the memory of what is trampled under the march of progress and its linear time.

Nonetheless, Benjamin's concept of secularization has been identified with the secularization of Jewish or Christian messianism in terms of a *Heilsgeschichte* (salvation history, soteriology), and his affirmation of Marx's secularization of the messianic idea might be (mis)understood in this way. If we follow Adorno's account in the context of his reading of Benjamin's critique of progress, the connection of messianic salvation with historical stages began with Augustine's *Civitas Dei* and was then secularized in the Enlightenment and in German idealism, especially in Kant and Hegel. From Kant to Hegel and beyond, this secularization is associated with a force in history that operates 'unconsciously' behind the backs of individuals, but eventually brings about the ultimate well-being of humanity. In this way, a ground of history—Kant called it the 'intention of nature' (*Naturabsicht*); in Hegel it famously appears as the 'cunning of reason'—is postulated. This ground operates as an alien subject outside of human power, but it is claimed to ultimately harmonize with the final purpose of humanity, and it brings the human (and moral) interest in history and society to a rational conclusion.[52] A hidden necessity, directed to its teleological resolution, is at work in the freedom of individual action. As is well known, Schelling referred to this problem of the harmony of necessity and freedom as the "highest [. . .] not yet resolved problem of transcendental philosophy."[53] We might also, keeping many differences in mind, relate this unconscious but progressive production of history to Adam Smith's celebrated "invisible hand" of the market economy.[54] Victor Hugo perhaps formulated this "God" of progress immanent in history best when he claimed that: "Le progrès, c'est le pas même de Dieu" (cited by Benjamin at V 905). While Marx is certainly very critical of the bourgeois idealization of progress, he inherited the theme of the unconscious and teleological production of history and turned it into the theory of a 'quasi-natural' (*naturwüchsige*) force moving history forward through the alienation of producers.[55] It is the task of the privileged agent of history—what Marx calls the proletariat—to reunite freedom and necessity in appropriating the 'capital' it produced, the alienated object of the capitalist stage of history. This is the meaning of Engels's famous claim that the proletariat is to become the heir of German idealism.

It has recently been pointed out how Benjamin's theory of the 'phantasmagoria' and the collective 'dream-sleep' of capitalism itself draws on this theory of the unconscious production of history, and thus on a teleological, divine, or natural force operating in history to bring it to a close.[56] "Capitalism was a natural phenomenon, with which a new dream-sleep came over Europe, and with it, a reactivation of mythical forces" (V 494), Benjamin writes. According to some commentators, the task is thus for Benjamin, as for Marx, to awaken from this slumber in the formation of the class consciousness of the proletariat (V 1033). Our analysis, however, demonstrates that Benjamin rejected the concept of a latent meaning of history to be freed in a supreme moment of awakening. Against the assimilation of Benjamin to the philosophy of history, one should note that, as I have argued, he rejects the idea of progress and of a historical teleology. Further, the connection between the unconscious production of history and the 'dream-sleep' remains unclear in Benjamin, as he saw himself.[57] What is clear is that Benjamin associates the theory of awakening—which for him is an awakening from the nineteenth century and its mistaken ideas about history—with the "now of recognizability" in which a historical constellation of past and present, formed as in a dream, becomes legible and demands interpretation (V 496). Thus, the fact that the receiving 'subject' of these images is not conscious of their formation, rather, that this "not-yet-conscious knowledge of the past" (V 1213, V 491) occurs to it in a moment of 'awakening,' does not really, despite Benjamin's own occasional formulations, agree with the Marxist concept of awakening to proletarian class consciousness. In the latter, as we saw earlier, the subject (the proletariat) actively forgets the ghosts of the past in order to accomplish the 'world-historical task' by consciously fulfilling the demands of history's rationality. By contrast, Benjamin's theory of awakening is part of a theory of memory—"Awakening is the exemplary case of memory" (V 491)—not part of a theory of the memoryless subject incarnating the future classless society. What Benjamin and Marx, however, have in common is the suggestion that the meaning of the past is not exclusively determined by the present, but also depends on the future. Benjamin expresses this by emphasizing the lack of control of the present over the past, a present cast in, according to Ernst Bloch's formulation, the "darkness of the lived moment" (V 491). Although the readings that reenclose Benjamin within the Marxist logic of fulfillment have their basis in some of Benjamin's formulations, we should not overlook Benjamin's explicit critique of Marx and neglect his rejection of this philosophy of history. (We will see in the third chapter that Benjamin's reformulation of the concept of the proletariat's political action, a reformulation that focuses on the nonviolent proletarian strike, further delimits the constitution of the subject of action by refusing its projection onto a goal.)

Given his critique of the idea of progress, and his refusal to conceive of the messianic as a goal, the task Benjamin faces in his inheritance of the promise is to retain its two sides while reconfiguring them. He must maintain the possibility of a critical analyses of capitalist 'phantasmagoria' without (teleologically) directing these analyses to a future utterly devoid of what Derrida will call 'spectrality,' without reducing human relations to the merely human. I want to suggest here (and in the following) that Benjamin wishes to inherit some of Marx's critical insights concerning the ideological effects of capitalism, specifically regarding the understanding of its own past, without aiming at the collective identity of a finally self-conscious subject in control of its history and its future. While Benjamin rejects the finalization of the past in all its guises—and therewith, a Kantian, Hegelian, or orthodox Marxist secularization of messianic eschatology—he is also aware of a certain danger in insisting on the utter unavailability of history to human action, as that would play into the history of victors. This is what Adorno called the danger of construing the promise of redemption as an "ahistorical theology" without any meaningful relationship to political action.[58]

Regarding the question of how we can inherit the two sides of Marx's emancipatory promise, it appears that Benjamin tries to think a certain kind of finitude within history that remains irreducible to the human and the living, an otherness that might the be experienced as the 'messianic claim' the dead have upon us. As will ideally become clearer as our exposition of the "Theses" and the "Critique of Violence" unfolds, Benjamin proposes to view the messianic *itself* as the finitude of the realm of political action, exposing every imposition of law, and indeed every decision and political struggle, to its inherent instability and transience. Benjamin then further suggests that certain kinds of political action—we might call them non-instrumental actions of resistance—have a privileged relationship to the messianic future insofar as they 'enact' this exposition without themselves imposing new law. I will argue in chapter three that this notion of revolutionary action must be linked to the assumption of a messianic claim.

The beginning of the "Theologico-Political Fragment" confirms that Benjamin rejects the mediatization of the messianic into a secular, immanent goal or *telos* of politics or history, one that could yield an idea of progress. Focusing on politics as the 'profane order,' Benjamin therefore rejects the political meaning of theocracy as the justification of state power by reference to the presence of the divine in it. "To have denied the political significance of theocracy with all intensity is the greatest merit of Bloch's *Spirit of Utopia*" (II 203). We might see Benjamin in a tradition of theological thought that rejects the 'incarnation' of God in nature or in the human world in all its forms, viewing an ecclesiastical establishment and all ritual as compromising messianic transcendence.[59] For Benjamin, the principal target here is not only historical "Catholicism"—"The problem of Catholicism is that of the (false, earthly) theocracy" (VI 99)—but "capitalism as a religion" that, as a "cultic religion," takes over the "satisfaction of the same concerns, vexations and insecurities to which formerly the so-called religions gave an answer" (VI 100).[60] It is thus for Benjamin not only (Social Democratic or 'vulgar') Marxism that claims to represent and embody the messianic, eschatological future, as we saw earlier. Rather, capitalism establishes itself as a cult that secularizes the religious tradition. And, further, Benjamin views the Marxist critique of capitalism as entangled in this cultic religion by continuing its logic. To confirm our previous reading of the later Benjamin, we may refer to his critique of Marx in the early notes.

In these notes, Benjamin presents Marx's idea of the transition to capitalism, along with Nietzsche's idea of the overman, as an attempt to capitalize on what Nietzsche called the death of God. At the time of the "blasting of heaven"—the breakdown of premodern religion as a secular, political force—both Nietzsche and Marx are seen to attempt to benefit from an "increased humanness," increased by having "grown through the sky" (VI 100f.). It would not be difficult to recognize in these comments a rejection of the Feuerbachian elements in Marx's critique of alienation. As is well known, Feuerbach "resolved the religious essence into the human essence," as Marx put it in the "Theses on Feuerbach," that is, he shows that the idea of God is a synthesis of idealized human perfections that are personified and projected into the heavens. In *The Essence of Christianity*, Feuerbach argued that, after humanity had alienated its own image in its creation of God, it was time to reappropriate this image. Marx then argued that the critique of political economy followed upon Feuerbach's critique of Christianity, where the former is more encompassing and radical in also viewing the conditions of alienation—capitalism itself—as a form of alienation that ultimately needs to be reappropriated. Benjamin sees this critique as an attempt to overcome capitalism with its own logic of 'interest' and 'guilt/debt': "And similarly Marx: irreversible capitalism becomes socialism with interest and the interest of interest, which are functions of guilt/debt [*der nicht umkehrende Kapitalismus wird mit Zins und Zinseszins, als welche Funktion der Schuld . . . sind, Sozialismus*]" (VI 101f.). Hence, Marx's attempt to overcome the logic of profit, while profiting from its historical creations (technology, labor as a new need of productively creative humans, global commerce, the universality of human relations, etc.), is doomed to failure from the outset.

Benjamin in particular rejects the idea of the human being—an idea that can be traced back to Kant's philosophy of history—as 'growing,' that is, as expanding its needs and capacities, even if the affirmation of this growth means taking into account, as we have seen in Marx, the sacrifice of large segments of past and present generations and their claim to a life without unnecessary suffering. Benjamin contrasts his conception of political action with the idea of the human, which Kant constructed as the teleological horizon, the regulative ideal, of history:[61] "My definition of politics: the fulfillment of non-increased humanity [*der ungesteigerten Menschhaftigkeit*]" (VI 99). We thus see that, from his first encounter with Marxism, Benjamin is critical of its 'idolization' of history and its elevation of humanity by investing it with secularized, religious categories. Benjamin's later critique of Social Democratic Marxism for its exclusive emphasis on humanity's "progress in the mastery of nature," an emphasis that neglects the "retrogression of society" (Thesis XI), must be seen in this context. The progress of human skills and technology is not to be used as a justification of present and past suffering.

This early and explicit critique of Marx's logic of an increasing humanity thus has to be read in conjunction with the critique of a messianic historical teleology. Not only can we not relate ourselves to the messianic by constructing it as our telos, but we cannot further reduce the future to the merely human by viewing it as the return of humanity from its alienation in the 'heavens.' With this in mind, we can summarize our review of Benjamin's critique of Marx with regard to the question of the memory of suffering and the inheritance of the promise of liberation. As we have suggested throughout, for Benjamin the promise cannot be construed as an overcoming or supersession of such memory, but must instead take it up and co-articulate the promise with it. In Marx, past violence and suffering appear inserted in a necessary course of history that is justified by its end (the classless society). So far, this critique of historical teleology agrees with other critiques of Marx's view of history (e.g., Löwith' s critique of *Heilsgeschichte* or salvation history, or Popper's critique of what he called historicism).[62]

Most significant, however, are the consequences Benjamin draws from this critique. Past suffering must be released from its insertion into a conception of historical necessity, and it must not be subjected to the concept of a just end, whether in Kant's liberal sense or in Marx's communist sense. Instead, we need a heightened awareness of the contingency of these acts of violence (dispossession, alienation, political atrocities, etc.), a contingency that first of all would allow us to face up to the co-responsibility that the present generation, as the heir and perhaps beneficiary of this history of violence, bears for it. But this exposition of contingency can, for Benjamin, also lead to a motivation for emancipatory struggles in the present. It is an action that assumes responsibility for the history of victors by resisting it in the present, by revealing its contingency and finitude, and by allowing different accounts of the past to be generated, thereby responding to the messianic 'claim' and 'address' of the dead victims.

Thus, despite his affirmation of Marx's secular classless society and his use of theological categories, Benjamin cannot be said to subscribe to the secularization of messianic eschatology in terms of the unconscious, rational, progressive production of history that orients it toward its end in a transparent and liberated humanity. Rather, Benjamin associates the messianic with those layers of history that are forgotten or cast aside by the progressive march of such history. Those are the layers that he connects with the suffering from a narrowly construed technological progress, from a capitalist modernity all too interested in downplaying the 'retrogression in society' it brings about on account of capital accumulation and the expansion of the productive forces. Benjamin views this suffering, the 'toil of the nameless,' as issuing a call to responsible action, a 'claim' of past generations on the present one. To respond to this call means not only to remember the 'enslaved ancestors' in 'unlocking' hitherto unrecognized 'chambers' of the past, but to resist those who benefit from their oblivion or occlusion in the present.

Such resistance, as I will elaborate, interrupts the 'progressive' handing down of power from one generation of 'oppressors' to the next. The interruption or 'messianic standstill,' as we will see, is possible on the basis of the inherent finitude of power itself, a finitude that Benjamin, accordingly, associates with the messianic dimension in history and politics. This dimension opens up if we view the future as non-telic and unknowable rather than as the *eschaton* that made its way into Enlightenment concepts of history. Benjamin, however, did not present a theory of secularized 'messianic time' that would have allowed him to intrinsically connect an open future, the discontinuity and interruptibility of historical time, and the memory of infinitely interpretable layers of history, including those that have largely gone unrecognized by present relations of power. It is for this reason that I will, in the next chapter, turn to the deconstructive, quasi-transcendental account of historicity, iterability, and the 'messianic promise'—an understanding of the promise and messianicity that Derrida, not by accident, largely develops in the encounter with Marx.

FOUR ISSUES IN THE "THESES"

Before we turn to Derrida's 'messianic' temporality as linking memories of injustice and promises of justice in a way congenial to Benjamin's project, however, we should investigate the latter a bit more with a view toward its sketch of the constellation involving memory, messianic time, and political action. If we go through the "Theses" more systematically, we see that its argument relies on four associations that remain rather allusive and desultory in the text. For the purposes of overview, I will now indicate possible explications with regard to these four relations, thereby indicating the tasks of future chapters. The "Theses" address past moments to be 'unlocked' as the "secret agreement between past generations and our generation," as the "expectation" or "claim" the past has on the present (Thesis II), the "true image of the past" prepared for its "recognizability" or readability in the present (Thesis V), as a "spark of hope" kindled in the past by the historian who knows that the dead may be forgotten by the conformism of a tradition dominated by the ruling classes, as the "tradition of the oppressed" (Thesis VIII), the "image of enslaved ancestors" that is lost if one focuses on a redeemed future alone (Thesis XII), or simply as the "oppressed past" whose rescue requires the seizing of the "revolutionary chance" of every moment in a "messianic cessation of happening" (Thesis XVII). The relation necessary to experience the crucial past that addresses itself to us is characterized both in terms of a novel method of writing history and in terms of political action. In broadly historiographical terms, Benjamin speaks of "memory" *(Erinnerung)* (Thesis VI), "remembrance" *(Eingedenken)* (Thesis B), "citation" (Thesis III, XIV), a "unique" experience rather than an "'eternal' image" (Thesis XVI), introducing, like the French Revolution, a "new calendar" (Thesis XV), and a "constructive principle" of materialist historiography that "arrests" thought in a "constellation pregnant with tensions" so that thought "crystallizes as a monad" (Thesis XVII).

The relation to the past that concerns us is, however, also characterized in more directly political, combative terms. As we saw earlier, in his notes to the "Theses," Benjamin says that political action in the present, at every moment, allows for a 'messianic' return of specific moments of the past (I 1231). The "Theses" speak of "wresting tradition from conformism" and from "the enemy" (Thesis VI), of "bringing about a true state of emergency" (Thesis VIII), of a revolutionary "struggle for the oppressed past" (Thesis XVII) on the part of the "enslaved, avenging class" as the "subject of historical knowledge" (Thesis XII). What needs to be explicated here above all are (1) the relation between the unknown future, on the one hand, and the "messianic cessation" or "standstill" of time (Thesis XVI), the interruption or "blasting open" of the continuum of history, on the other (Thesis XIV); (2) the relation between the concealed or 'locked' nature of the 'oppressed past' and oppression in the present; (3) the relation between political action in the present against this oppression and the messianic cessation that allows the unlocking; and (4) the relation between a new, 'constructive' writing of history and political action.

Concerning the first issue, the foregoing discussion indicates that the futural projection of an end to historical processes—whether as a goal implied by history's underlying laws or a regulative ideal to be approximated—results in a more or less linear conception of progressive history. Linear time and progress allow the utilitarian justification of past and present suffering by pointing to the promised gains of the future. Furthermore, they regard the past as lost, thus forgetting and surrendering its promises and energies, and weakening working-class struggles. They also contribute to a streamlining of historical accounts, leaving out those aspects of the past that have not, or perhaps not as visibly, entered the always contestable and interest-driven construction of tradition. To recover the richness and the promises of the past, it thus seems necessary to turn the view of historians and political actors away from the future as goal, and, on Benjamin's conception, even as a horizon with content to be anticipated. Benjamin opposes a notion of history governed by its 'end' or goal to a historical time of 'interruption' just as he opposes this version of totalized progress to a logic of the 'actualization' of specific moments in the past (V 574). He derides the lining up of historical events on the course of progress like "beads of a rosary" and attempts to attain the 'now-time' of a historical constellation into which "splinters of messianic time are blast [*eingesprengt*]" (Thesis A), rendering time not empty, homogenous, and continuous, but discontinuous and overflowing with images of the past.

As our reading of the "Theses" confirms, Benjamin's 'blasting open' of linear time refers the messianic 'splinters' or 'shards' (*Splitter*) neither to the past nor to the future, but problematizes the opposition between past and future, which is based on linear time. Rather than giving a detailed account of the temporality proper to a politics of memory, Benjamin conceptualizes this rift in time in the two different directions with whose relation the fourth issue is concerned: a new method for writing history and a concept of political action. Regarding the former, he sketchily suggests, in particular in the "Theses," a historiographical method that, not being based on narrative and linear construction, yields what he calls a 'constellation' of present and past that opens itself to the future. In this opening, the constellation achieves for Benjamin a passage to what is discontinuous and 'untimely' in history.

Benjamin's lifelong concern for the memory of, in his words, "the most endangered, most defamed and derided creations and thoughts" (II 75), for "what is unfulfilled, sorrowful and untimely" (I 343) in history, has often been pointed out. But this uncovering of unfulfilled images and promises, forgotten dreams, and claims of the dead reaching out to the present, requires at the same time a revisioning of the temporality of this present privileged by the emphasis on the writing of history. This is why Benjamin writes in his 'epistemological' notes to the *Passagenwerk* that he wishes to base his historical construction "on the differentials of time which for others disturb the 'major lines' of investigation" (V 570). Benjamin associates these major lines with a grand historical or 'epic' narrative with which a montage-like construction of history, arising from a discontinuity in time, has to break (I 1240). As we have seen, it is his critique of Marx's logic of progress, and his rewriting of the concept of the classless society in terms of a messianic future, that opens up the past for these differentials, these 'cracks' or 'leaps' (*Sprünge*, V 591), but that also exposes the present to the 'messianic' experience of the claim the oppressed of the past have on present generations.

It seems clear, however, that Benjamin's allusive comments on time do not amount to a philosophical theory that would account for the intended result: a concept of historical time that, while disallowing linear and archeoteleological conceptions, connects a 'disenchanted' future with the memorial retrieval of the past. Such a theory of time would no longer need to oppose "the image of enslaved ancestors" to the "ideal of liberated grandchildren" (Thesis XII), but combine both. It would even cultivate the latter while divesting it of the orthodox-Marxist or neo-Kantian logic of victorious progress, insisting on the need to interrupt it in order to seize the chances of the day, and render ideals contestable from an open-ended, 'disenchanted' future no one owns. As I will argue in chapter two, Derrida's account of time as 'another historicity' can fill this gap. Nonetheless, before engaging Derrida's reading of Benjamin more explicitly in the next chapter, we can glimpse that Benjamin attains a notion of temporality on which Derrida's engagement of Marx's promise focuses. For Derrida, as we will see, it is precisely this promise of a future, emptied of all content, that 'dis-joins' the present, so as to open it up to a plurality of specters from the past. Similarly, Benjamin's interruption or "messianic arrest (*Stillstellung*) of happening" (Thesis XVII) requires, as its condition, "disenchanting (*entzaubern*) the future to which those surrender (*verfallen*) who turn to the fortune-tellers for information" (Thesis B). It is the future that cannot be anticipated, what I will call a blind spot in the horizon of expectation, that opens up the present for its constellation with the past and to its inherited potential, thus rendering time discontinuous, irruptive, and, as Derrida would say, 'disjointed.' Thus, Benjamin indicates the desirability of conceiving a future beyond goal-directed anticipations, which, as a future present, can always be opposed to and played off against the past, that is, in the light of which the losses of the past might be cut and its promises abandoned.

As noted, Benjamin also addresses the 'messianic cessation of happening,' the 'rift' in time, by a reconceptualization of political action and revolutionary struggles. We saw him criticizing a Marxist concept of the revolution that relies on the progress of the economic base to provide favorable conditions for action. This concept results in a quietist or reformist understanding of action that is inadequate to the urgency and specificity of every political situation, and that does not tap into the energies of the past. Thus, he theorizes a non-instrumental political action that opens itself to the future by avoiding its projection onto a future end. In doing so, it frees the past for the sudden appearance of a unique image of the past crucially related to the present, and for an experience of the messianic claim the victims of history have on us. In a certain sense, of course, every action, decision, and event changes the past, which is never dead and gone. Every present is invested with the retroactive power of invention; to some extent, an event creates its precedents and causes and alters the conception of the past as well as of the future.[63] Benjamin, however, is not just concerned with changing and retrieving the past in any way whatever, with the uncontrollability of temporally disjointed dissemination. Rather, he wishes to uncover an 'oppressed past,' the 'tradition of the oppressed,' and to allow the experience of the claim the dead have on us. In my view, such uncovering requires the relation previously indicated (in issue three) between the oppressed past and oppression in the present.

Hence, only a fuller treatment of issues two and three will provide a satisfactory account of the way in which Benjamin associates messianic time, memory, and emancipatory action. For revolutionary action can arrest linear time, 'unlock' memorial images, and, at the same time, be nourished by them, only if access to such images is occluded by present power relations attacked by such action. In not directing itself to the future as a goal, a politics of resistance emerges that attacks present systems of domination and their imposition of a hegemonic view of history (the concept of 'victor-history'). In so doing, this action exposes the fundamental historicity, alterability, and finitude of all political systems by "calling into question every victory, past and present, of the rulers" (Thesis IV). At the same time, what I will later call 'memorial resistance' liberates different and each time unique conceptions of the past and assumes the claim of the dead on the present generation. In conjunction with the historiographical method discussed earlier (see issue four), the memory released here contributes to the present struggle by providing additional motivation, by highlighting the contingency of power relations, and by freeing the future from its 'enchantment' by the adherents of theories of progress (Thesis B).

Although Benjamin does not say very much about the connection between the historiographical method and political action, it is noteworthy that both issue from a messianic standstill of time: the arrest of thought and of events (Thesis XVII). Benjamin claims, in a well-known quip, "that things 'just keep on going' *is* the catastrophe" (V 592; cf. Thesis VIII), that is, that ruling classes still dominate in the present as they have in the past (Thesis VI) as mirrored in the linear, often progressivistic construction of historical thought and time. In turn, such constructions contribute to the hold of power and the prevention of a revolutionary breakthrough. In response to the ideological power complex—that, as we saw, cannot be neatly divided into base and superstructure—historical materialism must present the 'unity of theory and praxis' that Marxism always took itself to be. In Benjamin, this unity results in a reciprocal relation of resistance and historiography. While acts of resistance attempt to break the hold on power and ideology, thus uncovering heretofore buried images, materialist historiography motivates the struggle with images of past oppression and past revolutions, condensed in a constellation that, in short, presents the 'oppressed past' or the 'tradition of the oppressed.' Memorial action may also of itself give rise to such a historical "monad" (Thesis XVII) that "abbreviates" the history of humankind and its struggles (Thesis XVIII), as in the French Revolution: The introduction of the new calendar functions as a "historical time-lapse camera," providing for holidays as days of remembrance interrupting the linear time of the clock (Thesis XV). Such days of remembrance as well as a constructed monad connect one's individual fate with larger historical tendencies ("blasting a specific life out of the homogeneous course of history" so that "in a lifework, the epoch is preserved," Thesis XVII), thereby building communities capable of resistance.

As mentioned, I will further investigate the relation between an empty future and the interruption of time (issue one) by discussing Derrida's concept of historical time in chapter two. The relations among the oppressed past, present oppression, memorial resistance, and the interruption of time will be addressed in chapter three (issues two and three). Reading Benjamin's early essay on political action and power ("On the Critique of Violence") will show that he takes the rejection of projecting goals so far as to conceive the 'proletarian' strike as a radically non-instrumental action that exposes the finitude of institutionalized, ideologically dominant power. In the last chapter, I will return to the relation between such memorial resistance and Benjamin's proposal for a kind of historiography that responds to the claim of the dead (issue four).

TWO

Derrida's Reading of Marx

AFTER THE BREAKDOWN of 'actually existing socialism' in 1989, the discourse on Marx seemed abruptly changed in the East and the West. Marx's texts and the thinking of Marxism assumed a ghostly quality to which Jacques Derrida was one of the first to respond by attempting to keep this heritage alive and prevent its docile canonization in philosophy and sociology departments. The events that marked the end of more than a century during which Marxism functioned as an institutionalized and organizational doctrine—revolutionary events that now find us in post-euphoric disillusionment—positioned the question 'Whither Marxism?' at the forefront of a discussion concerning the future of social and political philosophy. This situation affords us the opportunity to see this discussion as truly opened up rather than closed, a discussion that I will take up in this chapter by considering Derrida's critical inheritance of Marx.

In particular, the events that opened up this discussion demonstrated once again what I would like to call the homelessness of Marx's promise for a classless society—that is, the absence of a (proletarian) subject embodying and carrying forward the promise—after the failure of the "social revolution of the nineteenth century," prophetically announced in "The Eighteenth Brumaire of Louis Bonaparte."[1] From the perspective of these events, what is most salient in Derrida's reading, as we will see, is his affirmative embrace of what Western Marxism experienced as a deplorable lack: the absence of the real prospect of finally realizing Marx's promise.[2] Derrida affirms the historical experience of the promise's 'homelessness' as a quasi-transcendental, structural opening through which, Derrida believes, emancipatory intentions may nonetheless be redirected: The promise, lacking incarnation in a unified subject, becomes 'spectral,' that is, neither present nor absent, but still practically effective.

Given that this historical experience is not entirely new, however, as Derrida himself points out, it may be seen as surprising that he does not take

up the reformulations of Marxism that previously resulted from it, beginning
with Ernst Bloch's *Spirit of Utopia* (1918) all the way up to the later writings
of the so-called Frankfurt School. We might say that it is largely this experience that accounts for the prevalence of a certain tone of mourning in such
writers as Horkheimer and Adorno. Their *Dialektik der Aufklärung* already
attempted a reformulation of Enlightenment promises by bending them back
on themselves, demanding that these promises of freedom and self-mastery
reflect on the 'regressive' elements their blind materialization brings about.[3]
Such a reflection on regressive tendencies would have to include an
'anamnestic solidarity' with the downtrodden of the historical process who
find no place in the future ideals of the Enlightenment. It could be shown
that Horkheimer and Adorno's book, written under the impression of the
Shoah and responding to some of Walter Benjamin's insights after his suicide
in 1940, already wrought changes on the utopian and progressivistic leanings
of Marxism precisely by taking up the memory of history's 'oppressed.'[4]

The only exception to Derrida's neglect of this tradition is Benjamin, to
whom Derrida appeals briefly in his book on Marx, primarily for Benjamin's
'messianism.'[5] This and the following chapters can thus also be viewed as
preparations for staging an encounter that was—almost—missed.[6] As we
have already seen in the case of Benjamin, and as we will see here for Derrida, what seems most problematic to both is the reading of historical events
in terms of a teleology, a movement and a promise toward the finality of a
goal. While one should note Marx's own critique of teleological constructions,[7] at crucial moments he promises his immanent, dialectical critique to a
final overcoming, or rather 'supersession' (*Aufhebung*), of what is criticized.
As we saw, Benjamin, like Marx interested in connecting the promise of justice with memories of injustice, rejects the teleo-logic on the basis of which
Marx effected such connection. Benjamin overcomes the promised *telos* of
the classless society by directing it toward a disenchanted future, and he precisely welcomes the images of the past that Marx thought were either to be
viewed as indices of the teleo-logic of victory or obstructing the 'poetry from
the future.' However, without an account that intrinsically connects these
two gestures of disenchanting the future and foregrounding memories of
injustice—that is, without conceptualizing the temporality of the relation
between the future and the past—Benjamin is in danger of falling back into
the logic that opposes the future to the past. It is such opposition, as we saw,
that allows past suffering to be reckoned up against, and redeemed by, future
gains. Merely disenchanting the future prohibits all future projections, even
those that are not connected to a logic of development or progress. It is here
that Derrida's critical inheritance of Marx's promise will help us to fill the
gaps in Benjamin's promise of memory. Derrida allows Benjamin to connect
more strongly the openness of the future with the differentials of time
through which the past may recover its richness and through which images

of repression may pass to enhance emancipatory action. First, then, we have to see how Derrida inherits and reformulates Marx's promise.

While the present chapter seeks to expose Derrida's reading of Marx with a focus on the resulting conjunction of memories of injustice and promises of justice, chapters three and four will then bring Benjamin's and Derrida's promises of memory into a more explicit dialogue. Chapter two proceeds in three steps. First, I will show, as briefly as possible, in what way Derrida's book on Marx, drawing on Benjamin, takes on Marx's promise by redirecting it toward the primacy of an empty future no longer opposed to the past. This analysis requires an elaboration of deconstruction's quasi-transcendental 'method' of reading, for it allows Derrida to argue that Marx needs the very openness of the future that a layer of his text denies. In this context, I will suggest a reelaboration of Derrida's own, problematic distinction between two ways to understand the inheritance of the promise. The second step will then elaborate the 'messianic' promise that is said to both make Marx's promise possible and to exceed it in a 'spectral' logic of disjointed time. Here, I will show that this promise, developed on the basis of the notion of originary repetition, requires a memory to which it cannot be opposed. The constellation of memory and promise raises the question of how we can, while rejecting what Derrida sees as Marx's exorcism of ghosts, retain that aspect of his Enlightenment promise that wishes to rid us of deceiving ghosts. In response to this question, I will argue in step three that Derrida's negotiation of Marx's promise yields a 'postutopianism' that attempts to reserve a place for utopian projections while continually questioning them in the light of a more radical, non-arriving future.

BENJAMIN AND DERRIDA: COMMON STARTING POINTS

The 'homelessness' of Marx's promise I just mentioned may be seen as one result of a more general experience of modernity, one that we might call, following Nietzsche and Heidegger, the nihilistic 'goallessness' (*Ziellosigkeit*) of the present after the 'flight of the gods' and the demise of ontotheologically grounded natural or historical teleologies.[8] This experience leads both Benjamin and Derrida to rethink a number of issues that have troubled Marxism for a while. If, on the basis of Benjamin's critique of Marx and Social Democratic Marxism as well as Derrida's reading in *Specters of Marx*, I briefly mention a few of the more salient issues, it is because they form the background against which Derrida's and Benjamin's rethinking of Marx's promise may be attempted. They form the context in which reflections on the promise of history must be understood, thus belonging to the ramifications of a reformulated promise.

There is first of all the theme of the 'end of politics.' The idea that the state is the expression of socioeconomic power led Marx to view the overcoming of class antagonism after the revolution as tantamount to the abolition of political institutions in which the decision-making process is negotiated between different individuals and groups.[9] As we saw in the first chapter, and will discuss further in the third, Benjamin, aiming at the primacy of politics over history, revised this theme in order to recover the political chances and urgencies of every moment rather than waiting for the base to prepare the revolutionary situation. Derrida will add to Benjamin's urgency the worry that action becomes deferred to the final overcoming of substantial differences. This revision has consequences for the 'critique of ideology' insofar as it is divested of the illusion of the final possibility of undistorted, free communication in a community transparent to itself. For what is perhaps most problematic in Marxism is the way in which a critique of social division and inequality lends itself to, or is nourished by, the phantasm of a completely transparent social order without radical internal differentiation—in a word, a totalitarian society.

The emphasis on the differences between political agents further leads to a skeptical glance at the Marxist construction of a unified macro-subject that is to enact the radical overturning of inherited, politico-economic circumstances. While Benjamin gave up on the hope of the economic base in unifying the proletariat, he attempted to motivate and unify revolutionary struggles by constructions of memory. Such constructions, however, must, as we saw, affirm the 'disenchanted' openness of the future and proceed from the 'differentials of time.' Recent developments in critical social theory as well as, in particular, French philosophy tend to view futural openness as installing an ineradicable, productive difference in all community. This amounts to a recasting of the 'subject' of history as marked by an 'internal' differentiation, or an 'external' excess, that it cannot present to itself.[10] It further leads to a rethinking of the Enlightenment topos of history—in the collective singular—as submissive to human action, and to an abandonment of the philosophy of history.

By determining societal, transindividual labor, even across history, according to the model of a macro-subject realizing its 'essential powers,' in an externalizing and reappropriating movement, Marx could both welcome and reject capitalist alienation.[11] Refusing the focus on technology in historical 'development,' Benjamin criticizes the idea of the human being as progressively 'growing,' as expanding its capacities, for its neglect of violence and moral-political regression in the past and the present (see VI 99ff.; Thesis XI). More generally, Derrida places in question the determination of what is 'proper' to the human by thinking an originary 'exappropriation,' epitomized by the role and place of language, death, and time—as well as the specters of 'history'—in human life. Indeed, the redirected and 'spectralized' promise itself, as we will see, turns into an ineluctable expropriation. Benjamin's focus on the rescue of images of past oppression is thus conceptually, by way of an analysis of historical time, connected with his rejection of a technocratic humanism. Vis-à-vis an originary displacement, the vulgar-Marxist analysis of capitalism as an expropriation of the property of the human, and the attempt to return what was alienated to the practical-historical subjects, is severely complicated and problematized.

These issues in reading Marx—the primacy of politics, the refusal of a transparent macro-subject, and a historical, non-teleological temporality—form the backdrop of Derrida's and Benjamin's recovery and sharpening of a certain 'messianic' structure in Marx. Derrida, as we will see, argues that the dimension of the future as an originary dislocation or 'disadjustment' of the human—the messianic future as unrepresentable and unmasterable—will lead to a rethinking of the very notion of finitude. It is the disavowal of this fini-tude, Derrida claims, that becomes the basis for the construction of the prop-erly human, of humanity's property, in the (humanist) Marxist discourse. Der-rida further views the disavowal as partly responsible for the historical violence in which the emancipatory discourse is implicated. Reflecting on the broad outlines of Derrida's approach, the attentive reader of *Specters of Marx* must then wonder whether the issue of memory and mourning—an issue that opens the book with its dedication and is frequently invoked as a necessary response to such disavowal[12]—is merely a polite, more or less conventional gesture, asking us to remember the 'victims' of struggles against injustice, or whether it is philosophically and conceptually tied to the emphasis on the dis-adjusting future and the remessianizing of Marx's promise through it. I will try to show that the latter is the case: a certain relationship to the future, a future not predetermined but nonetheless promised, promising itself to us, at the same time, and necessarily, opens up the past for a flood of memories. Thus, both Benjamin and Derrida link the opening of the future beyond the classless society to a particular attention to memory. Today, a rethought constellation of promise and memory, future and past, is necessary to inherit a promise that, linked by Marx to the victims of capitalism's institution and triumphal march, is now inseparable from the violence of its attempted institutionalization, a double violence the inheritors are called on to remember.

In this chapter, then, we will continue the investigation of the way in which a liberatory promise for the future may be conjoined with a memory of death and suffering. In the resulting constellation, the promise will have to be reconfigured so as to include—and not as a mere addition, a mere broad-ening of its scope—a memory of loss. Conversely, this memory will be seen to be invested with a promise that renders mourning interminable and, further, that combats its tendency to degenerate into the self-pity and the narcissistic or possessive mourning that Freud saw as the epitome of melancholia.[13] Avoiding melancholia, the promise of memory perhaps even allows it to fur-ther contribute to and energize political changes in the present and in the future. As we saw, it is this energizing that is central to Benjamin's concerns. In short, what I will try to bring to the fore here is a memory of promises as well as a promise of memory. The promise thus cannot be seen to surpass or overcome its own troubled history, but needs to revise the temporality that merely opposes the future to the past, that plays off a utopia, in a very broad sense of a future ideal, to a remembrance of the past. The Derridian account of 'originary repetition,' of the 'aporia' of time, and its attempt to think finitude as our exposure to an interminable future repetition, will here be seen as providing the means to approach such a constellation. It is an exploration of what Derrida has called a "messianic memory and promise."[14]

In thinking about the relation between memory and promise, we might begin by recalling two complications that, if we take the historicity of thought and action seriously, already suggest the inseparability of the two terms. First, the promise in question—Marx's promise for a classless society—may already be seen as a form of memory. Both Benjamin and Derrida follow (without naming) Moses Hess in viewing the socialist promise as part of a messianic tradition that began with the Abrahamic religions of the book.[15] Second, our time also inherits (or remembers) Marx's already inherited promise. Today, we are inheritors who have to negotiate not only the violence of subsequent attempts at institutionalizing the promise, but the religious imprint preceding messianisms might have left on it. In a way, the deconstructive relation to Marx's promise replays the relation of Marx's promise to religious messianism, even while this deconstruction recalls Marx to his debt. For Derrida, the religious prehistory imposes the most significant task on the deconstructive inheritance, for it connects it with a historical teleology that must be avoided above all. Insofar as, we might say, the 'onto-theo-logical' tradition thought God—which can here be defined, with Bloch, as "the problem of the radically new"[16]—according to various predeterminations—the 'metaphysics of presence,' which knows the future only as a future present—the question of how to inherit Marx's promise can be put thus: "Can one conceive an atheological heritage of the messianic?" (SM 168/266). In anticipatory brevity, we may say that Derrida attempts to inherit and 'radicalize' (SM 92/152) Marx's promise by emptying it of its content, by directing it to a future without horizon or predetermination, rather than to a utopia, a future ideal, or a blueprint that can be sketched out in advance. At issue is the move from a promise of the future that insists on the 'what' of the future, to the atheological, 'dry' promise *that* there is a future, before all else. Derrida tries to capture this latter promise, and the associated "indetermination that remains the ultimate mark of the future," in the formula "*il faut l'avenir*" ("it is necessary [that there be] the future," "there must be the future," SM 73/124). For Derrida, this is tantamount to saying that the inheritance of the promise involves, first of all, supplying what he calls the quasi-transcendental conditions of possibility of any prophetic promise (religious or Marxist). These conditions themselves bear a preeminent relation to the future. The 'atheological' inheritance, as a quasi-transcendental operation, turns the promise into a 'messianicity' or a 'messianic' without content and without religion, be it the (minimal) content of a classless society. It is the result of this operation that Derrida calls the *messianique sans messianisme* (SM 59/102), and, indeed, a "quasi-transcendental 'messianism'" (SM 168/297) that wishes to achieve a genuine openness and hospitality to the coming of the future.

TWO WAYS TO INHERIT MARX'S PROMISE

The inheritance of Marx's promise, then, plays itself out in terms of a quasi-transcendental reading, whose procedure we therefore have to investigate before assessing its outcome. Derrida himself, however, is (at least initially) unsure as to how exactly this methodical operation on Marx's promise is to be understood. Toward the end of *Specters of Marx*, he proposes two ways to construe the relationship between 'messianism' and the "messianic in general" (SM 59/102)—here, between the promise for a liberated future in the Marxist as well as the religious tradition, and its deconstructive 'radicalization.' On the one hand, the messianic, understood as a radical openness to the future that Derrida takes to be the very condition of experience, is arrived at and known by a process of "abstract desertification" (SM 167/266), that is, an after-the-fact, belated reinterpretation of the various messianisms. The assumption of the promise abstracts or extracts the formal features and structures of the "messianic eschatology" that Marx is said to share with the religions he criticizes (SM 59/102). An abstraction, of course, remains dependent on the 'absolute, irreducible events' of revelation in the religions of the book, and then in Marx (SM 91/149), such that the deconstructive promise could not have been discovered without the historical instantiations and events of messianic eschatologies. In this sense, the deconstructive, messianic promise would be made possible by historical events or, rather, by the codification in texts (religions of the book, Marx's texts) of an experience of historical time—in the sense, perhaps, in which inductively generated laws are unthinkable with a series of particular observations, or in which the conceptual procedure of abstraction requires the comparison of different units and their properties. Revelatory events would be "the only events on the basis of which we approach and first of all name the messianic in general" (SM 168/267).

On the other hand, one might think that the messianic promise precedes the historical messianisms as their "universal structure" and "originary condition" (SM 167/266). On this interpretation, the latecomers reach back to, and conceptualize, the conditions of possibility of the messianic eschatologies and their singular events of manifestations. "One may always take the quasi-atheistic dryness of the messianic to be the condition of the religions of the book, a desert that is not even theirs" (SM 168/267). According to this second way of understanding the relationship between Marx's promise and its deconstructive inheritance, the 'tradition of the Messiah' is not granted an absolutely necessary anteriority for the discovery of the universal structure of messianicity, for it names the futural opening of experience in general. As such, it can, at least in principle, be read off any experience.[17]

In *Archive Fever*, Derrida also describes the difference between these two ways to 'messianize' messianisms, this "aporia," in terms of an old theological question as to the difference, and relation of priority, between "revealability" as the condition of the possibility of manifestation, and "the event of the religious revelation" itself, in its irreducible singularity (AF 80/127). Viewed in this way, the question might be taken to concern the priority of either philosophy or religion. If we take the event of revelation as a historical event, however, the question will concern the relation between philosophy and history. In "Faith and Knowledge," Derrida describes the difference between the messianic and messianisms as one between, on the one hand, "the historicity of history" or the "historicity of revelation" and, on the other, the "history of historicity," asking again how they differ. In this context, Derrida points in a direction I will pursue, namely, that of their quasi-transcendental co-implication, for he adds the possibility that "the two overlap in an infinite mirroring [*en abyme*]."[18]

There is an additional complication here that we have to take into account: the revelatory events are, and ought to be respected as, singular, irreducible events that, in some sense, resist their abstractive reduction to a universal structure. For example, Derrida views Marx as the heir of the 'religions of the book' while granting him, the great critic of religion, that he bases it on a new ground without reference to positive religion. In this sense, Marx's promise, despite being an heir to the tradition of religious messianism—which already consists of singular events of revelation—remains "absolutely unique" and its event is "at once singular, total, and uneffaceable." As Derrida underscores: "There is no precedent whatsoever for such an event . . . [i]n the whole history of humanity" (SM 91/149). As we will see, the question is thus how we can respect the historical singularity of a promise while nonetheless thinking its universal condition of possibility, which also allows us to view this singularity as an altering repetition of previous events.

Thus, Derrida's 'oscillation' concerns three problems that are intricately, if not inseparably, linked in this question about the two ways of understanding the deconstructive inheritance of Marx's promise. The first concerns the question of whether transcendental conditions can be arrived at by a process of abstraction that operates on empirical, historical material, which is said to be conditioned by the transcendental. It concerns the relation between history and historicity: If the latter is moved into a transcendental, conditioning position, can we still think its history? How separate are conditions from what they condition? And second, can this separation be effected in thought, so as to secure the purity and uncontaminated status of the condition from what it conditions? How does thought come to know the conditions of its own activity, especially if the traditional distinction between the *ratio essendi* and the *ratio cognoscendi* does not help us here?[19] If historicity as a universal transcendental condition names the ineluctable insertion of thought into singular historical circumstances, does it not bend back on itself, so that the thinking of historicity has to be able, in principle, to give an account of its emergence within that which it conditions, namely history? This formulation suggests the third issue and its ethical overtones: How can a historically singular event contain at the same time universal elements? What is the relation between difference and identity here? If an event is made possible by universal conditions, do they not erase the irreducible singularity of the event? Does the extraction of formal, universal, and transcendental features from revelatory events not reduce them (in a way that does not befit an heir who wishes to respect the singularity of a tradition) to a mere example, a particular in contradistinction from a singular?[20]

Before suggesting how we can solve the paradox, let us note why this question is important for inheriting Marx in the attempt to interlace his promise with a memory of historical violence and suffering. From the perspective of such an attempt, as we already saw in the first chapter, teleological connections between memory and promise are deeply problematic, and the deconstructive operation is, among other things, to rule out an eschatological or teleological reading of history. Furthermore, the issue of singularity, and the ethical respect it deserves in the context of memory, is of great significance in the attempt to think the promise of memory. But there is more. For such a promise of memory, the possibility of granting philosophy the capacity to attain the 'pure formality' and aprioricity of transcendental conditions must seem troubling. In this case, we would 'purify' ourselves from the historical dangers with which the particular messianisms, including Marxism, are afflicted. While positive religion and Marxism, from both perspectives, only differ with regard to the content, the deconstructive, radicalized Marxism, in trying to abstain from giving content to the promise, would also avoid the atrocities committed in the name of both religion and Marxism. In fact, at times Derrida describes this way to assume the promise as an "*epokhê* of the content" (SM 59/102), which seems to arrive, by way of a traditional philosophical gesture, at the universal, the transcendental, the "purely" formal (SM 90/148, cf. SM 59/102, SM 73/124) structures making possible Marx's promise. The danger of thinking about the deconstructive operation in this way consists in the temptation to believe that one has attained those structures of the promise that are untouched by historical atrocities, for the operation would direct the promise to a contentless future that no one person or group could claim to embody or represent. In this case, the promise would have succeeded in inheriting Marx's promise from the past while 'purifying' itself from the violence associated with its attempted materialization in the past. Hence, there would be no necessary connection between the promise thus taken up and a call to remember the atrocities previously committed in its name. While, as I will hope to show, the deconstructive reformulation of Marx's promise gains immensely by the attempt to think its originary condition, the reformulation must still be marked as an inheritance, for both conceptual and political reasons. Marking it as an inheritance means seeing the conditions on which Marx's promise depends as conditions of historicity that cannot be severed from their own history: as *quasi*-transcendental conditions, precisely.

In *Specters*, Derrida writes that these two possibilities—"abstract desertification or originary condition" (SM 167/266)—"do no exclude each other" (SM 168/266). He later admits, however, that he "hesitates" and "oscillates"[21] between these possibilities, these two "messianic spaces" (SM 167/266). What I wish to argue here is that, if we take the notion of a quasi-transcendental—that is, of a deconstructive—reading seriously, the text of *Specters* is right to see no genuine alternative here, although more needs to be said. Maintaining the distinction, one risks falling back onto the idea of a clear-cut distinction between the empirical and the transcendental, between the example and the exemplar, or between the order of essences and the order of knowing. If deconstruction aspired to what Kant simply described as the "isolation" of transcendental conditions of experience in "pure understanding"[22] and, ultimately, of what goes by the name of history, it would be difficult to show that its inheritance of the promise, and the messianic promise itself, is an historically situated attempt to respond to the events of the twentieth century in particular and modernity in general.

THE EMPIRICAL AND THE TRANSCENDENTAL

We thus have to ask in greater detail about the quasi-transcendental conditions of possibility *and* impossibility (see SM 65), and especially about what justifies the use of the prefix "quasi" if we speak of conditions of possibility whose status has usually not been taken to be affected or challenged by what they condition. For the difference between the event of the conditioned and the condition, and the hierarchy it traditionally implies, goes to the heart of the deconstructive operation. Deconstruction, from the very beginning, is concerned with the space and the possibility of philosophy, and therefore, with its relation to "nonphilosophy" or "empiricism" (OG 162/232), in particular, to the human and social sciences (anthropology, literary studies, linguistics, psychoanalysis, political economy), which are largely concerned with the analysis of empirical material. Philosophy at least since Kant has had to contend with the debate between the specification of the ahistorical, transcendental conditions of experience, and the contestation of those conditions on the grounds of their historicity.[23] The general orientation that Derrida has taken—and continued to take, as in his more recent negotiation between Heidegger's *Sein und Zeit* and Philippe Ariés on the question of a 'culture of death' (in *Aporias*)—is to attempt to problematize the distinction between the transcendental and the historical domains so as to locate philosophy on the threshold between the two. He demonstrates that, briefly put, philosophy cannot legislate and govern in advance the empirical nature of human sciences, as the very facticity with which they occupy themselves always exceeds and, in unforeseeable ways, influences philosophy and its concept-formation. Philosophy thus remains tied to historical, factical contexts, and it remains afflicted with a certain contingency. As Derrida says: "The *departure* is radically empiricist. We must begin *wherever we are* . . ." (OG 162/232).

On the other hand, however, neither can the discourses that occupy themselves with this contingency and facticity encompass and predetermine philosophy in its entirety, since any such predetermination needs to draw on philosophical concepts in order to conceptualize this determination. If, for example, Marx argues that philosophy, as part of the superstructure, is not simply causally determined by a given, historically situated mode of production— a claim whose details would be difficult to establish empirically—but that its very concept-formation and articulation in general is conditioned by it, he needs to draw on the philosophical operation of specifying transcendental conditions of possibility for the exercise of philosophy. This operation makes Marx's concept of social praxis a transcendental concept, for it is presented as the world-constituting concept that at the same time forms the (normative) basis of the critique of its alienation.[24] This means that Marx needs to deny as derivative the very philosophical concepts and operations that he, implicitly or explicitly, uses to derive philosophy.[25] Especially when approaching Marx, philosophy needs to claim for itself the space of investigation and the right to speak on its own, lest it be encompassed in advance by Marx's critical reduction of philosophy to ideology. Therefore, as Derrida argues, "in order to avoid empiricism, positivism and psychologism, [. . .] it is endlessly necessary to renew transcendental questioning."[26] The thought of the quasi-transcendental is the result of the negotiation of this situation, a situation that will concern us mostly in terms of time and the law of originary repetition. The thought of originary repetition, as I now hope to be able to show, will help us to understand better both the promise of memory to an open future as well the reinscription of the empirico-transcendental difference.

Repetition, moved into a quasi-transcendental position as iterability, represents one way in which the originary condition, of which Derrida speaks in this debate between two 'messianic spaces,' can be understood. Since the originary condition of religious and Marxist messianisms is named the 'messianic in general' in the reading of Marx, we will have to link repetition to the messianic promise and its reference to an absolute future. It is this promise that Derrida views as the condition of possibility of Marx's promise. Thinking this condition of possibility means inheriting Marx's promise so as to inseparably join the promise to memory without relying on a logic of progress in history, an eschatology or teleology. It is the account of repetition, in its link to *différance* and *l'avenir à-venir*, that delivers the temporality of the past-future relation we found underdeveloped in Benjamin. At the same time, it affords an albeit precarious distinction between messianism and the messianic (or messianicity) that clarifies otherwise problematic theological ambiguities stemming from the attempt to, as Benjamin put it, 'return a messianic face' to Marx while affirming his secularization of messianism.

In order to join memory and promise in a philosophically novel and politically potent way, however, the notion of iterability or the messianic promise may not be viewed as a 'pure' formality arrived at by a philosophical discourse that is immune to its historical facticity. Rather, iterability, as a quasi-transcendental condition, must present both the transcendental 'historicity of history' and, at the same time, give an account of the history of the conditions themselves, that is, think the 'history of historicity' allowing us to speak of *quasi*-transcendental conditions that bend back on themselves. The reversal of perspective implied by the *quasi*, as I hope to show, comes into view above all if we underscore that repetition can as little be isolated from what it repeats as difference can be separated from the terms between which it holds. Differential repetition, while occupying a transcendental condition in relation to languages and the discourses (including philosophy) in which histories constitute themselves, nonetheless cannot be isolated by the transcendental philosopher from languages and histories. Rather, it can only be read, traced, and rediscovered in the always different contexts formed by languages and histories, thereby permitting us to account for the history of *différance*, iterability, the messianic promise, and so on. The originary condition is inseparable from what it makes possible, and therefore cannot be 'isolated' from it: it is not visible as itself—it has no 'itself'—but only in its effects or traces. The aporia of the two messianic spaces, two ways of understanding Derrida's inheritance of Marx's promise, is thus resolved in favor of neither alternative. While seeming to exclude one another on the model of linear time, both views hold true, but are one-sided without their aporetic relation to the other perspective. In discussing what I call the promise of repetition, I will not attempt to defend the idea of quasi-transcendental conditions in all of its admittedly difficult aspects, though I hope to present them sufficiently clearly so as to at least render their possibility and intelligibility plausible. Rather, I will keep to those features that are relevant to 'resolve' the question of the two messianic spaces and, thereby, to bring to the fore Derrida's reformulation of Marx's promise.

THE PROMISE OF REPETITION

Derrida situates himself in the transcendental tradition by beginning his account of objective sameness (of events and entities, of linguistic meaning and concepts, as well as of personal identity) not in confrontation with, for instance, an Aristotelian realist or essentialist ontology of natures, but with the Kantian and Husserlian account of objecthood and meaning. Kant and Husserl, of course, treat objects or meanings and their sameness not as given, but as constituted by the activity of a transcendental subject. Derrida aims at showing that objects and concepts, *as well as* subjectivity, are thus constituted only by potentially infinite repetitions of tokens. Like other contemporary attempts to refigure transcendental philosophy, Derrida's account decenters the transcendental subject, a move that here also goes along with a linguistic turn. Since meaning—including accounts of history—cannot be thought apart from language, we may focus on the repetition of linguistic units and signs as the element in which it is established. We should not think, however, that this account locks us up in language as idealism locked us up in subjective representations, as if the inside of language were opposed to the outside of the real world. Rather, as we will see, the notion of differential repetition will severely question such inside-outside distinctions.

If we think repetition from a transcendental viewpoint, it names the possibility of identity, and hence of the repetition of identity. Moved into the transcendental position, repetition is called *iterability*. Iterability attempts to think together the possibility of repetition *and* alteration in a single movement. According to this transcendental argument, the meaning, unity, and self-identity of a linguistic element are never given in advance, in full flesh and self-presence. Rather, such a unit of meaning, at any singular moment, must be repeatable in order to be what it is: namely, a meaningful element that can be understood by others and at different times. Otherwise, it could not be reidentified, remembered, reproduced, or signified. This possibility of repetition must be marked or inscribed in the unit, even in its singular occurrence, as a *trace of repeatability*.[27] This possibility of repetition implies the partial absence of the repeated, an absence supplemented or replaced by what comes to repeat it. If the unit were not already, from its 'first' appearance, marked by this possible absence, if it were entirely present to itself, it would not be repeatable. This does not imply the necessity of its actual repetition, but the necessity of its repeatability. Iterability makes possible the identity of a unit, but by inscribing its possible absence and repeatability in it, it also makes this identity impossible, if we mean by identity a given, self-present identity to itself.

Hence, there is no self-present origin from which a unit (of time, of meaning, etc.) emerges, and in whose terms it may be explained. This is why Derrida speaks of 'originary,' rather than 'original' repetition. (As we will discuss in a moment, nor is there any *telos* or goal to which it is directed, and which endows it with meaning.) Any unity or identity needs to be established by a never-ending process of relating to itself, of self-repetition. Repetition of a mark or of an identity-in-process is originary in that it is logically and temporally prior to a recognizable or identifiable unity. Repetition thus precedes the constitution of what is repeated. It is an 'originary' repetition, but one that never actually took place, in present time. If iterability is prior to any identity and unthinkable apart from what it repeats, every identity of a mark is preceded by a zero point, a gap, a nothingness: there is no origin other than an anterior otherness. Derrida has described this otherness in various ways, for instance as a trace, a *déjà* (already), the "irreducibility of an always-already-there," and an "absolute past" (OG 66/97). "Everything begins with reproduction. Always already: repositories of a meaning which was never present, whose signified presence is always reconstituted by deferral, *nachträglich*, belatedly, *supplementarily*" (WD 211/314; see also WD 246/361f.). This is why Derrida, inheriting Marx's love of Shakespeare, relishes the beginning of *Hamlet*: Hamlet's ghost-father's first appearance on stage is a 'reentering,' his second appearance for the characters of the play (SM 4/22). A ghost, as a *revenant*, always comes back; it never comes for the first time. Like the ghosts that Marx is said to have chased away for their lack of presence, originary or 'spectral' repetition is neither present nor absent. Repetition 'is' nothing without or apart from the terms of the repetition, and therefore cannot be represented. As previously indicated, the quasi-transcendental condition is not to be separated from its 'effects,' from what it makes possible.

Furthermore, iterability renders every unit inherently *contextual* and *relational*. Every repetition differentiates and defers. It differentiates insofar as we can distinguish the first and second appearance in a repetition, and it defers from one time to another. However, iterability does not only, as we saw, prevent the self-same presence-to-itself (*présence à soi*) of a unit in its repetitions. Rather, it also prevents the identification of a nonrepeated unit as identical to itself. This is so because a unit can only establish its identity by differing from other units in its context. As de Saussure argued for a system of language—*la langue*—it consists of differences without positive terms.[28] This account of language, or any economy or conceptual system that consists of different units, produces unities such as words or concepts not by the intrinsic properties or substance of such unities, but by the differential relationship, the 'spacing' or the 'gap,' between the unities. Hence, a unit, in order to be a unit, must be inserted in a structure of referral in order to achieve a minimal, repeatable identity. If a unit can refer to itself and establish its identity only by taking a detour through other units from which it differs, we can say that it differs from itself. What I referred to earlier as the inscribed trace of iterability, now reveals itself as a *trace of difference*, and repetition shows itself to be differential repetition.

If the context of differential repetition were a closed context—that is, if a unit could take the detour through all other units and then return to itself, giving it only one identity—self-identity as presence to itself would still be possible. If we could formalize differential repetition and its possibilities by limiting the system—for example, by establishing a finite number of possible repetitions in a taxonomy, as John Searle does with speech acts and their types[29]—we could close the context of repetition. However, Derrida argues against de Saussure, Searle, Husserl, and others, that this would imply that language had been paralyzed, frozen in its limitless play and processes of differential repetitions and inventions. It would imply that one could exhaustively determine the *future* of possible repetitions. However, just as repetition is potentially infinite, so is the process of differentiation. This is so because contexts keep on shifting and changing, and cannot be paralyzed by conceptual decisions. I will return to this structural opening in a moment.

What I want to show now is that this notion of a differential iterability—whose contexts cannot be limited to formal systems or exhaustively enclosed in theoretical taxonomies—can be seen as an account of historicity. Repetition as self-relation does not take place in a neutral terrain, or in an abstract, objective, and closed conceptual system of differences, but in discourses, traditions, and determinate sociohistorical contexts. Any identity necessarily repeats, and thus borrows from, these traditions and languages. For example, when it comes to the identities of human subjects in history, Derrida writes: "[W]e *are* insofar as we *inherit*" (SM: 54). There are always already others ('others' understood as widely as possible) when an identity appears on the scene, and it is essentially related to these others, bearing them within itself. This trace of otherness in every identity (and every subject)—the trace of differential iterability—names, at one and the same time, the ineluctability of history, that is, historicity, and a certain reference to the future. Let us look at this link between historicity and the future more closely, for it is this link that Derrida thinks in the messianic promise, and that helps us to establish, as a conceptual (not merely political or psychological) necessity, the relation between Benjamin's 'disenchanted' future and memory, a memory that Benjamin configured as one of suffering and oppression.

The account of the relation between historicity, iterability, and the messianic future may be understood as explicating the following Derridian passage. In this passage, Derrida connects historicity with the only 'apparently' formalist nature of the messianic promise to a disenchanted, radically open future without content, a content that makes the difference between the messianic and the messianisms that project futural horizons:

Apparently 'formalist,' this indifference to the content has perhaps the value of giving one to think the necessarily pure and purely necessary form of the future as such [*l'avenir comme tel*], its being-necessarily-promised, prescribed, assigned, enjoined, in the necessarily formal necessity of its possibility—in short, in its law. It is this law that dislodges any present out of its contemporaneity with itself. Whether the promise promises this or that, whether it be fulfilled or not, or whether it be unfulfillable, there is necessarily some promise and therefore some historicity as future-to-come [*l'historicité comme à venir*]. It is what we are nicknaming the messianic without messianism (SM 73/124).

The crucial link between the future to come and historicity can best be explicated by beginning again with repetition. As we saw, every repetition draws on contexts that, broadly understood, we may characterize as historical. These contexts are themselves constantly shifting due to their structural openness to processes of possible repetition. It is in this sense that Derrida writes axiomatically "no future without repetition" (AF 80/128), and, we may add, no repetition without future. In other words, repetition is to the future as memory is to the promise: the one implicating the other. Iterability refers to the *possibility* of repetition, and thus of recontextualization. As a possibility, it contains a reference to future actualization. But this actualization is not to be thought teleologically, that is, it cannot be foreseen or determined in advance due to the nonparalysis of history. Thus, while iterability implies that every identity can only be adequately understood if it is seen against its background of emergence, such as a tradition or a history, this tradition and history are subject to the same law of repetition (and not a closed system). Hence, 'adequate understanding' involves an infinite process, a process open to an unforeseeable future. For a heritage is never a given but always a productive reconstruction in new circumstances, and these will alter the heritage itself. In Derrida's words, inheritance is a "critical and transformative filter" (SM 102/168) structurally open to the infinite possibilities of the future. Every interpretation of history or lineage, and thus every identity of meaning, or of a constituted subject (e.g., of a macro-subject like Marx's proletariat), is projected onto the future, but may be criticized or revised by rival interpretations, thus keeping history open to the future. This future is thus not simply beyond 'history,' but names precisely the infinite movement in which history (better: histories) constitutes itself. These features of the repetitive constitution of history—precedence by otherness, relationality or contextuality, and radical instability—imply the infinity of processes of (self-)constitution and hence, a certain relation to the future. It is this relation to the future that Derrida names in the messianic promise. Let us then see in what way the process of repetition and the concomitant notion of an anterior otherness are linked to this messianic future.

Insofar as the (minimal) identity accomplished by the process of repetition is never final but continuously requires a renewed repetition to be what it is (and to be otherwise), it is deferred to a future that never arrives as such. As is well known, Derrida's neologism *différance* tries to capture this deferral of repetition as economically as possible, for it names both the movement of repetition in difference and that of deferral. The movement of repetition 'promises' the establishment of an identity that, however, is constantly undermined and referred again to repetition. As indicated previously, no final and closed identity is ever accomplished by repetition. Repetition thus promises what it constitutes to a future that always defers its 'itself,' that never comes as such, in full presence, but that comes in the form of provisional, minimal, and internally differentiated moments of an incomplete, fragile identity. What I have called an anterior otherness, as a past that was never present, bears an essential relation to the future to come that never arrives, and therefore disallows the simple opposition between past and future. Originary repetition as well as the messianic promise are located in an 'absolute past' that never took place as such. This is what Derrida means by a 'messianic' promise to a future that always remains to come. It is not a promise with a specific content, and not a promise issued by (thus presupposing) a subject. Rather, as part of repetition that generates (thus being prior to) subjectivity in the first place, the messianic promise is directed toward the utterly indeterminable aspect of the future beyond horizons of expectation, planning, or awaiting.

For Derrida, a preceding alterity or nothingness is intricately bound up with the 'promise' of the future, a promise that precedes us and yet opens the future. The alterity and nonpresence of this future is so radical that it cannot be restricted to a particular domain of beings or appearances, nor can it be conceptualized. It is not a horizon of expectation or of possibilities projected onto the future (such as a utopia), but precisely names what I would call the blind spot in any horizon whereby it gives way to other horizons, other hopes and interpretations. As an essential possibility on which every (self-)determination of an identity must draw in order to establish itself, the promise of the future is that which places such a (self-)determination in 'anachrony,' at odds with itself.

Before turning to the issue of what originary repetition implies for the relation between the empirico-transcendental difference, let me note that the messianic promise, while referring to the indeterminability of a constantly deferred future, is nonetheless inseparable from the future present of specific futural projections. As the image of the blind spot in futural horizons indicates, neither can be thought without the other. If repetition is inseparable from what it repeats, the promise cannot be thought without the identity it promises, and such an identity implies the projection of a futural horizon. The promise is always filled with specific content, and yet, if we think the "being-promise of a promise" (SM 105/173), we will see that the establishment of this content structurally depends on a repetition that is referred to the empty future to come. We can thus see that messianism (as the projection of a specific content, say, the classless society) and the messianic are inseparable: while the latter supplies the 'originary condition' of the former, the messianic cannot appear as such, apart from specific historical contexts in which we always already find ourselves situated, and which determine 'our' hopes and projections. I will return to the question of the way in which the messianic promise may be thought of as conditioning Marx's promise, and I will also return, in the last section of this chapter, to the ineluctable interplay of what I will term postutopian projections and the future to come.

The quasi-transcendental conditions, named in iterability, *différance*, and the messianic promise, are, then, inseparable from what they make possible. Philosophy can think the universal conditions of experience in attaining to 'formal' structures, but these structures and conditions turn back on philosophy by also conditioning its discourse. This paradoxical bending back can only be thought if the historicity of history and the history of historicity imply one another. The two 'messianic spaces' are implicated in one another. Likewise, while Marx's historical materialism may account, with some justification, for philosophy, philosophy may think the transcendental trait in historical materialism. By elevating historicity to the status of a transcendental concept, deconstruction thinks the possibility of historical materialism as well as the inescapability of its own insertion into historical contexts.

FOUR FEATURES OF THE QUASI-TRANSCENDENTAL

Let us now turn to a more detailed treatment of the problem of how, on Derrida's quasi-transcendental account, the relationship between the conditions of possibility and the conditioned thereby made possible, is to be understood. Derrida has tackled this problem in a number of texts that all gesture toward a renegotiation of the empirico-transcendental difference.[30] Rather than discussing these texts in detail, we will restrict ourselves to schematic remarks here. These remarks will extract features regarding the relationship between condition and conditioned from the earlier account of originary repetition and historicity. The following points in this regard may be seen as so many ways of approaching and circumscribing the same problem of explicating a relation that may be said in many ways, and yet refers to 'the same' difficulty in thinking the 'quasi' in quasi-transcendental.

1. We have just seen that to think iterability, difference, and historicity as transcendental concepts means that this historicity needs to be bent back on the concepts themselves, to think their history, their possibility of becoming conditions of possibility of a field without closure. In *Of Grammatology* Derrida calls this bending back, this inquiry about the condition's possibility, genesis, and power of conditioning, an 'ultratranscendental' inquiry: a transcendental inquiry regarding the conditions of possibility of conditions of possibility. In his early engagement with transcendental phenomenology, Derrida follows Husserl in speaking of "transcendental historicity."[31]

Granting historicity the status of transcendental concept necessitates that the concept be subject to its own conditioning power. From the side of the condition, the quasi-transcendental operation questions its conditioning power, its possibility to delimit itself from that which it conditions. Here, we see that conditions such as iterability and historicity are not separable from their effects: A repetition is nothing apart from the repeated, difference nothing apart from the 'differents,' and historicity nothing apart from history. Historicity precisely names the ineluctability of transcendental thought's insertion in historical contexts; this is why the thought of historicity requires a thought of the history of historicity. From the side of the conditioned (empirical history), this co-implication of condition and conditioned has to explain the possibility of it (the conditioned) being affected, traversed, and fissured by the conditions. As we have seen, iterability precisely names this possibility of being affected, the trace of repeatability in units of meaning and identity.

2. This self-reflexive bending back of the conditions, as we have noted, further implies that the transcendental cannot be demarcated by a clear dividing line from the empirical. This is ultimately so because the quasi-transcendental concepts we looked at—difference, iterability, historicity—are not concepts in themselves, as Kant's concepts of the understanding are. Rather, they are limit-concepts, or what we may call essentially *relational* concepts: they are literally nothing, refer only to a gap, an absence, which, however, is traced in presences, identities, and so on. We cannot, therefore, isolate them from what they make possible and rigorously divide them from it.

This impossibility may also be described in the following way. As we saw, the dependence of any identity on processes of differential repetition introduces—originarily and not merely 'after' the constitution of an identity—a trace of otherness into the unity that relates 'it' (even prior to its 'itself') to other minimal identities. Already this indicates that it will not be possible to differentiate clearly what belongs 'properly' to the identity and what to the trace of differential iterability it bears within itself. Hence, the distinction between the conditions of possibility and the field of their effects is difficult to draw in a clear manner. What holds for the identity of a unit of a system of differences, also holds for such systems.

3. The inseparability of condition and conditioned, then, further implies the impossibility of closing systems of differences, and thus raises the issue of the relation between the inside and the outside of a system. Such a distinction seems to be called for by the very structure of a transcendental argument, which indicates—or, in Kant's words, 'isolates'—the conditions of possibility of something else. Insofar as historicity and differential iterability name the condition of possibility of conceptuality, or of conceptual systems, we should have to say that these conditions do not belong to the very order of concepts they make possible. Yet, the only way in which we can articulate these conditions is within the system. As conditions of possibility must be articulated in terms of the system that is made possible by them, it is always already too late to be its conditions: They defer their final, secure establishment, leaving the system structurally open. Thus, Derrida speaks of a quasi-transcendental account that does not claim to master a field—history, language, conceptuality—from without.

Given that the thinking of the quasi-transcendental questions the estab-lishment of closed systems (such as a system of transcendental concepts), it supposes that a system can only establish itself, its coherence, univocity, and universality, by exclusions that cannot be thought from within itself, but nonetheless make it possible. In this sense, the excluded is both inside and outside the system, needed simultaneously on both sides of a dividing line.[32] The dividing line must be seen as fissured and transversable, and the quasi-transcendental names this opening of any structure or closure as a necessity. In this context, Gasché speaks of "an opening that is structural, or the struc-turality of an opening," or simply a "transcendental opening."[33] This struc-turally inescapable opening is named in the future to come to which the promise of repetition directs any attempt to establish meaning or identity.

4. Insofar as the promise, however, directs us not only to the future to come, but to the establishment of identity, the condition of possibility of identity is also the condition of the impossibility of that identity, if we think it in traditional terms as a self-present identity, and not as what I have called a minimal identity, a nonpresent remainder. Derrida thinks we cannot think this co(i)mplication of identity and difference other than as, in the final analysis, contradictory, so that the promise of repetition commits us to con-tradictions a priori.[34] Historical contexts, inscribed in linguistic meaning-units or marks by the trace of differential iterability, render their minimal rerecognizability possible, after what I called the detour through all other units from which they differ. However, since these other units are themselves engaged in this self-reference, this detour is potentially infinite. Hence, the trace of difference and iterability renders identity as given and self-present impossible in the very process that allows it to establish itself. We will see later on that Derrida, in his reading of Marx, indeed treats the messianic promise as making possible and impossible the promise of a classless society.

Before we return to the deconstruction of Marx's promise, however, I would like to emphasize that the previous account of originary repetition and the reinscription of the empirico-transcendental difference renders Derrida's distinction between the two messianic spaces, two ways of inheriting Marx's promise, problematic. There can be no distinction between supplying Marx's promise with the 'originary condition' and formally extracting from it, as part of 'our' heritage, its transcendental features by a process of 'abstract desertifi-cation' (SM 167/266). To recall, the problem of the two messianic spaces won-ders whether we arrive at the deconstructive radicalization of Marx's promise by way of a process of belated abstraction and desertification, emptying the promise of its content, or whether we must think the messianic promise as the originary condition of possibility of Marx's promise, making possible both Marx's formulation of it and our inheritance of the promise. But since the mes-sianic promise, once it is moved into the quasi-transcendental position, is inseparable from an originary deferral and an anterior otherness without any presence and phenomenality of its own, entirely dependent on its effects that are always after-effects, Derrida's problem of the two messianic spaces, named in *Specters of Marx*, should not arise. Posing the question of inheriting Marx in this way risks underestimating the fact that the historicity Derrida links to the messianic promise, in the way I have explicated, forces the 'originary condition' to bend back on itself. Thinking the messianic in general as the condition of possibility of Marx's promise does not preclude the distillation of this same messianic from its critical inheritance. Since the messianic promise, like iterability and historicity, is traced in the field it constitutes, its comprehension must always proceed from this field, and continuously return to it. Attaining these formal and universal structures does not mean that they are immune from history, and that no historical account of their emergence—as Benjamin would say, their passage into readability—can be given. The thinking of originary conditions is itself, again in Benjamin's terms, 'historically indexed,' and we can given an historical account—in the history of ideas as much as in the history of society—of their coming to be read and theorized.[35] As I will emphasize in a moment, this further implies for any deconstructive reading that it must borrow its resources from its object, demonstrating the efficacy of these structures anew with each reading, as Derrida does with regard to the semantics of ghosts and specters in Marx. In fact, quasi-transcendental structures are only readable as traces.

The messianic, in its link to originary repetition and *différance*, derives its 'disjoining' as well as its constitutive effect—as a condition of im/possibility—from the inescapable deferral of identity and meaning. It is on this basis that Derrida sought an 'aporetic' resolution of the conundrum. A passage from *Archive Fever*—written shortly after *Specters*—tells us that, concerning the empirico-transcendental difference and the two messianic spaces, the logic of originary delay "turns out to disrupt, disturb, entangle forever the reassuring distinction between the two terms of this alternative" (AF 80/127). To be sure, in this text Derrida does not explicate this disruption and entangling. Our reflection on the co-implication of history and historicity, however, should have demonstrated that the messianic promise, as a quasi-transcendental thinking of the future, always requires particular, archived events (such as Marx's texts) in order to be accessed, retrieved, experienced, and known. It does not designate a present, transcendental structure governing these archived events from the outside. But this does not mean that these archived events are merely empirical. For it remains true that these events and their experience are interlaced and interwoven with the condition that made them possible, and that cannot be described apart from these events. The singular event of the revelation or manifestation, such is the claim of the quasi-transcendental operation, must already harbor its condition of 'revealability,' which is also a condition of unrevealability, rendering impossible the clear and self-present manifestation of the manifest.

MODERNITY, TRAUMA, AND DEFERRED ACTION

Let us look more closely at Derrida's proposed 'resolution' of the paradox of the two ways of understanding the inheritance of Marx's promise, for this proposal will also force us to reconsider the violence of modernity in which the promise is caught up. When Derrida came to rethink the distinction between the two messianic spaces, he treated it "from the point of the view of the archive" and put the matter in the following terms:

> [D]oes one base one's thinking of the future on an archived event—with or without substrate, with or without actuality—for example on a divine injunction or on a messianic covenant? Or else, on the contrary, can an *experience*, an *existence*, in general, only receive and record, only archive such an event to the extent that the structure of this existence and of its temporalization makes this archivization possible? In other words, does one need a first archive in order to conceive of originary archivability? Or vice versa? [. . .] Is it not true that the logic of the after-the-fact [*après-coup*] (*Nachträglichkeit*) . . . turns out to disrupt, disturb, entangle forever the reassuring distinction between the two terms of this alternative, as between the past and the future? (AF 80/127).

In order to resolve or suspend the aporia, Derrida here suggests that we reconsider the very opposition between the past and the future, between the event of the 'Abrahamic' messianisms in the past and their belated rethinking in terms of their originary condition, on the basis of Freud's logic of "deferred action" (as it is usually called in English). Looking at this logic will help us understand Derrida's (psychoanalytic) account of the violence of modernity and the structure of mourning. Furthermore, the logic of deferred action further explicates the 'messianic' temporality that connects the promise for a radically open future with memory and inheritance.

Freud uses the notion of *Nachträglichkeit* frequently to denote, generally speaking, the psychic or unconscious temporality according to which experiences or memory traces can be revised at a later date to accommodate and integrate new experiences. While this general formulation still lends itself to existential psychoanalysis—which argues that consciousness constitutes its own past by continually revising its meaning for the present—Derrida's discussion of Husserl's living present of protentions and retentions seeks to show that the concept of *Nachträglichkeit* operates "a delay that is inadmissible to consciousness" (OG 67/98). Fundamentally speaking, Derrida wishes to demonstrate that the meaning of the past is not in the first instance defined by the present, especially not by the presence of a consciousness or a subject. Instead, the present is itself subjected to and fissured by a future that opens up the past in the first place. That the concept of the 'after-effect' does not operate on the level of consciousness is, as we will see in a moment, crucial to its being able to solve the problem of the two 'messianic spaces.' Derrida radical-izes the notion of *Nachträglichkeit* to have it designate the delayed effects of an originary, preceding alterity that is not recoverable within consciousness, lead-ing to a 'trauma' on the individual as well as on the cultural level.

In the context of Lacanian psychoanalysis, it has been suggested that a closer analysis of Freud's use of the concept of deferred action actually reveals that "it is not lived experience in general that undergoes a deferred revision, but, specifically, whatever it has been impossible in the first instance to incor-porate fully into a meaningful context. The traumatic event is the epitome of such unassimilated experience."[36] In his reading of Marx, it is indeed for Der-rida a matter of a trauma, a trauma to narcissism giving rise to a certain kind of mourning about which we need to be on guard. Today, Derrida argues, it is not only a matter of responding to the three 'blows' to mankind that Freud listed in "Eine Schwierigkeit der Psychoanalyse" and associated, metonymi-cally, with proper names: the cosmological (Galileo), the biological (Darwin) and the psychological (Freud himself) trauma (SM 97/160). But further—and this should be of particular interest to us—Derrida describes as "perhaps the deepest wound for mankind" the contemporary experience that the Marxist promise resulted in terrible failure, for this failure condenses the traumas on Freud's list: "The Marxist blow is as much the projected unity of a thought and of a labor movement, sometimes in a messianic or eschatological form, as it is the history of the totalitarian world (including Nazism and fascism, which are the inseparable adversaries of Stalinism)" (SM 98/161).

If the Marxist *coup* "accumulates and gathers together," or even "carries out" (ibid.), the previous three lesions of narcissism, Derrida here opens up the negative side of what is usually called modernity, the side we need to remember in inheriting the promises of modernity. He reveals this negative side on the basis of a quasi-transcendental account of the messianic promise that shows, as we will see, the promise's impossibility of materializing itself in the classless society. The contradictory fate of modernity and of the Enlight-enment comes to a head in the inheritance of a promise that is afflicted with a totalitarian perversion. Our question concerning the inheritance of Marx's promise—as we saw already in discussing Benjamin's critique of Marx—then also concerns the relationship to the process of secularization, thought as a 'trauma' whose consequence is a mourning work that tries to forget and repress its occurrence in the very manner of facing it. (In chapter four, we will return to the theme of the trauma as what, being inaccessible to conscious-ness and subject to the logic of retroactivity most of all, nonetheless 'affects' and traverses experience. For Derrida's frequent return to the notion of deferred action[37] is, from the start, linked to Levinas's thought of the anorig-inal trace of the other, the 'trauma' of the other's precedence in an unrepre-sentable past.[38] As we will see, Derrida links a notion of inescapable, 'origi-nary' violence to a responsibility that is no less originary.)

What is central in this context is the task that results from these reflections for the quasi-transcendental inheritance of Marx's promise. The quasi-
transcendental account would have to show how Marx's promise in particular,
itself an heir to the Enlightenment, led to totalitarianism while also contain-
ing the elements that destructure and exceed all totalitarianism. As we will
see, Derrida attempts to reveal the connection between Marxism and Stalinism by Marx's 'exorcism' of ghosts and specters generated by the messianic
promise, that is, by originary repetition through which all identity (of the
nation, of the proletariat, etc.) is constituted. On the other hand, by contain-
ing its own condition within itself—the messianic promise—Marx's promise
can be inherited in such a way as to reveal the impossibility of reaching the
full identity sought by totalitarian movements and regimes. For Derrida, it is
this structural impossibility that accounts for the failure, and homelessness, of
Marx's promise, rather than a mere empirical failure of the progressive movement of the economic base that Marx had predicted. However, this impossibility, as we can already gather from the ineluctable connection between repetition and the deferral to an open future, also allows us to connect the
promise with memory. On account of its pointing to a determinate future—
the classless society, to be brought about by the unified proletarian subject of
history—as well as beyond it—the messianic promise of an indeterminable
future—Marx's promise finds us caught in a "double bind," the "double bind
of any inheritance" that is amenable to a double reading (SM 169f./269).

Inheriting Marx's promise in the quasi-transcendental mode, then, does
not purify us of the violence with which the promise is afflicted. On the contrary, this inheritance raises the stakes of a memory of violence, a violence
that Derrida views as part of every inheritance, as part of finitude, calling on
us to be aware of its pitfalls. Awareness of this violence involves rearticulat-
ing the messianic promise so as to be inseparable from a memory of finitude,
and that means a memory of the dead whose specters Marx, according to Derrida, wished to exorcise. As we have seen, the Derridian understanding of the
messianic promise is inseparable from repetition, and thus from memory;
there can be "no future without repetition" (AF 80/128) and, as we noted,
also no repetition without a deferred and differentializing future (what we
called the promise of repetition). As in Benjamin, any promise of 'history'
that opposes the future to the past, that calls for an exclusive focus on the
(utopian) future, and thus for a forgetting of the past, misunderstands the
very nature of the promise. It is important to remember in this context that,
as we saw in chapter one, the Marx of the "Eighteenth Brumaire" envisaged
as the bearer of the future—the home of the promise—a historical subject
that had to abandon a memory of the dead to fulfill its 'world-historical task.'
Today, after Marx's promise led to violent victimizations in totalitarian perversions, such a memory of the dead (and, specifically, of the 'victims' of
totalitarianism) appears necessary for ethical and political reasons. This

explains the dramatic appeal of Derrida's critique of Marx, for example, when he speaks of the "absolute evil" of Marx's call to abandon the spirits of the dead for emancipatory struggles (SM 175/278).

How far, then, does the law of iterability help us to understand the totalitarian violence in which Marx's promise is entangled for us? It first of all indicates why Derrida chastises Marx's call to abandon the specters of the past in order to constitute the unity of the communist movement. Holding on to the promise in a reformulated form means connecting it with an ethical injunction that Derrida develops out of the quasi-transcendental rereading of the promise, an injunction that allows us to assume the heritage of Marxism while still rejecting its "totalitarian perversions" (SM 91/149). Every historical account has to recognize an irreducible and anterior otherness, as the spectrality of time, within life. Even every revolutionary moment, possibly the fullest outburst of energies of life, has to acknowledge the moment of the (nonpresent) anteriority of originary repetition—what Derrida calls an 'absolute past'—within itself. The revolution, on pain on turning against itself, has to "answer for the dead, respond to the dead [répondre du mort, répondre au mort]" (SM 109/177). Inasmuch as Derrida sees Marx as a philosopher of life, of the real and living individual, he concludes that Marxism neglected this spectral injunction, the ghost of the other. Only thus could it lead to a totalitarian society that is totalitarian precisely because it is panic-ridden, Derrida argues. It is obsessed with a spectral otherness within itself that it does not admit and thus projects onto an external enemy. In this way, the proletarian revolution turned against itself, and scared itself by a "reflexive return of a conjuration" (SM 105/171) according to which those who seek to inspire fear—like the specter of communism that opens the Communist Manifesto—frighten themselves.

This would apply above all to the aftermath of Marx's call for the incarnation of the specter of communism in 1848, which, according to this argument, contributed to the disasters of the twentieth century. The disasters began with Marx's fear of the ghosts of the past, ghosts that are necessarily generated by a repetition that passes through the messianic future. The response to this fear is the call to give flesh and blood—in party form—to the specter of communism; this is the moment of the Communist Manifesto. The Communist Party unifies the—differentially constituted—proletariat as the subject that, in knowingly moving with the laws of history, may actively forget the ghosts of the past former revolutionaries needed. Even as—or precisely as—specter it inspires fear in capitalist Europe, which responds with a panic-ridden, ruthless war to drive out the ghost and extinguish the critique of capitalism. By way of an antagonistic logic in which both opponents fear the "ghost in general," this war in turn engenders even more obsessive attempts to incarnate the communist specter, to make the ghost go away: this is the moment of Leninist and Stalinist totalitarianism with its "cadaverous rigor" (SM 105/171).[39] Derrida's claim is, therefore, that it took the terrible

European history between 1848 and 1989 to rid the specter of communism of its will to incarnate itself, and to maintain it as a specter—and even that accomplishment is not certain, insofar as the fear of the specter is at work again today, this time, for instance, as the attempt to bury Marx and avoid the inheritance of his spectral-messianic promise.

According to this historico-philosophical thesis, Stalinism must be seen as falling prey to the peril of all messianisms: the belief in the chosen people and the finality of 'history.' The peril lies in the attempt of the Communist Party to embody, and unilaterally represent, the future of universal liberation, an incarnation that would authorize the violent removal of individuals and groups that contest this exclusive claim to the future, and the repression of spectral otherness (as figured in 'the dead') within itself. Marx may be said to have feared the spectrality of his own promise, a promise to a future beyond cognitive or political control by a subject laying claim to making world history. The active forgetting of the dead which Marx had advocated in "The Eighteenth Brumaire of Louis Bonaparte" turns out to make the revolution, the opening toward a wholly different future, impossible. As in Benjamin, we are led to the necessity of a different concept of the revolution, one that does not project itself as a clean cut from the past, ending the 'prehistory of humanity,' one that does not "cease to inherit" and that includes and is open to a "revolutionary memory," a "mourning work in the course of which the living maintain the dead" (SM 113/185). Thus, Derrida's insistence on—and problematization of—the necessity of mourning and of a thinking of loss for an openness to a promise for a different, wholly other future, is also an attempt to come to terms with the European legacy of the last 150 years.

RESPONSIBILITY IN DISJOINTED TIMES

The capitalist and anticapitalist fear of the ghost, then, makes two mistakes at once, both rooted in the metaphysics of presence and to be negotiated by the recognition of the spectral-messianic promise: This fear neglects to respond to the dead and to accept the unownability of the future. The messianic promise at the heart of Marx's promise cannot only explain why its institutionalization had to fail, but also allows us to retrieve a call to responsibility, a responsibility that, as spectral, takes into account not only the living but also the dead and the unborn. In chapter four, we will examine more closely how the promise of the future leads not only to the 'spectral' anteriority of an otherness that cannot be appropriated by subjects, and that therefore "shoulders" them "always with a cadaver,"[40] but also with a responsibility whose origin remains unlocalizable. I will also discuss there the problematic nature of the gesture that, in an attempt to inherit Marx's promise and Benjamin's messianic claim of the dead, extends specific violence in history—the instituting violence of capitalism, including slavery, dispossession, and economic exploitation—to

not only include Stalinist violence, but also the unavoidable, originary violence associated with *différance*. Let us note here, however, that for Derrida,
Marx's promise is not only connected with the latter two sorts of violence. As
a deconstructive, 'radicalized' inheritance of Marxism, it also contains an
injunction to criticize and tackle the violence of capitalism.

For Derrida, our times are destitute and bleak, full of injustice, from
unemployment, homelessness, and economic as well as interethnic wars to
the contradictions in relation to the so-called free market, the arms industry
(including the spread of nuclear weapons) and the shortcomings of international law (SM 78ff./134ff.). For Derrida, this bleak state of affairs is epitomized in Hamlet's cry of despair "The time is out of joint." As is well known,
this cry of despair was triggered by the appearance of Hamlet's dead father as
a ghost, calling on his son to 'set things right,' to do justice by an act of
revenge. Derrida uses this opportunity to point out that, in fact, one always
inherits from a crime that asks to be corrected, the primary crime, from the
viewpoint of narcissism, being the uncontrollable otherness originary repetition introduces into every identity. "[R]epetition as tragedy" (WD 247/362),
as "the spectral anteriority of the crime—the crime of the other, a misdeed
whose event and reality, whose truth can never *present themselves* in flesh and
blood, but can only allow themselves to be presumed, reconstructed, fanta-
sized. One does not, for all that, bear any less of a responsibility, beginning at
birth" (SM 21/46). The originarity of the otherness, of the 'absolute past,'
thus signifies that that which precedes every generation in its uncircumventable lateness, is both a crime (a trauma) and a call to responsibility. "One
never inherits without coming to terms with [*s'expliquer avec*] some specter,
and therefore with more than one specter. With the fault but also the injunction of *more than one*" (SM 21/46). This injunction points to a responsibility
"that comes from nowhere."[41]

Hence, for Derrida, that the time is out of joint not only means that
'something is rotten in the State of Denmark' but refers to the disjointure of
time itself. This disjointure is a movement in the future anterior, following
the logic of an originary delay we analyzed earlier. Every moment is exposed
to a future repetition that, while allowing its minimal or spectral presence,
also divides it against itself. Hence, there is no 'living' present, insofar as
every event is "always already" future-indexed—it always already defers its
full presence—and past-indexed inasmuch as a "date always repeats" (SM
118/192). Derrida further argues, however, that this disjointed time does not
simply lead to the necessity of injustice, as one might think. On the contrary,
it affords the possibility of justice by opening up the relation to the other.[42]
Since the exposure to this radically open future, the iteration from the future,
disjoins the present and the past alike, the present is always open to and
haunted by a past to which the present is not related in continuity. This
thought gives rise to Derrida's neologism 'hauntology,' a quasi-ontology that

concerns itself with the analyses of the specters of the past and of the future that, neither present nor absent, come to haunt the living. These specters, of course, have to pass through the repetition from the future, which is why Derrida can show that at bottom, the ghosts always face us from the future (SM 39/71), that the *revenant* is an always other *arrivant*. Further, however, these specters, as 'our' tradition—its unity and ownership thus being put into question—precede and determine us (since we are our tradition), and they look at us before we look at them, before we can respond—the 'visor effect' (SM 7/27). It is against this background that Derrida suggests that justice cannot be rendered to the living alone. Responsibility cannot only concern itself with the presently living, but must include an address to, and a being addressed by, the specters of the dead and the unborn. We have to listen to—and, in fact, have always already heard—the contradictory 'injunction' that the specters, the dead and the unborn, address to us. Otherwise, we are in danger of violently suppressing the self-difference that, always already, entered the self with its positioning, its self-repetition. For Derrida, however, this violence is co-originary with the 'absolute past' that separates any identity and event from itself. "The One, as self-repetition, can only repeat and recall this instituting violence. It can only affirm itself and engage itself in this repetition. This is even what ties in depth the injunction of memory with the anticipation of the future to come" (AF 79/125f.). In a certain sense, memory, as a form of repetition, is always promised to the future. Ethically and politically speaking, it makes all the difference whether this "originary violence,"[43] this 'traumatism,' has been recognized. It would be a recognition of the fact that one's heritage is necessarily internally differentiated—that there is always more than one specter—and that it therefore can be repeated against itself. That it remains open to the future on account of the promise that already divides it against itself.

WHY MARX'S MESSIANISM NEEDS THE MESSIANIC

Having discussed originary repetition in its link to the messianic promise, and having demonstrated that the inheritance of Marx's promise, however transcendental, cannot be thought without taking into account the history of this promise, we can now discuss in greater detail the relation between Marx's messianistic promise and Derrida's messianic promise. As discussed, the latter presents the originary condition of the former. The condition, as the 'being-promise of the promise,' shows why the institution of Marx's promise aiming at the classless society had to fail. However, what specific features of Marx's formulation of communism, apart from its nature of a promise, allow, and even demand, its reformulation in terms of the messianic in general? If the co-implication of historicity and history in the originary condition demand that the latter not be imposed from without, but rather revealed in its particular effects, how does the condition manifest itself in what it conditions, namely, Marx's promise? Let us remember that the quasi-transcendental inheritance implies, among other things, two consequences for a deconstructive reading. First, it means that there is no clear dividing line, and thus no hierarchy, between the constituted and the constitutive. For a practice of reading, this means that deconstruction must find the condition of possibility of the text under discussion in the text itself. A deconstructive reading 'borrows' the resources of its reading from its 'object.' The object is thus not just an object opposed to an interpreting subject, nor does deconstruction amount to a 'method' external to its object. Second, this condition or operation also signifies that the condition of possibility is at the same time the condition of impossibility. Referring a text to its enabling conditions also means to unground it, to reveal its failure of achieving self-transparency, and to read its unreadability. Repetition is constitutive of reading and meaning, but by virtue of its openness and deferral to the future, it necessarily alters and deconstitutes what it constitutes.

The '*quasi*-transcendental' operation thus indicates that the conditions of possibility to which it refers—the conditions of (im)possibility of Marx's messianism—cannot be seen to precede, and thus govern his text from the outside. A deconstructive or 'double' reading both returns its object to the metaphysical 'closure' or conceptuality, and shows how it itself, by virtue of the play and work of its conceptual structure, its aporias, contradictions, and slippages, necessarily exceeds that closure. Such excess, then, need not be imported from without and imposed on the text by a schema of reading.[44] Thus, like any deconstructive procedure, the reformulation of Marx's promise must be able to locate in Marx's text itself those conditions that make his communist promise possible. In other words, Marx's very notion of the promise of emancipation must already contain its own principle of deconstructive reading within itself, just as—to refer to one of Derrida's more familiar readings—the ambiguous *pharmakon* allows Plato's texts to be deconstructed from inside out, thereby radically complicating the distinction between inside and outside.[45] In order to graft the notion of a messianic promise, a promise to a future that cannot be anticipated in our horizons, onto Marx's promise for a 'classless society' or for 'communism,' Derrida has to argue that the promise, and its formulation in Marx, already lived off, and was constituted by, its more open, messianic version. The inheritance of his promise would attempt to filter out this messianic promise located at the heart of the promise of communism. Thus, Derrida claims that "communism *has always been* and will remain spectral: it is always still to come" (SM 99/162; my emphasis).

The following considerations revolve around an attempt to show how Derrida practices such a quasi-transcendental reading in *Specters of Marx*. I will isolate, and briefly discuss, three features of Marx's promise that allow and demand their reinscription in the field transversed and fissured by originary repetition as its ineluctable condition. The first of these features is the most consistent focus of Derrida's reading, while the latter two require that we go beyond the text of his book on Marx. The first concerns Marx's promise to rid us of the 'specters' of past revolutions, of ideology and of commodity fetishism, all of which are said to share a symptomatic, 'spectral' hovering between presence and absence. Here, Derrida argues that Marx's critique relies on an ontology of life on the basis of which he (implicitly) promises the classless society as the end of the spectral. The second feature I discuss concerns the unity of theory and praxis in Marx. The truth of his discourse depends on the (promised) future realization of scientific prognoses. Finally, I will turn to a logic of incarnation at work in the construction of the proletariat as the subject of history. Regarding the promise of fully incarnating the 'specter of communism,' I will attempt to show how Marx's 'messianism' presupposes the 'messianic in general.' Derrida's deconstruction of Marx's concept of critique, of the unity of theory and praxis, and of his logic of incarnation thus show how the messianic promise at the heart of Marx's promise renders it both possible and impossible.

In his book on Marx, Derrida does not always spell out such a detailed deconstructive reading of Marx's various formulations and pronouncements of the promise but prefers to speak, in a more general fashion, of "that 'spirit' of emancipatory Marxism whose injunction we are reaffirming here" (SM 167/266). In my view, this is in part due to the fact that Derrida is most interested in the ethico-political aspect of Marx's promise. It is the call to criticize and act against injustice that we must inherit. Hence, Derrida operates the quasi-transcendental procedure by considering the Marxist concept of critique. As its title indicates, *Specters of Marx* focuses on the specters and ghosts of Marx—the specter Marx and his injunction turned into after his death, especially after 1989, but also the ghosts Marx himself was obsessed with—and his attempt to 'exorcise' them. The operation of the deconstructive procedure of reading may, then, first of all be observed by focusing on the concept of critique, which Derrida claims is grounded on an 'ontology'[46] of the living individual and of living work (SM 187/178f.). Consequently, Derrida focuses on the relationship of Marx's "*ontologie*" to "*hantalogie*," and on the semantics of specter, ghost, *Geist*, *Gespenst*, *Spuk*. Insofar as Marx's texts are populated, to the point of obsession, with ghosts, Derrida tries to inhabit this semantic field in order to show how Marx's various attempts at a distinction between *Geist* and *Gespenst*, for example, are untenable, and how, therefore, his attempt to rid us of bad and deceiving ghosts remains problematic and needs to be reinscribed in a generalized, hauntological field. Derrida's analysis of the relationship between an ontological critique of ghosts and a hauntological "fantasmatics" disrupts what he views as Marx's "pre-deconstructive ontology of presence" (SM 170/269). According to Derrida's reading, this ontology grounds Marx's critique of 'specters' such as ideology and the commodity fetish by "bring[ing] this representation back to the world of labor, production, and exchange, so as to reduce it to its conditions" (ibid.). (Derrida thus recognizes that Marx employs a transcendental procedure of his own, one that focuses on a world-constituting concept of praxis, as previously indicated.)

This disruption of Marx's ontology is undertaken in order to arrive at the spectrality of *différance* that Marx—according to the deconstructive 'double reading' mentioned earlier—is said to recognize by analyzing the inevitable autonomization and idealizations of these specters (cf. SM 170/269). The hauntological spectrality thus functions as the aporetic, undecidable, and groundless ground making possible and undoing the efficacy of the ontological critique. Derrida wishes to reinscribe historical time in this differential, disadjusted, spectral time that maintains us always already in an openness to the (repressed) ghosts of both the past and the future, making of life itself a "being-with specters" that is itself the 'proper' politics of memory (SM xvi-iif./14f.). As we will see, this spectral time inhabits Marx's promise from the beginning, and can be said to come to the fore in the wavering between the constative (the revolution will happen, according to a scientific analysis of capitalism's contradictions) and the performative (let us make the revolution happen) formulations of the promise.

With the example of the spectral deconstruction of Marx's notion of critique, we see that Derrida employs the deconstructive procedure of reading. According to this procedure, Marx's promise, especially where it is directed toward the final reduction of specters to their material conditions, is founded on an 'ontology' of social relations within a mode of production (where the task is to achieve a conscious self-transparency of these relations). Many specters (ideology, fetishism, the specters of the dead, even the 'specter' of communism itself), however, can be shown to escape a reduction to this ontology if the latter is reinscribed in a more general field of spectrality that Derrida also calls a general 'fantasmatics.' Marx, as Derrida puts it, "did not begin where he ought to have 'been able to begin,' namely with haunting, before life *as such*" (SM 175/278). This reinscription puts questions to Marx's "critical ontology [which] means to deploy the possibility of dissipating the phantom" (SM 170/269), questions that are not just theoretical but derive from "seismic events [that] come from the future" (ibid.). Such events ultimately render the reduction of the phantom impossible. The future to come dislocates the order of events such that they cannot be reduced to their material conditions alone, but, as 'seismic' or 'spectral,' require a hauntological analysis rather than an ontological critique. In other words, Derrida suggests here that the deconstructive, quasi-transcendental reinscription of the Marxian promise of critique reveals it as sustained by, but also as ignoring or attempting to dispel, seismic events that are produced by the messianic in general as a promise of a future beyond horizons. Reinscribing Marx's promise means to recall it to a more originary promise of the future, one that dislocates time in such a way that specters emerge that cannot be reduced to the dialectic of the forces and relations of production. The efficacy of Marxian critique, as well as of Marx's promise, then, requires the reduction of specters that, however, can be shown to be irreducible. In a quasi-transcendental fashion, *Specters of Marx* deconstructs Marx's formulations of the promise with regard to the promise of a Marxian critique, the ontological promise of a world without spectrality (without alienation, ideology, and commodity fetishism).

Before we turn to another area in which *Specters* attempts to show the quasitranscendental priority of the messianic promise—namely, the analysis of Marx's call for revolutionary action and for the incarnation of the 'specter' of communism—let us turn to the second feature mentioned earlier. The consideration of this feature further supports, even beyond Derrida's own analysis, the claim that a quasi-transcendental reading does not simply impose its own concerns and presuppositions on a given discourse, but inhabits a discourse from within in order to open it onto a more general, quasi-transcendental field. Marx's text furnishes the possibility, and even necessity, of the quasi-transcendental reading of the promise by virtue of the projected self-sublation of the Marxist discourse. Marx's text performatively calls on the future to realize its theoretical program, where the efficacy and the truth of the discourse is not primarily to be judged by its scientific or constative value, but by its power to bring about a fundamental change in the world, as the eleventh Feuerbach Thesis famously proclaims. This self-overcoming discourse marks its date and its material inscription by promising itself to a future transition to praxis. This praxis will have to prove that what the young Marx called the 'human essence'—the potential of social humanity to objectify itself through labor—is capable of transcending capitalist alienation so as to make communism possible, thus corroborating Marx's visionary critique of capitalism. What Derrida wishes to save of this theoretical promise to praxis is "Marx's injunction not just to decipher but to act" (SM 32/61). However, he argues that this injunction must proceed from, and take account of, the messianic future, rather than the future of a determined communism. The future that Marx has to invoke for the coherence and truthfulness of his discourse could then be shown to be the future that at the same time undoes or disallows this projected self-sublation, the full materialization of the promise, that would coincide with a complete objectification or externalization of all human 'essential powers' (*Wesenskräfte*).[47] Such a demonstration would correspond to a quasi-transcendental reading insofar as the promise of the future would be shown to simultaneously render possible and impossible the Marxian promise of liberation. It is this self-negation of a theoretical discourse promising itself to the future that allows Derrida to revisit the messianic structure of an injunction upon Marx, while declaring the essential non-arrival of the future.

The claim that Marx's discourse presupposes and inscribes the more rad-ical, messianic future could thus be justified by the fact that it has to draw on this future to which it promises itself. As textual evidence, one could refer to Marx's double determination of the notion of communism. In the same text (and not just in different phases of his writing), communism is determined as, on the one hand, a future (present) state that can be described and antici-pated on the basis of a dialectical analysis of the contradictions, and the internal laws of movement, of the history of capitalism. On the other hand, Marx describes communism as a practical movement toward the abolition of capitalism.[48] Despite the passionate critique of capitalism, a certain spirit of Marx—the one that Derrida calls 'ontological' and that also criticizes the suf-fering capitalism causes—believes it can retain all the riches capitalism pro-duces, and therefore, like Hegel, cannot think nor mourn for the real losses of historical 'development.' For Marx's 'ontological,' that is, world-constitut-ing, concept of 'labor'—determined variously as social or species-being praxis, as human production, or life activity—in alienating itself in capital-ism, speculates on a good return of historical humanity's investment in capi-talism. This investment hopes to benefit in terms of the maturity of the human 'essential powers' and needs, and thus in terms of technological devel-opment. Like Benjamin, Derrida refuses to connect the promise with mem-ory on the basis of humanity's technological, teleological development.

With this speculation and investment, Marx's critique of political econ-omy entangles itself in an economy that Derrida, in his essay on Hegel, called a 'restricted economy,' and the attempt to overcome capitalism remains within the orbit of its logic. This investment is what explains the almost hymnic celebration of the historical role of the bourgeoisie in the *Communist Manifesto*. "The human being had to be reduced to this absolute poverty in order that he might yield his inner wealth to the outer world," as Marx writes elsewhere.[49] Thus, the self-sublation or practical supersession (*Aufhebung*) of the Marxian discourse—which also has a self-critical thrust that Derrida wel-comes, an openness to self-transformation (SM 88/145)—turns at Derrida's hands into a self-*relève*, an effect of substitution and difference that takes account of the possibility, and even necessity, of a real *loss* on the investment in capitalism. According to a deconstructive reading, this investment results in a "restricted economy that takes no part in expenditure without reserve, death," and that thus lives off a "general economy" and a "*différance* that misses its profit."[50]

This reinscription of Marx's limited economy in a general economy cor-responds to the aforementioned reinscription of Marx's ontological promise in a spectral, messianic promise. This general economy, and the disadjust-ment of time it analyzes, conceives of a play "in which one loses and wins on every turn" (ibid.). It is on the basis of these consideration that I suggested that the reformulation of Marx's promise must be able to take up and consider

a memory of loss. The loss in question here, however, is not only represented
by the suffering capitalist alienation brings about, and by the increasing dis-
persion and competition into which capitalist development throws the working classes themselves, thus rendering the practical realization of Marx's revolutionary promise more difficult. Marx was quite aware of these negative
effects of capitalism, undermining the very movement that is dialectically
determined as their overcoming. But the loss Derrida's reading keeps coming
back to is also, and primarily, figured as an unrepresentable excess of the community of producers who, according to Marx's promise, have to appropriate
the technological advancements of capitalism at the moment these advancements have become unmanageable and uncontrollable by the bourgeoisie. It
is an excess that prevents the projected self-transparency and collective will
of the proletariat in that it refers to the 'spectrality' and ultimate uncontrollability of the differential play at work in social relations in general. On this
score at least, Derrida's reading of Marx agrees with Habermas's and Apel's
claim that Marx neglects the irreducible and nontotalizable aspect of social
interaction in his concept of critical praxis and labor.[51] Derrida thinks this
excess precisely as the irreducibility of time to all forms of political organization, as an excess of the unrepresentable future.

With this discussion of the differential field of social relations, we have
already moved on to the third feature mentioned earlier. The analysis of the
promise of Marx's discourse to a future transition to praxis—allowing, even
necessitating, the grafting of Derrida's messianic promise onto Marx's discourse—leads us now to a closer examination of this concept of future praxis
and Marx's revolutionary program. Here, the task is to show that the promise,
more often than not in Marx, is subjected to a (Hegelian, Christological) law
of incarnation that ultimately renders the Marxian promise impractical and
impossible. The future classless society is embodied by the revolutionary
working class that, being the immanent contradiction, the "negation of the
negation," of capitalism, is already "in itself the expression of the dissolution
of all classes."[52] In *Specters of Marx*, Derrida criticizes this logic, apart from his
earlier treatments of Hegel, not only in Marx, but even more so, in his reading of Fukuyama's *The End of History and the Last Man* (SM 56ff./97ff.), a book
that has generated a leftist, and even a Marxist school of interpretation.[53] By
extrapolating Derrida's comments on the inevitable autonomization and proliferation of specters, we can see that he criticizes this logic in Marx by directing the promise away from the classless society to the messianic future and
the ineluctable repetition from the future. The latter engenders a flood of different specters and ghost within the members of the 'class' that is supposed to
be unified by this promise and the revolutionary task it assigns to them. As
discussed in the first chapter, it is such ghosts of the past that the "Eighteenth
Brumaire" wished to dispel in the name of the poetry of the future. On the
basis of originary repetition, Marx's concept of the revolution would then not

be able to draw an advance credit on the future, following a 'logic of incarnation' whereby the future universal of history is embodied in the present, in the privileged agent of history.[54] The future envisaged as a future present, as a utopia, supplies the illusion of a unified subject-agent of history that is present to itself and not haunted by a 'spectral' otherness within itself. It is this conception of the future as a 'utopia' that does not keep history open to a different future, but forecloses it.

Let us look more closely at this deconstruction of Marx's logic of incarnation with a view to the question of the relationship between Marx's promise of emancipation and its deconstructive and messianic 'radicalization.' The following analysis of Derrida's reading of the opening sentences of The Communist Manifesto draws on the quasi-transcendental law of iterability and the originary lateness or delay of time to itself. In his book on Marx, Derrida analyzes the promise in texts of Marx that one might group under the heading of a revolutionary program. I cannot reconstitute these analyses in detail here. Suffice it to point out that it is in these calls to action, to overcome capitalism, that one can show that Marx neglects the spectral disjointure of the present most of all. For in his call to "create something that does not yet exist,"[55] for the institution of the future communist society in the movement of the present, Marx submits to a theory of revolution and political invention that, at the same time, draws on and disavows the disjointure of time, and therewith the 'messianic in general.' The institution of the Communist Party by way of the Communist Manifesto both describes and enacts, both states and performs, the "final incarnation of the specter [of communism], the real presence of the specter, thus the end of the spectral" (SM 103/168). Like any instituting language—a language Derrida analyzes more closely in "Declarations of Independence" and also in "The Force of Law"— the Manifesto hovers between the constative and the performative mode. It both presupposes, as already instituted, the communist movement that gives itself a party program, and, simultaneously, it performs the inauguration of this movement and gives birth to it. The Manifesto both claims that communism, as a movement, already exists, and produces this existence in the first place. This inadequation testifies to the 'out-of-jointness,' the spectrality of time itself, which for Derrida can only be denied in the act of inauguration. The 'incarnation' of the specter of communism that Marx aims at is thus only possible in a disadjusted time, a time marked by the originary lateness (Nachträglichkeit) of the event—a deferral that depends for its 'first time' on a repetition that never took place.

Communism, then, must promise itself to its appearance in flesh and blood, giving body to the fearful specter of communism Marx announced in 1848. But due to the disadjustment and spectrality of time, especially the time of inauguration and manifestation in a manifesto, the specter cannot ever fully incarnate itself: "The specter that Marx was talking about then, communism, was there without being there. It was not yet there. It will never be there," Derrida argues (SM 100/165). This aporia of time's noncontemporaneity with itself expresses itself in Marx's language as the undecidability between the performative and the constative mode, which is, for this reason, highlighted by Derrida as running through Marx's revolutionary program (SM 103/168). What is original about Marx's language is that he seems to recognize this disadjustment and lateness by describing the presupposed movement of communism as a 'specter' and not as a living presence. However, he proceeds to call for the overcoming of the specter, so that the Party may represent the future as "the end of the spectral," even as "the end of the political as such" (SM 102/166f.): the communist society rid of the ghosts and mystifications of capitalism. In this way, we can say that Marx both recognizes the spectrality of time and attempts to overcome it once and for all. In this tension, the heritage of Marxism is to be found as, precisely, always more than one specter of Marx. The future to which Marx promised himself is still outstanding, giving us his legacy from the future beyond his promise, for the latter has to draw on, and cannot overcome, a more radical promise, the one that spectralizes and disadjusts time.

As the analyses of these three features—the promise of Marx's critique, the unity of theory and praxis, and his call to give body to the specter of communism—have shown, Marx's promise can be and must be reinscribed in a logic of spectrality that is more originary than his promise, making it both possible and impossible. The basic structure of argumentation here is to inhabit Marx's promise for the future, a promise that makes his discourse possible, in such a way as to direct it to a more radical, nonhorizonal future. The resulting, more 'radical' promise is then shown to disjoin the order of time, thereby making Marx's promise impossible at the same time.

As in Benjamin's critique of Marx, the inheritance of the promise is directed toward a disenchanted, open future. By virtue of the quasi-transcendental concept of originary repetition, Derrida can show more precisely that it is this future that, by exceeding the classless society, disallows the teleo-onto-logic on whose basis Marx connected the promise of justice with the memory of past violence. Naturally, this does not mean that the future to come is without reference to memory. On the contrary, the messianic promise of the future to come derives its disenchanted emptiness from the inescapable deferral of repetition. As a form of repetition, memory itself harbors the promise within itself, installing a future 'in' the past that Benjamin associated with the implicit and explicit promises of past generations. The call to remember at the same time refers us to the future. If, as we said, any subject or unit of meaning can only establish its minimal and unstable self-identity by virtue of remembering and thus repeating itself, then repetition always defers to an unreachable future the identity it nonetheless promises. Memory, repetition, and the promise form an indissociable constellation. Derrida describes this constellation in his consideration of the archive, of tradition and its exposure to the future: "This is even what ties in depth the injunction of memory with the anticipation of the future to come. The injunction, even when it summons memory or the safeguard of the archive, turns incontestably toward the future to come. It orders to promise, but it orders repetition, and first of all self-repetition, self-confirmation in a *yes, yes*" (AF 79/126). The promise of self-identity is always undermined by the necessity to repeat this identity, by the messianic promise that is directed to a non-arriving future. This future to come never arrives since the need to remember and repeat will not go away, and no final *telos* or *eschaton* is available. Again, Derrida does not hesitate to name this latter, quasi-transcendental and 'axiomatic' promise, and the memory of the past as well of the future it implies, a "messianic memory and promise":

> Of a discourse to come—on the to-come and repetition. Axiom: no to-come without heritage and the possibility of *repeating*. No to-come without some sort of *iterability*, at least in the form of a covenant with oneself and of a *confirmation* of the originary *yes*. No to-come without some sort of messianic memory and promise, of a messianicity older than all religion, more originary than all messianism. No discourse or address of the other without the possibility of an elementary promise.[56]

These 'axiomatic' statements certainly indicate that we are here dealing with a quasi-transcendental discourse. Indeed, the messianic promise of repetition is 'older' and 'more originary' than all particular promises, whether those of religious messianisms or of Marx's promise for the classless society. What the latter have in common, as previously suggested, is the fact that they give content to the promise, a content that would eliminate the necessity of repetition. As Marx put it: "The reality, which communism is creating, is precisely the real basis for rendering it impossible that anything should exist independently of individuals."[57]

HOW TO TELL GOOD FROM BAD GHOSTS

After having discussed the quasi-transcendental law of iterability, and the disjointure and delay of time it implies, we will now turn to this law's consequences for an understanding of the emancipatory promise and its relationship to memory. The overall argument here will be that the Derridian promise of the future is best understood as what we will call a postutopian, rather than an antiutopian promise of politics (despite Derrida's own misgivings about the term "utopia" as a future present). I call it postutopian because it does not deny, but rather implies, the possibility and importance of the projection of horizons of political change, although it directs us to a 'messianic' future that, being beyond all horizons, radically exposes all horizons to their instability and reinterpretability, such that no utopia can harden into a dogmatic eschatology or teleology. What is more, I will suggest that the inescapability of factically and historically determined contexts, as implied by the account of iterability and its promise, also renders uncircumventable the projections of specific horizons, an argument whose significance for political purposes should not be underestimated. The relationship between utopian horizons and the messianic future, contrary to what some of Derrida's own formulations might seem to suggest, thus cannot be thought as a mere opposition.

As we have seen, by insisting on the primacy of the future to come, Derrida attempts to inherit Marx's promise by redefining it as nonrealizable and as an infinite otherness. This redefinition takes the form of an analysis of what I called the homelessness of the promise of the future as, precisely, the condition of finitude in general. Recalling this finitude prevents the conception of a privileged bearer of the future totality of history incarnated in the present, in a class or a people. For the future in question here is beyond any 'logic of incarnation' in that it precisely exceeds the constitution of any subject, making possible and demanding its ever new reconstitution by way of repetition.

As in Benjamin, Marx's promise is to be articulated with a certain dimension of a mournful memory, a memory that alters the conception of the promise no less than being altered by it. At the beginning of *Specters of Marx*, Derrida associates 'mourning' with Marx's 'exorcist' ghost hunt, a mourning defined by the attempt "to ontologize remains, to make them present . . . by localizing the dead" (SM 9/30). This localization would be the attempt—ultimately doomed to failure, but nonetheless full of problematic consequences—to prevent the dead from returning as specters. The reconceptualization of the promise must then also affect the notion of a mournful memory with which the promise is to be articulated. It would have to be, perhaps paradoxically, a 'mourning' directed to the future by the promise, that is, a mourning that is aware of, and acquiescent to, the pluralizing work of the repetition from the future. The 'object' mourned for always exceeds the mourner(s) and their interiorization of the lost object by virtue of its link to the future.[58] It is in this spirit that Derrida opens his book on Marx with the desire "to learn to live *with* ghosts" (SM xviii/14).

In what follows, I want to briefly present Derrida's rejection of Marx's 'exorcism' of the ghosts from the past, insofar as it allows us to further approach, via the negative route, a notion of mourning in the context of what I call Derrida's postutopianism. Along this path of investigation we encounter a difficulty concerning the inheritance of Marx's call for revolutionary action and critical analysis, a difficulty that Benjamin prefigures and that Derrida has to face as well. For the inheritance of the Enlightenment promise of emancipation and freedom is, in particular in Marx, inseparable from a notion of critique, which in turn is, as its etymology tells us, linked to critical distinctions. Derrida leaves no doubt that, although deconstruction is not a critical procedure in any traditional sense—it does not, as indicated, presuppose a given norm or a regulative ideal—he wishes to hold on to the critical spirit of Marx above all (SM 88/145). The difficulty then concerns the necessity to distinguish between specters, between, for instance, the 'mystifications' of capitalism and the ghosts of the past whose suffering we are called on to remember. It consists in the necessity to inherit the two sides of the emancipatory promise. On the one hand, we are asked to retain Marx's critical analysis of certain specters like ideology and fetishism, analyses that seem to imply that the reenchantment of social relations in the midst of a modern and capitalist process of disenchantment and secularization can be overcome. It is, moreover, difficult to think this notion of critique without at least implicitly envisioning a utopian future that would be freed from these 'ghosts.' On the other hand, however, we need to discard the reduction of specters to the merely human, to an 'ontology' of the living individual that privileges life in its presence. Given this emphasis on a mournful memory of specters and ghosts, part of the question here is in how far the spectralized promise can still criticize specters—like those of ideology and fetishism—and whether there is room for a utopia freed from such specters in Derrida's conception.[59]

As discussed in the context of Benjamin's reading of Marx, at times the latter does not hesitate—his and Engels's critique of 'utopian socialism' notwithstanding—to demand a 'cheerful' forsaking of ghosts and memories when it comes to the task "to create something that does not yet exist."[60] Marx's response to his mourning for the missed proletarian opportunity in 1848 Paris is thus instructive: instead of placing his hope in memory, he opposes the latter to the future and argues that

> the social revolution of the nineteenth century cannot draw its poetry from the past but only from the future. It cannot begin with itself before it has stripped off all superstition in regard to the past. Earlier revolutions required world-historical recollections in order to drug themselves concerning their content. In order to arrive at its content, the revolution of the nineteenth century must let the dead bury their dead.[61]

In his analysis of the "Eighteenth Brumaire," Derrida draws attention to the Nietzschean resonances of Marx's call for an "active forgetting" (SM 114/187) and links it to what he sees as his exorcism. This exorcism consists in a repeated and seemingly constative reassurance that the dead are really dead and will not return (SM 48/84), a performative death certificate that does not want to know or hear about death (SM 175/278). Such a repression of the ghosts of the past ultimately denies its own mortality, Derrida argues, viewing, as we have seen, the "pre-deconstructive" (SM 170/269) layer of Marx's texts as a philosophy or ontology of life and the living guilty of the metaphysics of presence. Derrida recognizes a certain necessity in such a cheerfulness, of course, but, according to his overall argument, this necessity always has to be limited by a 'but' or a 'however': "However alive, healthy, critical, and still necessary his burst of laughter may remain," Derrida thinks that Marx's cheerfulness is inserted in a general ontology that "should not have chased away so many ghosts too quickly" (SM 174/277).

One might wonder here whether the critical difference between an exorcism and a responsible inheritance, the one that wishes to welcome ghosts, is a matter of quantity and speed, or whether the difference lies in the fear driving the ghost hunt whose outward sign would be this quantity and speed, a fear of the other in the self haunting every self-identity and self-determination: for example, that of the proletariat in the moment of revolutionary action. How far does Derrida—in aiming at the inheritance of Marx's 'critical spirit' more than anything else, to the exclusion of "almost everything" else in Marx (SM 89/146)—actually succeed in assuming the legacy of this cheerful side of the emancipatory promise? And can one learn to live with the specters of the past and the future while nonetheless allowing the establishment of, if only temporary and fragile, political identities and communities that will continue the struggles, thereby assuming the promise of the ones who gave their life for them?[62] As might have been expected, the argument has been made that Derrida welcomes too many specters too quickly, thus depriving himself of the means to distinguish good from bad, mystifying from emancipatory ghosts.[63]

There is, however, no point in simply opposing Marx's (or Nietzsche's) cheerfulness in forsaking unhealthy ghosts to a generalized welcome of all specters, regardless of their effects. Thinking the ineluctable spectrality of any inheritance not only means, against a suppression of death in 'exorcism,' to recognize an ever renewed repetition of the past from the future, and thus the necessity of memory for the promise of the future. It also means—according to Derrida's association of an 'originary exappropriation' with an originary forgetfulness as the law of finitude—that a certain relinquishing of specters is inherent in every inheritance of them. As previously argued, the reinscription of Marx's promise in a "general economy" configures a differential play "in which one loses and wins on every turn."[64] The necessity of loss here would not only be due to the limits of memory's capacity, but stem from the fact that every inheritance represses other possibilities of constructing and interpreting a 'heritage,' and thus is necessarily exclusive. This is why Derrida emphasizes that the work of inheritance— and we *are* 'our' inheritance, unless we wish to complicate this adjective to the point of suppressing our complicity with the unnecessary violence it also stands for—is a "critical and transformative filter" (SM 102/167), a reaffirmation "by choosing" (SM 16/40) according to a selectivity that "will fatally exclude in its turn. It will even annihilate, by watching (over) its ancestors rather than (over) certain others." It will even end up "killing the dead: law of finitude" (SM 87/144).

The concept of finitude Derrida invokes here does not circumscribe the limits of a given field, such that the heritage or memory in question would be, empirically speaking, too large and thus inexhaustible. Rather than being an 'empiricist' concept, it focuses on the infinite substitutability within a discourse. As Derrida writes in one of his clearer expositions of this concept of finitude: "This field is in effect that of *play*, that is to say, a field of infinite substitutions only because it is finite, that is to say, because instead of being an inexhaustible field, as in the classical hypothesis, instead of being too large, there is something missing from it: a center which arrests and grounds the play of substitutions" (WD 289/423).[65] According to this law of finitude, every heritage must be viewed as afflicted with annihilation and exclusion, and thus with a certain sense of loss. The spectral future imposes a 'double bind' on inheritors; it signifies that forgetting is not only the antonym of memory. It reminds us, for example, that a mindlessly and automatically repeated ritual of mourning or gesture of memory, as in highly mediatized memorial events, may be, depending on the context, the best kind of forgetting. A certain kind of inheritance, as Benjamin knew well, is the worst kind of memory: "There is a [way of handing down phenomena] (*Überlieferung*) that is a catastrophe" (V 591), he wrote in an effort to combat the reduction of works of art to a mere stage or phase in a continuous history, thereby suppressing their critical impact, their promise for the future. This complexity upsets any simple call for mourning or memory, a call that would aim at the acquiescence of a good conscience in the face of the past. It is what Derrida has in mind when he analyzes the contemporary response to the "trauma"—"[m]ourning always follows a trauma" (SM 97/160)—of this "century of Marxism": "This trauma is endlessly denied by the very movement through which one tries to cushion it, to assimilate it, to interiorize and incorporate it" (SM 98/162).

The response to our being asked to remember the victims of history can thus not only consist in a more inclusive memory, in widening the scope of 'our' heritage. Derrida's insistence on a certain sense of originary loss, on the fact that every inheritance is selective and thus repressive in a certain sense, should not simply be read as a generalized mourning for the condition of finitude itself—although, as I will discuss in chapter four, it may easily undermine Benjamin's attempts to highlight political exclusions and the suppression of the 'oppressed past,' which is why I will call for a productive oscillation, an always new and provisional renegotiation between Benjamin's and Derrida's call to responsible action in the face of a history of violence. Despite these difficulties, originary loss may be read as a paradoxical attempt to remember even those victims whose names have been forgotten or erased, in what Benjamin called a "memory of the nameless" (I 1241). It is further directed against the comfort and good conscience that can lie in an ostentatious mourning, and it highlights the very disappearance of memory, of witnesses, beyond the redressable violence of exclusion and foreclosure. It attempts, says Derrida, to "make the absolute destruction reappear" (*Points* 390/404).

If we are then looking in vain for a universal standard of a critique and de-cision about specters, this is because our exposition to the future—the future that, according to Derrida, demands our "blind submission" or affirmation (SM 7/27)—precisely inserts us, according to the account of historicity, into a specific context in the midst of which alone we can decide about hospitality and exorcism, welcome and relentless critique. The thinking of this future does not ask of us to welcome any specter, including those of 'ideology' and 'fetishism,' however understood, but to affirm the work of a spectralizing repetition from the future to which all specters owe themselves. In this sense, "the specter is the future" (SM 39/71), born of the rift, of a certain undecidability, that the future to come institutes in the heart of the present (SM 107/174). For the interminable repetition from the future also divides the present against itself insofar as it is the constant possibility of repeating this present against itself, keeping it open for a repetition of the past that can bring with it the specters one might want to exorcise. In this way, the thinking of this future radically opens up and disadjusts the present, letting the past, in the form of specters, overflow this present.

POSTUTOPIAN MARXISM:
KANTIAN AND DECONSTRUCTIVE

If it is correct that Derrida's messianic in general, the quasi-transcendental promise of the future, while not being empiricist, inserts us into specific 'empirical' contexts on the basis of which anticipations of the future are made, how then can this promise direct us to a future without determinable outlines? Since every specific context implies and necessitates the specificity of its future horizons, must we not say—as some commentators have[66]—that the 'pure formality' and utter lack of content of the future at which Derrida aims is likewise unthinkable? Given the earlier exposition of the quasi-transcendental nature of Derrida's messianic promise, we must insist here, following Derrida himself, that the *determinability* of these historical conditions, or their historicity, still requires more than this insistence on their facticity. The quasi-transcendentality of these conditions is not to be mistaken for a lapse back into precritical empiricism. For the messianic in general—Derrida's "quasi-transcendental 'messianism'" (SM 168/267)—is precisely an attempt to account philosophically for the historicity of such conditions. In the treatment of the quasi-transcendental promise of repetition, I have attempted to specify how the messianic promise returns us to the necessity of repeating, and thus altering, a specific heritage, thereby inserting us into specific historical conditions. The ineluctability, that is, the very historicity, of factical conditions itself requires a philosophical account—which is, to be sure, not immune from those condi-tions, but neither is it reducible to them.[67] Thus, the messianic promise is nei-ther merely historical and factical nor merely transcendental and formal. While it insists on the historical nature and empirical specificity, and thus on the limit, of all future horizons, it also thinks the necessary instability and versatil-ity of such horizons. This instability consists in their exposure to altering repe-titions from the future, to reinterpretations and reinventions that necessarily change such horizons. Therefore, just as there cannot be a binary opposition between the empirical and the transcendental, so there cannot be such an opposition between utopian projections and the messianic future, in Derrida's sense. While the necessity of horizons of the future puts the pure formality of Derrida's promise in question, this promise questions the stability and limited-ness of such horizons. In addition, the messianic promise points to the ethical urgency of interrupting alleged progress toward, for instance, a regulative idea, as in Benjamin's concern with seizing the political chances of the day.

Thus, the fact that the messianic promise—which Derrida, without fur-ther ado, associates with the "idea of justice" or the "idea of democracy" (SM 59/102)—is an 'ethico-political idea' does not mean that it is already compro-mised by its specificity and historicity. For Derrida indeed thinks that the mes-sianic promise, with its lack of content, may still be associated with a ('leftist') politics,[68] with justice and democracy, despite its quasi-transcendental status. We will discuss the political import of Derrida's messianic promise and mem-ory in greater detail in chapters three and four. Here, let me just indicate that, apart from a general desire for change referenced in the open-ended future, the messianic promise allows its association with democracy not because of a par-ticular set of ideals and programs for the future, but because of its insistence on the necessity and inescapability of constant reinterpretations of (and 'from') the future, and thus of the past and the present. The messianic promise aligns itself, therefore, with the openness of public space, which is inseparable from a concept of democracy. It is further connected with the lack of a political identity fixed by reference to extrapolitical concepts, and with the general lack in democracy of a permanent and incarnated locus of power.[69] In this light, the totalitarianisms of this century, including Stalinism, might indeed be seen as a response to the modern loss of a theologico-political logic guaran-teeing and stabilizing such a locus of power, as Claude Lefort has shown.[70]

We can only indicate here, however, that utopian horizons of the future are no less crucial to political invention and transformation, despite the sense of (an unproductive) impossibility associated with the word 'utopia,' as Der-rida insists.[71] Not only for motivational purposes, but also in order to prevent Derrida's insistence on what he terms 'the impossible' from being misunder-stood as such an unproductively impossible utopia (in the pejorative sense), utopian horizons are necessary. Otherwise, Derrida's deconstructive radical-ization of the Marxist promise, pointing out its impossibility in favor of an empty and formal promise, could turn out to block emancipatory movements and political invention guided by horizons of change. In the same way in which the formality of the messianic promise may not be misunderstood as freeing its inheritance from a violent past, so its emptiness may not rule out the projection of liberating horizons.

I indicated earlier that the very idea of inheritance as a "critical and transformative filter" (SM 102/167), which attempts to highlight and politicize the ineluctable forsaking of aspects and dimensions of a tradition due to the 'law of finitude,' implies the necessity of future horizons devoid of those aspects and dimensions. The projected overcoming of certain specters thus still requires 'utopian' horizons. Derrida cannot dispense with horizons, but they are not irreconcilable with the insistence on a quasi-transcendental messianic without messianism. Despite his own critique of utopian thinking—unless it is of the wildly speculative, Fourierian type that cannot be tied to quietist logics of progress (Thesis XI)—Benjamin showed an awareness of this by noting that "the function of political utopia [is] to highlight [abzuleuchten] the sector of what is worthy of destruction" (I 1244). However, such a horizon must be prevented from allowing the justification of past and present suffering, as happens easily with a utopia viewed as the goal of a progressive development, as we saw in Benjamin's objections to Marx.

With this in mind, the distinction I am making here between the nonpresent future 'beyond' horizons of anticipation and those horizons themselves, in which the future is a modification of the present, allows me to speak of Derrida as a postutopian, rather than an antiutopian thinker, a significant nuance easily missed. For Derrida, our relation to the future is not a matter of deciding between a 'messianistic' (or utopian) and a 'messianic' future. Derrida does not turn against Kantian Marxism as radically as did Benjamin, who, addressing it only in its progressivist, Bernsteinian form, saw in it a pernicious *embourgeoisement* of Marxism that disallows the memory of past suffering and the motivation of urgent struggle in the here and now. While distinguishing the nonhorizonal future from regulative ideals, Derrida attempts to capture the virtues of a Kantian Marxism that criticizes empirical reality in the light of a regulative ideal. We do not have to decide between the latter and a 'radicalized' questioning of this ideal—and the temporality it involves—in the light of the spectralizing future beyond such ideals (SM 86/143). The latter procedure would ultimately question "the concept of the human" (SM 87/143) in the name of which, since Kant, the Enlightenment ideal had been formulated, an ideal that, for Kant, precisely required the disowning of a debt owed to the past.[72] The former strategy, however, would still allow the projection of future horizons devoid of mystifying ghosts that ultimately lead to an unenlightened affirmation of the status quo.

In this sense, as I will elaborate in the next chapter, Derrida not only supplies Benjamin with the temporality of the relation between a disenchanted future and memory, but also prevents the former's radical critique of Kantian Marxism and progressivism from leading to a wholesale rejection of all utopian horizons. Such projection, and the critique of ghosts it permits, allows Derrida to model the 'New International' after the specter of communism in 1848 (SM 85/141), divested of its tendency to incarnate itself in the one class, the bearer of the future. Indeed, Derrida characterizes his idea of a new political and emancipatory community by the call for "a kind of counter-conjuration" (SM 86/142) against, for instance, the neoliberal and media-tized—that is, spectralized—triumphalism that speaks of the death of Marxism and the end of history, the exemplary target being Fukuyama's book by that title. If, as I will suggest later (in chapter four), Derrida's 'New International' is to avoid the indistinguishability of 'good' and 'bad' specters in an insistence on the 'originary violence' inherent in all memory, and if Derrida's 'democracy to come' (SM 64f./110f.) is to combat the death of Marxism that is so convenient to neoliberal capitalism, he will have to welcome those kinds of nonteleological utopian projections that point beyond, and thus highlight, the severe politico-economic constraints today's democratic procedures have inherited from what Marx called 'primitive accumulation,' and what we discussed as the instituting violence of capitalism.[73]

As noted earlier, we can think of the postutopian future beyond any horizon—what Derrida calls a future to come (*l'avenir à-venir*)—as a *blind spot* in the horizon, reminding us that there are always other horizons contesting a given ideal projection, such that it never petrifies into a dogmatic doctrine or an idea of automatic progress; one horizon will have given way to another. The promise to repetition—and, we recall, there is "no future without repetition" (AF 80/127)—severs any utopia from a logic of progress and finality, insofar as this 'absolute' future never arrives as such, and insofar as it includes in its 'general economy' a thinking of loss that thwarts the logic of investment and speculation. Enabling the possibility of the contestation of different utopian imaginaries, the messianic future names the possibility of a horizon's constitution as much as of its unraveling. Even while one may think that Derrida is still too hesitant to obligate his New International to a given, 'leftist' horizon, this 'radicalized' Marxism has not done away with utopian strivings altogether. Further, as we have seen, the promise to a future we cannot own at the same time brings with it an opening of the past to an always new inheritance and memory. It opens it up for new specters and new spirits to be selected and transformed in a present that does not possess the final meaning of the past. In his interpretation of Benjamin's "Theses," Derrida reads Benjamin's "strait gate" or "narrow door" [*kleine Pforte*] through which the "Messiah might enter" at any second (Thesis B), and which "turns in the hinge called memory [*Eingedenken*]" (I 1252), as naming what I called the blind spot of horizons of anticipation (AF 69/110).

For Derrida, both of these critical and conflictual procedures—the projection of a regulative ideal and its questioning in view (or, rather, blindness) of the unanticipatable future to come—exist side-by-side in Marx's spirit, the one we must inherit: "Here are two different reasons to be faithful to a spirit of Marxism. They must not be added together but intertwined. [. . .] Without this strategy, each of the two reasons could lead back to the worst, [. . .] namely, to a sort of fatalist idealism or abstract and dogmatic eschatology in the face of the world's evil" (SM 87/144). Such dangers are thus to be averted by a co-implication of two strategies, adjusted within each context to its demands. It is not difficult to recognize them as the problems of a degraded Marxism that, for Benjamin in the 1930s, was embodied by the German Social Democrats, leading him to severely criticize their abstract and fatalistic interpretation of Marx and to demand a 'messianizing' of Marx's concept of the classless society (I 1231f.), as we have seen. For one of the problems with an unquestioned regulative ideal is that it affords a notion of progress according to which the suffering of past generations can be played off against the benefits of a distant future.

We can thus say that, insofar as we think finitude—with Derrida, who is here following Heidegger's insights[74]—as the exposure to a future that can never be mastered or overcome, the inheritance of the promise of the future at the same time asks us to remember death—and with it the dead. Hence, as I have argued, we are called on to ask what becomes of the thinking of loss and suffering in history. It is this loss that Marx is said to have forgotten or repressed in his analyses of the specters of the past that were to be overcome for the constitution of the revolutionary subject. In this regard, Benjamin makes a crucial contribution to the concerns under discussion, for at the same time that he suggests to return a messianic 'face' to Marx's concept of the classless society, he associates this messianic dimension with the claim the dead have on us, and thus with a memory of suffering. Combating in particular the link between a progressive view of history and its projected goal or 'end,' Benjamin rejects the reduction of what Derrida calls specters to the logic of history. This reduction takes on a particular significance with respect to the issue of inheritance, insofar as this reduction led Marx—most notably, as we saw, in the "Eighteenth Brumaire of Louis Bonaparte"—to construe the proletariat, and the proletarian revolution, as both freed from a memory of the dead, and as the victorious inheritor of a history of violence. As noted, Benjamin refuses this "triumphal march of a victorious procession" (Thesis VII) and the utopian conceptions of the future in the name of which the downtrodden of the victor's history can be forgotten or sacrificed. Derrida's renegotiation of Marx's promise helps us to see that Benjamin's attempts to retrieve and redirect a messianic dimension of Marx's emancipatory promise insists on the radical otherness of a non-instrumental future that is neither an end nor a goal. Furthermore, we are in a better position to understand in what way this revisioning of the messianic allows Benjamin to conceive of it as an interruption of history that, as the 'differentials of time,' as a "messianic cessation of happening" (Thesis XVII), makes possible an experience of the dead's claim on us. Taking up this claim or address of the dead is then seen as necessary for revolutionary struggle. I will now turn to Benjamin's nonviolent and radically non-instrumental concept of such struggle. As we will see, this concept, developed as a critique of power, is antithetical to its institutional-ization in a legal framework. The debate between Benjamin and Derrida regarding law will allow us to investigate further the constellation of promise and memory afforded by the interweaving of these two thinkers.

THREE

The Critique of Violence

IN THE FIRST CHAPTER, I argued that Benjamin, in turning against Marx's projection of an end to history, also rejects the conception of a law-governed history. The latter afforded Marx a link between a memory of past victimization and the promise of history. The promise would then 'redeem' past loss by 'expropriating the expropriators,' thereby fulfilling and simultaneously overcoming the laws of history. In this sense, history is the site of politico-economic violence and class struggles in which the end alone is just. In the present chapter, I will discuss how far Benjamin takes his rejection of such teleology. We will see that Benjamin, in developing a concept of political resistance in a history of violence, criticizes not only teleological concepts of history, but also teleological concepts of action and power—two concepts that Marx did not analyze sufficiently. Above all in "On the Critique of Violence," Benjamin wishes to expose the violence of instrumental action and the imposition of power by means of law. For Benjamin, such imposition may be viewed as undertaken by the 'victors' of historical struggles in order to secure their victory. Acts of imposing law derive their justification from the postulation of just goals. Benjamin's concept of ethico-political action takes as its starting point the refusal of such a justification, and it reflects on the possibility of non-instrumental action devoid of the violence of means legitimated by reference to just ends.

Thus, if Benjamin's early "Critique of Violence" allows us to give clearer contours to the later "Theses'" concept of 'victor-history' as successive impositions of legally codified rule that legitimizes itself by reference to supposedly just ends, a non-instrumental concept of action may serve as the politically crucial bridge that connects another history—the 'history of the oppressed'—with emancipatory hopes for the future. This bridge would not, as in the Marx Benjamin criticizes, link memory and promise by way of a teleological history, but by way of nonteleological action. Thus, for Benjamin, a radical refusal of a politics of goals or ends in history is one of the preconditions of severing Marx's link between the notion of progress and the assumption of a memory of violence, and of reconstituting the connection between such memory and the promise. An instrumental politics, referring itself to its end, might justify present suffering and violence in light of the greater benefits to be derived from this end, from a 'utopia' seen as a future present on which an advance credit can be drawn.

A reading of Benjamin's early text on law will thus prove indispensable to a further understanding of the use of the term "messianic" in the context of the "Theses on the Concept of History" almost twenty years later. As we saw, Benjamin rejects an ultimately teleological secularization of messianism in Marx's account of law-governed history, but he also wishes to return a messianic structure to Marx's promise "in the interest of revolutionary politics itself" (I 1232). Benjamin thus indicates the necessity of a close relationship between emancipatory action and a messianic dimension of history. In contrast to Marxism's progressive teleology and ultimately quietist eschatology in scientific garb, the messianic dimension must bring to the fore the contingencies of history and the urgency of emancipatory struggles: Every political situation has its store of untapped possibilities (I 1231), and the class struggle, which Benjamin continues to see as central to politics, may not be inserted into a law-governed development that promises a victory whereby today's oppressed merely profit from past oppression (see chapter one). If we reject this 'messianism' and its 'victory history,' we can reconceive the messianic dimension as the opening up of history for the injunction that past oppression, now uncovered from the history of victors and freed from the promise of victory, addresses to the present generation. Such opening up of history, according to Benjamin, will occur by a kind of emancipatory action whose very 'unlocking' of history characterizes the action as 'messianic' in the first place (I 1231).

Here, then, I will try to show how Benjamin's early study on violence and the nonviolent mass strike proposes a concept of political, revolutionary action as 'messianic'; a political act that breaks through a violent history of the 'victors' responds to what the "Theses" present as the messianic claim of past generations. The contrast between 'victor-history' and its messianic interruption appears in the "Critique of Violence" as the opposition between 'mythical violence' and what Benjamin calls 'divine violence.' The 'revolutionary' and transformative possibilities of 'every historical moment' (I 1231), as we will see, derive from what we might call the 'finitude' or self-alienation of law-positing, 'mythical' power, such that its messianic, 'divine' interruption proceeds from this finitude itself. For this finitude signifies the necessary openness of political and legal power to its own transformation.

Such a reading of Benjamin's understanding of power as finite prepares the way for seeking a more detailed and mutually complementary rapprochement between his and Derrida's connections among memories of injustice and promises of justice. For apart from deepening our understanding of Benjamin's constructive critique of Marx, the further task of this chapter is to present a denser interweaving of Benjamin and Derrida's conception of the promise of memory. On my interpretation of Benjamin, it is the finitude of power as permitting its messianic 'interruption' and the assumption of the messianic call of the slain that allows us to spell out more fully Derrida's reference to Benjamin in the context of the deconstructive inheritance of Marx's promise. We will see, however, that a full appreciation of these references has to go beyond Derrida's own interpretation of Benjamin in *Specters of Marx*, and necessitates a much more generous reading of Benjamin's "Critique of Violence" than the one Derrida presents in "Force of Law." An indication—one that is to be pursued beyond Derrida's own references to Benjamin—of the rapprochement sought here consists precisely in the recognition of a messianic force associated with the powerlessness of power, as I will suggest here before presenting Benjamin on power.

Benjamin's "Theses" are first cited in *Specters* in a footnote that, as we have seen, focuses on the messianic injunction of history's victims (SM 181f./95f.). The note is to a passage in the body of the text that discusses the relation of oppressors and the oppressed. Derrida suggests in that passage that Benjamin's 'messianic' must be thought as overturning the simple hierarchy of dominant and dominated, in an insistence on the power of powerlessness. The critical analysis of the neoliberal "dominant discourse" on the final death of Marx and Marxism, Derrida writes, is already indebted to Marx in the claim that a hegemonic (socioeconomic and political) force is represented in a dominant ideology and rhetoric. However, this debt must—as is always the case, with every 'critical inheritance'—expose itself to repetition from an open future that allows its reinterpretation. Hence, the "simple opposition of *dominant* and *dominated*," as well as the "idea that force is always stronger than weakness," must be complicated: "Nietzsche and Benjamin have encouraged us to have doubts on this score, each in his own way, and especially the latter when he associated "historical materialism" with the inheritance, precisely, of some 'weak messianic force' ['*faible force messianique*']" (SM 55/95).

The present chapter can thus be read as an explication of the claim regarding the connection of a weak force with a strength that compromises the simple opposition of oppressors and the oppressed. Rather than dismissing these suggestions as a feeble consolation of the dispossessed, we have to understand the connection between the messianic promise—which, as we saw in the preceding chapters, is also a messianic memory for both Benjamin and Derrida—and the exposure of the finitude of politics. This connection must show that a certain kind of finite power—the 'power of powerlessness'—is invested in political action itself, an action aware of its historical situatedness and belatedness, which means, at the very least, its coming 'after' a history of violence. Despite the curious fact that Derrida, in the "Force of Law" as well as in *Specters*, missed this aspect of Benjamin's text, the self-alienation of power in its connection with the messianic claim and the motivating memory of past violence may be seen as giving more concrete expression to the power of powerlessness.

What is it, in Benjamin and also in Derrida, that allows us to associate the resistance of seemingly dominated groups with a messianic promise, a messianic claim of the dead that in some sense might surpass the domination of the dominant? Derrida affirms Benjamin's idea of the inheritance of a messianic claim from the heritage of the oppressed. Hence, as Derrida argues in a slightly different context, deconstruction "is the memory of some powerlessness [. . .], of the limits of mastery—there is some power in that," and he continues to claim that "the monster [the figure of the future] is too powerful or too threatening for the powers that be" (*Points* 385/399). We have seen that the promise of the future—the insight *that* there 'is' an unownable future—is for Derrida the mark of an uncircumventable finitude that necessarily implies a 'spectral' return of the dead, a spectral memory. Benjamin and Derrida may thus be read together on the question regarding the political nature and import of the power and memory of powerlessness.

I will begin by locating, in a close reading of the "Critique of Violence," the complication of the binary opposition between dominated and dominant in the link between the finitude of power and its messianic interruption. The interruption shows itself to be open to the assumption of the weak messianic force and the claim of the past on the present and its future. This link will lead us to specify in greater detail the concept of political history that is implied in the later Benjamin's notion of a history of victors. The elaboration of the concept of victor-history demands that Benjamin's early essay be read alongside the much later "Theses on the Concept of History." I will then link the messianic interruption to the notion of 'divine' or 'pure violence' that contrasts with the 'mythical' violence characterized by the 'oscillation' between law-positing and law-conserving violence. The interruption is thought by Benjamin to lie in what he names the 'depositing' that accompanies all law imposition. Explicating further Benjamin's concept of justice as tied to singularity, I will show in what way justice requires such depositing of law. Depositing reveals the finitude of power and is made manifest in what Benjamin names 'pure means.'

Regarding Benjamin's call for a 'politics of pure means,' most central to our concerns is the 'example' of pure means represented by the Sorelian proletarian strike. The discussion of this strike will explicate Benjamin's concept of what we might call memorial resistance: a form of political action able to break through a history of violence, retrieve the memory of the oppressed, and seize the political chances of every moment. In this context, I will, with Sorel, return to a critique of Marx's concepts of power and of revolutionary action as seizing state power in the 'dictatorship of the proletariat.' This discussion will confirm and explicate, in action-theoretic terms, my earlier excavation of Benjamin's critique of Marx's link between promise and memory. Toward the end of this chapter, I will turn to Derrida's reading of Benjamin's "Critique of Violence" to show how some of Benjamin's conceptual identifications, notably the concept of victor-history and its messianic interruption, need to be reconsidered on the basis of a deconstructive procedure in order to highlight, and perhaps avoid, some problematic ambiguities.

LAW AS VIOLENT MEANS

Let us begin with a careful examination of Benjamin's essay on violence (or power) in order to arrive at the notion of political action as messianic resistance. In this examination, particular care is called for because Benjamin presents his thought and his conceptual demarcations often, and not only in this essay, by way of implication rather than by an elaborate unfolding of the argument. Benjamin initially defines power or violence (*Gewalt*) as a cause that intervenes in moral relations (*sittliche Verhältnisse*; II 179/CV 132). Since such relations are situated within the sphere of law or right (*Recht*) and justice (*Gerechtigkeit*), a critique of violence and of violent actions consists in the discussion of the relationships among violence/power, the legal order (*Rechtsordnung*), and justice. It is important to note at the outset that the relationship between the latter two terms is problematic for Benjamin (as for Derrida, as we will see); laws do not exhaust or even attain justice, for justice goes beyond and constitutively exceeds any legal order. Indeed, we might say that, for Benjamin, a demonstration of why justice necessarily escapes law is the fundamental task of a critique of the violence and power of a legal order. The excess of justice over violence and law constitutes one of the main concerns of the essay, for it reflects on the finitude of politico-legal power in order to think justice, and indeed a critical memory of justice.

Given these concerns and definitions, Benjamin's approach to the question of violence circles around the 'violence' a legal (and political) order must necessarily assume to assert itself.[1] A legal order, Benjamin explains, is characterized by a means–end relationship as its "most elementary basic relation" (II 179/CV 132). In it, violence is seen as a means to an end (*Zweck*). Two claims are, more or less implicitly, contained in Benjamin's opening remarks. First, the claim that violence or power is, first and foremost, expressed and articulated in law, and, second, the claim that violence pertains to laws as means, not as ends. Laws must be seen as violent means to the end of (a claim to) justice, or, as Benjamin attempts to show, to the end of maintaining the legal order itself—a maintenance of stable order that might very well, as the classical sociologists from Durkheim to Weber and Parsons as well as, more recently, Habermas have argued, require a claim to justice and the appearance of legitimacy.[2] Concerning the first of these claims, we will see in a moment that the claim most central to Benjamin's critique is the necessity of power to materialize and institutionalize itself in a legal order, that is, to posit and maintain law, in order for power or violence to ensure its permanence and stability. Indeed, a little later he terms this claim the "only secure foundation of the critique of violence" (II 185/CV 137). With regard to the second claim, Benjamin argues that the most crucial ethical issue regarding a legal system that uses its laws as violent means to an end, consists in the mutual co-implication of means and ends. Before returning to the first issue, let us look more closely at Benjamin's discussion of this co-implication, which he calls the circle of justification (II 181/CV 133).

That the critique of violence must concern itself with laws as means to an end does not mean, for Benjamin, that such a critique merely has to postulate a "system of just ends" (II 179/CV 132) as its criterion for determining the justice of laws. For such a procedure would leave unanswered the question whether violence or power can on principle—*as* a principle—be justified, that is, whether violence can be justified as a means *even* to a just end. Although such a system of just ends could evaluate the practical application of violence, it cannot justify violence itself. For Benjamin turns against the 'popular' idea—which, he suggests, has been nurtured by Darwinism—that violence is a 'natural' condition of political and interpersonal conflict. Indeed, as we will see, Benjamin's essay devotes crucial reflections to detecting nonviolent means of conflict resolution both in the private and the political realm (II 191f./143f.).

If violence or power, in the specific sense Benjamin intends, were a "natural product" (II 180/133), it would have to be subjected to a natural law directed toward a system of natural ends, which in turn would allow the separation of just from unjust violence. In this way, the tradition of natural law, from Hobbes's *homo homini lupus* onwards, can justify a state power's monopoly over the exercise of violence, for it assumes that in the state of nature, before the founding of the state and the transfer of power to it, the individual disposes freely over her or his power, having the (moral and legal) right to exercise the power given to him or her by nature.[3] In turning against the modern idea of an individual's natural right to exercise violence, and in implying a sense of responsibility more original than such a right, Benjamin implicitly anticipates his claim toward the end of the essay that not individual life as such is 'sacred,' but sacred in human life is the possibility of justice (*Nochnichtsein des gerechten Menschen*, II 201/152), the possibility of being claimed by a justice beyond law (II 202/CV 153). The factical holding of power does not morally or legally justify its use, Benjamin argues, thereby turning not only against Thrasymachus's famous insistence on the law of the stronger (Plato's *Republic* 338c), but also against the natural law tradition, which would subject this strength to a just end deemed natural. For the tradition of natural law can, he argues, criticize existing law only with regard to its ends. Since it assumes violence as a 'natural product'—a premise that, according to Benjamin, provided an 'ideological foundation' for the terrorism of the French Revolution—it cannot criticize violent means if they are employed toward what it considers just ends.

Thus, Benjamin identifies two traditions of thought that share a "common basic dogma" (II 180/133): the naturalistic and the positivistic schools of law. While the former specifies ends that are claimed to be 'naturally' just, in order then to evaluate given violence and power in view of this end, positive law insists on the historical origin and nature of law and violence. Since it does not stipulate natural ends of justice, it criticizes not ends but means, trying to guarantee the justice of ends by the appropriateness of the means employed. What both schools have in common, Benjamin argues, is the premise that "just ends can be attained by justified means, justified means used for just ends" (II 180/CV 133). It is this common dogma that prevents them from posing the question regarding the justice of violence itself. This 'circle' of just ends and just means could only be left behind by specifying "mutually independent criteria both of just ends and of justified means" (II 181/CV 133, cf. II 196/147). Benjamin's essay devotes its reflections to a possible breaking of the "spell" of this circle (Bannkreis, II 196/147), which is not the only 'mythical' circle Benjamin will specify.

But how can means and ends be thought at all if not as concepts reciprocally implying each other? Benjamin admits the difficulty of this problem, and suggests the "final undecidability of all legal problems" and the impossibility of the "redemption from the spell circle of all world-historical conditions of existence hitherto" (II 196/CV 147). Nonetheless, he advances the idea of ends that do not rely on means, and, more important, means that do not serve the pursuit of ends. He searches for "a different kind of violence [or power]" that would not relate to just ends as a means (II 196/CV 147). With regard to the latter, he calls for a "politics of pure means" (II 193/145), which we will discuss with regard to the question of political action.

Before returning to the problems posed by this 'common dogma,' and the irreconcilable conflict between legal means and just ends it implies, we should look more closely at Benjamin's treatment of positive law. For he suggests a certain superiority of this school of legal thought over the tradition of natural law, and extracts a distinction between natural and legal ends from positive law as a "hypothesis" (II 181/CV 134) for further investigation. The superiority of positive law lies in its focus on the justification of means, for Benjamin rejects the criterion of (naturally) just ends, in part because he defines, as we have seen, the violence of law in its function as a means and disclaims all naturally just ends. We might surmise, however, that Benjamin rejects the idea of naturally just ends also because, as indicated earlier, he tends to see in natural law an unwarranted secularization of a theological tradition, the nostalgic response of the West seeking to find in 'cosmology' what it lost in theology, thereby problematically tending to sacralize human existence itself (II 202/CV 153).[4]

The positive theory of law, however, in acknowledging the historical origin and evolution (*historische Gewordenheit*, II 180/CV 133) of law, distinguishes between kinds of violence independently of their application in particular cases. Historically recognized and thus sanctioned violence (or power), which Benjamin describes as a violence directed toward legal ends (*Rechtszwecke*), is demarcated from violence not so sanctioned, as it is governed by ends (posited by individuals or groups) that lack such a historical recognition as legitimate ends (*Naturzwecke*, II 182/CV 135). Benjamin wishes to use this distinction as a "hypothetical starting point" only and warns us that it does not yet help us to inquire into the justice of violence as such. Such an inquiry must be reserved for a "historico-philosophical consideration of law" (II 182/CV 134) that is situated "outside of positive legal philosophy" and reflects on the "meaning" (*Sinn*) of this distinction (II 181/CV 134). (I will return to this 'philosophy of history' and ask what makes Benjamin's consideration a 'critique' of violence and power.)

According to Benjamin, this distinction reveals an insight into the nature of power and violence that surpasses legal naturalism because it prepares us for the claim that violence and power are essentially law-positing (*rechtssetzend*), an imposition of law that naturalism masks by casting law as naturally given. The 'meaning' of the distinction between legal and natural ends is to expose the (necessary) attempt by a legal order to understand its own ends as legitimate ends and all others as natural, illegitimate ends, thereby monopolizing violence and power. By denaturalizing law, violence, and power, legal positivism shows that law is always posited by power or violence, that violence is therefore law-positing (for Benjamin, necessarily so) and, further, that such a law-positing power must always aim at the deprivation of individuals (or groups) of the legitimacy to use violence in order to pursue their legal ends. Law-positing power uses the positivistic distinction to replace all natural ends by legal ends. A European legal system, Benjamin writes, "tries to erect, in all areas where individual ends could be purposefully [*zweckmäßigerweise*] pursued by violence [*Gewalt*], legal ends that can only be realized by legal power [*Rechtsgewalt*]" (II 182/CV 135). Despite the right of self-defense, Benjamin argues, modern European states view the individual as a potential danger undermining the legal order itself. Since these politico-legal orders do not only condemn (individual) violence or power directed to illegal ends (*rechtswidrige Zwecke*), but *all* violence positing its own natural ends, we must take seriously the surprising possibility that "the law's interest in the monopolization of violence vis-à-vis individuals is not explained by the intention of preserving legal ends but, rather, by that of preserving the law itself" (II 183/CV 135f.). Benjamin indicates here a 'logic' of self-preservation that will become important for his overall argument, and to which we will return: Once power has instituted itself, it must preserve itself in its institution.

OSCILLATION OF INSTITUTING
AND CONSERVING POWER

Benjamin identifies this logic as another 'mythical spell' that follows from the circle of means and ends, and concerns the justice of a legal order. As noted, Benjamin argues that the violence of means must materialize in institutions, must posit and preserve law in order to achieve stability and permanence. Otherwise, it remains merely "predatory violence" (raubende Gewalt), the violence of a mere means to an arbitrary end (II 185/CV 137), devoid of the possibility of "founding or modifying, in a relatively stable manner, [legal] conditions" (ibid.). This necessity of institution—a law-imposition that is always violent, and never natural, as legal positivism understood—and, hence, of the conservation of the power thus instituted, implicates legal and political orders in an ambiguity and undecidability concerning law-imposing and law-preserving violence, subjecting it to what Benjamin calls, as we will see, a 'law of oscillation.' In order to show the necessity of institution, but also the inherent weakness of such institutions, Benjamin discusses the (significant) examples of organized labor's right to strike, and of military violence and its need to secure its victory by way of a legal codification of peace. These discussions of military violence and the class struggle (the right to strike)— discussions that deliberately limit themselves to (contemporary) European legal and political conditions (II 182/135)—aim at showing that violence or power does not posit law from time to time, but that it is essentially and necessarily law-positing. We must understand this necessity of power to institute itself, and to subsequently monopolize violence in the interest of its own self-preservation, for Benjamin claims that this necessity provides the critique of violence with its "only secure foundation" (II 185/137), a foundation that will lead us to approach the possibility of pure means and pure violence free of this necessity.

Benjamin introduces the right to strike to show that, as we have seen, power must institute itself in relatively stable (legal and political) conditions, and that it, in so doing, monopolizes violence by depriving all other subjects of the right to posit its own laws. For this reason, it casts all ends other than its own as 'natural ends'—in the sense given it by legal positivism—rather than as legal (and thus legitimate) ends. For while it may grant the right to strike to organized labor in its class struggle, it does so only on condition that it be limited to purely economic concerns, as determined by specific legislation, excluding legal and political concerns. The state power, as the functionary of the legal order, views with suspicion the natural ends of nonstate powers as undermining its monopoly. Nonetheless, "organized labor is, apart from the state, probably today the only legal subject entitled to exercise violence [or power]" (II 183/CV 136). What the state fears in organized labor's right to strike, which the state itself grants to the working class, is precisely the law-positing function of power, and it is this function that it tries to contain by special acts of legislation that limit the very right the state feels pressured to grant. Thus, the state and organized labor differ with regard to the interpretation of the right to strike. Organized labor sees in it the "right to use violence for the attainment of certain ends" (II 184/136), ends that appear as mere natural ends from the state's point of view. The state, however, sees in it merely the permission to pursue limited economic interests. Since these cannot be the same in all industries, a revolutionary *general* strike, which might be aimed at the eventual overthrow of state power, cannot be tolerated. Benjamin sees in this attitude of the legal order—it grants a right that it then tries to contain—not a "logical contradiction of law" but only a "material contradiction" (*sachlicher Widerspruch*, II 185/137), which not only permits, but necessitates the state to resist the strikers by violent means under certain conditions. The 'logic' of law is not contradicted because, as Benjamin showed, this logic consists in law's own monopolization and self-preservation. When the state uses violent means to contain and limit the strike, it feels provoked and threatened in its claim to be the only power positing law. Law imposition by another power—which, in the 'crisis' of the revolutionary strike, uses the right granted to it by the state in order to attempt to overthrow it—threatens the monopoly of the state over violence. In defining this monopoly, Benjamin implicitly draws on Max Weber's definition of the modern state as claiming "(successfully) the monopoly of the legitimate use of physical force within a given territory."[5] The right to strike thus shows that power or violence is law-positing, and that it is so in excluding all other law-positing powers. As we have seen, the resistance of the state to all (individual, nonsanctioned) violence shows the state's monopolization of law-positing violence and, hence, the need to preserve itself. This 'logic' of law imposition and self-preservation by way of exclusion furnishes the critique of violence with a foothold, since it forces power, as we will see, to turn against its own principle of positing.

All violence (*Gewalt*) must posit law, and all law owes itself to an imposition that cannot do without violence. All law, as Benjamin shows in discussing the right to strike, must therefore be posited, and remains dependent on the original violence of this positing. This original violence reappears each time the politico-legal order tries to assert itself against real or potential adversaries, such as an external enemy (in the case of war) or an internal one (a revolutionary working class, for example). That this self-assertion turns into self-preservation is no accident but a necessity inscribed within essentially law-positing violence. In order to show this, Benjamin further discusses military violence and power after World War I, and it is in this context that he first explicitly introduces the distinction between law-positing (*rechtsset-zende*) and law-conserving or law-preserving (*rechtserhaltende*) violence, what he calls the "duality in the function of violence" (II 186/CV 138). After a military victory, a (new) political order is instituted and codified in a 'peace' treaty. The military power thereby ensures the relative stability of its victory, such that 'peace' implies the lasting imposition of the will of the victor. Subsequently, the institutions of this political and legal order must seek to maintain peace by preserving themselves. Instituting power necessarily turns into conserving, administrative power. Benjamin refers to militarism and the enforcement of universal conscription (*Wehrpflicht*) as exemplifying the law-preserving function of violence:

> Militarism is the compulsory, universal use of violence as a means to the ends of the state. [. . .] In it, violence shows itself in a function quite different from its simple application for natural ends. It consists in the use of violence as a means of legal ends. For the subordination of citizens to laws—in the present case, to the law of universal conscription—is a legal end. If that first function of violence is called the law-positing function, this second will be called the law-preserving function (II 186f./CV 139).

Benjamin defines these two different forms of violence as follows: "If [law-positing violence] is required to prove itself in victory, the second is subject to the restriction that it may not set itself new ends" (II 189/CV 141). The original positing violence must now, according to the law of the self-preservation of political and legal bodies, view itself as its own end, and thus turn into self-preserving violence. Since violence or power is essentially law-positing, it also necessarily falls into the circle of means and ends, such that the violent means are always ultimately directed toward the end of preserving the politico-legal order itself. Next to his earlier claim that the circle of means and ends cannot pose the question of the justice of violence itself, since just ends might still not justify violent means, Benjamin now suggests that legal ends are always (also) the ends of the self-preservation of a given power, of the asserting of a particular way of life, or particular political formations. The need to preserve itself compromises, and even usurps, the interest in preserving certain legal ends. Any claim as to the (natural) justice of an order's legal ends would mask this interest in self-preservation and monopolization. This is how Benjamin describes the complication:

> For the function of violence in law-imposition (*Rechtsetzung*) is twofold, in the sense that law-imposition pursues as its end, with violence as the means, *what* is to be instituted (*eingesetzt*) as law, but at the moment of the institution of its end as law, violence does not abdicate; rather, at this very moment, violence first of all becomes law-positing violence, in the strict

sense and immediately, not by instituting as law an independent end free of violence [Gewalt], but one necessarily and intimately bound to itself under the title of "might" [Macht]. (II 197f./CV 149; Benjamin's emphasis).

Violence or power thus becomes 'might' by necessarily positing itself as its end, that is, by turning into law-conserving violence. The abdication of violence once it has instituted and expressed itself—for instance, in view of just ends independent of its imposition—is therefore an illusion. The oscillation between the two functions of violence allows Benjamin to associate all imposition of law with 'mythical ambiguity,' and the monopolization of violence leads him to compare state power with a "fateful order" (II 187/139) that insists on its sovereignty and unchallengeable status. It is clear here that, for Benjamin, an answer to the question of justice cannot be found within this dialectic of imposition and conservation, just as the question of violence as a principle cannot be answered from within the circle of means and ends. We will return shortly to the question of a notion of justice that would escape this dialectic.

Benjamin draws a further conclusion from the circulation of positing and conservative violence. In trying to preserve itself, a form of power or violence—now posited as, and materialized in, a legal, political order—turns against its own principle. For, as we have seen, it must exclude and suppress other forms of positing violence (like that of organized labor, of the 'great' criminal, or of other military forces). In order to preserve itself as the violence of law imposition, such violence must become law-preserving, and thus collide with itself in turning into a different function of violence, while opposing other, potentially hostile forces of its own principle of law imposition. Power does not reside within itself, so that all its actions and expressions are mere accidents. Rather, it must express and expose itself in order to be effective and preserve validity. "All violence as a means is either law-positing or law-preserving. If it lays claim to neither of these predicates, it forfeits all validity" (II 190/CV 142). In thus expressing itself, however, it must turn into a different form of violence and hence, as law conservation, exclude its 'own' form of law-positing. Violence (or power) must repeat itself continuously, return to itself by excluding what is other than itself. In this repetition, it opens itself up to historical change and internal transformations. We might say here that Benjamin discovered for politico-legal orders the law of repetition or iterability—a law more powerful than posited law—that we discussed in chapter two, and to which we will return.

For the moment, let us note how Benjamin describes this law of repetition, and what conclusions he draws from it toward the end of his essay. As mentioned earlier, Benjamin argues that neither legal naturalism nor legal positivism attain to the question of the justice of violence as such. Only a "historico-philosophical consideration of law" (II 182/134) can respond to the demands of a genuine 'critique of violence.' We are now in a better position to understand this claim. A critique of violence must be philosophical in order to reflect upon the enabling conditions of politico-legal power, which may be formulated as a version of what Derrida discusses as the law of repetition. Otherwise such a critique will be, as Benjamin suggests, 'too close' to understand this law of repetition, or what he calls the 'law of oscillation.' Since this law also concerns the uncircumventable necessity of violence to express and institute itself, and hence governs the historical transformation of law-imposing forces and their succession, it must also be a historical critique.

> The critique of violence is the philosophy of its history. [. . .] A gaze directed only at what is closest at hand can at most perceive a dialectical up and down in the law-imposing and law-preserving formations of violence. The law governing their oscillation [Schwankungsgesetz] rests on the circumstance that all law-preserving violence, in its duration, indirectly weakens the law-positing violence represented [repräsentiert] by it, through the suppression of hostile counter-violence. [. . .] This lasts until either new forces or those earlier suppressed triumph over the hitherto law-positing violence, thereby founding a new law [Recht] for a new decay [Verfall] (II 202/CV 153).

Political history, the history of the succession and transformation of different forms of state power and its institutions, is thus the history of the changing forms of positing violence, their decay and reinstitution. Law-positing violence always becomes a mere means of its own end, the end of preserving itself. Falling into the circle of becoming its own end, this violence weakens its own principle of law imposition by compromising itself in law-preserving, administrative violence. The history of state power is governed by a model according to which a victorious power institutes itself only to degenerate into a mere instrument for the conservation of its victory. In this ineluctable decay—in its finitude—positing violence compromises and forgets itself until it is challenged or transformed from within or without by other positing forces, which in turn are subject to the same law of oscillation. Historical change proceeds from this internal complication of positing forces. Their decay is not only a suppression of other forms of positing violence, but is its own self-alienation and self-obstruction as positing violence insofar as it has to materialize and hence preserve itself. Violence or power, due to its need to express itself in institutions, also, and from the outset, compromises itself in its own conservation. In its historical dialectic of means and ends, positing violence is always already conserving violence.

PARLIAMENTARY AND RADICAL DEMOCRACY: HOW TO MAKE THE REVOLUTION PERMANENT

An outward sign of this internal complication and weakening may be seen in the violent suppression of revolutionary forces, as when a state crushes the

advances of a mass strike. For in doing so, a state institution forgets the revolutionary, law-positing power to which it owes itself, a forgetting made possible, and even required, by the structural and necessary self-alienation of
law-positing power. Benjamin refers to the example of the German parliament, instituted after the 1918/1919 revolution, and its brutal suppression of
the Communist rebellion in 1920. "When the consciousness of the latent
presence of violence in a legal institution vanishes, this institution decays. In
our time, parliaments provide an example of this. They offer this familiar,
woeful spectacle because they have not remained conscious of the revolutionary forces to which they owe themselves" (II 190/CV 142). In suppressing other revolutionary forces, the state insists on its monopoly over violence,
but indirectly (and necessarily) weakens its own positing force. Benjamin's
evaluation of this weakening, however, does not imply that the forgetting of
a debt to revolutionary forces could be overcome easily, for, as we have seen,
the forgetting proceeds from the internal structure of violence as such. Nor is
this forgetting limited to parliamentary democracy since any political and
legal system must, above all, be concerned with its own duration and thus
restrict all other instituting forces. Thus, while Benjamin goes on to criticize
political compromises, as emblematic of parliamentary conflict resolution, for
their mere *appearance* of nonviolence, and while he tentatively subscribes to
the "Bolshevist and Syndicalist critique of present-day parliaments" (II
191/143), he describes working parliaments as comparatively desirable:
"However desirable and gratifying a flourishing parliament might nonetheless
be by comparison, a discussion of means of political agreement that are in
principle non-violent cannot be concerned with parliamentarianism. For
what parliament achieves in vital affairs can only be those legal decrees that
in their origin and outcome are attended by violence" (II 191/CV 143).

Thus, parliaments, despite their improvement relative to other political
forms of decision-making, are not exempt from the law of oscillation, and do
not achieve (as no political state does) the status of pure nonviolence that
they often claim, thereby masking the violence or power vested in them.
Benjamin's discussion of parliaments can therefore not be characterized as
'antiparliamentarian' in general, as Derrida does. The latter criticizes the former for the critique of parliaments as such, and very quickly generalizes to
democracy in general and the entire Enlightenment tradition, speaking of
Benjamin's "hostility to parliamentary democracy, even to democracy as such,
or to the *Aufklärung*" (FL 977). For Derrida limits the law of oscillation, and
the "amnesic denegation" of instituting violence it brings about, implicitly to
the "structure" of parliaments (FL 1017), while suppressing Benjamin's claim
as to the comparative desirability of these institutions. However, as I have
argued, and as Werner Hamacher, in a brilliant reading of Benjamin's essay,
has shown in advance of Derrida's reading, Benjamin's discussion by no
means amounts to a critique of the institution of parliamentary democracy as

such.[6] Moreover, neither Hamacher nor Derrida considers the link that has often connected the attempt to preserve the 'spirit' of the revolution with the 'council' system as, compared with parliamentary democracy, a more radical and participatory form of democracy. Rather than being hostile to democracy in general, Benjamin's concern with preserving the memory of revolutionary violence may be seen as placing its hopes on a conception of radical democracy that was exemplified in the workers' and soldiers' councils. In 1921, these councils must have been fresh on Benjamin's mind, for they played a large role in the 1918/1919 revolution, as in many others.

In 1918/1919, Benjamin witnessed a victorious power—while brought into power by revolutionary forces operating from the ground up, such as the councils—turn against these forces and the working masses as soon as it occupied the state apparatus and its legal institutional means. Benjamin's disappointment with the Social Democrats who assumed power in Berlin in 1919 can still be heard in 1940. As we saw in the first chapter, the "Theses" accuse them of 'conforming' to a history characterized by the mere replacement of one elite by another (Thesis VII, XI), thereby "cutting the sinews of its [the working class's] greatest strength" in forgetting and forsaking its revolutionary spirit (Thesis XII). The 1921 essay is a philosophico-historical reflection on the problem of maintaining the revolutionary 'spirit' to which large-scale legal-institutional transformations owe themselves. Merely instituting a constitution (like the *Weimarer Verfassung*) that guarantees formal democratic rights to participation, as Thomas Jefferson knew, and as Hannah Arendt has argued forcefully, is radically insufficient.[7] Benjamin, like Arendt, is concerned with the maintenance of the revolutionary energies of (past) action in order to energize present struggles, thus calling for a 'permanent revolution.' One way of achieving the perhaps paradoxical duration of the revolution is the retaining of the radical democratic council system, rather than its abandonment in favor of a representative, parliamentary system. Benjamin's objection to the latter must be seen in this historical context, to which he seeks a philosophico-historical answer. His references to the nonviolent problem-solving capacities of language as a medium, as opposed to the centralized state apparatus that monopolizes violence, may be, in this context, seen as an endorsement of the councils, and might have been understood in this way by contemporaries.

Furthermore, Benjamin's lifelong concern with the "remembrance of [. . .] defeats" (I 1240), of lost promises and previous revolutionary struggles, aims at retrieving the revolutionary spirit and at energizing present struggles in the memory of the dead and oppressed. In Benjamin's philosophico-historical perspective, however, such retrieval must break through the dialectic of law-positing and law-conserving violence that brings with it the fateful forgetting of revolutionary energies once positing turns into conservation and administration. To prevent the 'indirect weakening' of positing violence through its forgetting and self-obstruction—a self-alienation that characterizes, according to Benjamin, the political history he later names the history of victors (Thesis VII)—the revolution must become permanent. In resisting the present rulers, contemporary struggles thus break through this history of violence toward a subterranean, oppressed history of revolutionary struggles that are also oppressed by contemporary rule through legal-institutionalized means. Before I elaborate the ways in which the "Critique of Violence" and the "Theses" reciprocally illuminate each other, let us explore further the concept of history presented in the former text. (Toward the end of the present chapter, I will return briefly to Benjamin and Derrida's discussion of democracy, as well as to Benjamin's relationship to the Enlightenment.)

VICTOR-HISTORY AND ITS MESSIANIC CESSATION

According to the "Critique of Violence," history is the realm of victorious powers forced to institute their victory and, hence, forced to deteriorate in the interest of their monopoly, their duration and security. Positing violence turns into an instrument of its victory in positing its own conservation as its end, an end that justifies the violence of its legal order. Benjamin's text characterizes this history as the history of victorious impositions of power and their transformations according to the internal and necessary self-alienation of violence. For Benjamin, it is a history of "might" (*Macht*, II 198/149), a characterization that draws on Sorel's notion of a history of violence as might or power (*force*). It is a history that, Benjamin and Sorel charge, the orthodox Marxists merely want to continue, as is evident in the idea of the "dictatorship of the proletariat," by which state power is, allegedly temporarily, used to extirpate any opposition.[8] As we have seen, for Benjamin violence turns into might as soon as it posits itself as its end, instituting and monopolizing its power as law or right. The territorial demarcations of "peace" can be seen as the "primal phenomenon" of such impositions of might (II 198/149). The "positing of limits" or the "instituting of frontiers" (*Grenzsetzung*) demonstrates that what law-positing power must guarantee is, "more than the most extravagant gain in property," its own might (ibid.).

Law-positing violence is thus characterized by the double imposition of limits: in order to establish a domain for the exercise of its power or its 'might,' it must establish territorial boundaries (such as those of a nation-state). Furthermore, for the internal conservation of its order, a law-positing power must establish legal limits defining crimes, and enforce legal contracts that, even if peacefully concluded, ultimately depend on the instrumental violence of the enforcing institution (II 190/142). "Where frontiers are established [firmly imposed: *festgesetzt*], the adversary is not simply annihilated; indeed, he is accorded rights even when the victor disposes over the most superior power [*überlegenste Gewalt*]" (II 198/CV 149). Benjamin characterizes these limits as mythically and 'demonically ambiguous,' for while they claim and demand equality before the law, they cannot take into account the singularity of those judged by the law. He quotes Anatole France: "'Poor and rich are equally forbidden to spend the night under the bridges'" (II 198/CV 149f.). As we will see, this lack of singularity requires the interruption of the circle of means and ends, of the circulation of imposing and conserving violence, by a 'divine justice' and a 'divine violence' attuned to singularity.

Since the question of the justice of violence as such cannot be answered within the ensuing dialectic of mutually legitimating means and ends, the history of victorious powers is necessarily devoid of 'pure justice,' of a justice that does not lend itself to the justification of violent means. We can here already intimate that this characterization of political history anticipates and specifies the later Benjamin's notion of a 'history of victors,' which necessarily suppresses and seeks to forget the memory of those who contributed to, or who resisted, this history. Victor-history is to be challenged by the memory of a justice—a "memory of the nameless" (*Gedächtnis der Namenlosen*; I 1241)— that cannot be subsumed by this history, and by its systems of representations. In a way we will have to analyze later, this justice, and this memory, must in some way be linked to the inherent weakness and finitude of the oscillating history of victorious power, "annihilating" (I 1231) its power in order to invigorate the struggle against it. Benjamin will find this link in the "interruption" of the circle of means and ends, in the "breaking" of the mythical spell of politico-legal forms (II 202/153). Before returning to the text of the "Critique of Violence" and its conception of a resistance to such a spell, I will now argue that the "Theses on the Concept of History" draw on this interruption in defining it as the—famous but recondite—"messianic cessation of happening" (Thesis XVII) and the "blasting open" of the continuum of history (Thesis XIV). In arguing that "[a]ll rulers are the heirs of those who conquered before them," and that the historical materialist must "brush history against the grain" (Thesis VII), Benjamin returns to his concept of a political history of violence (or, more precisely, of 'might'), a history of the succession of victorious impositions of law and power. In fact, the theoretical link between these two texts, as we will see, is so central to Benjamin's thought that many of the crucial claims of the famous "Theses" can hardly be understood without recourse to the "Critique of Violence." It is all the more surprising that this link goes almost entirely unnoticed in the still proliferating secondary literature on Benjamin.[9] We must, then, elaborate this link to intensify our discussion of Benjamin's nonteleological politics of memory.

In the first chapter, I discussed how Benjamin connects the hegemonic rule of the 'victors' with the inheritance of power relations and the transmission of power from rulers to rulers—"from the privileged ones to the privileged ones," as the "Critique of Violence" puts it (II 194/CV 145). We saw him link the history of victors with an 'epic' and linear continuity and a

bourgeois historicism that merely recounts the apparently most visible story
of great victories, forgetting the "nameless drudgery of the contemporaries"
of the rulers (I 1241; cf. Thesis VII). The circle between law-positing and
law-conserving violence can help us to account for a connection implied by
the "Theses": the connection between the instrumentalizing of state power
by the rulers and the narrative continuity of bourgeois historicism, both of
which, according to Benjamin, have to be interrupted by a form of political
action that then liberates or triggers a different conception of history. In the
"Critique of Violence," Benjamin presents the law of oscillation according
to which state power, as we have seen, can only maintain itself by its (self-
alienating and hence discontinuous) transformation and 'representation' in
administrative violence. Benjamin further argues that the monopolization of
violence by the state demands of it a suppression of its own law-positing violence to which it necessarily owes itself—hence its necessity to represent
itself by positing legal ends masked as naturally just. A conserving violence
is interested in maintaining the status quo and must thus, as we have seen in
the discussion of parliaments, delimit and restrict the law-positing violence
"which is represented in it [law-preserving violence] through the suppression
of hostile counter-violence" (II 202/153). Administrative power attempts to
suppress and 'actively' forget the law imposition of the "revolutionary forces
to which it owes itself" (II 190/142). Not only does the alienation of law
imposition in law conservation 'weaken' the former, but the latter has to
deny and forget its origin in a violence that cannot be justified by, as legal
positivism understands, superior, preexisting laws (such as natural or divine
laws). The legitimacy of a founding act can only be established in hindsight,
after the fact (nachträglich), as Derrida also emphasizes (FL 993).

The representation of law-positing violence by conservative violence is
thus also a dissimulating substitution, a forgetting and a suppression of the
violence of every founding act. From this perspective, a politico-legal order
must hide its own finitude, that is, the discontinuity of the law of oscillation.
It must be interested in recounting history as one of the continuity of power
relations, for not only will this fortify the position of the current rulers, with
their domination appearing as unalterable, but it will suppress the violence to
which this domination ultimately owes itself. Hence we have Benjamin's critique of bourgeois historicism, the one-sided construction and use of a cultural tradition, and its linear narration of history—the history of the victors—as the ideological complement to political hegemony. One has to ask,
the "Theses" insist, "with whom the adherents of historicism actually
empathize. The answer is inevitable: with the victor. And the rulers of the
day are the heirs of all those who were victorious before them" (Thesis VII).

What does Benjamin's association of presently hegemonic forces with a
narrative ideology of conformism and progress imply for a concept of 'destruction' or resistance to the hegemony represented in state power? The "Theses"

further explain that the necessity of violence to hide its origin in ultimately unjustifiable acts of law imposition leads it to appropriate cultural traditions and present linear historiographies for its own purposes of retrospective self-legitimization. Thesis VI warns the oppressed classes of the "danger [that] affects both the content [*Bestand*] of the tradition and its receivers. The danger is one and the same for both: that of lending itself to the ruling classes as a tool." The insistence on the discontinuity that makes political history possible, and thus the subsequent critique of the notion of progress for its linear understanding of time (Thesis XIII) is the only way to show an awareness of this danger. By denying the toil of the nameless who allowed a certain tradition to form in the first place, and by constructing this tradition in a linear fashion that also denies its constructedness, the content of this history and this tradition becomes a tool of the presently ruling classes. Hence, the more liberating and energizing aspects of this tradition cannot articulate themselves in such a way that the finitude of power, its lack of transcendent justification, becomes clear. Contrary to this dangerous linearity, Benjamin argues, "revolutionary classes in the moment of action" are characterized by an "awareness that they are about to make the continuum of history explode" (Thesis XV).

The (heretofore unseen) images of the past that are born of this discontinuity at the heart of history—both at the heart of the history of power, but also at the heart of every representation of history—record this awareness: "The Great [French] Revolution introduced a new calendar. The day on which the calendar sets in [*einsetzt*] functions as a historical time-lapse camera" (ibid.). As in the "Critique of Violence"—which, as noted, criticizes the German parliamentary institutions for losing the consciousness of the "revolutionary forces to which they owe themselves" (II 190/142) after the 1918/1919 revolution in Germany—the question is how such a knowledge of the discontinuity of historical, revolutionary events can be maintained and turned against the 'continuity' of an administrative violence seeking to legitimate the oppressive status quo. In Thesis XV, Benjamin only indicates that revolutionary calendars that "do not measure time as clocks do," "reserve blank spaces" (*aussparen*) for "holidays, which are days of remembrance," days that recall and repeat the historical time-lapse camera.[10]

The connection between narrative continuity and the justification of administrative violence leads Benjamin to attempt to oppose, as a "fundamental aporia," "the tradition [of the oppressed] as the discontinuum of what has been [*des Gewesenen*] to historiography [*Historie*] as the continuum of events" (I 1236). He continues this self-consciously aporetical and experimental opposition in his notes to the "Theses":

Basic aporia: 'The history of the oppressed is a discontinuum.'—'It is the task of history to take possession of the tradition of the oppressed.' [. . .] 'The continuum of history is the history of the oppressors. Whereas the idea of the continuum levels everything off [*alles dem Erdboden gleichmacht*], the idea of the discontinuum is the basis of a genuine tradition.'—The consciousness of historical discontinuity characterizes revolutionary classes in the moment of their action (I 1236).

This last sentence here again returns us to the "Critique of Violence," for it attempts to show that a revolutionary situation suspends law in a moment that, as the "Theses" put it, is "not a transition" and hence not present (Thesis XVI). Benjamin seems quite aware of the problematic nature of the binary opposition between continuity and discontinuity. The idea of a discontinuous tradition of the oppressed does not mean that there should be no consciousness of the continuity of a struggle, for example, of the history of the labor movement. Rather, it indicates that political action, in order to be effective—in the sense of effecting a change in the legal codification of exploitative relations, for example—must challenge and suspend law, and thus draw on the very self-alienation and finitude of law itself. This is why Benjamin argues, despite the association of a tradition of the oppressed with discontinuity, that in certain contexts a sense of continuity may be required for the struggle of the marginalized and oppressed, in particular to offset the fleeting temporality—what Benjamin calls the 'logic of the new'—of an increasingly commodified modernity (V 459f.). In particular in our discussion of Derrida's deconstruction of the pairs of opposites structuring the "Critique of Violence," we will see that Benjamin's seemingly binary and pure dichotomy between the history of the oppressors and the history of the oppressed must be complicated precisely because of the discontinuity that is at the heart of political history itself. For, according to Benjamin's argument, it is only the discontinuity of every imposition of law, and its discontinuous and self-alienating transformation into the conservation of law, that allows the fundamental alterability of political formations, and hence the "constant" "calling in question of every victory, past and present, of the rulers" (Thesis IV). Such a calling into question thus requires an exposure of the discontinuity underlying, or rather undermining, every claim to continuity. A heightened awareness of this discontinuity, this finitude of the political itself, complicates the simple opposition between the oppressed and the oppressors, as Derrida said about Benjamin (SM 55), for it endows the oppressed classes with a "weak messianic force" (Thesis II).

Thus, the reception of this messianic force, and the response to the 'claim' the dead have on us, demand a sense of this discontinuity fissuring history. The 'danger' of missing this discontinuity implies a missing awareness of the challengeability affecting every victorious imposition of law and its representation in its administration. Hence, the danger consists in becoming a mere tool of the ruling classes. Such a challenge to present *and* past victories, their messianic 'destruction' or 'annihilation'—in a less dramatic and violent sense than these words connote, as we will see—becomes a necessity. This is how Benjamin continues Thesis VI:

> In every epoch, the attempt must be made anew to wrest tradition from the conformism that is about to overpower it. The Messiah comes not only as the redeemer, he comes as the subduer of Antichrist. Only *that* historian will have the gift of fanning the spark of hope in the past who is firmly convinced that even the dead will not be safe from the enemy if he wins. And this enemy has not ceased to be victorious.

'Fanning the spark of hope in the past' thus refers to the reception of the messianic claim of the dead. This reception requires generating radically alternative readings of a cultural tradition, readings that, at the very least, articulate the toil of the nameless—what Benjamin usually calls an operation of 'rescue' (*Rettung*). But it also demands resistance to a conformism that legitimates the existing power structures, structures whose alterability and ultimate lack of legitimation need to be recognized in order to energize struggles in the present. This resistance is both a resistance to the present rulers—and thus a foregrounding of the nameless dead whose toil and oppression allowed the rule of the present—and an assumption of the promise of those nameless ones for liberation, a liberation that will always have been too late for them. As we will see, in the "Critique of Violence" Benjamin tries to specify such a resistance in a nonviolent mass strike whose hallmark is that it can suspend and interrupt state power and its law without imposing new law. We will also see that whereas Benjamin is interested in the possibility of responding to the messianic address by the dead, of defending the nameless dead against their second mortification by the hegemonic and self-legitimating forces of the present, Derrida emphasizes above all that the dead will never, in Benjamin's words, be safe from 'the enemy,' no matter who that enemy is.

DEPOSITING: THE FINITUDE OF POWER

Let us review Benjamin's argument thus far and observe how he continues the analysis of power in the study of violence. Benjamin's essay "On the Critique of Violence," as we have seen—and as has been pointed out by a number of commentators recently, following Derrida's crucial reading[11]—makes and employs two fundamental distinctions: that of the difference between law-imposing (*rechtssetzende Gewalt*) and law-conserving violence or power (*rechtserhaltende Gewalt*), and that between "mythical" and "divine" or "pure immediate violence" (*reine unmittelbare Gewalt*, II 199/CV 150). The dialectical oscillation between the terms of the first pair (imposing and conserving violence), which together form mythical violence or what Benjamin calls 'might,' demands a third figure—divine violence or justice—which in some way opposes this oscillation. As we will see, however, the distinction between, or the comparability of, these two distinctions—that is, their very nature—is in dispute among commentators, partly because it is these oppositions and distinctions that make the essay a test case for a deconstructive reading. While Derrida construes both oppositions as binary pairs to show their self-deconstruction and necessary contamination, others have argued that 'pure violence' cannot be viewed as the binary opposite of 'mythical,' law-positing violence but must be seen as its necessary interruption or 'breaking apart' (*Durchbrechung*).[12] The distinctions go to the heart of the essay as it concerns itself with 'critique,' the critique of violence and the violence of critical limits, as the deciding and dividing power of thought and of human institutions. We have analyzed the first two-thirds of Benjamin's essay in view of the concept of history, and with regard to the finitude of politics. In an effort to show the inefficacy of current critiques of violence, this part of his essay attempts to establish the difference between the imposition or inauguration of law and its maintenance.

Derrida emphasizes this opposition in particular (FL 981) and attempts to deconstruct it, claiming—in good deconstructive fashion—that it deconstructs itself in Benjamin's text, in an "auto-hetero-deconstruction" (FL 981) beyond Benjamin's intentions. We have argued so far, however, that it is Benjamin's explicit aim to expose the way in which every legal order has to maintain itself by maintaining this distinction: for example, the difference between the legislative power and the executive power in a modern state. Benjamin attempts to show how this distinction is necessary for, and constitutive of, the violence of a legal system, but that it cannot clearly and cleanly maintain this distinction, due to the immediate and original self-alienation of law-positing power. According to Benjamin, in constituting itself, violence again and again produces the "circulation" [*Umlauf*] of law-conserving and law-imposing violence "under the spell of the mythical forms of law" (II 202/153). Furthermore—and here we approach the second major distinction of this text—the essay wishes to show at what point and in what manner this 'spell' or the 'circulation' of the two kinds of violence can be, must be, or is already interrupted. Benjamin refers to this interruption or breaking apart as a deposing or depositing (*Entsetzen*) that would accompany any positing of law: "Upon the breaking of this circulation [*Durchbrechung dieses Umlaufes*] under the spell of mythical legal forms, upon the depositing of law [*Entsetzung des Rechtes*] with all the forces on which it depends as they depend on it, finally therefore upon the breaking of state power, a new historical age is founded (*begründet sich ein neues geschichtliches Zeitalter*)" (II 202/CV 153). We find an ambiguity in this last part of the text concerning the 'depositing' of law and the 'founding' of a new epoch, an ambiguity to which we will return in the discussion of the proletarian strike, which Benjamin describes as possibly "the highest manifestation of pure violence by human beings" (II

202/154). The ambiguity concerns the question of whether the law of oscillation, and with it the circle of means and ends, can (only) be interrupted, or
whether it can be overcome altogether. While depositing, and the nonviolence of 'pure violence' Benjamin associates with it, refers to the 'internal'
complication and self-alienation of law and power (what we have referred to
as its finitude), Benjamin appears to think that this self-alienation may or
will lead to the founding of a new epoch, an epoch that may be free of the
finitude of power and its necessary self-alienation. This ambiguity is thus at
the same time the question as to how the two sets of distinctions relate to
each other, that is, what relationship 'pure' or 'divine violence'—which is
also nonviolent as it does not posit law—maintains with the circulation of
law-positing and law-preserving violence. We will analyze this relationship in
its ambiguity, an ambiguity that appears almost consciously explicit in the last
part of Benjamin's study, by focusing on the interpretation of depositing.

Benjamin seems to suggest not only that there are forms of social and
political interaction that are very different from law imposition (such as private conflict resolutions by means of conversation and language), but also
that these 'nonviolent' forms (in the sense Benjamin gives to the word "violence") could lead to the end of the dialectic of law imposition and law conservation, allowing a new form of politics to take root. One must ask here,
however, how the founding of a new age—a founding whose passive form
(*"begründet sich,"* "is founded") indicates with good reason a nonsubjective
act or enactment *(Vollzug)*—can be liberated from the necessity of power to
institute and preserve itself. Inasmuch as the depositing of law and state
power of which Benjamin speaks remains dependent on the finitude of
imposing violence, it is highly doubtful that it could overcome imposing violence, and not merely interrupt it (unless the interruption leads to the ultimate disintegration and decay of law-positing power). We may anticipate
here that the founding of this new and other historical age cannot be understood as another imposition, such that the 'breaking of state power' would
aim at another state, another law, or another power. If we were dealing with
another imposition, the new historical age would be its goal, and the imposition would itself fall into the 'dialectic' of law-imposing and conserving violence. This is why the inauguration of another history is described as a
depositing *(Entsetzung)* that interrupts the dialectical cycle. Benjamin, as we
have seen, further characterizes this depositing as every imposition's inherent
weakness, its necessity to expose itself to another positing. The imposition of
law is never final; on the contrary, depositing exposes the ends of law as
posited, and hence as finite. On the one hand, every imposition necessarily
turns into the conservation of law; on the other, an imposition remains
exposed to the future of new positings that cancel, alter, or supersede it.

Let us characterize this depositing, and the 'pure violence' it implies, in
greater detail, before we look at its link to what Benjamin calls 'divine justice'

and its 'manifestation' in the proletarian strike. A better understanding of the nature of depositing will allow us to assess Benjamin's own ambiguity concerning the capacity of divine violence to 'end' the mythical age of imposing violence, and will clarify the reasons that disallow its being conceived as standing in binary opposition to the 'mythical' violence of law and might. For depositing names the finitude of positing in demanding of any imposition to reaffirm itself, to return to itself in order to maintain itself. It names the withdrawal of an identity given once and for all to a legal order or a political formation. It demands of every positing force to 'represent' and transform itself immediately into a conserving force, thereby directly alienating and indirectly weakening itself in excluding other positing forces. With this requirement, depositing opens the circle of means and ends, of a law-positing violence that immediately compromises its positing character by becoming its own end in a law-conserving violence. It thus belongs to the finitude of law-positing violence; its self-alienation not only implies that it has to become law conservation, but also that the alternation between imposition and conservation always exposes violence to hostile counterviolence, to other law-positing forces, and thus to challenges from without that are made possible by its internal structure. The structural transformation of law-positing violence, whose law of oscillation we saw as characterizing political history, proceeds from the withdrawal of power's stable self-identity, its constant necessity to posit itself anew and thus maintain itself.

Furthermore, depositing reveals that the legal ends and political goals of a power are always posited and never natural or pregiven. They are thus not situated beyond the law that views itself as its own end. It follows from the necessity of political and legal power to materialize itself in the imposition of laws and limits that it posit legal ends whose violence cannot be justified by reference to external standards, such as a natural or divine order. (In this context, one might recall Benjamin's rejection of 'theocracy' in the "Theologico-Political Fragment," II 203). And further, even if such an external "system of just ends, assuming it to be secure against all doubt" (II 179/CV 132) were given, as we saw Benjamin argue, it could still not adequately pose the question of justice. For this question cannot satisfy itself with the derivation or postulation of just ends even if these could be attained without a shadow of a doubt, but would have to show the valid justification of violent means without reference to these ends. This was the reason for Benjamin to reject the starting points of legal naturalism and positive law. If legal ends as well as the legal means used to attain them are always general, their justification does not fully transfer to applications of law in always singular circumstances. Making a connection between justice and singularity that will also prove to be crucial to Derrida's deconstruction of law, Benjamin implies that this justification cannot be given or fully assured since legal and political means are always deployed in singular cases that escape their full determination by legal ends. "For ends that for one situation are just, generally acceptable, and valid, are so for no other situation, no matter how similar it may be in other respects," Benjamin writes (II 196/CV 148).

Since depositing exposes legal ends as always posited and imposed by means of violence, that is, without prior criteria and independent (eternal, natural) laws free of such positing violence, it refers to the withdrawal of such criteria in every law imposition, and, in fact, in every decision. Every decision lacks criteria and laws that fully ensure its justice—not only are the ends and laws for decision-making possibly violent (as they are set up by a monopolizing power preserving itself), but the transition from ends (even if they were 'indubitably' just, as Benjamin says) to means (to the particular decision) can never be guaranteed or fully ensured. In Derrida's words, the transition cannot be calculated or programmed. There is thus always an interruption in this transition. The finitude of power and legality, then, excludes justice, but it might also be seen to make justice possible in the necessary transition from general law to the singular case. Derrida—who, as we will see, describes this finitude of any legal order as the 'deconstructibility of justice'— has this double structure, the Janus face of law's finitude, in mind when he writes that the deconstructibility of law "is not bad news. We may even see in this a stroke of luck for politics, for all historical progress" (FL 943f.).

As we have seen, Benjamin associates this interruption—this lack of full justification in the transition from (posited) ends to means, from universal laws to particular decisions—with the question of justice, even with 'divine justice.' Only if we focus on this interruption can we ask the question of justice, he argues, because only then can we ask whether violent means can be justified by (general but finite) ends. For even if the ends were just without a doubt, and would justify means, those means, applied to a particular, singular case, would still remain violent, subsuming the particularities of a case to a general end (which, moreover, is only stipulated as just by a legal order trying to preserve itself by monopolizing violence). It is this singularity, as Derrida points out correctly, that Benjamin associates with divine justice. Depositing thus makes possible and leads to the question of justice, allowing it to emerge as a question in the first place. The 'breaking' of the circle of means and ends allows the question of the justice of means themselves to be asked in the first place, for only in this interruption can the question of justice intervene on the mutual justification of means and ends. 'Divine justice,' a justice attuned to the singularity of circumstances and individuals, can therefore not be manifested in means serving as instruments to ends, but only in what Benjamin calls 'pure means': means that do not serve ends that claim to be situated outside of the means themselves, but that are "immediate" in the sense of a "non-mediate function of violence" (II 196/CV 148). Let us now discuss such pure and nonviolent means as well as examples of it that Benjamin gives.

PURE MEANS: THE PROLETARIAN STRIKE

As we have seen, only a focus on the necessary deposition of all imposition and conservation of violence can point up the singularity that is always in danger of being crushed by the victorious administration of political and legal violence. In explicating the disjunction between legal ends and violent means, Benjamin foregrounds the issue of singularity in the domain in which means operate. Singularity, and with it, justice, is foregrounded by its being situated in the sphere in which alone law can assert itself by using violent means, the sphere of the application of law. Law-positing violence is dependent on the domain of mediacy, for it can only impose itself by relying on possible (and violent) means of its defense and maintenance. The depositing of every imposition, the interruption and necessary self-alienation of law-positing violence, exposes this dependence. If we can now point to means that, in some sense, reveal and make manifest the ineluctable force of depositing attending all positing, we would have discovered means that expose the finitude of power and foreground justice. Benjamin terms such means pure means. Pure means, as we will see shortly with the example of the proletarian strike, do not refer to ends outside of themselves, but only to themselves. This self-reference, however, does not imply that pure means seek their self-preservation, as law-positing violence does. Rather, they only refer to their own enactment. In this, they have no reference to the future present or horizon implied by the *telos* of self-preservation, but require an utter openness to the future. In this openness, they highlight the necessary prior givenness of the instruments of instrumental violence and the objects to which they apply.

Pure means may be characterized further in the following way. Given the definition of violence as law-positing, a definition that might include the positing of 'natural' ends contrary to dominant legal ends, pure means, in abstaining from such positing, are nonviolent (*gewaltlos*). After having explained the relative preference of parliamentary politics, which is still not without recourse to violence, Benjamin asks: "Is the non-violent resolution of conflict possible at all?" (II 191/CV 143). He answers in the affirmative and refers to the interpersonal, private sphere: "Non-violent agreement is possible wherever the culture of the heart gave human beings pure means of agreement. For legal and illegal [*rechtmäßigen und rechtswidrigen*] means of every kind, which are all violent, may be contrasted with pure means as nonviolent ones" (ibid.). Nonviolence thus consists in the refraining of pure means from being directed toward ends that may or may not be deemed just. In any case, as we have seen, ends can never fully justify violent means. Pure means are therefore without instrumentality and purposiveness, as they lack ends that could determine their validity. Their validity, and thus their morality, derives from this absence of ends and from their self-referential character as a 'medium.'

Insofar as pure means are devoid of posited ends, and ends always imply a subject of positing (a victor, a state legislature, individuals), we may surmise that pure means are also devoid of subjectivity. Indeed, it seems that, for Benjamin, pure means cannot be the means of an action that originates in an identifiable subject.[13] This is why a human subject is desubjectified if it becomes the 'manifestation' of pure means, as in the example of an expression of "anger," which is "not related as a means to an end previously posited," Benjamin explains (II 196/CV 148).[14] This subjectlessness of pure means, combined with their inaccessibility to human cognition, control, and determination, further implies that no political subject can be formed as the instrumentalizer of pure means, as we will see with the proletarian strike. "Less possible and also less urgent for human beings, however, is the decision when pure violence was effective in a particular case," Benjamin writes (II 203/CV 153). This inaccessibility of pure means to human cognition implies the impossibility to delineate the boundaries of any subject. It also implies that the 'manifestation' of pure violence cannot be thought as a determinate and recognizable historical event, but precisely withdraws from the order of visible, repeatable events and their temporality. As previously mentioned, depositing names the withdrawal of (a stable and pregiven) identity from positing power, and exposes the latter's necessity to permanently reconstitute itself in a discontinuous manner, passing from positional to conservative power. This withdrawal and this discontinuity cannot be recognized as such, but, as Benjamin explains, only by virtue of their "incomparable effects" (ibid.).

Consequently, Benjamin also characterizes the pure violence of depositing as "law-annihilating" (*rechtsvernichtend*) as opposed to "law-positing" violence (II 199/CV 150). He specifies that "pure or divine violence" is characterized by the "absence of all law-positing" (II 200/CV 151), and that its force is only "relatively" annihilating, with regard to law, goods, life, but that it spares the "soul of the living" (ibid.). The soul of the living (*Seele des Lebendigen*), or what Benjamin also calls simply the living (*das Lebendige*), is here associated with the singularity of human life, rather than with life pure and simple, human existence as such, which Benjamin calls "mere life" or "bare life" (*das bloße Leben*). "For a human being cannot, at any price be said to coincide with the mere life of a human being" but must be referred to the "not-yet-being of the just human being" (II 201/CV 153). We have already seen that depositing, as the force that undermines or, if we use Benjamin's terms, annihilates law and its imposition, and thus interrupts the circular justification of means and ends, thereby allows the question of 'divine justice' to resonate in the first place.[15] For justice is tied to the singularity upon which the means of law and power are exercised. Mythical power, on the other hand, is said to exercise a "bloody violence" over 'mere life' (II 200/151).

Benjamin now specifies two realms of pure mediacy, realms in which pure, nonviolent means without a view toward an end operate. These two

realms, he then argues, are 'analogous' (II 193/145) to one another (he does
not specify the *tertium comparationes* of this analogy). They are circum-
scribed by the domains of language and of politics; the former is seen as
underlying and making possible peaceful conflict-resolution in the private
realm, whereas the latter circumscribes the public arena.[16] Benjamin gives
examples of the sphere of pure mediacy and its possibility of nonviolent conflict resolution first of all on the basis of nonviolent private ethical behav-
ior, in which language, considered as a 'technique' of conversation, plays a
particularly important role, for language may be said to be a medium of pure
means. Benjamin considers as the subjective precondition of pure means in
the private realm "courtesy, sympathy, peacebleness, trust, and whatever else
might here be mentioned" (II 191/CV 143). He also notes that diplomacy
represents an analogy of private conflict resolution in the political realm
"between states" without the latent presence of violence (II 195/CV 147).
All these nonviolent means depend on "the proper sphere of 'understanding,' language" (II 192/CV 144).

     In elaborating the link between depositing and pure means, we have seen
that depositing foregrounds the givenness of the means themselves, their
prior self-reference, on which the use of means in view of an end is dependent. As Hamacher has elaborated, this givenness in the sphere of language
refers to the 'already-being-there' of language whenever it comes to be used
as a means of communication.[17] An act accomplished by means of language—
whether a constative or a 'performative' speech act—must already be in language as the sphere of mediacy, as Benjamin's essay "On Language as such and
the Language of Humans" explains. For language is there defined by its "communicability" or its "impartability" (*Mitteilbarkeit*) from whose perspective
any communication (*Mitteilung*) of a 'content' appears as derivative: "There
is no content of language; as communication, language communicates a spir-
itual essence [*geistiges Wesen*], that is, communicability itself," Benjamin
explains (II 145f.). The instrumental use of language remains dependent on
the self-referential impartability or givenness of language as a pure means.
The "Critique of Violence" extends this insight, by way of "analogy" (II
193/CV 145), to the political and legal realm, where all instrumental use of
violence appears dependent on the prior givenness of means of violence and
their sphere of operation. Benjamin's notion of a pure language (*reine
Sprache*), expounded in the essay "The Task of the Translator," might thus be
said to correspond to the notion of pure violence: Pure language is, according
to Derrida's reading of the essay on translation, the "being-language of language" as a 'messianic' promise inherent in language, prior to its use.[18] (Benjamin's discussion of language, and its analogy to politics, has been examined
in greater detail by commentators, including Derrida.[19] For lack of space, I
forego such an analysis here.) It is, however, important not to interpret this
dependence of posited ends on their enforcement by means as a 'fall' from the

purity of means to the impurity of the circle of means and ends. This is a temptation to which Benjamin succumbs at times in both texts, thereby allowing Derrida's severest strictures, as we will see.

Before turning to Derrida's reading, let us discuss Benjamin's "politics of pure means" (II 193/145), which centers on the concept of the proletarian mass strike. The concept of political action as a pure and nonviolent means is geared toward the suspension of posited law as depositing 'annihilates' or interrupts it. This suspension of law and power is also a suspension of the political history governed by the perpetual transformation of law-positing power and the victorious impositions and administrations of new law—"from the privileged ones to the privileged ones," as we saw the "Critique of Violence" put it (II 194/CV 145). The strike thus presents a model for the kind of political action that, as discussed in chapter one, Benjamin came later to interpret as 'messianic,' as 'annihilating,' and as opening up a "heretofore locked chamber of the past" (I 1231). Drawing on the early study of violence, we are thus able to specify in greater detail what kind of action, and what kind of an interruption of history and time, Benjamin had in mind when he spoke in "Thesis XVII" of the "messianic arresting [*Stillstellung*] of happening, or, put differently, a revolutionary chance in the fight for the oppressed past." The messianic arresting or 'divine' annihilation, according to our argument, must be viewed as proceeding from the interrupting deposition of law and power, such that the arrest belongs to what I called the finitude of the political itself. The proletarian strike can expose the arbitrary imposition of power in the 'history of victors' only because it itself, being nonviolent rather than instrumental, escapes the logic of the position and conservation of power, and its circle of means and ends. This interruption or arrest of political history must then also be critically directed against the Marxist conception of the proletariat as the victorious inheritor of a history of violence. To stay true to Marx's idea that the proletarian revolution will not just, like earlier ones, replace one ruling elite with another, power and resistance have to be radically rethought.

In the wake of the Marxist tradition, it is clear that Benjamin, despite the critique of the proletariat as final victor of history, considers it the only real political force next to the state and the owners of the means of production. Apart from state power, organized labor, as we have seen, is described as "the only legal subject endowed with the right to violence" (II 183/CV 136). It is therefore no accident that Benjamin immediately turns to the "class struggle" in discussing the politics of pure means (II 193/145). When Benjamin first turns to the discussion of strikes in the essay on violence, he wonders whether such modes of political action in the context of the class struggle would not always have to be considered nonviolent insofar as they do not posit ends. Since a strike, as a mere refraining from action, might be said to be nonviolent per se, Benjamin discusses in what way the strike is a violent means to the attainment of 'natural ends.' As it turns out, even an omission of action, such as the strike, can be, and usually is, directed toward such ends. In contrast to the 'active' use of violence in the revolutionary strike, which heightens the class struggle to strive for the goal of a new legal order, a passive use is given in all cases where the stoppage of work is willing to resume work if certain conditions are met, conditions whose attainment thus becomes the goal of the "non-action" (*Nicht-Handeln*; II 184/136). Benjamin characterizes such action as "extortion" (*Erpressung*; II 184/136), and appears critical of the 'passive' strike as well as the utopian thrust of the revolutionary strike (although he does not unequivocally reject them either).

Instead, in anticipation of his distinction between the political and proletarian strike, Benjamin wonders here whether a strike, as the omission of action, can also be engaged in without goals or ends in mind. In such a case, the strike would be a pure means, and without violence, since it only withdraws from power rather than positing its own laws or ends. We may note, then, that 'without violence' (*gewaltlos*) does not mean 'without causing any suffering whatsoever,' for a work stoppage might very well result in lack of profit and reduced consumption. 'Without violence' implies that the politics of pure mediacy does not fall prey to the logic of the circle of imposition and preservation, for 'violence' here means 'law-positing power' (*rechtssetzende Gewalt*). As we have seen, in not positing an end outside itself, a pure means does not posit law, for it is not undertaken in view of ends outside itself. It thus exemplifies the politics without a goal, especially without the Communist goals, which Benjamin had criticized in his letter to Scholem (May 29, 1926; see chapter one).

In turning to the concept of the general strike, Benjamin intervenes in contemporary discussions between communists and anarcho-syndicalists as to revolutionary strategy and the efficacy of the mass strike. The debate, sparked by the controversies between Bakunin and Marx in the First International (1864–1876), revolved around the democracy of the revolution, the role of striking, and the relationship to state power.[20] Benjamin intervenes in this debate by aiming at a concept of revolutionary action that will be neither reformist nor justify revolutionary violence as a means of attaining a revolutionary imposition of law. A truly democratic revolution must remain democratic and nonviolent at every moment instead of postponing democracy and nonviolence to a postrevolutionary future when the means of power will have achieved their ends.[21] As we have already seen, Benjamin is above all concerned not to defer the question of justice to indefinite ends (from where they can justify all kinds of violence), but to let this question, and the singularity of persons as of situations that it implies, accompany any political strategy. This was behind Benjamin's rejection of the politics of the German Social Democrats and their Kantian Marxism, in which the 'classless society' had become a regulative ideal without urgency, leading to the squandering of the revolutionary chances of every moment (I 1231, Thesis XI, XIII). Benjamin criticizes Social Democratic as well as 'vulgar' Marxism for the fateful combination of the politicians' "stubborn faith in progress and the trust in their mass basis" (I 1240).

To attain a different concept of revolutionary action, Benjamin, following Sorel, distinguishes the proletarian strike from a revolutionary and from a political strike. Unlike the revolutionary general strike, which aims at the imposition of a new state in the course of the revolution, and unlike the political strike, which ultimately strengthens state power by merely 'extorting' advantages, and hence by positing determinable purposes beyond the strike, the proletarian strike refrains from positing ends. The proletarian strikers do not aim at new and improved legislation or labor contracts, nor do they promise the resumption of work within the legal and political constraints of state power. "While the first form of the cessation of work [the political strike] is violent since it causes only an external modification of labor conditions, the second [the proletarian strike], as a pure means, is nonviolent" (II 194/CV 146). The 'aim' of the proletarian strike is the abolition of state power and the relations of production on which it depends and that it legalizes.

Benjamin points out, however, that even this language of the revolutionary aim of the strike is still inexact. For this general strike is not so much the instrument of a resolution with a definite goal, but, more precisely, "consists in the determination to resume only a wholly transformed work, no longer enforced by the state, an overthrow that this kind of strike not so much causes as enacts [vollzieht]" (ibid.). The relationship between the strike and its outcome cannot be thought as a means relating to its end, as a step in the direction of the ultimate goal. Rather, this relationship is an 'enactment' that suspends the projection of goals and interrupts the positing of ends, thereby revealing ends as posited. In the interruption, the end of the state's self-conservation is exposed as such and shown to be dependent on a sphere of 'pure mediacy.' The interruption severs the relation between means and ends just as the strike severs the (exploitative) relations of production (Abbruch der Beziehungen; II 184/136). We may say that Benjamin calls the strike 'annihilating' (vernichtend) for it is directed toward nothing (nichts), proceeds from the finitude of power and the 'nothingness' or absence of unposited, naturally just ends, and in its sheer enactment deposits and desiccates state power. As the interruption of the domain of positing violence, nothing is produced, planned, or projected in the strike; it remains a "nonaction" (II 184/136).

Benjamin construes the proletarian strike as interrupting the 'continuity' of means–end relations, as having no end outside of itself, and thus as a nonutopian enactment, as a pure means. In the deployment of such a pure means, the end is not attained by the means but is in enactment, the event of the discontinuity or interruption itself. This is an enactment for which language, understood as a medium rather than as a means, provides an analogy (II 191/143), as we have seen. Just as the transmission of a semantic content is not to be reduced to an intention preceding and producing it, but is the temporary offshoot of the prior medium of language itself, so the result of such a strike is not the end of its means, but is its process of enactment. As such an enactment, the interruption does not present itself as a pure break with past impositions of power, but proceeds from, or 'taps into,' the discontinuity or self-alienation that separates any founding and law-imposing act from itself. It exploits the depositing to which every imposition remains subject, and hence reveals the fundamental alterability of power itself.

The enactment exposes the uncircumventable violence of positional power, and foregrounds the dependence of such power on violent means. For, as we have seen in the discussion of pure means, no legal and political ends can do without recourse to instrumental violence, a violence that operates in the realm of singular cases. The proletarian strike draws on and proceeds from the necessary finitude of political and legal violence, as expressed in what Benjamin calls depositing: the necessary withdrawal of the identity and security of law imposition, and its need to produce and reproduce itself again and again.[22] The power of the state reproduces and preserves itself by administrating its power, in, say, enforcing labor contracts as a means of maintaining what Marx called the extortion of surplus labor. By radically refusing to participate in this constant reproduction of legally institutionalized power, the proletarian strike interrupts the state power's return to itself and enacts its depositing. The state power is 'deposed' by drawing on the inherent finitude of power to reproduce itself; it is, if you wish, dried up as its life is drained out of it. By refusing to participate in its reproduction, the finitude of power is thus exposed and thwarted in one act.

If the interruption of communication brings to the fore the medium of communicability itself—namely, the self-reference of language as a pure means—what then is the medium that is foregrounded in this strike, if both domains are analogous to one another? On what sphere does the imposition and operation of power remain dependent when it instrumentalizes violence? Power operates in the domain of a human 'community' in which it constitutes and articulates itself, and that it in turn constitutes by imposing limits: territorial boundaries (such as the borders of a nation-state), but also legal limits that regulate and circumscribe the life of a political community. If the word "community" did not already imply the setting of boundaries (*communire*), we could say that it 'is' a community, a relationality or sociality, before any community, before determinate sociopolitical and legal relations. Hence, it is a community that can never appear as such but is nonetheless presupposed by the operation of power. Hamacher conceives this "manifestation of the social *tout court*" as manifested in the strike, thus having the

advantage of being conceptualized apart from the modern production para-
digm of the political. Benjamin does not address the question of this sociality in any detail; the only possible reference to it is to be found in his notion
of "bare life" (*das bloße Leben*).[23]

For Benjamin, therefore, the proletarian strike is not so much, as in the
Sorelian discussion from which Benjamin derives it, a 'social myth' whose
efficacy is to be judged by its constitution of a unified political subject.
Rather, it is the action that 'deposes' any subject of positings. Its primary aim
is not the unification of dispersed subject positions and the creation of an
antireformist determination of the proletariat, but the interruption of a history of violence governed by the oscillation and transformation of law-
imposing power. In this interruption, no subject is constituted but the—forever inaccessible and withdrawing—presupposition of any group acting as a
political subject is brought into relief: the sociality or politically and legally
'unrestricted' and unimposed 'mere life' on which any imposition and
administration of violence depends. Since, according to Benjamin, we cannot decide with certainty "when pure violence was actually present in a certain case" (II 203/154), a determinate subject of the proletarian strike cannot be identified, for it would reposit the violent logic of the thetic,
positional act. The proletarian strike might thus not be limited to a general
strike by the proletariat, but opens up the political possibilities of "every second" (Thesis B, cf. I 1231) by exploiting the "law of oscillation" according
to which law-conserving violence necessarily "weakens" law-positing violence from the beginning (II 202/153).

BENJAMIN'S UTOPIAN AMBIGUITIES

With this last comment, we have entered a domain characterized by Benjamin's ambiguity toward the possibility of pure violence, an ambiguity that
has not gone unnoticed by commentators.[24] Let us now look at some passages
that reveal Benjamin's ambivalent characterization of pure violence's relation
to law-positing violence. I have already had occasion to point out that Benjamin not only associates depositing with the withdrawal and self-alienation
of violence—that is, with its 'interruption'—but also with its overcoming,
that is, with the 'founding' of a new historical epoch (II 202/153). This
founding would have to be free of any law imposition, and yet would have to
inaugurate a different political community. Benjamin's word for the 'interruption' of the law of oscillation that binds law-imposing and law-preserving
violence together reflects this ambiguity. *Durchbrechung* (II 202/153), literally
a breaking through, can mean, and usually implies, the final breakthrough as
the overcoming of what is thus broken, and must be seen as distinct from
Unterbrechung, an interruption or a pause that implies the resumption of what
is broken apart and temporarily halted. However, in appropriate contexts—

for instance, the *Durchbrechung* of enemy lines in a siege—the word may also assume the more moderate signification of breaking through a line or a continuity that may, after the break, reconstitute or reclose itself. In question is thus whether the 'circulation' (*Umlauf*) of law-positing and law-conserving violence would have to close itself again and return to positing law, or whether the interruption of the circle destroys, or simply leaves behind, the circle itself. The same ambiguity is to be found in Benjamin's reference to his concept of the revolution in texts from the late 1930s. In his notes to the "Theses," as we saw, Benjamin speaks of the reconceptualization of revolutionary political action by emphasizing that the "classless society is not the end-goal [*Endziel*] of progress in history but its often failed [and] finally accomplished interruption [*endlich bewerkstelligte Unterbrechung*]" (I 1231). Although this time Benjamin uses the less ambiguous *Unterbrechung* ('interruption'), he interprets the non-goal of political action as a long-awaited (though not necessarily final) accomplishment.

The question here is how the history of power can be interrupted without imposing new law. Must we say that a utopian horizon devoid of positing violence and might silently animates Benjamin's thought here? It would be a utopia not as a goal, but as the opening up of the possibility of a political life without the imposition of borders, boundaries, laws, without the enforcement of contracts and parliamentary compromises, and without revolutionary or administrative violence. Its conflict resolution would have to rely on pure means alone, on 'pure immediate violence,' that is, on nonviolent conversation and diplomacy, without any recourse to laws, rules, and regulations whose institution requires an imposing force and whose enforcement depends on a conservative administration. Can there be justice without laws and their enforceability? Referring to Pascal, Derrida denies this in his reading of Benjamin's essay (FL 935f.). However, the thought of this utopian possibility is not so far from the ("Greek") Enlightenment—for example, Kant's reading of Plato's ideal state[25]—and not as exclusively "Jewish," as Derrida suggests in accusing Benjamin of anti-Enlightenment strategies (FL 973, 975, 981, 1044).

Benjamin seems to have been unsure himself about this utopian possibility, as the use of the conditional in the following passage might indicate: "But if the existence of violence outside the law, as pure immediate violence, is assured, this furnishes the proof that revolutionary violence [the proletarian strike], the highest manifestation of pure violence by human beings, is possible, and by what means" (II 202/CV 154). Benjamin thus leaves open whether a sociality without laws can be attained. The continuation of the preceding sentence makes his uncertainty and hesitation even more obvious: "Less possible and also less urgent for human beings, however, is the decision when pure violence was effective [*wirklich*] in a particular case" (II 202f./CV 153). I have already pointed out that any 'manifestation' of divine violence and its annihilating force cannot be recognized and identified with certainty in concrete cases. The indeterminacy of human cognition indicates the difficulty of the concept of divine violence and the depositing to which it is linked. No recognizable, temporally and spatially defined event can fully embody such a manifestation and satisfy the cognitive criteria we might be tempted to specify. It remains recalcitrant to any logic of incarnation, hovering in a zone of indistinction between the level of historical events and their conditions of manifestation, recording, and remembrance.

The necessary ambiguity Benjamin seems to recognize renders it all the more problematic that he, drawing too much on (Jewish) "religious tradition" as the "witness" to divine violence (II 200/151), does specify such criteria at all, in an effort to oppose divine and mythical violence point by point (II 199/CV 150). Submitting to the temptation inherent in his ambiguity, Benjamin describes divine violence as unbloody, as 'expiating' (sühnend), and as 'striking' (ibid.), thereby triggering Derrida's severest criticism—a criticism that goes so far as to accuse the concept of divine violence of an in-advance justification of the Holocaust, as we will see.

The question of the 'interruption' of the circle of ends and means in conjunction with the cognitive indeterminacy of divine violence also complicates the distinction between the political and the proletarian strike. If the purity of divine violence in the proletarian strike cannot be determined cognitively, with certainty, then we can never be sure that the proletarian strike is not a clandestine political strike. Just as it is impossible in Kant to determine (even for the agent herself) whether an act was undertaken merely in accordance with duty or from duty, so it is impossible to be sure of the purity of the proletarian strike.[26] Self-serving ends that involve a compromise with the employer or concessions from state power might always, at least retroactively (once advantages have been gained that were perhaps not aimed at), play a role in entering and conducting the strike, thus positing ends to which the strike is employed as a (violent) means. The proletarian strike is, in this zone of indistinction, always threatened by its fall back into a goal-directed strike, and therewith by the circle reclosing itself. We will see that one might call this reclosing of the circle an 'interruption of the interruption,' a possibility Benjamin is forced to admit due to the cognitive indeterminacy of pure, mediate violence.

Now, I have argued that the proletarian strike, if read alongside the "Theses on the Concept of History," allows us, above all other forms of political action, to inherit and respond to the messianic claim of the dead and oppressed of a history of violence, a claim that expresses the "incompleteness of suffering" (das Unabgeschlossene des Leids; V 589). It is a privileged site of the memory of what we today generally call the 'victims' inasmuch as it, aware of the promise of 'redemption' implied in this memory (Thesis II), does not inherit the promise of the forgotten and vanquished nameless ones for a liberated future by continuing and fulfilling the logic of the history of victors, as we saw in Marx. Rather, it breaks through and interrupts this history and its notion of power (Benjamin's *Macht*, Sorel's *force*)—a power that appropriates and instrumentalizes the state, for example, in the Marxist notion of the 'dictatorship of the proletariat.' This interruption is a "blasting open" (*Aufsprengung*; Thesis XIV) or a "messianic standstill" (*Einstehen, messianische Stillstellung*; Thesis XVI, XVII) of the continuity of history insofar as this history is characterized by instrumentalizing and law-positing power. If, however, the distinction between the proletarian and the political strike is undecidable, as Benjamin is forced to admit, we must conclude that the reception of the 'weak messianic force' in this interruption is not assured, and cannot be determined cognitively and conceptually. No criteria can be given to determine when such a memory occurred in all its purity; it is a (prosopopeitic) voice from the past that may always miss its destination.

Perhaps this is why Benjamin speaks of the 'secrecy' of the agreement or the appointment (*Verabredung*) between the victims and those engaged in the struggles of the day: "There is a secret agreement [*geheime Verabredung*] between past generations and the present one. Our coming was expected on earth" (Thesis II). The singling out of a privileged subject of this memory, of the awareness of this expectation, is thus thwarted by the secrecy of the contract or the clandestinity of the place of the rendezvous. And further, we cannot pretend that "the truth will not run away from us" and wait for redemption to fulfill the expectation, to make good on its promise to connect the past and the present by redeeming the past: "For it is an irretrievable image of the past that is under the threat of disappearance with every present that does not recognize itself as intended by the image" (Thesis V). The intention may fail to arrive at its destination, and must be aware of the possibility of failure. However, this does not lead to a melancholic withdrawal from politics, but rather to a heightened sense of the political urgencies of the present moments of 'danger' (Thesis VI). For every situation has its political opportunities (I 1231), "every second" must be regarded as the "small gate through which the Messiah might enter" (Thesis B).

Nonetheless, we should emphasize again that if a 'new historical age,' liberated from the fateful law of oscillation, could be founded, then Benjamin would at the same time allow the possibility of defining the political history of violence characterized by this law, namely, the history of victors, in direct opposition to the 'tradition of the oppressed.' The history of victors could achieve a closure, a totality from which the memory of the suffering of the nameless ones was excluded. However, the indeterminacy of the messianic claim's destination is also reflected from the other side—not from the side of the addressee, but from the side of the addressor: History, subjected to the infinity of interpretations and the constant regeneration of images, does not seem to allow a clear distinction between the 'victors' and the 'victims.' Perhaps this is the reason that Thesis II speaks not of the oppressed in the past, but simply of 'past generations.' Benjamin's ambiguity about the possibility of the utopia of nonviolent and pure means, and the cognitive indeterminacy of divine or messianic violence, allow us to reconceive this relationship between competing versions of history. As we will see in our discussion of Derrida's critique of Benjamin, to which I now turn, the complication of the simple opposition between the dominant and the dominated, and the uncovering of a 'power' in 'the limits of mastery,' as I said in the introduction to this chapter, must thus also entail a significant complication of the binary opposition between a history of victors and the tradition of the oppressed.

DEPOSITING AND ITERABILITY
IN THE FOUNDING OF A STATE

After some preliminary notes, I will facilitate the discussion of Derrida's "Force of Law" by stating where the latter's reading of Benjamin's "Critique of Violence" agrees with the one I just presented. I will then expand this explicit agreement into areas in which Derrida sees disagreements that are, on my view, caused by his less generous reading. Lastly, I will discuss aspects of Benjamin's text Derrida rightly criticizes, largely revolving around what I referred to as its problematic ambiguities. We will see that, on my reading, the primary agreement concerns what I called the finitude of power in its inevitable depositing, made possible by the law of repetition. It further concerns the link between this law and the possibility of justice, understood as, in part, necessitating an attunement toward the singularity of situations and persons. The primary difference between Derrida and Benjamin concerns the need to maintain systems of positive law: pace Benjamin, but without clearly spelling out its pragmatic or normative justification, Derrida insists on this need and connects it with an originary, unavoidable violence beyond the violence of law critized by Benjamin. Apart from this disagreement on the definition of violence, the law of repetition does, however, suffice to undermine a clear, once-and-for-all identification of a history of power/violence, as the history of law impositions, with the victor-history that we could then oppose, in a binary fashion, to a history of the oppressed and the reception of a messianic claim beyond law and power.

Derrida makes it clear that the deconstruction of law is concerned with the Enlightenment promise of emancipation and with a memory of responsibility. Similar to the inheritance of the Marxist promise for a classless society in *Specters of Marx*, the meditation on law and justice in "Force of Law" is to demonstrate "at the heart of deconstruction" the responsible assumption of "the legacy we have received under the name of justice" and of "the task of a historical and interpretative memory" (FL 953f.). The reading of Benjamin's "Critique of Violence" thus belongs to the negotiation of the inheritance of the *Aufklärung* and its emancipatory promise, a concern that has animated us throughout. Derrida writes with regard to the latter: "Nothing seems to me less outdated than the classical emancipatory ideal" (FL 971). In this context, we will see that Derrida accuses the early Benjamin both of uncritically subscribing to questionable assumptions of the Enlightenment and, at the same time, belonging to a problematic anti-Enlightenment wave whose deconstruction must defend the 'classical' emancipatory promise.

In our reading of Derrida's negotiation of Marx's promise of history, we witnessed a 'radicalization' and 'messianization' of the promise. The spectral inheritance of the promise directs it away from utopian horizons of anticipation, such as a regulative ideal or Marx's classless society, in order to turn it toward a 'blind spot' in these horizons. This blind spot figures the future of the infinite repetition and interpretation of a heritage, such that its openness and incompleteness, but also its critical filtering through—a filtering that necessarily excludes and loses certain dimensions of a tradition—come into focus. I further described the postutopian future beyond any horizon as a reminder of the existence of other futural horizons that contest any singular utopia or 'messianism,' thus disallowing the latter to harden into a dogmatic doctrine or an idea of automatic progress. The promise of repetition renders inescapable the memory of an inherited injunction, as well as a memory of loss and finitude.

This promise of an infinite repetition from the future also plays a crucial role in the negotiation of justice and law in "The Force of Law." Derrida presents the blind spot in the horizon as that which allows deconstruction to situate, and, to some extent, withdraw from the competition (*concurrence*) of various historical forms that the idea of justice as a horizon has assumed. Derrida argues that the singularity of "our historical place"—a singularity marked by the exhaustion of several utopianisms in the course of the twentieth century—allows us to think the "type" of all previous messianisms and distinguish the deconstructive messianic promise from them as from any regulative idea in the Kantian sense (FL 965f.). For the messianic promise of repetition, as we saw in the preceding chapter, relates to all messianisms as the condition of possibility as well as of impossibility: Messianisms relate themselves to an essentially nonarriving and indeterminable future whose determination, and even incarnation in the present, they nonetheless claim.

Deconstruction thus inherits a call to responsibility 'without limits' from all these messianisms "in face of a heritage that is at the same time the heritage of an imperative or of a sheaf of injunctions" (FL 955). This multiple inheritance must include, as one of the senses of a promise of memory, a critical investigation of the origin and determination of the injunctions and horizons of justice in view of the task of preventing "a good conscience that dogmatically stops before any inherited determination of justice" (FL 955). The messianic promise, as a promise of justice, is a call to memory in the sense of questioning the history of all determinate conceptions of justice, in particular those that were and are institutionalized in a given political and legal order. Proceeding from the promise of repetition—a promise without determinable horizons of justice and yet crucially necessary to it—deconstruction thus focuses on the blind spot in all these horizons in order to keep justice open and prevent its delimitation or confinement to a particular utopianism or definite political system. Hence, the promise of repetition is a promise of memory and a promise of justice.

Thus, the "Force of Law" calls for a "politicization of law" as a way of responsibly inheriting the "emancipatory ideal" (FL 971). In conjunction with the exposure of law to a constitutively indeterminate future, this means that no particular political formation can, and should be taken to, embody justice. The very nonlocation and undecidability of justice signifies that it is situated outside the public institutional realm so as to remain as a call to responsibility and a source (not a standard) of the critique directed at institutions. Neither is justice to be confined to the private realm pure and simple, to the private life of singular individuals. For Derrida, justice is situated best in a 'democracy to come' (la democratie à venir), what Derrida calls "a democracy that must have the structure of a promise," that is, not a determinate form of democracy, but the one that remains open to the future of its own transformation.[27] Only this openness preserves the indeterminate status of justice in the interstices of law, its nonlocation or, if you wish, its postutopian position on the indeterminable threshold between the private and the public realms, between the present and the future.

Before turning to a closer discussion regarding the interdependence of the promise of repetition and the idea of justice, let us note Derrida and Benjamin's agreement on the law of repetition—an agreement that, in the end, permits us to graft a spectral temporality onto Benjamin's suggestive hints about memory and an open future. Despite his severe strictures of Benjamin's concept of a divine violence that might overcome law itself by depositing and annihilating it—strictures we will return to—Derrida does not deny that Benjamin noticed the structure of repetition at the heart of law-positing and law-preserving violence. Commenting on the passage in which Benjamin speaks of the 'law of oscillation' between law-positing and law-conserving violence (II 202/153), Derrida acknowledges that this law indeed discovers the necessity of an originary repetition of power: "For here Benjamin to some extent recognizes this law of iterability that insures that the founding violence is constantly represented in a conservative violence that always repeats the tradition of its origin and that ultimately keeps nothing but a foundation destined from the start to be repeated, conserved, reinstituted" (FL 1033). On the basis of our previous reading of this law of oscillation, we can elaborate Derrida's claim as to Benjamin's recognition of the law of repetition. For we saw that, for Benjamin, power not only represents itself in legal institutions, but it must also preserve itself by returning to itself continuously, a return that excludes what is other than itself (the hostile counterforces of positing). In repetition, it opens itself up to historical change and internal transformations: iterability implies for legal systems a historicity that renders law deconstructible (FL 943f.).

For Derrida, it is the structure of time itself, as a self-differing self-repetition, that implies the necessity of power to institute and preserve itself. This structure of time contains *in nuce* the thought of inescapable and originary violence. Due to the disadjustment of time, the performative act of the institution of law, which is to be reconfirmed in every instance of its application, necessarily involves some measure of violence, even if the law is applied in the interest of justice. This corresponds to Benjamin's insight that even perfectly just ends (if such ends exist), inasmuch as they justify violent means exercised upon singular cases, involve an element of violence that can be traced back to the inescapable instituting violence of all law-positing power. Derrida often points out that this violence, as the act of self-determination in a differential field of infinite possibilities, must be repeated for the constituted 'self' or 'one'—in this case, the legal and political order—to endure (AF 78f./125).

The idea of originary violence also determines Derrida's rejection of the Marxist (and, in his view, early Benjaminian) critique of law as superstructural, to be overcome in the classless society (the end of the political as the end of the spectral, as *Specters* sees it). Derrida notes the possibility and desirability of a (Marxist) critique of legal codifications of the capitalist mode of production, but he also wishes to go beyond it. He attempts to reach a level at which the need of law to cover up the illegitimacy of its founding act, the necessary violence of any act of law imposition, is not a question of ideology, but one of the aporia of time 'itself,' that is, a violence derived from the paradox (and promise) of originary repetition. He calls this more originary level "a more intrinsic structure, one that a critique of juridical ideology should never overlook" (FL 941). This structure is the structure of the "performative force"—not an Austinian performative whose enabling conventions are firmly in place, but a performative that has to create and suspend its conditions of possibility and legitimacy, and that Derrida names, employing a phrase from Montaigne, the "mystical foundation of authority" (FL 939, 943).

If, as we will see, the application of a law to a unique situation always implies a momentary suspension of this law itself, such suspension holds above all for the founding moment of law, a moment that is never authorized by preexisting laws and hence "rips apart" the "homogenous tissue of a history":

> [T]he operation that amounts to founding, inaugurating, justifying law (*droit*), making law, would consist of a *coup de force*, of a performative and therefore interpretative violence that in itself is neither just nor unjust and that no justice and no previous law with its founding anterior moment could

guarantee or contradict or invalidate. No justificatory discourse could or should insure the role of metalanguage in relation to the performativity of institutive language or to its dominant interpretation (FL 941f.).

Since this metalanguage is not available, the founding moment can neither be justified nor described or stated in a metadiscourse. Such a description or justification can only be given after the event, but the event itself requires this description to be recognized as an event, in order to have taken place in visible history.

In his commentary upon the "Declaration of Independence," which delivers a clearer exposition of this problematic, Derrida shows that the unification of the American states, as the constitution of the subject that declares its independence from the British Crown, is described as preceding the signature of the document. However, this unity of the subject is only performatively posited through the very signing of the Declaration, so that the founding of the United States can only be stated after the event but needs to be claimed to predate this event for the United States to claim its independence. The ineluctable violence of the founding act lies in this temporal disjointure marked by what Derrida calls the "undecidability of a performative and constative statement" and the "fictional retroactivity of the signature."[28] This disjointure or constitutive retroactivity (Nachträglichkeit) of time, as we saw in chapter two, implies that the final justification of the event, and its recognition, is constantly deferred to an open future that never arrives as such. The attempt to cover up this violence of time 'itself' is thus not primarily a question of hiding the violence of an instituting power that merely instrumentalizes violence, but is a necessary disavowal of time, of the 'impossibility' of experiencing this aporia—and hence, an originary violence besetting all power formations in the course of their history.

Benjamin, however, combines the insight into the self-alienation of all founding power, its altering self-repetition as an inevitable and discontinuous move from founding to administrative violence, with the hope of its overcoming by way of the non-telic and non-thetic strike. The discontinuity at the heart of history permits the thought of a 'messianic cessation' in which the continuity of history and stories of progress are exposed as ideological masks of law-founding power. We saw earlier that Benjamin's depositing renders law transformable and open to challenges from without and from within. We also saw that, for Benjamin, the suspension of law implies a suspension of a history of victorious impositions of law, and thus allows a placing in question of "every victory, past and present, of the rulers" (Thesis IV) in the moment of a nonviolent revolution that 'blasts open' the continuity of history and historiographical narratives. Relying on Derrida's account of the promise of repetition, we may now understand the suspension of the past, and the revolutionary interruption, as an exposure to an open future of the necessary and productive reinterpretation of the past. The open future is, as we saw in the preceding chapter, a spectral future that divides and 'dis-joins' the present against itself. Hence, it makes possible first of all the 'messianic standstill of time' as the countertemporal or untimely interruption.[29] This reading makes more precise what in Benjamin's "Theses" remains largely implicit: the conceptual constellation linking the messianic future, covered by the ban on graven images (Thesis B), the "messianic standstill" or explosion of time (Thesis XVII, XV), and the assumption of, or the response to, the messianic claim of the dead on us (Thesis II). The messianic promise of redemption, directed to an open and indeterminable future, unhinges and halts the 'empty and homogenous time' of a history of victors and of bourgeois historicism, thereby allowing a plethora of 'images' to overflow the revolutionary moment whose action is thereby enabled to receive the messianic claim otherwise buried under a narrative and linear history.

JUSTICE AND SINGULARITY: DERRIDA'S OBJECTIONS TO BENJAMIN'S CRITIQUE

There is another broad area of explicit agreement between Derrida and Benjamin: the (non-exhaustive, partial) understanding of justice in reference to singularity. We will see, however, that Derrida denies Benjamin the insight into the constitutive connection between the iterability or depositing of law and the opening up of singularity. This is what leads Derrida to accuse Benjamin of ignoring not only the indispensability, but also the deconstructibility of law, and hence, of not contributing to its politicization. Let us begin with Derrida's discussion of the aporia of justice. In the first section of his essay, Derrida presents three aporias of justice that originate in "one" aporetical structure concerning the relation between law and justice (FL 959). The reflection on these aporias does not wish to overcome them, and thus overcome this relation, but wishes to release a productive tension between justice and law by negotiating the uncircumventability of these aporias. In fact, Derrida claims, justice is an aporia as an impossible experience: "Justice is an experience of the impossible" (FL 947). The experience is impossible because a justice beyond horizons will never present itself as such (such that we can say: 'that was just' or 'that will be just'). Nonetheless, the experience of this impossibility of experiencing justice is necessary for justice to have a chance, for only the experience of the ultimate inadequacy of all laws and all political systems to justice, and to the singularity it implies for Benjamin as much as for Derrida, allows the transformation of all law in view of what Derrida once called a philosophy of "the lesser violence" (WD 313n21/136n1). This is why Derrida does not call out for better utopias but for 'the impossible.' We will understand this impossibility better if we reflect more carefully on the relation between law and justice.

The 'classical emancipatory ideal' whose injunction Derrida wishes to inherit usually thinks justice as ensured by, or at least dependent on, the universality of law. (We would only have to think of Kant's 'kingdom of ends' as made possible by the universalizability test of the categorical imperative.) The universality of laws, it seems, is necessary for justice because justice constitutively requires a reflective equilibrium between the needs, interests and goals of a singular self and those of its others. Such equilibrium requires a universal and impartial perspective that transcends singular viewpoints and a language that does not speak in the voice of any of them. And yet, this universal perspective or language, which modern law attempts to embody, cannot possibly do full justice to the singularity of a situated self and the unique circumstances of a situation, for such an appropriateness to the singular self implies the use of the self's own language and perspective. Derrida puts it this way:

> To address oneself to the other in the language of the other is, it seems, the condition of all possible justice, but apparently, in all rigor, it is not only impossible (since I cannot speak the language of the other except to the extent that I appropriate it and assimilate it according to the law of an implicit third) but even excluded by justice as law [droit], inasmuch as justice as right seems to imply an element of universality, the appeal to a third party who suspends the unilaterality or singularity of the idioms (FL 949).[30]

In his insistence on 'private' and nonlegal conflict resolutions, Benjamin seems to deny the absolute necessity of this third party while wishing to retain the openness to singularity. Thus, he appears to dream a dream that stands in an oblique relation to the Enlightenment tradition. Benjamin indicates the possibility of an overcoming or even 'annihilation' of law-positing violence, and with it the overcoming of this element of universality and the necessity of a third perspective. We may begin to understand here how Benjamin comes to be charged by Derrida with an anti-Enlightenment strategy that, Derrida argues, we need to resist today (FL 975, 1044).

For Derrida, there is an irreconcilable conflict between two kinds of responsibility in the domain of ethics, politics, and law. Apart from the universal perspective of equality that is embodied in the social, political, and legal institutions of modern states, there is the singular perspective of the infinite demands of the Other on the self and on the institutions of law. Derrida makes it clear that this latter perspective is communicated to him above all by Levinas's insistence on the heteronomous relation to the infinity of the personal other (FL 959; see also SM 23/48). This perspective defines justice, the idea of an infinite justice, precisely as a heteronomous relation to the singular other whose infinite needs and ethical demands suspend the egocentric attitudes and instrumental rationality of the individual. What Derrida now insists on above all is the impossibility of a continuous and fully legitimate, or fully just, transition between both demands, between the universality and equality of law and the singular demands of the other. The focus on the singular other always neglects the other others and the reciprocal recognition between autonomous individuals. This focus is thus always exclusionary to some extent, and may be called violent in this sense. On the other hand, the application of law always encounters singular people in singular 'cases' in which justice can only be attained if, suddenly and abruptly, the perspective of the welfare of the singular other is adopted. Since the move from law to singular cases is not itself justified, or even justifiable, by law or by a superordinate morality, it is also violent to some degree.

Violence, then, is unavoidable not only in the founding of the rule of law; the lack of full authorization by prior laws also shows up in every instance of its application, and must be assumed if the law is to be inventively attuned to the singular. The deconstructibility of law, then—that is, its necessary exposure to, and interruption by, a nonhorizonal future of repetition—makes justice possible. This connection between iterability and justice corresponds to the link between Benjamin's law of oscillation and the singularity of justice. For we have seen in our reading of the "Critique of Violence" that it is only depositing itself that makes possible the question of justice itself, as a question of the violence of means and hence a question of the singularity of the situation in which these means are employed. It seems that Derrida would have to admit not only that the law of oscillation respects the law of repetition, but also that this law is associated by Benjamin with the possibility of justice. If Derrida accepts that "God" in Benjamin's text, "above reason and universality, beyond a sort of *Aufklärung* of laws," stands in for the singularity of every situation and the uniqueness of persons (FL 1023), then one might argue that he must also accept the link between 'God' or 'divine violence' and the necessity of depositing.

However, Derrida does not connect Benjamin's notion of 'divine' or 'pure' violence to the insight into the necessity of repetition, as we did when we pointed out that this other form of violence, this third figure, proceeds from the depositing and self-alienation of all positing violence. Despite granting Benjamin the law of repetition, Derrida continues to merely oppose divine and mythical violence (FL 981), an opposition he attributes to Benjamin's 'intentions' but that, he claims, is deconstructed by the letter of his text itself. One must wonder here how Benjamin can be said to "recognize" the law of repetition "to some extent" (FL 1033) and yet attribute to him intentions or "explicit purposes" (FL 997) that imply a simple and binary opposition between the two forms of violence that are caught up in the law of oscillation.[31] Especially if, as Derrida points out, it is this very law of repetition that blurs the borderline separating law-positing from law-conserving violence: "What threatens the rigor of the distinction between two types of violence is at bottom the paradox of iterability. [. . .] This iterability inscribes conservation in the essential structure of foundation" (FL 1007f.).

As we have seen, iterability makes justice possible, and hence prepares a path for its politicization. Denying Benjamin this insight, Derrida can then claim that at least Benjamin's early texts do not contribute to such politicization. According to "Force of Law," these texts reject any political and legal order and oppose justice to them, a justice that thus remains wholly exterior to orders denounced as 'mythical.' The "Critique of Violence," read alongside the 1916 essay on language, is said to rely on an "archeo-teleological" model of history and a "messianico-Marxist" model of critique (FL 1045). Referring to Benjamin's earlier essay "On Language in General and the Language of Man," Derrida accuses Benjamin of criticizing all kinds of representation as "evil" from the viewpoint of an original language of names (FL 975).[32] He is said to resist political and linguistic representation in general as causing the fall of original presence in the name, where the rejection of formal and parliamentary democracy would be part and parcel of the "great anti-parliamentary and anti-*Aufklärung* wave" of the interwar period that generated Nazism (FL 975). However, we already saw that the presentation of parliamentary democracy as an example of the disappearance "of the latent presence of violence in a legal institution" (II 190/142) does not entail a rejection of this institution as such; indeed, Benjamin notes its comparative desirability, though he might have wished to radicalize democracy in the indeed less representative and more participatory council system. For Benjamin, the parliament of the early Weimar Republic in particular is an example of the fact that political institutions deteriorate when they begin to exclude the revolutionary forces to which they owe their existence, as in the violent repression of a mass strike. Benjamin analyzes this deterioration, however, as a general process exposing the weakness and alterability of all legal orders, thus providing the possibility of its transformation despite its claim to a monopoly of power.

Derrida not only thinks that the Benjaminian distinctions between law-preserving and law-conserving violence—and between the political strike with its continuation of the instrumentalist logic of positing aims and the proletarian strike that refrains from positing any goals—are in need of deconstruction, but also that his critique of violence aims at a final overcoming (and not interruption) of the 'mythical' order of law altogether. This overcoming is, according to Derrida's reading, also the attempt to purify once and for all the Jew of the Greek in an effort to transcend the fateful 'complex of guilt' (*Schuldzusammenhang*), as Benjamin defines mythical power (FL 973). Thus, Benjamin's critique is said to be inserted in and backed up by an "archeo-teleological, indeed, archeo-eschatology," a triadic philosophy of history that "deciphers the history of *droit* as a decay since its origin" (FL 1015). The *arché* here would be the state and the language before the fall into representation and the *telos* its final return to the origin. In discussing, in chapter one, Benjamin's critique of progress as applied to history in toto, I already pointed out that he explicitly rejects archeo-teleological concepts of history. Emphasizing, like Derrida, a 'disenchanted' and open future over the projection of history onto a goal, Benjamin argues that concepts of progress lose possibly critical functions when they designate the automatic and lawful passage "between a legendary beginning and a legendary end of history" (V 596). While the "Critique of Violence" hesitates with regard to the (utopian) possibilities of the future, I have, in this chapter, read his critique of a politics of positing ends as a radical extension of his refusal to stipulate goals of history, as discussed in the first chapter.

Apart from locating Benjamin firmly in the metaphysics of presence that deconstruction is bent on delimiting, Derrida reads Benjamin's "Critique of Violence" as belonging to what the first part of his essay calls a "modern critical philosophy" of law as a "critique of juridical ideology" (FL 941). Such a critique, aiming at clean distinctions, consists in questioning the superstructure of law as to its simultaneous reflection *and* suppression of the economic and political interests of the hegemonic forces of society. It presupposes the clear separation of power and law, in that the bearers of power—say, those who have the means of production at their disposal—may either use these laws or not use them, but in any case remain exterior to the law itself. Law would be nothing but the "docile instrument" (FL 941) of the dominant power. The reading of Benjamin's text advanced earlier shows, in contrast, that the text not only does not separate power and law, but regards their inseparability as the "only secure foundation of the critique of violence" (II 185/CV 137). Derrida misses this starting point in the need of power to institute itself. For Benjamin, this need implies the necessity of the law of oscillation, that is, the transformation of instituting violence into conservative violence. This starting point for critique and the resulting 'finitude' of power, I have argued, most consistently, and on the basis of Benjamin's texts themselves, vindicate Derrida's own claim, in *Specters of Marx*, that Benjamin's messianic claim of the oppressed troubles the distinction between the latter and the oppressors.

And yet it is true that Benjamin and Derrida present different relations to a Marxist critique of law as superstructural, differences that have consequences for the account of victor-history. The fundamental difference concerns the question of whether one permits the utopian projection of a society without law to govern one's assessment of its ideological effects. As we saw, Benjamin is ambiguous on this score; his text does not resolve the question of whether the history of power can be interrupted without imposing new law. If one allows such a utopia to animate one's thought, one may still recognize the law of oscillation as a law of repetition in Derrida's sense, but only 'to some extent.' For the law of repetition, for Derrida, characterizes language and human sociality as such, and, hence, would not be overcome even if it were possible to constitute a society without enforceable law. On the other hand, the confrontation with Benjamin's ambiguous utopia shows us that the extension of iterability to language and sociality in general, as a mode of originary violence, leads Derrida to simply assume the necessity of enforceable law—despite his noted interest in also maintaining a Marxist critique of legal codifications of the capitalist mode of production. While we may assume that Derrida, with good reason, would subscribe to both a normative justification of the rule of law—in the interest of ensuring universal justice and equality— and a functional one—with a view toward system maintenance in highly complex modern societies—the real confrontation with Benjamin here is missed in that Derrida does not even assume the responsibility to deliver such a justification.

THE DISUNITY OF VICTOR-HISTORY

Let us now turn to the consequences of Derrida's extension of the law of repetition for the relation between the tradition of the oppressed and the history of victorious impositions of law. As we saw, Benjamin's conception of a promise of memory connects the law's necessity to conserve itself in a retrospective legitimation of its instituting violence with its reliance on bourgeois historicism as projecting a continuity of history that contributes to this legitimation and the covering up of positing, ultimately unjustifiable violence. In focusing on the more visible history of the victors (Thesis VII), bourgeois historicism reflects the continuity of violence that is handed "from the privileged to the privileged" (II 194/CV 145), but also conceals the discontinuity implied by the self-alienation of law-imposing in law-conserving power, a discontinuity Derrida extends to all applications of law. Benjamin thus sees ideological effects as deriving from the finitude of power, but he also sees them as legitimating a power or violence to be resisted and, perhaps, overcome, whereas Derrida emphasizes only the former.

While Derrida admits that law must always retrospectively legitimate itself, this necessity is part of the movement of any law, a movement that always takes place in the time of the future anterior: "As this law to come will in return legitimate, retrospectively, the violence that may offend the sense of justice, its future anterior already justifies it" (FL 991). Thus, law-positing violence *will have been* justified, but 'is' not in the present of its institution and interpretative application. Derrida continues to argue that the covering up of this disadjustment in time that makes the founding of law possible is not a mere ideology that could be dispelled, but is a necessary and constitutive illusion of presence (FL 991f.).

Let us draw some conclusions from Derrida's reelaboration of Benjamin's law of oscillation as a law of iterability. We will see that this reelaboration counters Benjamin's temptation and tendency to identify the law of oscillation with mythical 'might' and the history of violence such that justice could only intervene on this totality from without. This tendency is above all implied in the ambiguity of the *Durchbrechung* (breaking apart or interruption) of mythical law that Benjamin says is based on the depositing of law. As I argued earlier, if this breaking through implies a wholesale overcoming of the complex of law-positing and conserving violence, then the divine violence that is based on this depositing names both this depositing, and the horizon of justice holding sway in a 'new historical epoch.' That divine violence may also name the latter, messianistic future, is indicated in the fact that Benjamin opposes it feature-for-feature to mythical violence, rather than letting it stand for what we called the finitude of power and the necessity of depositing. Derrida's reading now clearly suggests that if the law of oscillation is the law of iterability, or what we called the promise of repetition, then it is exposed to the openness of a future that cannot be anticipated or predetermined as a utopian new epoch. Rather, divine or pure violence must refer to the self-withdrawal of power from itself, its inherent need to materialize and, in a discontinuous shift, preserve itself. Divine justice, the justice of singularity, is only made possible by this finitude of power and the discontinuity at the heart of law.

This clarification, by removing Benjamin's ambiguous interpretation of divine violence, has significant consequences for our understanding of the relationship between a history of violence and the 'tradition of the oppressed.' Benjamin's text, as indicated, vacillates on the possibility and desirability of overcoming mythical violence, as the complex of law-positing and law-conserving violence characterized by the law of oscillation. If we now deconstruct the claim that the history of state power, as representing the 'victors' of history, must be abolished altogether, and if we admit with Derrida that any legal and political order contains its difference, as the self-difference and self-deferral of repetition, 'within' itself, then we must complicate the opposition between the order and the ones it oppresses in the past and in the present. The transmission of a 'weak messianic force' between the oppressed of the past and those struggling against contemporary orders cannot be viewed as taking place altogether outside the order and its 'law of oscillation.' The history of the victors cannot be identified with the fateful law of oscillation. For this law, recast as the law of iterability, introduces a difference into this history that disallows even the simple identification of the oppressed. The oppressed, both in the past and in the present, are, in some sense, a part of the system of power and violence, which is, as Benjamin points out, also a system of representation, a historiography, and a cultural tradition. As participants in this system, and as contestants of its dominant interpretation of itself, the oppressed cannot claim 'pure violence' (the nonviolence of refraining from positing law) for themselves, though their political action, as nonviolent in Benjamin's sense of law-positing and law-conserving power, may take on forms that must indeed be analyzed by different action- and power-theoretical means. The radical refusal to participate in this system—a refusal Benjamin presents, as a kind of limiting case, in the nonviolent proletarian strike—still depends on, and proceeds from, the differentiation and self-deferral of the system itself, what we called the finitude of power. Within this system of representation, the distinction between the oppressed and oppressors, however politically necessary, is always subject to a contest of interpretations that is itself not without its investment with power.

Therefore, Benjamin's often straightforward association of bourgeois cultural history, and a scientific historicism that suppresses all "lament" in history (I 1231), with 'the rulers' and their need to cover up and legitimate the instituting violence of the order from which they benefit, must be revised. This association, however real and effective, is not simply pregiven in a totality we may call a history of victors, such that the only resistance to it would consist in the complete abolition of this totality. This history is itself the result of an interpretation, an interpretation that attempts to achieve greater justice. Justice, however, is not merely external to the system, but is located in the cracks and fissures of the legal order itself. Insofar as the legal order of modern states may be politicized and directed toward a greater openness to justice, it admits its finitude and its violence, and opens itself to a deconstructive politics of the 'lesser violence.'[33]

Correspondingly, the assumption of the messianic claim, and the call for justice inherited from previous generations, cannot be restricted to a 'tradition of the oppressed.' If the history of victorious impositions of power is no totality, the messianic claim cannot be located beyond it. That Benjamin is aware of the impossibility of limiting the response to the dead and oppressed by singling out a unique subject follows from his theory and practice of precisely radical and alternative rereadings of the canons of cultural history. He calls it the operation of 'saving' or 'rescuing' a tradition against the 'danger' of its becoming a legitimating tool of the ruling classes: "To perform 'rescue operations' [*Rettungen*] on the great figures of the bourgeoisie also means to understand them in the most decrepit [*hinfälligsten*] part of their effectiveness, and to precisely tear and cite out of them what remained buried as inconspicuous under them because it helped the powerful ones very little" (V 460). Rather than reconstituting a tradition in simple opposition to a dominant canon of interpretations, Benjamin suggests that we disrupt this canon itself in an effort to 'brush' tradition against itself, as we will see in greater detail in the next chapter.

In conclusion, I would say that Derrida's call for a 'memory of responsibility' from our historical vantage point, a call for a critical investigation of inherited concepts of responsibility, justice, and the ideal horizons of politics, registers, and responds to, the political experiences of the twentieth century. In the course of the twentieth century, the claim to embody the only and hence final just political order has led to the totalitarian excesses that we must avoid in the future, especially the Stalinist perversions of the Marxist promise, but also the Western correlate (Derrida would say, problematically: response) to these perversions (e.g., in European fascism, but also today's neoliberal triumphalism). Derrida's cautious and vigilant assumption of this heritage extends its critical and investigative stance to all legal, political, and ethical concepts of the Western tradition, while tentatively holding on to human rights and to a 'democracy to come' that remains open to its own self-questioning and transformation. Today, what Benjamin simply calls the enemy appears a lot less well defined as we live in political constellations where the demarcation between the victims and the victors is often harder to attain. Consequently, we would have to be more critical of viewing the modern democratic state as nothing but a tool of the ruling classes.

From this vantage point, Derrida is critical—overly critical, I would say—of what he perceives as an anti-Enlightenment messianism in Benjamin. That messianism seems to him to criticize the achievements of the Enlightenment, and of modernity, from without, drawing on resources that seem opposed to the modern Western, European, and North American tradition (such as Judaism, in Benjamin's case, or the pre-Socratics, in Heidegger's case). At a time when deconstruction came to be—hastily and uncritically—associated with a Heideggerian critique of modernity, Derrida thus saw the necessity of distinguishing the deconstructive endeavor from such a 'messianism' or an 'archeo-eschatology'—hence, the surprisingly direct and, seen against the background of my reading, fairly unjustified assimilations of Benjamin's critique of power to Schmitt's and Heidegger's projects (FL 977, 1045).

While Derrida at least to some extent accounts for the possibilities of placing Benjamin in such a lineage, possibilities that Benjamin's texts themselves furnish, I have tried to show that a more careful and more generous reading of the "Critique of Violence"—a text I have placed in closer proximity to the "Theses" rather than to the early study of language, as Derrida does—can reveal the fruitfulness of Benjamin for a reconsideration of the Marxist promise of history. Benjamin's strategies are then seen to be neither simply opposed to the Enlightenment, to parliamentary democracy, political representation, and human rights, as Derrida's summary judgment would have it, nor are they simply "messianico-marxist" in the sense of an "archeo-eschatology" (FL 1045). Instead of simply succumbing to an interpretative "temptation" that disregards and crushes the "victims of the final solution, to its past, present or potential victims" (ibid.), Benjamin's reformulation of the Marxist promise—and not only in the "Theses" but from the early 1920s onwards, as the preceding chapters have tried to demonstrate—is precisely undertaken to give the suffering of 'victims' a voice in the promise itself. It was for this reason that Benjamin reconceived proletarian resistance to capitalist oppression—in an almost prophetic register anticipating the Stalinist disasters resting on the dictatorship of the proletariat—as a nonviolent polit-

ical action that draws on the limits of the political itself, and that is responsive to the forever incomplete voice of the vanquished and forgotten.

What this chapter has demonstrated is the difficulty of identifying and
defining a subject, or a singular concept of political action, that inherits and
responds to the messianic call of the nameless 'victims' of history. While Benjamin attempts to read the finitude of politics in such a way that a messianic
and memorial resistance to it becomes conceivable in a nonviolent strike,
Derrida emphasizes the finitude of politics as the inescapable violence of self-
determination and the disavowal of spectral time. Such insistence on an
'originary violence' and a necessary misrecognition of time invites the question of the politically necessary distinction between a juridical ideology
masking its violent power in a self-declared legitimacy—thus, for Benjamin,
necessitating a destruction of this ideology in order to respond to the
oppressed—and an uncircumventable disavowal of time. As we have seen,
however, for Derrida the suspension of law in an act of originary violence is
by no means unproductive or unethical, but must be considered the very possibility of justice. Since, for Derrida, this originary violence is also an originary loss and forgetting, as the necessity of exclusion in an act of self-determination, there is a tendency in his writings to equate the reception of the
messianic call with recognition of this originary loss. It is this problem of the
assumption of the messianic call that I will negotiate in the final chapter. It
has to be placed in the context of the question of originary violence.

At the end of chapter two, I showed that Derrida's dislike of the word
"utopia" and his strong emphasis on the messianic, absolute future as opposed
to messianistic or utopian horizons of change did not disallow a double, postutopian strategy. The strategy demands the projection of horizons such as regulative ideas—in what Derrida, in both *Specters* and "Force of Law," views as
a legitimate and potentially fruitful 'Kantian Marxism'—while subjecting
them to infinite revision and criticism through the messianic promise of repetition. In the first chapter, I indicated that Benjamin's preference for the
"image of enslaved ancestors" rather than the "ideal of liberated grandchildren" (Thesis XII) was in danger of reproducing the opposition between the
past and the future he criticized in Marx and some Marxists. Here, with
regard to the "Critique of Violence," I have attempted to demonstrate that
the proletarian strike's utter openness to the future, in the sense of refusing to
posit ends, cannot be maintained, as the cognitive inaccessibility of pure violence implies that the strike might always include latent anticipations or
unconscious wishes and demands.

Despite this demand for utter openness in a radically nonteleological
concept of action, Benjamin intimated the beginning of a new historical
epoch, thus projecting a future horizon of political-legal transformation. In
ambiguously suggesting the absence of legal-political institutions supported
by enforceable law, the horizon would be one of absolute nonviolence or of

the absence of power, in the sense Benjamin gives to these words. Derrida finds this horizon deeply problematic, mainly for two reasons. First, he sees it as the *telos* of a messianic and Marxist 'archeo-eschatology'—a view that, as we saw, neglects Benjamin's explicit rejection of such a teleology or escha-tology, and stems from a rather ungenerous reading of "On the Critique of Violence" and "On Language in General and the Language of Man." Sec-ond, Derrida rightly thinks that Benjamin's horizon indicates the utopia of a society devoid of institutionalized law, a utopia he—unfairly, I argued—sees as connected to an antidemocratic, anti-Enlightenment stance on Ben-jamin's part.

I think the foregoing analysis suggests, however, that Benjamin's ambigu-ous stance on the possibility and desirability of such a utopia—indicating utter futural openness in the proletarian strike while quietly hoping for and anticipating the end of law—might be brought into agreement with Derrida's double strategy. Benjamin radically criticizes—partly from a Kantian and Marxist perspective devoid of dogmatism and teleological progressivism—institutionalized law for its violence, thereby projecting a future free from such violence. However, he also indicates the need for a future even more radically open, a future that—if we bring in Derrida's conception of the absolute future of infinite repetition and the deferral of identity—permits the critical and careful revision and democratic criticizability of the projection. As I suggested, Benjamin's attempt to avoid a centralized state that monopo-lizes violence and keep the revolutionary spirit alive—a spirit also of democ-ratic criticism and antidogmatic openness to revision—tends to favor the anarcho-syndicalist and radical-democratic council system, a system that, however, would be hard to imagine without institutionalized law.

A further, more critical point is connected to the commensurability between Benjamin and Derrida that I merely wished to indicate here. On Derrida's view, in line with the second reason mentioned earlier, Benjamin's utopia of nonviolence is problematic because it denies originary violence, the violence that Derrida sees as inseparable from the law of repetition in its link to the 'disjoining' future that upsets all identity. It is this violence that makes Derrida suspicious of hopes for 'perpetual peace,' and it is a violence that ren-ders institutionalized law, as the channeling of violence, indispensable. Utopias of nonviolence, Derrida seems to say, have allowed themselves to be implicated in the 'worst violence,' according to the terrible logic we analyzed in preceding chapters: drawing an advance credit on the future justifies the violence necessary to arrive at the utopian future. And yet, like Adorno, at least the early Benjamin implicitly retains such a horizon. This horizon is not simply antithetical to an open future in that it, devoid of dogmatism, teleol-ogy, and fine-tuned contours, does not in advance rule out the possibility of human politics wholly apart from legal institutions and the violence of (legal) means. Given that the future Benjamin seems to project is one of nonviolence, and given Derrida's double strategy, the confrontation with the "Critique of Violence" forces Derrida to admit the desirability of an at least rough distinction between juridical ideology and the uncircumventable disavowal of time, between, as we saw in chapter two, ('utopian') future horizons and ('messianic') future openness, between nonviolence, political violence, and originary violence. In the next chapter, I will argue that the inheritance of Benjamin's messianic claim of the dead and oppressed requires the possibility of such a distinction, an albeit fragile, contextually alterable distinction that permits us to tell preventable, unnecessary violence from originary violence, and keep originary forgetting apart from the occlusion that, deliberate or not, serves the interests of oppression.

FOUR

The Claim of the Dead
on the Living

IN THE CONCLUDING CHAPTER, I will seek to connect various lines of investigation, with a focus on the history of culture and the source of responsibility to the oppressed in the past as well as in the present and the future. At the end of the first chapter, we sought a more detailed account of the relations Benjamin suggests between a past oppressed by the dominant (usually progressive) view of history and oppression in the present, between politically responsible action and the messianic cessation of historical time, and between such action and a different, decidedly nonbourgeois historiography. In the preceding chapter, we saw that Benjamin regards dominant views of history as necessary accompaniments of a history of victorious impositions of legally codified state power. Continuous, often (especially in the nineteenth century) progressive views are necessary to suppress and legitimate—indeed, legitimate by suppressing—the inevitably violent institution and administration of state power. The dominant state power monopolizes the means of power in a legal structure that supports the property institutions of capitalism. In doing so, it has an interest in suppressing, in particular, the instituting violence of capitalism that Marx recounts as 'primitive accumulation,' from the violent expropriation of European serfs to North American slavery and the dispossession of aboriginals. Resistance to contemporary capitalist state power is thus at the same time resistance to oblivious histories of progress, preparing a way for liberating the 'oppressed past.'

According to Benjamin's charge against Marx and the orthodox Marxists, however, such political resistance may not be thought of as a continuation of victorious impositions of state power, for instance, by way of the dictatorship of the proletariat whose violent use of state power may be justified with a view toward the *telos* of the classless society. Instead, by at least attempting to refrain from positing goals and ends altogether, the proletarian strike proceeds from the 'depositing' or finitude of power, that is, its need to institute, maintain, and dissimulate itself. In what Benjamin describes as a messianic standstill of historical time, the strike thereby exposes state power's violence, self-alienation, and dissimulation. As a form of memorial resistance, it may thus 'unlock' hitherto buried aspects of the past and give rise to a different form and content of history—the nonprogressive 'tradition of the oppressed,' condensed into a fleeting 'image' that concerns and calls on present generations. Such resistance, then, taps into a 'weak messianic force' by exploiting the finitude of power and the 'differential' nature of historical time. It seeks to assume the 'messianic claim' of the dead as a form of responsibility not restricted to the presently living.

There are three arguments that this chapter would like to present to further our understanding in this context. First, we should note that the relation between political action and alternative, materialist images of the past does not seem to be restricted to the unilateral fashion indicated here. While non-instrumental political action may give rise to images of the hitherto oppressed past, already Benjamin's arduous search for an alternative, nonbourgeois method of reading the history of culture, in a time when revolutionary action seemed far from imminent, suggests that the causal relation may also work in the opposite direction: Retrieving images of historical oppression and resistance is to motivate present struggles. Second, such a historical method, by operating upon the dominant view of the history of culture, implies that the reception of the messianic call cannot be sought beyond the history of power, taken as a unified totality. The call to responsibility in relation to a 'tradition of the oppressed' is not to be opposed to the history of violence in a binary fashion, but must precisely be seen as produced and carried along by this history, as if in spite of itself. While Benjamin's utopian ambiguities might have left open the interpretive, and deeply problematic, possibility of such a unified totality, Derrida's extension of Benjamin's law of oscillation to a law of iterability operative not only in power but also in all interpretation (including historiography) rules it out. Third, however, the deconstructive law of iterability implies an unavoidable, 'originary' violence that threatens to obscure Benjamin's and Marx's efforts at rendering legible the avoidable violence suppressed by capitalism and bourgeois stories of progress. Derrida connects his account of the source of responsibility with an originary violence, whose 'absolute victim' cannot be made legible, and whose "unreadability of violence" (FL 993) demands of us to wait, sometimes for generations, in order to determine whether the founding of a state, or any other institution, was justified and beneficial. While there are good reasons for Benjamin to take this absoluteness, as a form of finitude, into account, Derrida's originary violence will be seen to equally need the productive oscillation with a call to responsibility that arises with those who, while rendered nameless by dominant discourses, are in principle identifiable and memorable.

CRITIQUE OF CULTURAL HISTORY

Let us begin with the main lines of Benjamin's critique of the history of culture as well as of historiography as a history of victors, with a focus on this critique's association with a memory of suffering that can be said to be a source of responsibility, a responsibility that comes to assume what was once meant by the promise of history. The critique, as we saw, addresses itself to what he calls historicism *(Historismus)*. By historicism, Benjamin means primarily an objectivism about knowledge of the past 'the way it really was' (Ranke), as discussed in the German Historical School of the late nineteenth and the early twentieth century. Furthermore, Benjamin often relates historicism to the idea of history as progress, derived from the Enlightenment philosophy of history (to which the Historical School, in Ranke and Droysen in particular, largely constitutes a response, as does Marxist historical materialism).[1] In Benjamin, this ambiguity between an objective history based on empirical data and the philosophy of history of a Hegel or a Kant, condensed in the vacillating concept of historicism, is an attempt to expose the hidden assumptions shared by seemingly opposed concepts of history prevalent in the nineteenth century.

What is often overlooked, as we also saw, is that Benjamin's critique of historicism is also addressed to a Marxist historicism or "vulgar Marxism" (I 1160) that projects the classless society as the *telos* of an infinite progress. Benjamin rejects Marx's idea of a scientifically accessible, lawful movement of history, for the laws turn out to result in a history of victors that construes the proletariat as the victorious heir of a history of violence, asking it to "move with the current" (Thesis XI). Rather than being remembered and permitted to motivate present struggles, the violence is suppressed by the glorification of technological progress—which is confused with social and political advances—and justified by an end that alone is viewed as just. Consequently, vulgar Marxism in particular misconceives the relation between a memory of injustice and a promise of justice.

Benjamin then finds that bourgeois historicism and vulgar Marxism—which he tends to accuse of an *embourgeoisement* of the working classes—share the faith in science, universality, and linear time. He criticizes bourgeois historicism's method as a method that is supposed to guarantee objectivity, and exposes it as an interpretation whose typically modern "absolutism of method" misses the "richness of layers" in history (VI 95). In addition, it denies the significance of accounting for its "own concrete historical situation" that gives rise to "the *interest* in its historical object" in the first place (V 494), and, hence, ends up legitimating a continuity of oppression and a political history of power. Historicism also seeks a linear movement of history discovered by an objective science that borrows its tools from the natural sciences, thereby missing or explaining away suffering. The positivistic

concept of history merely collects facts and claims to represent them 'faithfully' as what 'really happened,' an objectivist empiricism that requires the
abstractive overcoming of one's own situatedness in favor of unbiased 'empathy' with past actors. Given that past actors are customarily construed as
those who left the most visible traces, who imposed law as a result of war and
politics, the empathy turns out to favor the victors, resulting in a history of
rulers and victorious law imposition (Thesis VII). Due to its positivism and
objectivism, historicism denies its interpretive construction of history, and
suppresses the singularity of past events as well as the uniqueness of every
experience of the past in the present:

> Historicism gives the 'eternal' image of the past; historical materialism sup-
> plies a unique experience with the past. [. . .] Historicism rightly culminates
> in universal history. Materialistic historiography differs from it as to method
> perhaps more clearly than from any other kind. Universal history has no
> theoretical armature. Its method is additive; it musters a mass of data to fill
> the homogenous, empty time. Materialistic historiography, on the other
> hand, is based on a constructive principle (Thesis XVI, XVII).

By presupposing a universal but empty time line along which events may be
lined up "like beads on a rosary" (Thesis A), a time that is then claimed to
be natural or cosmological, historicism assumes a neutral and objective gaze
that disavows the interpretive character of its time line and regards the past
as irretrievably lost. It is better, Benjamin argues, to acknowledge the
necessity of interpretation and "construction" so that it may be "dedicated"
to the nameless ones (I 1241). Moreover, the past is denied its voice of suffering as well as its claim on us, which may still be heard. Benjamin mobilizes a memory of suffering against scientific historiography: "[The 'scientific' character of history] is purchased at the expense of the total
extirpation of all that which reminds it of its original meaning of remembrance [Eingedenken]. The false vitality of representation [Vergegenwärti-
gung], the removal of every echo of 'lament' [Klage] from history, signifies its
final subjection to the modern concept of science" (I 1231). Benjamin's
point here has been explicated, in a different context, by Lyotard's argument that scientific historiographical representation is inadequate to a
memory of suffering, and that the attempt to explain it exhaustively, without remainder, is perhaps the best way to forget.[2]

What scientific and merely cognitive representations first of all forget,
suppress, or dissimulate is the echo of 'lament' issued by a history of suffering. As has been pointed out by commentators, Benjamin shares with, for
example, Emmanuel Levinas's critique of the 'history of survivors' a concern
for what we might see as a second victimization of the dead, in all their singularity, at the hands of the survivors and historians.[3] Unlike Levinas, however, Benjamin—as might be expected, given his critical inheritance of

Marxist concepts—historicizes the account of history and historiography rather than focusing on the inevitable violence every survivor inflicts on the dead by appropriating their works.[4] The history of suffering does not indiscriminately affect singularities in the same way; suffering is not seen to issue first and foremost from the inevitable alienation affecting the works of a singular being through its death. Instead, Benjamin argues that the suffering of some groups and individuals is forgotten precisely in remembering the deeds and works of others. A heritage owes its existence "not only to the efforts of the great minds and talents who created them, but also to the anonymous toil of their contemporaries. There is no document of civilization which is not at the same time a document of barbarism" (Thesis VII). This barbarism stems from oppression in the past and from a process of cultural-historical transmission (*Überlieferung*) that dissimulates both past oppression and contemporary domination.

Calling for a "memory of the nameless" (I 1241) rather than a memory of the dead in general, Benjamin distinguishes between different forms of historiography, notably between materialist historiography whose task it is to "brush history against the grain" (Thesis VII) and a universalizing historiography that contributes to a construction of the history of the victors. He does this in an effort to show that a call to responsibility is assumed especially by those who resist an objectifying historiography that is in complicity with oppression and disenfranchisement in the present. For, in Benjamin's view, it is not inevitable that historiography continues the oppression of the forgotten and nameless ones. However, historiography must sever its link to present oppression and a power that can be resisted in the here and now. For this reason, the primary task is to "wrest tradition from conformism" (Thesis VI) and to endow what I called memorial resistance with the "retroactive force" to "call into question every victory, past and present, of the rulers" (Thesis IV). This resistance—which, for Benjamin, as we know, can take the form of political action, but also calls for a rethinking of historiography—would thus simultaneously free the present for a memory of the downtrodden in history. It is in this way that resistance can be said to inherit a certain "weak messianic force" or a "claim" from the dead and oppressed of a history of violence (Thesis II).

Benjamin suggests that the scientific removal of 'lament' plays into the hands of currently dominant groups in the social and political hierarchy. These groups, the victors of history, as we saw, consolidate their position by the construction of stories of progress, and by repressing the memory of the oppressed of this progress. Consequently, Benjamin is particularly opposed to the method of abstraction from current events in order to achieve neutrality and objectivity about the past, for such an abstraction would only play all the more perniciously into the hands of the current oppressors of the working classes and other oppressed and marginalized groups. Like Horkheimer's crucial essay "Traditional and Critical Theory" (1937), with which he might have been familiar, Benjamin criticizes the social sciences for the ideal of imitating the natural sciences in attaining a 'view from nowhere.' Apart from their epistemic impossibility, attempts to attain an objective and contextless standpoint on history, and thus to "empathize" with the past by "blotting out every thing one knows about the later course of history" (Thesis VII), inadvertently assume the standpoint of the victors of history, insofar as they forget and suppress the fact that the present inherits power relations and past injustices.

Benjamin rejects the method of empathy (*Einfühlung*) for its claim to objectivity as well as for its faith in an immediate access to its object, be it historical or aesthetic, as in his discussion of Aristotelian catharsis.[5] With regard to historical objects, he notes that this method, by contrast to materialist historiography, is based on *acedia*, the "indolence of the heart" (Thesis VII), which the *Origin of the German Mourning-Play* had associated with a melancholic attitude (I 332f.). The critique of empathy, then, not only targets historicism's neglect of the history of reception and interpretation of historical objects (such as cultural artifacts, but also historical events in general), a history Benjamin sees as mediating and co-constituting the object in the first place (cf. V 587). Rather, empathy, as an expression of idle or even lethargic melancholy in the guise of disinterested science, also attempts to eliminate those features of the historian or survivor that seem merely subjective, including individual or collective cognitive interests and capacities for experiencing and responding to human suffering—especially suffering that may be viewed as being continued today.

In this sense, Benjamin calls for the recognition of the vulnerability and mortality of all human beings, a vulnerability the bourgeois historian is said to deny in aiming at objectivity and neutrality, the "purity of a gaze into the past" that is "impossible to attain" (V 587). Benjamin appeals to the survivor to give up a melancholic attitude that, as characteristic of modern experience, merely succumbs to the 'empty' passing of time, to the "ticking of the seconds" (I 642).[6] For only a consciousness aware of the discontinuity of time, and the possibility of its interruption, may seize the political chances of the day and 'rescue' the images of the past that most concern the present (Thesis V). Benjamin names this consciousness *Geistesgegenwart*, the 'presence of mind' that allows a historical agent to register the fleeting images of the past to be rescued from the mere flow of time, as well as to notice the political opportunities of the day, precisely by being aware of the discontinuity and ultimate cognitive inaccessibility of the present (V 586, IV 141f.).[7] Historicism's and vulgar Marxism's refusal to seize these chances and the image of past suffering, their aiming at a false semblance of objectivity and indifference, thus turn out to be in agreement with the continuum of oppression in history.

COMMODIFIED CULTURE AS FETISH

Benjamin sums up this continuity in the following formula: "All rulers are the heirs of those who conquered before them" (Thesis VII). I suggested that this claim is best understood against the background of Marx's powerful argument, presented in Part Eight of *Capital, Volume One*, that the birth of capitalism was made possible by atrocities Marx summarizes as expropriation: the active dispossession of the rural (mostly serf) population of feudalism, for example, which led to the formation of the modern working class free of all property and thus 'free' to sell its labor power, as well as genocide and slavery in the colonization of what was to become the United States.[8] Insofar as this expropriation was necessary for capital formation and the generation of capitalist relations of production, all capitalists and all those who benefit today from this past injustice are 'the heirs of those who conquered before them.' Apart from a number of legal challenges to the rule instituted by property rights, today's political landscape, for example, in North America, makes a feeble attempt to recognize and react to what seems to many, perhaps problematically, the most visible side of past injustice—racialized and sexualized exploitation—with affirmative action practices, geared to the rectification of past injustice and its lasting effect on the present. Even the most outright philosophical justifications of capitalist property rights and the private ownership of the means of production are forced to admit the enormity of a problem that cannot be solved on the terms of these justifications themselves.[9]

It would not be difficult to show in greater detail than I can do here that, for Marx as well as for Benjamin, the recognition of the violent origins of capitalism is hampered by what the former calls commodity fetishism. Although Marx never makes the link between the critique of fetishism and the memory of the genesis of capital explicit, one may argue that fetishism—as the forgetting of the social origins of exchange value and its amortization processes—blocks the understanding of the historical origins of capital formation. According to Marx, fetishism names the suppression, by the operation of the market itself, of qualitative aspects of production as well as of the particular characteristics of the producers (the transformation of 'living labor' into 'abstract labor'). By bringing different commodities into equation, the capitalist market gives rise to the constitutive illusion that products possess their abstract exchange value, expressed in money, within themselves, rather than this value being an expression of a relation between products. Moreover, these relations are *social* relations mediated by *things (res; Dinge)*; the forgetting of these social relations in the commodity is thus the origin of what became known, since Lukács, as reification (*Verdinglichung*).[10] As Marx notes, "the relative value-form of a commodity [. . .] expresses its value-existence as something wholly different from its substance and properties, as the quality of being comparable [. . .]; this expression itself therefore indicates that it conceals a social relation" (*Capital* 149). The forgetting involved here is akin to the belief that a king is king by virtue of his innate properties, rather than being made king by his subjects believing him to be king, and acting accordingly (ibid.).

The critique of fetishism is thus a critique of presence:[11] of the presence and availability of products on the market whose exchange value, taken to increase 'mysteriously' as if all by itself, is viewed as inhering in them rather than being dependent on the market and the exploitative relations of production that gave rise to their existence. This critique then asks us to remember the labor and the laborers invested in the product. Fetishism systematically hides the origin of value in the social division of labor in favor of an abstract means of exchange—namely, money in its correspondence to what Marx calls abstract labor, measured in terms of homogenous, linear time rather than in terms of the heterogeneous quality and substance of the productive process. The achievement of a "socially uniform objectivity" of value and of labor (*Capital* 166) thus works by the projection of qualitatively different processes on a presupposed timeline, the very same one historicism presupposes to line up historical events. Historicism's 'objective' time line then reifies singular events and robs them of their specificity in the way that the uniform and linear temporality, risen to dominance with the modern form of production, commensurates labor and its products. From this perspective, historicism represents an (unreflective) part of modern capitalism, which brought the homogenization of labor time as the time of abstract labor (the universal equivalent) along with the standardization of world time in terms of the 'time of the clock.'[12] Benjamin's virulent polemic against 'empty and homogenous' clock time as well as his association of historicism and uncritical ideas of historical progress with the rule of capital may be seen in this context.

By generating the illusion that products amortize themselves on the market and thus produce surplus value and capital to be reinvested, fetishism denies the exploitative social relations behind processes of amortization in general, and disavows the violence at the origin of capitalism in particular. By suggesting that, as Marx argues, capital is "the source of its own increase," or that it is essentially credit—the most fetish-like form of capital, namely, "money creating money"—fetishism conceals that capital is a relation between propertied and propertyless or laboring classes.[13] Thus, it suppresses the memory of the labor and suffering that made capitalism possible. By forgetting that exchange value is "something purely social" (*Capital* 149), we forget that objects have their power of amortization and capitalization only if labor power is invested in them, labor power that may be bought, like any other commodity, on the market. But the availability of labor power for capital, the very existence of a labor market, had to be created violently by expropriation; as Marx's "Modern Theory of Colonization" demonstrates with reference to the emergence of North American capitalism, in the absence of poor proletarians who own nothing but their labor power, such as former serfs, slavery of both Native Americans and, later, Africans had to fill the gap (*Capital* 931ff.).

As we briefly mentioned in chapter two, Derrida's critique of fetishism as a reduction of spectrality to presence—justified insofar as Marx views the critique of fetishism as a critique of interpersonal alienation *in general*, directed to its teleological overcoming in communism—acknowledges that this critique is itself a critique of presence.[14] Nevertheless, Derrida's claim that what he calls capitalization—and which he, without necessary qualifications, seems to derive from the concept of iterability—"began before culture" (SM 160/254) might inadvertently support the idea that commodities can increase their value by themselves, forgetting that the amortization of value on the market requires human labor. We can insist on the need for the critique of fetishism (to which Derrida would not be opposed in general)[15] even if we also wish to be mindful of the danger of viewing all autonomization of products and their meaning—what Derrida calls an 'originary expropriation'—as an alienation that is to be overcome in the 'classless' future. Yet, as a critique of presence as well as of forgetting, the critique of fetishism contributes to a memory of suffering in history, the very memory that Derrida sees as crucial to the inheritance of Marx's emancipatory promise.

Returning to Benjamin's critique of historicism, we should thus not be surprised that he characterizes the scientific-positivistic belief in the immediate accessibility of historical objects as fetishistic. The suppression of the 'drudgery of the nameless' results in the reduction of a heritage to a dead possession or inventory whose origin in labor and a history of expropriation is forgotten. Thus, a heritage takes on a fetishistic aspect in historicism. In the essay on Eduard Fuchs, Benjamin attempts to formulate a historical materialist method for reading cultural history by, in part, applying Marx's insights to the concept of culture itself.

> The concept of culture is a problematical one for historical materialism, just as culture's disintegration into goods which are to become an object of possession for humanity is an impossible idea for it. For historical materialism, the work of the past is not complete. As the complex of objects which may be looked at independently of the production process, or at least independently of the process in which they endure, the concept of culture bears fetishistic features. It appears reified (II 477).

Referring again to the 'barbarism' at the heart of the origin as well as of the transmission of culture, Benjamin continues to note that as this dead inventory, it does not allow any "genuine, that is, political experiences" (ibid.; see also V 822). Political experience of cultural history is thus again associated with a memory of the barbarism that gave rise to a tradition. Overcoming the fetishistic, historicist notion of cultural history, in the crafting of a new historiographical method, contributes to a memory of suffering that, in turn, motivates political resistance against those who profit from the fetishism. (Moreover, commodity fetishism in general is said to hamper active intervention into political processes in that it contributes to the melancholic boredom characteristic of modernity.) Here, we begin to see that, for Benjamin, it is not only the proletarian strike, as a model of political action, that can give rise to the hitherto buried 'image of enslaved ancestors' and their resistance to oppression. Rather, the reciprocal interplay of counter-historiography and political action may also work in the opposite direction.

We should first note, however, that Benjamin does not exempt Marxist historians of culture from this fetishism. Here, the fetishism does not so much consist in the mere denial of the historical mode of production from which an object, like a work of art, is inseparable, but in the neglect of the history of reception and the violent processes of transmission: "For it is a vulgar Marxist illusion to be able to determine the social function of a material or a cultural product without considering the circumstances and the bearers of its handing down [*Überlieferung*]," Benjamin writes in a short methodological fragment (I 1161). In line with his insistence that an account of the 'interest' a historian has in a particular object must be given (V 494), Benjamin argues in this fragment that the historical materialist must ask above all about the origin of the developmental processes unified in a "stream of transmission [*Strom der Überlieferung*]": "Whose mills are driven by this stream? Who utilizes its rapids? Who contained it?—thus asks the historical materialist" (I 1160f.). Thus, Benjamin's materialist historiography includes a critical reflection both on the conditions of production and on those of reception and transmission of a cultural artifact as well as of material goods in general.

For Benjamin, the process of handing down is mediated by the sociohistorical context of the production of a work, of its transmission, and of its reception. Benjamin's materialist theory of cultural history registers this by insisting on the "fore- and after-history of historical states of affairs" that produces the states of affairs "in a new way, never in the same way" (V 587). Works of historical subjects are never immediately accessible "things in themselves," and the question is not how they are "in truth" (I 1160). This is so not only because the object always already appears under the determinate perspective of a finite subject, but because, prior to a receiving subject, it is mediated by a heterogeneous objectivity that conditions subjectivity itself. In Benjamin's early work, for example, in "The Task of the Translator," this objectivity is mostly thought as the autonomous movement of language in which cultural artifacts survive and grow, such as in a translation (IV 10ff.). While Benjamin never gives up on this emphasis on language in which all historiography takes place, the writings of the 1930s place the sociohistorical processes, analyzed in Marxism as the conditioning mode of production, in the foreground as the mediating instance.[16] Reception and transmission must be seen in the context of human socioeconomic and political praxis, and that means, for Benjamin, in the context of social domination, the economic and exploitative relations of production, and in hegemonic discourses. (As we saw, this also means for Benjamin, at least for the bourgeois period of history, that the mediation of works occurs under the conditions of commodity production, which generates the illusion of the immediate accessibility of objects.) Not only cultural artifacts, but material inheritance in general is subject to the social institutions that regulate the production, consumption, distribution, and transmission of the works of previous generations. In modern Western history, these institutions at the same time defend the existing laws of property and inheritance through the legal order. As we saw in the preceding chapter, Benjamin sees these social institutions and the legal order as controlled by state power whose 'interruption' thus becomes the task of a memorial political action aligned with a materialist historiography. It is in this way that Benjamin suggests to merge political praxis and critical theory.

READING THE VOICE OF THE NAMELESS IN HISTORY

At the end of chapter three, I indicated that Benjamin's concept of action, if we read it as imagining a utopia devoid of state power, enforceable law, and domination, could be taken to suggest that the reception of the messianic claim and the articulation of the voice of the nameless must bypass the violent form of power characterized by the 'law of oscillation.' Reading Benjamin in this way would allow for the exclusionary opposition, on the level of action, between state power and memorial resistance (in the form of the proletarian strike), and, on the level of historiography, between the history of victors and the tradition of the oppressed. The closer discussion of this latter level in this chapter, however, shows that Benjamin does not construe such a binary opposition. The critical reflection on origin and transmission of what survives is not undertaken by a historical materialist situated simply outside the 'stream of transmission,' free from the guilt by association that the inheritance of this culture implies. While ambiguities in Benjamin's early "Critique of Violence" seem to allow for the possibility of altogether excluding from a political history of violence the messianic claim and the oppressed past, the discussion of the historical-materialist method disconfirms this possibility. The stream of transmission does not form a totality for Benjamin, to which the voice of the nameless could only appear from without, in binary opposition to the history of violence. Several reasons for this may be extrapolated from Benjamin's discussion of historical materialism.

First, if the violence in question, insofar as it concerns cultural history and historiography, must be observed at the level of origin, transmission, and reception, the participants in this violence will be multiplied and their identification rendered very difficult. This is so in particular if one stresses, as

Benjamin does, the 'primacy of politics over history' and the writing and rewriting of history out of the present. Second, if the violence in question does not only concern a history of state power, within which power is transferred, but must be seen to pass through the fluctuations of capitalist markets and its 'rulers'—of course, in connection with state power—the beneficiaries of past violence and capital formation will not be easily separated from the 'victims.' (Predictably, the problem of clear identification is sometimes turned into an argument against reparations and affirmative action.[17]) Third, commodity fetishism cannot be construed as a deliberate construction aimed at concealing the true relations of power and their historical emergence. Already Marx's account of fetishism implied the necessity of its emergence for those engaging in market transactions. Given generalized commodity production, participants in exchange cannot help abstracting from concrete use value and living labor. "They do this without being aware of it," Marx writes famously (*Capital* 166). If fetishism is a necessary illusion not simply to be dispelled by the superior knowledge of the theoretician, Benjamin's account of cultural history cannot claim its deliberate and ideological construction on the part of rulers while exempting a group of nonrulers, under favorable conditions, from its effects.

The result of these considerations is that no one may easily claim a good conscience with regard to history and the appropriation of a culture by the survivors. However, this carefulness may not lead to an indistinct generalization of the 'guilt' of survivors. It is important to recognize that not only 'the rulers' participate in the 'barbarism,' but they may be said to benefit from it most of all. Benjamin does not wish to generalize the survivor's guilt because for him, as we have seen, the liberation of the voice of the nameless precisely requires a resistance to the rulers in the present. According to Benjamin's Marx-inspired view, not all heirs are equally implicated in the suppression of the claim past oppression has on present and future generations. A historicization of what Levinas calls the history of survivors yields necessary distinctions within history, cultural heritage, and its receivers. Rather than being given in advance, these distinctions remain subject to a struggle of interpretations in the present. As we will see, Benjamin's method of reading cultural history confirms the insight that such struggles of interpretation do not permit the voice of the nameless to be altogether excluded from a history of victorious violence.

Regarding the distinctions between rulers and oppressed, however, there remains a tendency in Benjamin, as we saw in the previous chapter, to construct them—perhaps, like Marx's scientific prognoses, in a performative rather than a constative mode—in too binary a fashion, opposing the 'history of victors' to the 'tradition of the oppressed.' The seeming exclusivity of this distinction, as indicated, is in danger of specifying a uniquely situated subject whose political action receives the messianic call. Without distinguishing his voice from the one he attributes to Marx, Benjamin writes: "The subject of historical cognition is the struggling, oppressed class itself. In Marx it appears as the last enslaved class, as the avenger that completes the task of liberation in the name of generations of the downtrodden" (Thesis XII). It is this subject that is motivated by the call from the past rather than the utopian ideals of progress, according to which the struggling class only has to wait for the 'revolutionary situation.' As we saw, Benjamin introduces the conception of a form of political action that, in a revolutionary situation, breaks through the continuity of power relations and, hence, liberates other 'images' of the past, remembers the toil of the nameless forgotten by the state power's self-representation, and responds to the messianic call of previous generations.

For Benjamin, I suggested, returns to his account of a history of violent impositions of law and power in the "Theses on the Concept of History" in order to argue that state and class domination cover up the instituting violence to which they owe themselves by relying on a complacent cultural history and an objectivist historiography. Benjamin argues that a revolutionary action that interrupts or overturns the sociopolitical order thereby also interrupts the continuities and narrative linearities of its ideological discourses, thus altering our relationship to the "triumphal procession" of the victors and its booty called "cultural treasures" (Thesis VII). Such an interruption liberates (and is in turn supported by) alternative readings of a cultural heritage, revealing its 'origin in horror.' At the same time, it generates alternative views or 'images' of history by focusing on what the history of transmission and reception of a cultural history neglected. These alternative images would be more aware of the messianic claim of the nameless dead, and thus reveal our political responsibility to remember as well as to achieve justice in the present.

While generally affirming Benjamin's (practical and theoretical) critique of cultural history, I demonstrated the difficulties and dangers of delimiting the concept of political action that may respond to the messianic claim. First of all, it is not clear that a revolutionary action that would remain nonpositional is conceivable, that is, that would not eventually have to found or modify legal political institutions that attempt to ensure justice (despite the inevitability of the failure to do justice to singularity). Benjamin's insight into the cognitive indeterminacy of the distinction between the proletarian and the political strike is an implicit admission of this problem. All past revolutions have turned out to posit new law, and such law is often necessary precisely to try to 'rectify' past injustice and its effects on the present. At present, modern legal institutions seem indispensable to this process and to the defense of human rights, however utilizable the concept of human rights may be due to its 'mystical ambiguity.' Moreover, as Derrida points out, the moment of institution itself is unreadably violent, and can only be judged adequately in hindsight, a temporality of 'deferred action' or *Nachträglichkeit* of whose significance for politics Benjamin is quite aware.[18]

Further, I suggested that Benjamin's concept of the law of oscillation at the heart of law-positing power must be radicalized in view of Derrida's promise of repetition, which, as we saw, renders all strict lines of demarcation between the rulers and the oppressed difficult, and makes these lines an object of political interpretation, too. Economic relations can thus not be seen to alone draw the lines between political groups, a view we discovered (in chapter one) as one of the major problems in Marxism. Likewise, the inheritance of Benjamin's weak messianic force, which is to strengthen the oppressed classes (see SM 55/95), if read through the lens of Derrida's messianic promise of the future, turns out to blur the simple opposition between dominant and dominated. Hence, the specification of a 'subject of historical cognition' to which the reception of the messianic call is restricted is both conceptually impossible and politically dangerous, in that it might repeat the logic of a 'chosen people' uniquely incarnating the messianic future—the very logic that Benjamin criticized in contemporary Marxists. As we also noted, cultural discourses do not always and unilaterally represent state power and class domination, so they do not necessarily suppress the messianic call of history's oppressed. We will see in a moment that Benjamin indeed specifies a materialist method that outlines a way of reading cultural treasures so as to reveal their origin in violence and hence render them unusable for ideological functions (see II 435).

It is perhaps not surprising that for the Benjamin writing under the impact of European fascism in general and the Hitler–Stalin pact of 1939 in particular, political action can presuppose, and perhaps also requires, a well-defined 'enemy.' However, if we look more closely at Benjamin's concern for a rethinking of historiography rather than his thoughts on political action (without denying the close connection between them), we see that Benjamin is quite aware of the necessity of viewing cultural and material heritage as a political force-field that is internally differentiated (rather than forming a totality). While Levinas, whose opposition between the totality of history and the infinite responsibility to the other Derrida also attributes to the early Benjamin,[19] views the 'history of survivors' as such a totality, requiring the location of the origin of responsibility outside of that totality, Benjamin sees the call as precisely produced and borne along by this history. The voice of the oppressed is precisely produced—*as* forgotten or repressed—by the injustice in the past as well as by the suppression of this injustice in the heritage and its transmission. For a heritage is, as Benjamin points out, always constructed, selected, and filtered by a history of reception. As a result, a heritage in the context of violence must carry along the voice of the nameless as if in spite of itself. Every work of (bourgeois) culture and every material good inherited is affected by this 'barbarism' in its origin and its transmission. The task of a critical inheritance and materialist history of culture is thus to bring out this violence in it, to make it legible as a way of retrieving the claim of the nameless dead on us.

CONSTRUCTING A MONTAGE OF HISTORY'S RAGS

That Benjamin sees the paradoxical voice of the voiceless—the memory of past violence—as produced and carried along by the history of violence that suppresses and disavows it, becomes clearer when we take a closer look at his proposals for a method that would respond to the messianic call. Benjamin devoted most of his research efforts in the 1930s to developing such a method, which also was to become the method of presenting the vast stock of material and citations he had amassed for the *Arcades Project*. This method has generated many debates, beginning with Adorno's opposition to it, and I cannot treat it in great detail here.[20] I will limit myself to a closer look at the relation between a memory of the "oppressed past" (Thesis XVII) and a memory of responsibility.

Benjamin's method aims at the "rescue" *(Rettung)* of phenomena from their "appreciation as a heritage," from the "catastrophe" or "danger" of "a certain kind of their transmission" (V 591). It consists of a 'destructive' gesture of interruption targeting the 'stream of transmission,' and a careful and 'constructive' unfolding of the result of this interruption. In a well-known formula, Benjamin writes that "'construction' presupposes 'destruction'" (V 587). The constructive process need not occur chronologically after the destructive one, since Benjamin often suggests that the unfolding of the fragments broken out of the stream is predelineated or prestructured by a discontinuous movement taking place 'underneath' the visible stream, endowing a phenomenon or an image with a "historical index" suggesting its legibility to a particular time (V 577f.). Similar to the way in which nonviolent political action, such as the proletarian strike, draws upon the discontinuity at the heart of law-positing power, the critical gesture of the materialist historian consists in proceeding from the discontinuity at the heart of this stream. As discussed in chapter one, Benjamin suggests in his epistemological notes to the *Passagenwerk* that he wishes to base his historical construction "on the differentials of time which for others disturb the 'major lines' of investigation" (V 570).

This discontinuity makes possible the tearing of individual works of art, for example, out of their established place in the history of reception, out of their insertion into the 'stream.' This 'ripping out of its context' Benjamin names 'destruction' or "a citation without citation marks" (V 572), a practice that, according to Benjamin, makes the object historical in the first place: "To write history means to cite history. But the concept of citation implies that any given historical object must be ripped out of its context" (V 595).[21] While it may seem here that the object is already constituted when removed from its context, we need to take into account that the interrupting gesture is itself demanded by the object's peculiar structure: "If the historical object is to be blasted out of the continuum of the historical process, it is because the monadological structure of the object demands it. This structure only becomes evident once the object has been blasted free" (V 594). The blasting free in the 'messianic cessation of happening,' the happening of transmission itself, thus does not precede the construction of the object, but only lays bare its structure, which Benjamin names monadological.[22] Dormant or latent processes in history that Benjamin, drawing on Proust's *mémoire involontaire*, calls the "involuntary memory of humanity" (I 1233), demand the reading of images as they "flash up" (Thesis V) out of history, and the point is to recognize, seize, and interpret them. This brings us to the constructive process of Benjamin's method.

The second gesture now interprets and unfolds the work, 'rescued' from its context by a "brutal grasp" (V 592), and reads it as a "force-field" in which prehistory and posthistory of the work polarize themselves (V 587). The task here is to show how the work owes itself to the (violent) sociohistorical processes, but also how a history of reception might have constructed the work as part of a progressive, linear, and developmental process. Furthermore, the constructive element of the task of the historian consists in a constellative rearrangement of the elements or works broken out of the stream of tradition so as to break with the power of received interpretation and what Gadamer calls effective history *(Wirkungsgeschichte)*. Benjamin notes explicitly that this constellation or construction, which he associates with the surrealist method of montage (V 575), is undertaken in order to remember the toil of the nameless: "It is more difficult to honor the memory of the nameless than that of the famous and celebrated ones, the poets and thinkers included. The historical construction is dedicated to the nameless" (I 1241).

The 'memory of the nameless' thus must be won against the construction of a forgetful canon of received interpretations that suppress the dependence of a work on the 'barbarism' of its origin and of its transmission. The critical constellation focuses on those "most decrepit [*hinfälligsten*] parts of the effectiveness [of the great figures of the bourgeoisie]," and the point is "to precisely tear and cite out of them what remained buried as inconspicuous under them because it helped the powerful ones very little" (V 460). It is in this sense that the memory of the nameless requires a destruction of the bourgeois apologia for its heritage: "The appreciation or apologia only gives weight to those elements of a work that have already generated an aftereffect. It misses those points at which the transmission breaks down and thus misses those jags and cracks which call a halt to those who wish to move beyond it" (I 658, see also V 591f.).

Moving beyond it means to focus on what Benjamin sometimes calls the "trash of history" (V 575), what fell by the wayside, and was left out of consideration by a heritage. It is for this reason that Benjamin's historian or historical materialist, like Derrida, has been named a *chiffonier*, a collector of the rags of a tradition in order to read its truth out of them.[23] In capitalist modernity, with its rapid outmoding of commodities, the rags, the cracks and jags, may not only refer to undiscovered and neglected strata of great bourgeois works, but to the refuse of industrial processes themselves. In his essay on surrealism, Benjamin extends the idea of inheriting 'revolutionary energies' from the past to the derivation of energy from the blandness of consumer culture and its casting away of commodities, the "enslaved objects" that in turn "enslave us" (II 299). The point is to resist the political passivity that a commodified, fetishistic cultural landscape generates.[24]

Thus, moving beyond the dominant and canonical interpretation of a tradition or heritage also names Benjamin's hope that the constellation, constructed from the rags of a tradition, forms an image of the 'oppressed past' that will contribute to political resistance targeting the primary beneficiaries of a tradition. The constellation responds to and remembers a latent promise—the messianic call—of the nameless ones for whom hope will always have come too late: "Only that historian will have the gift of fanning the spark of hope in the past who is firmly convinced that even the dead will not be safe from the enemy if he wins" (Thesis VI). By reading the dominant tradition and its underlying industrial processes in such a way as to point out its losers and its oppressed, and thus by remembering the violence of this tradition's origins and construction, the survivor may remember the messianic voice of the dead and at the same time interpret it as a promise to resist suffering and its denial in the present and for the future.

For Benjamin, there is then a crucial link between contemporary rulers, the currently dominant discourse, and the dominant view of history, the one that has an interest in removing lament from history. The victors of history, directly or indirectly, benefit from the dominant view of the past, and that means that historiography seeks to eliminate or downplay alternative versions of history that would be responsive to the tradition of the oppressed. Further aiming at the philosophy of history, or its secularized version as progress, according to which the more prosperous future allows a justification of suffering in the present and the past, Benjamin argues that resistance to such suffering must be "nourished by the image of enslaved ancestors rather than by the ideal image of liberated descendants," for such a "solidarity with the dead" (I 1237) preserves the claim of the oppressed on the present.

For, as we saw, Benjamin suggests that the past, the past of suffering and victimization, has a special claim on the present. "There is a secret agreement [appointment: Verabredung] between past generations and the present one. Our coming was expected upon earth. Like every generation that preceded us, we have been endowed with a *weak* messianic force to which the past has a claim. That claim cannot be settled cheaply" (Thesis II). Past suffering has a claim to be remembered, but it also carries with it the promise to resist suffering in the present. For that resistance alone frees the present for the assumption of this claim, this responsibility that is also a promise. In this way, "every lived moment" becomes "Judgment Day" (ibid.), a judgment that here, for Benjamin, not only issues from the oppressed and marginalized in the present, but that also decides about the memory of oppression, from whence it draws its sustenance.

Thus, by viewing a specific cultural memory as suppressing the voice of the nameless, in particular those crushed by the birth and march of capitalism, Benjamin sees the struggle for the memory of the messianic call as taking place in a political domain that the currently dominant discourses must share with those who resist it. The 'totality' of a history of oppression excluding the 'others' of this history must be seen as the result of an interpretation by those who understand themselves as the inheritors of the oppression. No clear line of separation between the oppressors and the oppressed can therefore be drawn in advance of the moment of politics, for example, by relying on purely economic criteria (as in orthodox Marxism). The totality of the history of victors is always provisional and is to be challenged in the same way that past and present victories are to be challenged. For Benjamin, the victors and their 'spoils,' the cultural heritage dragged along in the triumphal march, also drag along the cry of outrage that the nameless forgotten ones address to the present generation. The call to political responsibility in the present thus emerges from within tradition itself, and it even promises 'revolutionary energies' to those engaged in struggle today, provided the critical historian knows how to read the cultural heritage against itself and condense it in a powerful image, montage, or constellation: to do historiographically what Celan's "In One," cited at the beginning of this book, did poetically, perhaps so as to blur the distinction between the two.

THE ANTERIORITY OF RESPONSIBILITY

Although the early Benjamin seemed, albeit not unequivocally, to permit an exclusionary opposition between the history of power and a call to responsibility, we saw that his later materialist method for reading history sees the call as to be uncovered precisely in that history. In exposing Levinas's notion of survivor-history, I have elsewhere analyzed Derrida's, if you wish, more philosophical reasons for agreeing with Benjamin (and against Levinas) on this question.[25] (This agreement, however, requires that we resist the application of Derrida's 'critique' of Levinas to the early Benjamin.) According to Derrida, Levinas considers history a "finite totality" (WD 107/158; 141/207) that, qua finite, does not allow the infinity of responsibility within it. By a finite, violent totality, Derrida means a totality that cannot think the infinity of its movement between totality and infinity. This finite totality implies that Levinas cannot view the call and memory of responsibility to issue from the 'victims' of history, for insofar as they appear within it, within historiography, they are no longer singular beings capable of issuing the call. By contrast, Derrida suggests that what Levinas indicates in the other's transcendence or eschatology '*is*' history (WD 123/180): as we saw in chapter two, the infinitely transcendent or messianic future, by way of the promise of repetition, names the infinite movement in which histories first of all constitute themselves.

Derrida thus argues that the Levinasian relation to the transcendent other as to an unforeseeable future be viewed as a relation to a future that is productive of history. As a result, the relation in question is to an alterity that is neither restricted to the human face nor opposed to history since it generates the movement of history in the first place. Thus, Derrida agrees with Benjamin that what the latter names the messianic claim or address (*Anspruch*) cannot be thought as arising from outside of the history of violence, but is carried along by it. Derrida indeed clarifies Benjamin's thought here, for in Benjamin, the necessary link between openness to the future and the reception of the messianic call, which expresses the incompleteness of suffering in history, remained unclear. Drawing on Derrida, we can now see that the promise of repetition at the heart of history's movement installs a discontinuity that, as we argued, is for Benjamin the very possibility of interrupting the history of victors and the stream of transmission; it is this interruption that in turn makes possible the recognition of the messianic claim. Thus, if we read Derrida and Benjamin together, an openness to the future beyond horizons is the very possibility of receiving and responding to the messianic claim that the oppressed of history have on us. Radicalizing Benjamin's ban on representations of the future (Thesis B) in terms of Derrida's open promise of memory yields an understanding of history and heritage that explains its infinite reinterpretability and its discontinuity as a "revolutionary chance in the struggle for the oppressed past" (Thesis XVII).

However, for Derrida, the altering and deferring repetition that constitutes histories cannot be thought without violence, insofar as every appearance within the order of the visible or memorable, every linguistic reference, and every phenomenalization implies violence. Without this "originary violence" (OG 106/156; 110/162)—this is what Levinas is said to overlook most of all—the other cannot even appear, in language or in history, as the other (WD 125/184). In this context, as we will see in greater detail, violence consists of (a) the quasi-transcendental opening of the subject of responsibility, which prevents the final or 'authentic' self-identity and self-sufficient plenitude subjects are said to desire, (b) the necessity of choosing among different, even contradictory, injunctions, which requires ultimately unjustifiable exclusions, and (c) the deconstructive erasure and reconstitution of singularity in historical relations. In this latter sense, violence first of all consists in the fact that the appearance of the other that always occurs in a particular context and under a horizon of intelligibility is destructive of singular identity insofar as every repetition is a repetition from the future beyond horizons, and that means a repetition in difference. Hence, history again and again rewrites and alters identity, affecting the singularity of the event and of the other in the historical relation. Since it is the singularity of the other from which the ethical call, for Levinas as well as for Derrida, proceeds, and since singularity is not exterior to but produced by history, the call to responsibility must be seen to be generated by history and its movement itself.

The link between history and responsibility thus implies an inevitable violence—*"une violence pré-éthique"* (WD 125/184) that, while being structurally necessary as the "nonethical opening of ethics [*ouverture non-éthique d'éthique*]" (OG 140/202), may obviate Benjamin's hope that a memory of redressable violence become the primary motivation of emancipatory struggles. If Derrida's account of the call to responsibility sees it originating in a future that is part of the movement of history itself, what relationship might it have to a memory of what Benjamin means by the oppressed of history? Does not Derrida's reinscription of the root of responsibility in a more heterogeneous, nonhuman otherness, despite its refusal to simply oppose a call to responsibility to a history of violence tout court, make it impossible to conceive a link between this call and the 'victims' of history? Between an ethico-political promise of change and a memory of suffering? Before seeking to negotiate this conundrum by discussing Derrida's originary responsibility and Benjamin's claim of the oppressed of history, it is advisable to explore in greater detail the connections between the violence of differential iterability and a preceding otherness prior to the determination of the human other, an otherness that is then claimed to constitute the very 'origin' of responsibility.

The account of the promise of repetition in chapter two should help us to grasp the relation that Derrida sees between the originary otherness implied in differential iterability and the 'origin' or 'root' of responsibility. Iterability refers the promise not only to the future but to the past, in the form of an anterior, unpresentable otherness. Insofar as there is "no future without repetition" (AF 80/127), the promise simultaneously returns us to the past to be repeated. The paradox of originary iterability implies that whatever appears *as* something determinate must already be repeated for it to establish its determination. There is thus no self-present first time, no pure origin of a phenomenal appearance, of a semantic content, or of a subject. To be itself, a subject, content, or phenomenon must already relate to itself as to an other, for the closure of its self-relation (as self-self, not as self-other) is only promised, but never given or presupposed. In this sense, alterity, by virtue of the promise of repetition, precedes identity, but as an otherness that itself lacks positivity or identity. It is an otherness 'in' the same, not outside of it, lacking any phenomenality itself but subtending, contaminating, dividing, and opening any phenomenon. Since the repetition that, as a prior differentiation, precedes what is repeated, 'is' nothing without or apart from the terms of the repetition, it cannot be represented by itself, as such. As men-

tioned in chapter two, Derrida calls the resulting unrepresentable and anterior otherness a *déjà*, a radicalized unconscious, the "irreducibility of an
always-already-there" and an "absolute past" (OG 66/97).

On the basis of this structural insight, Derrida has analyzed originary otherness in a range of accounts regarding various phenomena. Naturally, the
ineluctable coming-too-late in question shares with Heidegger's thrownness
(*Geworfenheit*) in the *Da* ('there') of *Dasein* the sense of the necessary anteriority of other subjects, languages, and traditions. However, Derrida also
argues that the promise of repetition casts us in the anteriority of an alterity
that is even more radical than thrownness. Here, I do not wish to go into the
details of Derrida's demonstration in *Aporias* except insofar as the mediation
between Heidegger and Levinas on the question of the 'mineness' of death
expands the thought of a heterogeneous and preceding alterity, and moves us
closer to the political and ethical responsibility connected with it. Whereas
Heidegger thinks the projection on *Dasein*'s future, on the mineness of death,
as the possibility of the impossible that returns me to my thrownness and
hence to the taking over of the 'there' and its potential, Derrida argues that
the very impossibility of my death's appearance signifies the impossibility of
the recognition of death as such. "'Death' is the disappearance, the end, the
annihilation, of the *as such*," Derrida writes.[26] He continues to draw a radical
consequence from the unrepresentability of death 'as such':

> [M]an, or man as *Dasein*, never has a relation to death as such, but only to
> perishing, to demising [*Ableben*], and to the death of the other, who is not
> the other. The death of the other thus becomes again "first," always first. It
> is like the experience of mourning that institutes my relation to myself and
> constitutes the egoity of the ego as well as every *Jemeinigkeit* in the *dif-
> férance*—neither internal nor external—that structures this experience.[27]

The anticipation of death does not confirm the futural potential to be
repeated or retrieved (*wiedergeholt*) by *Dasein*, but points to an otherness
before *Dasein*, an otherness that now means that the experience of death is
always mediated by an other. The other here, however, need not necessarily
be a personal other, whose death would thus precede mine, as Levinas argues.[28]
Rather, its anonymity (or even 'anhumanity') allows it to be myself as another,
divided from myself by the law of differential iterability, indicated here by the
reference to *différance*. It is because of this division within myself—which con-
taminates and overturns Heidegger's distinction between the authentic and
the inauthentic—because of this fundamental "expropriation" and "inauthen-
tication" at the heart of the subject that it is open to the other.[29] There are
always already others (others understood as widely as possible, in the sense of
otherness) when the subject appears on the scene, and the subject owes its
constitution to this otherness. In short, the promise of repetition, as an originary violence (in the sense of [a] mentioned above) to the authenticity of the

self—indeed, to the very possibility of an authentic self—installs an originary otherness that at the same time names the enabling condition of responsively opening the self to the other. Originary violence and responsibility—or what I have elsewhere called responsiveness as the ineluctable fact that we have always already responded to spectral others (languages, ancestors, histories and traditions)—must be seen as inseparable.[30]

Derrida's concept of anterior otherness, however, while accounting for the condition of possibility of responsibility, does not yet give us a *call* to responsibility. Derrida has to show how the enabling condition, while inseparable from their constitution, can appear to human subjects as a recognizable voice. For this reason, his reading of *Being and Time* elaborates the alterity preceding the 'self' as Heidegger's "voice of the friend which every *Dasein* carries with it."[31] The preceding alterity that, on Derrida's quasi-transcendental account, makes subjects possible is always already mediated by or expressed in particular languages, traditions, and ancestors, which in turn appear to the subject in an 'inner' dialogue as a polyphony of voices. Metonymically, the 'voice of the friend' stands for this prosopopeitic polyphony. For Derrida, it is a nameless voice that, before every subjective determination, articulates the 'call of conscience' calling the subject to its originary being-guilty (*Schuldigsein*).[32] Whereas in Heidegger, the call calls *Dasein* to the 'authentic' taking over of its inherited possibilities (*Sein und Zeit*, §§ 55–60), it names in Derrida a call that opens up every subject to its responsibility prior to its self-determination (which is, however, always already under way). The 'guilt' or 'debt' (*Schuld*) to which *Dasein* responds in this primordial responsibility is not a debt to be assumed in the self-fashioning of an authentic subject. Nor is it a specific debt to be paid off, a guilt defined by a specific (moral or legal) code that has been violated. Hence, the guilt in question here is not (yet) to be translated into a specific guilt that would stem from one's co-implication in, or one's benefiting from, a history of violence. Likewise, it is not (yet) the debt one owes a given tradition or heritage, in the sense in which Derrida argues that "to be" means "to inherit" (SM 54/94). Thus, it is not yet Benjamin's debt owed to the toil of the nameless. However, insofar as this primordial and "anhuman" or "inhuman"[33] responsibility—in advance of the constitution and every definition of the human—is "at the root of all ulterior responsibilities (moral, juridical, political)" (*Points* 276/290), one must suppose that the primordial, nonspecific guilt/debt is also at the root of Benjamin's notion of the claim of past generations. We will return to this question of priority in a moment.

Derrida thinks this anterior otherness further as the givenness of language, the 'promise' or 'being-language of language' prior to our 'use' of it, a priority to what Benjamin, in his early essays on language, sees as the bourgeois, instrumental conception of language as a tool. Derrida retrieves this prior givenness of language from Heidegger's thinking of the essence (*Wesen*) of language as an original affirmation, promise, or agreement (*Zuspruch*, *Zusage*) as well as—in a, compared to the interpretation of the "Critique of Violence," much more generous reading of the early Benjamin's 'messianic'—from the notion of pure language (*reine Sprache*).[34] For Derrida, this originary affirmation of the gift and promise of language is prior to the possibility of the question, insofar as it makes the latter (which must always be linguistically formulated) possible. This affirmation—which I am not free to choose since language is there before me—is also, for Derrida, an affirmation, a (non-determinate) promise, and hence, an opening to the other. Language forces me to commit to the other on account of its own givenness as well as its structural openness to the future to come. By preceding me in its givenness so as to promise my words to a time and to effects beyond me and my control, it makes me promise to the other to respond to her or him and continue speaking. According to Derrida, the promise of language, in what Habermas would call a transcendental-pragmatic presupposition of speech, even forces me to promise to speak the truth, even if I lie, insult, or threaten the other by means of speech (*Points* 384/397f.).

This is one of the ways in which Derrida thinks the promise of repetition, which is always a promise of language, as the origin of an unchosen responsibility for the other "before any kind of freedom—in the sense of mastery" (ibid.). We might say that we contract this promise with the nameless voice of the 'absolute ancestor' (what Levinas would call God). Benjamin thinks this nameless and secret voice as an 'echo' of past voices in present ones, an echo that articulates the messianic claim of the dead on the present. For before Benjamin comes to speak of the secret agreement between the past generations and ours and the weak messianic power whose source remains unnamed by Benjamin, he writes of the promise of the past:

> The past carries with it a secret index by which it is referred to redemption. For does a breath of air which had been about the earlier ones [*die Früheren*] not brush against [*streift*] us? Is there not in voices to which we lend our ears an echo of voices now grown silent [*ein Echo von nun verstummten*]? [. . .] If that is so, then there is a secret agreement between past generations and ours, then our coming was expected on earth, and then we, like every generation before us, have been given a *weak* messianic power to which the past has a claim (Thesis II).[35]

As indicated earlier, the generation, transmission, and reception of cultural history are, for Benjamin, not only mediated by socioeconomic and political circumstances, but also by language. Here, Benjamin seems to suggest that, in a certain sense, the debt the present owes to the past, the agreement by which the past 'intends' the present to redeem it, happens in language itself. The present generation owes the possibility of speaking, of language, to the past, and indeed in such a way that language also represents a reservoir of the past, of singular events, and speakers who impressed themselves on language. For Benjamin as for Derrida, in (necessarily) affirming this debt and the prior givenness of language, we respond to the dead and 'contract' the 'secret' messianic agreement. We will come back to this notion of affirmation as an affirmation of one's necessary position as an heir, a born latecomer; for Derrida, as noted, it is also a 'nonpositive affirmation,' as he says with Foucault (WD 335n15/380n1), not of a specific future, but of the necessity *that* there be a future.[36]

In the passage from *Aporias* cited earlier, Derrida further characterizes the subject's relation to the nameless voice of originary otherness, the one that asks us to respond first of all and to promise to speak to the other, as a 'mourning' of the self for itself and for its 'death' at every instant, an "originary mourning." It is this mourning that makes an ethical opening onto the other possible: "If *Jemeinigkeit*, that of *Dasein* or that of the ego (in the common sense, the psychoanalytic sense, or Levinas's sense) is constituted in its ipseity in terms of an originary mourning, then this self-relation welcomes or supposes the other within its being-itself as different from itself."[37] Derrida thinks originary otherness as a *prévenance* (coming-before) of specters (like traditions) as well as of the spirits of the dead. Originary mourning names the subject's self-relation in difference, a relation that, at the same time, installs the other in the originary violence—violence in the sense of (a) mentioned above—that separates the self from itself—the "violence of an appeal [*appel*] from the other" (*Points* 381/395). It figures the self's movement in the future anterior, its original lateness as the delay of time itself. As indicated, this lateness, figured as an anterior alterity, implies a responsibility to heed the call of otherness.[38]

THE ABSOLUTE VICTIM

With this discussion of the relations among iterability, anterior otherness, originary violence, and responsibility, we are in a better position to confront Derrida's responsibility with Benjamin's messianic claim. How can we think a link between political responsibility in the present and the victims of history? How does Derrida respond to Benjamin's messianic claim? As noted, Derrida's originary responsibility, as developed out of a quasi-transcendental account of the constitution of identity (rather than from narrowly defined ethical or political considerations), is not (yet) responsive to specific otherness in the past, one that could be determined on the basis of historical data. Insofar as Benjamin's distinctions within a history of violence, notably between the history of victors and the tradition of the oppressed, cannot do without such data, its determination of the 'debt' owed to the past is not to be equated with Derrida's thought of an originary culpability. Likewise, Benjamin's messianic claim, if we see it as emerging with history's oppressed, will not be identical to Derrida's call, injunction, or appeal from the other—"who is not *the* other."[39] However, as we pointed out in chapter three, Benjamin's second "Thesis" does not explicitly restrict the messianic claim to the 'oppressed,' with which the rest of the "Theses" are concerned, but speaks of the "secret agreement between past generations and the present ones." There is thus an ambiguity to be negotiated here, an ambiguity that concerns the double difference between, on the one hand, an anterior otherness and past generations or the dead in general, and, on the other, between the dead in general and the oppressed.

As we have seen, Derrida's reading of Benjamin's "Theses" suggests that the secrecy of the agreement or appointment with the past as well as the weakness of the messianic force to be inherited show that the messianic force must be read in terms of the "messianic without messianism" (SM 181/96). Hence, the past's claim to redemption cannot be understood in a religious sense as promising an afterlife to all the dead in a future present. Moreover, Derrida assimilates Benjamin's messianic claim to his notion of the appeal from an originary otherness: "What Benjamin calls *Anspruch* (claim [*pre-dentin*], appeal, interpellation, address) is *not far* from what we are suggesting with the word *injunction* [*injonction*]" (SM 181/96; emphasis added). We have seen, however, that Benjamin's messianic claim, the echo of past voices in present speech, refers primarily to the call of the oppressed and the nameless whose suffering is drowned out by objectivist historicism and ideologies of progress, including a Marxism that derives the promise of history, as the promise of past generations, from the laws of history. The very critique of bourgeois cultural memory, which pays homage to a few heroes and geniuses while forgetting the nameless and the lament of the oppressed, presupposes that we differentiate between the dead and the dead. Hence, we must ask *how* far Derrida's injunction is from Benjamin's *Anspruch*.

As we have seen, Derrida's injunction, as the 'anhuman' origin of responsibility, is prior to any definite political or ethical responsibility in that it makes it possible. In contrast to Levinas, Derrida does not think this opening, and the call to responsibility, as limited to the face of the human other. As the opening of the subject to its own internal self-difference before any self-identity, the call of the other is radically anonymous, heterogeneous, 'inhuman,' and indeterminate. For Derrida, the location of the call's origin in the human other is already a secondary determination of what is originarily without determination but that—like the blind spot in future horizons, like death—can never be accessed *as such*. In Derrida's view, views such as Levinas's deny the violence of this secondary interpretation. This violence, which is ultimately inevitable but must be taken into account, reveals itself most conspicuously in the exclusion of other others from the hospitable response given to a singular other, or in the exclusion of the animal or even "the living in general."[40] Insofar as the exclusion of others is inescapable, the point is not to overcome this inevitable violence (in the sense of [b] mentioned above) but to recognize it as 'originary' in an "economy of violence" (WD 117/172). As Derrida put it in "Violence and Metaphysics:" "[W]ithin history—but is it meaningful elsewhere?—every philosophy of nonviolence can only choose the lesser violence [*la moindre violence*] within an economy of violence" (WD 313n21/136n1).

In light of Benjamin's concerns about rendering legible the violence of capitalist modernity, as a double oppression in the primary form of dispossession and exploitation as well as its subsequent foreclosure in bourgeois history, it is crucial to negotiate Derrida's insistence on the inevitable violence of defining the address of responsibility as well as the violence of all historiography. The necessity of choosing between addressees of responsibility, the anterior heterogeneity that requires us to exclude certain possibilities in favor of others, and hence make decisions that are not without violence, as well as the productivity of iteration that reconstitutes what it repeats, introduce the necessity of an originary loss at the heart of every inheritance and historical account, including those of Benjamin's critical historical materialism. The original 'crime' of every inheritance as of every responsibility is that the necessarily 'inauthentic' heir, as latecomer, must choose between the demands of conflicting specters and conflicting others, but also that repetition introduces into memory a forgetting whose responsibility appears to be without (human) addressee (though not without beneficiaries). We will now look more closely at the double bind that Derrida sees as based on an originary violence in all inheriting, and at the responsibility it implies but also obviates. The subsequent confrontation with Benjamin's notion of the history of victors will then allow us to ask about the risks of the insistence on originary violence in relation to a politics of memory.

Like Levinas, Derrida thinks the past not, as the Heidegger of *Being and Time*, as (potentially) 'my' past, but as the gift of the other to me, to the present generation. This thought, however, leads to a paradox. As a gift, a heritage requires the ingratitude of the inheritors, for gratitude would return the gift to an economy of exchange;[41] and yet, the heirs are asked to remember the singularity of the dead and acknowledge their indebtedness. The gift will never be a 'pure' gift, as we have to repeat the past and thus "respond to the dead" (SM 109/177), a response that closes the circle of exchange, thereby contaminating the purity of the gift as a gift. This paradox encapsulates Derrida's thought of the 'double bind' (SM 16/40)[42] in our relation to the tradition. While we should be grateful to those who worked for the riches of 'our' heritage and be mindful of its victims, we must also be ungrateful in order to accept the gift as a gift.

The promise of repetition tells us why, according to Derrida, we cannot evade this paradox but only negotiate it in a critical inheritance. Born latecomers, we must first of all affirm, repeat, and work through our traditions and languages; we can try to be faithful to them. But we cannot help being unfaithful because a repetition is never a repetition of the same; it is promised to an open future, which, moreover, asks us to choose between contradictory injunctions—for instance, different and even mutually exclusive concepts of responsibility, of history, and so on. The memory of the 'victims' will therefore not simply be a memory turned to the past, but will always be a memory turned toward the future, toward the promise (see *Points* 383/396). Memory, as a form of repetition in difference, will reconstitute the singularity of victims and hence go beyond them. This is why *Specters of Marx* speaks of the "the spectral anteriority of the crime" (SM 21/46), a crime that first of all consists in the paradox of repetition itself.

Derrida's politics of memory is thus always caught between the necessity of inheriting, repeating, and borrowing from one's tradition, with all the debt and faithfulness that implies, and the (transcendental and moral) necessity of going beyond that tradition. Indeed, the double reading Derrida practices in reading texts of the (largely Western and philosophical canon) attempts to negotiate this double bind *en miniature*. Double reading consists of a faithful commentary on a text, placing it in the orbit of the 'metaphysical' tradition, while at the same time opening up the text—brushing it against the grain, as Benjamin would say—so as to show how and where it escapes metaphysics in its exposure to the future. The promise of memory binds us and promises us to the otherness of a tradition and a heritage that we cannot not choose to repeat, that we must affirm blindly (SM 7/27), but to which we also cannot be entirely and strictly faithful. This is also why Derrida suggests that Benjamin's *weak* messianic force to be inherited from previous generations is weak because it names a messianic *without* messianism, where the messianic names the promise of repetition, requiring us always to go beyond the laws of history or a logic of fulfillment that messianism would espouse. Derrida's conception of memory ultimately comes to a head in the suggestion that we can remember the dead only if this memory is also, at the same time, a memory and a promise of the future that is not a future present, but a future otherness 'in' the past no less than in the present: "the past as absolute future" (SM 17/41). Only a present disjoined by the future can let the nonliving haunt the living, can give way to the heterogeneity of a *prévenance* of the other.

Hence, the promise of the future is necessarily aporetic, insofar as the future, as the inscription of the law of originary repetition, is not only opening the present to the nonpresent, but thereby also destroys, while reconstituting, the singularity of what is always already inscribed in the system of iteration. The contingency of time signifies the exposure to a future that is productive of an excessive remainder, consisting of that which inevitably remains unthought, unread or unappropriated, what Derrida calls the *restance* of any inheritance.[43] At the same time, repetition from the future is destructive in that it brings about the possibility, even the necessity, of an absolute loss. This loss has to be thought beyond a "teleological optimism" and a "politico-psychoanalytic concept of repression" according to which the unconscious of a culture "never loses a thing."[44] Derrida's reflections on the date and the proper name as privileged figures of memory try to take this precariousness and finitude of memory into account. A memory of the name, which Derrida proposes at times (e.g., FL 1042), might be seen as an adequate response to Benjamin's concern with the 'nameless' of history, but Derrida insists that the names are not available and that a name immediately withdraws the singularity it keeps: It is effaced in the system of language that preserves it. Likewise, as Derrida argues in *Shibboleth*, the openness of a date to the future is its readability and repeatability by everyone, by a public structure like the calendar. But this structure also effaces the singularity we try to remember by dating an event, and threatens it with its complete erasure.

We pointed out that the memorial response to the fate of the nameless victims of history cannot merely consist in a more inclusive memory, in widening the scope of 'our' heritage. This is why Derrida radicalizes the figure of the victim by speaking of the "absolute victim" who is always already erased as a victim and reduced to 'ashes,' remaining unidentifiable in the history of survivors: "One of the meanings of what is called a victim (a victim of anything or anyone whatsoever) is precisely to be erased in its meaning as victim. The absolute victim is a victim who cannot even protest. One cannot even identify the victim *as* victim. [. . .] He or she is totally excluded or covered over by language, annihilated by history, a victim one cannot identify" (*Points* 389/403).

Like the growing ashes of a burning cigarette, time leaves traces of its passage, of transitoriness. Ashes and cinders are traces that keep what they point to only in the form of annihilation.[45] Derrida's concept of 'cinders' is designed to stand in for what is lost due to originary repetition, namely, the very disappearance of the witness, the "destruction of memory" (ibid.). It is a concept that, beyond the redressable violence of more or less self-serving exclusion and foreclosure, and in a hopeless paradox, tries to "make the absolute destruction reappear" (*Points* 390/404), that is, it attempts to reveal originary loss as inescapable. Repetition "carries forgetting into memory," and we are asked to keep to "the memory of forgetting itself,"[46] a memory, ultimately, of the future to come. To 'save the name' (*sauf le nom*) of the victim is thus always a double-sided, and hence perilous, undertaking, insofar as the very inscription of the name irretrievably loses what it wishes to retain—in the very act of retaining it (OG 112/164f.).[47]

It should be clear here that Derrida's insistence on the inevitability of victimization in all historical representation, on the absoluteness of the victim, draws at least some of its plausibility from a focus on the singularity of the victim. It is this singularity that cannot but be deconstructed, that is erased and reconstituted, in historiography. An originary violence in history and inheritance is tied to the ineradicable finitude of human life, a finitude that becomes the very source of responsibly acting in the present. I indicated earlier that Benjamin resists a generalization of the guilt of the survivor and the dehistoricization of the historical relation. Such generalization, as perhaps to be found in Levinas, would disallow a close link between responsibility in the present and concrete violence in the past. Hence, it might demotivate resistance to contemporary rule, a resistance that is motivated by, and at the same time generates, the rewriting of history in the name of its oppressed. In the remainder of this last chapter, I want to ask about the link Derrida allows between the origin of responsibility and the doubly oppressed of Western modernity in the face of Benjamin's challenge. Let us then turn again to Derrida's notion of originary responsibility.

WHY DERRIDA'S INJUNCTION NEEDS BENJAMIN'S CLAIM

Since the promise of repetition makes possible responsive-responsible subjects in the first place, including collective subjects such as Marx's proletariat or Benjamin's working class, an affirmation of emancipatory historical subjects must also affirm the open-endedness of repetition, and that means the impossibility of ever constituting the subject once and for all. The originary violence of the promise of repetition that we have to affirm, however, also opens up the subject to an originary responsibility. This responsibility, as I have indicated, refers to the fact that subjects owe their constitution to processes that will always already have installed a nontransparent otherness within them. Such otherness implies a relation to language, history, and ancestors that can never be shaken off, but inscribes the very condition of responsibly relating to others, and thus of more concrete concepts of ethical and political responsibility. Responsiveness to the dead in Derrida, the *Schuld* of this responsibility, thus does not (yet) refer to a particular debt owed to determinate human beings, dead or alive. Rather than a particular guilt or debt, it names the "possibility of being guilty, a liability or imputability" (*Points* 275/289f.). While Derrida, as demonstrated, agrees with Benjamin that the origin of the call to responsibility cannot be located beyond the history of violence thus totalized, but originates from 'within' it, he nonetheless views this call as a quasi-transcendental condition, that is, as logically prior to any determinable debt and to determinate 'victims.' To suggest a productive oscillation between Derrida's and Benjamin's account of responsibility and its link to the dead, it is necessary to recall that quasi-transcendental conditions are not isolated, or even definitively separable, from what they make possible, and therefore not only allow, but demand their translation into the concrete contexts and histories one inhabits.

It is noticeable that a number of 'originary' concepts that Derrida introduces in discussing ethical and political relations have a direct relationship to quasi-transcendental concepts such as *différance*, iterability, and historicity. These concepts are then, at least provisionally, contrasted with what they make possible. So originary violence or 'arché-violence,' as the loss of self-presence brought about by differential iterability and exposure to the future to come, is said to make empirical moral and political violence possible (OG 112/164f.). Similarly, what I called responsiveness, as the installing of relations to otherness in the very act of constituting subjects, is said to be at the root of 'moral, juridical, and political' responsibility. Openness to the messianic future names the very possibility of responsibility for others inasmuch as the exposure of subjects to open-ended repetition will always already have opened them for the reception of an injunction from what is other than the subject. Furthermore, Derrida's quasi-transcendental operation appears to require distinctions between the debt owed to the anonymous identity-constituting structures and concrete debts to specific others and traditions. As we have seen, Derrida also speaks of the 'absolute victim' forgotten due to iterability and the victim of more or less redressable foreclosure, as well as of an 'originary mourning' for inevitable loss and mourning for a concrete, perhaps ultimately avoidable loss.

However, we should recall that one of the structural features of Derrida's quasi-transcendental arguments is precisely the impossibility of isolating the transcendental from the empirical once and for all. I argued that conditions such as iterability and *différance* are not separable from their effects: Repetition cannot be thought apart from the terms it repeats, difference is nothing apart from the elements it keeps distinct, and historicity is nothing apart from concrete histories. Historicity precisely names the ineluctability of transcendental thought's immersion in historical contexts: this is why, as we saw, the thought of historicity requires a thought of the history of historicity. Thus, while we can and must distinguish between the condition and conditioned, the distinction is not to be viewed as isolating two inviolable levels from one another. What this means, in the present context, is that Derrida's concept of originary responsibility not only allows, but demands, its articulation with the more concrete moral and political concepts of responsibility of which Derrida speaks. With regard to history and its victims, Benjamin's link between the responsibility of historians as well as political actors and the oppressed of history presents such an articulation, indeed a politically necessary and promising one. At the same time, however, this articulation or translation requires us to distinguish, always in a provisional way, between the originary level of violence and victimization and the historiographical violence of a foreclosure and forgetting that benefits contemporary oppression, and may be challenged.

So while the quasi-transcendental element in Derrida's originary responsibility might be seen to call for and harmonize with Benjamin's messianic claim, the former also remains distant from the latter on other grounds. As

we have seen, Benjamin insists on making readable the violence that constructs a dominant history or culture, a domination that must be broken in
order to open oneself to the messianic claim. If we merely equate Benjamin's
'claim' with Derrida's 'injunction,' this opening has always already been
effected by the inevitable paradox of iterability itself. There is thus no need
to first resist or interrupt the present relations of power in order to free the
claim of the past upon us. This is not to say that the call cannot be, or is not
always, dissimulated, covered up, or disavowed. But the messianic claim as
what Derrida, in *Specters of Marx*, calls an injunction, has always already
reached us and opened us. Hence, if we follow Derrida's reading of Benjamin's
"Theses," the messianic claim cannot be limited to the 'victims' of a determinate history and a determinate construction of the past that removes the
lament, claims, and promises of the "oppressed past" (Thesis XVII). The victim in question, as indicated, must for Derrida be thought as the 'absolute victim' absolved from such determinations, while the address or injunction
issues from the 'absolute ancestor.'

Thus, from Derrida's perspective, restricting the reception of the call to
certain kinds of political action and certain subjects is itself the result of a
violent and secondary (yet inevitably necessary) interpretation, just like Levinas's restriction of the call to the human face. As Derrida argues, "the origin
of the call [. . .] comes from nowhere, an origin in any case that is not yet a
divine or human 'subject'" (*Points* 276/290). We would thus have to say that
Benjamin's messianic claim, if we understand it as originating with the dead
and oppressed of history—with "the slain" or the "enslaved ancestors" (Thesis XII)—is a specific interpretation or translation of Derrida's originary otherness. At the same time, as Derrida is well aware, the violence of such a secondary interpretation is unavoidable (OG 112/164f.). Is there not also a
certain degree of violence in interpreting Benjamin's claim as the condition
of all responsibility, in its link to an anterior otherness and an inevitable violence that appears to thwart Benjamin's efforts? Derrida chooses to read Benjamin's weak messianic force as indicating an originary responsibility issued
in an absolute past and yet (dis)continuously emerging from within history
or, rather, out of the originary opening of history. Given, however, that such
an originary call to responsibility cannot be removed from history and be simply opposed to it; given that, as Derrida's quasi-transcendental historicity
shows, we always find ourselves in a specific history attended by specific violence, would we not have to say that the originary opening always appears as
attached to the specificities of history? Is not Benjamin's ambiguity—which
does not decide whether the messianic claim of past generations originates
with human finitude and past generations in general or with the oppressed of
a specific history, the history of capitalist modernity and its violent dissimulation in bourgeois canons of culture—ultimately a necessary, at least a productive ambiguity?

This question gains its significance from the following consideration. If the originary responsibility cannot be opposed to anything we might call history, as in Levinas, but can only be activated, so to speak, from within it so as to exceed it, then it must appear in a given heritage, memory, and history. Since Derrida argues "that the *being* of what we are *is* first of all inheritance" (SM 54/94), there is the danger that we are asked to affirm a *particular* heritage, and not just the fact that we must always, in general, inherit, remember, and repeat a given heritage. As Benjamin has warned us, however, a particular heritage, here capitalist history and its canons of culture, is a construction in danger of disavowing its very constructedness as well as the 'barbarism,' the 'toil of the nameless,' on which it is founded. One might think that in this thought of an originary affirmation, Derrida asks us to affirm a particular canon, a given inheritance whose barbarism is dissimulated in its appearance.

If originary responsibility appears only in, not beyond, a finite history, and if the ineluctable affirmation of this origin or anterior otherness, as the promise of the future and of language, has to be more than a faithful, traditionalist affirmation of inherited languages, canons, and dominant hegemonic discourses of the past, it must affirm what is oppressed and forgotten by these canons above all. Thus, as Benjamin showed, the barbarism must be made legible from within history, and even *as* the history of the modern West. Derrida's reading of the messianic call, his notion of an originary otherness prior to a codified duty or debt, cannot be cut off from the resounding of the call originating with the oppressed and slain, but demands its articulation with the latter. The affirmation of an originary otherness must be translated into the affirmation of what Benjamin simply, perhaps too simply, calls an oppressed past. In this way, Benjamin's ambiguity, rendered legible by Derrida's reading of the messianic claim of the past on the present as an originary injunction, turns into a productive oscillation between two senses of responsibility, two senses of memory. On the one hand, for the inheritors and, in varying degrees, for the victims and beneficiaries of the history of capitalist modernity, the memory of the promise must first of all issue in the 'fight for the oppressed past,' both in political praxis and within and against the hegemonic discourses that establish the canons and script the way most people understand the past. On the other hand, the originary otherness, as the thought of an uncircumventable originary violence of exclusion, reminds us that there will always be an oppressed past and that no final day of redemption will ever be available. The productive oscillation moves between an originary violence and the unnecessary, redressable violence of foreclosure and exclusion that fortifies presently unjust institutions. In this way, the productive oscillation I am sketching here negotiates what Derrida calls the double bind of any inheritance.

Derrida gives little consideration to the link in Benjamin's "Theses" between the messianic call and history's oppressed. He does not call for a responsible memory of the barbarism Benjamin addresses. And yet the notion of responsiveness or originary responsibility needs a more concrete concept of responsible ethical and political action, such as the one Benjamin names in the claim of past generations—especially those whose oblivion in the present repeats their oppression in the past—on the present, and which he elaborates in terms of the materialist writing of history and a memorial resistance (for which he, in his time, suggested the nonpositional general strike). Derrida's responsiveness cannot avoid this translation or articulation. As indicated, the "blind submission" or "first obedience" to the "secret" of "absolute anteriority" (SM 7/27) must avoid the conflation of such anterior otherness, as the 'spectral anteriority of a crime,' with inherited canons and their redressably violent exclusions. Likewise, originary violence is not be confused with, or easily translated into, the exclusions and dissimulations that allow untainted national or individual identities, and justify contemporary rulers and beneficiaries of past oppression. In recent writings, especially in *The Politics of Friendship*, Derrida precisely attempts to translate originary responsibility into, for instance, the more concrete demand for the hospitality of nations toward the stranger, the immigrant, and the asylum-seekers, and demands recognition for the exclusion of the 'sister' from political friendship in general and democratic fraternity in particular. If the very 'anessence' of the political is at stake in the responsiveness to the ghosts of the dead,[48] the repetitive construction of political identity and the porousness of a nation's borders as well as the openness of democratic social relations demand, first and foremost, the memory of those among the dead whose secondary, historiographical oppression permitted, and continues to permit, untainted identities and fixed borders. There can be no democratization without the recognition of past violence.

While we must thus distinguish between the traditionalist affirmation of the past for the sake of untainted identities and originary responsiveness, such distinction, as I pointed out, cannot simply fall back on the empirico-transcendental difference. Insofar as Derrida's responsiveness names the ineluctable fact that subjects, as part and parcel of their constitution, have always already responded to and affirmed an anterior or spectral otherness as the source of responsibility, such otherness never appears as such, but is always mediated by the concretion of languages, politico-legal institutions, histories, and traditions. Given the history of capitalist modernity, the response of its inheritors must come to terms with the preventable social, political, and economic violence with which it is afflicted. If, then, the response that has always already occurred, and continues to be reproduced, is to deserve the name of ethical and political responsibility, Benjamin's materialist historiography seems inescapable as it is poised to retrieve the voice of the nameless against the irresponsible submission to, or affirmation of, dominant identities, institutions, and values.

Lastly, Derrida's originary responsibility requires Benjamin's more specific claim of the dead due to its insufficiency on more strictly normative grounds (although Benjamin's claim is not absorbed by such grounds either, especially not if we contrast 'moral' discourses of justice with 'ethical' discourses concerning a community's inevitably historical self-understanding). As Derrida himself points out, originary responsibility, as a constitutive openness, names the condition of possibility of more concrete moral and political responsibilities. But, as Ernesto Laclau, for one, has argued, if constitutive openness has to be affirmed as it makes subjects possible, no ethical injunction to cultivate that openness follows without further arguments of a normative kind.[49] I have argued elsewhere that the quasi-transcendental argument by itself does not permit Derrida to translate the responsiveness of constitutive openness into the more concrete ethico-political injunctions in favor of a democracy to come, for example. This is so because the quasi-transcendental argument puts into doubt the logic of noncontradiction that would be needed to ask subjects to follow through on those obligations that appear logically derived from what makes subjects possible, on pain of contradictions. From the fact that subjects are always already indebted, and have always already responded, as their condition of possibility, to an anterior otherness, no ethical injunction to cultivate this otherness and to recognize the debt need to follow.[50] For these reasons, I suggest that Benjamin's memory of the oppressed of capitalist modernity be regarded as a necessary contribution to Derrida's insistence on the memory of specters, especially in light of the political responsibility that follows from Benjamin's considerations. Since originary responsibility is not yet responsibility in the face of capitalist modernity, Benjamin's claim is needed to allow a deconstructive affirmation of the "emancipatory promise" (SM 59/102).

WHY BENJAMIN'S CLAIM NEEDS DERRIDA'S INJUNCTION

Derrida, however, may be said to recognize the necessity of such a productive oscillation between the memory of the oppressed wrested from an oppressive canon, and a memory of originary responsibility. Given the anterior alterity and heterogeneity of every inheritance—and it is this heterogeneity, not a particular canonical inheritance that we must affirm—Derrida cannot be said to simply affirm the specific violence of the construction of a canonical cultural memory, although this misunderstanding of the deconstructive affirmation is always possible. This is why, as we saw, Derrida speaks of a "(nonpositive) affirmation" that does not affirm a given gift that could be described in positive terms (*Points* 357/368; WD 335n15/380n1). Nor does Derrida's quasi-transcendental procedure, as I showed in chapter two, seek to extricate itself from the complicity with metaphysics in which those engage who, in a paradoxical movement, totalize history as the history of totalizing violence, as has been argued.[51] I will return briefly to the contribution of Derrida's memory of forgetting, the forgetting that cannot be avoided, to the productive oscillation I am sketching here.

Nonetheless, as I stressed throughout, the perils of Derrida's insistence on originary loss and the "unreadability of violence" (FL 993), on the ultimate opacity of history, may not be taken lightly. In the face of such unreadability, Benjamin's attempts to render violence readable, by remembering past violence and struggle against its effects on the present, might appear futile from the beginning. This futility will be felt especially in a melancholic mind that surrenders to the powers that be, confusing them with the power of time and finitude itself. Benjamin's attempt to make legible, partly for motivational purposes, the violence of oppression in the past as well as the violence of suppressing its memory, runs up against Derrida's insistence that the latter violence is, at least to some extent, inevitable. The field of what is to be remembered is too large, a decision in favor of one construction of memory leaves out another, as the inevitable constitution of identity—for example, the identity of resisting subjects—cannot do without exclusions, and differential repetition cannot help recontextualizing and altering what it maintains in repetition. For this reason, I have called for always renegotiable and precarious distinctions between originary violence and the violence of ideological exclusions and oppressions that help maintain present institutions. For political reasons, the distinction must always remain renegotiable, as it is part of emancipatory movements to redefine violence, to gain social recognition of practices as violent that might not have been seen as violent before. As Benjamin argued in "On the Critique of Violence," existing definitions of violence, insofar as they are legally codified, need to be challenged as to their justification of violent means by reference to just ends. As Benjamin shows in conjunction with Marx's account of primitive accumulation, the claim to legal justice of modern constitutional states in particular can be exposed as resting on the violence of law imposition, especially if they institute and defend property rights of productive capital.

The distinction between the violent exclusion of the voice of the nameless and the inevitable erasure of the name will always be fragile, although Derrida is certainly aware of this distinction's necessity as he recognizes, as I showed in chapter two, the need for horizons of change. For apart from the unreadability of the past produced by arché-writing, generating the absolute victim, he discusses another violence:

> But there is also the unreadability that stems from the violence of foreclosure, exclusion, all of history being a conflictual field of forces in which it is a matter of making unreadable, excluding, of positing by excluding, or imposing a dominant force by excluding, that is to say, not only by marginalizing, by setting aside the victim, but also by doing so in such a way that no trace remains of the victims (*Points* 389/403).

What remains too disarticulate in this discourse on an originary forgetting is the relationship between, on the one hand, the politics of forgetting Benjamin elaborates—a system of explanations and narratives that repress a second time the tradition of the oppressed, and thereby fortify the present—and, on the other, the inevitability of originary loss that makes Derrida move, by way of the 'but' that emphasizes the posterior conjunct, from the Shoah as "the hell of our memory" to the "holocaust for every date, and somewhere in the world at every hour."[52]

The productive oscillation that seeks to combine Benjamin's memorial resistance against bourgeois canons with Derrida's originary responsibility as an originary violence, again proves necessary here. Before we give in to the melancholic attitude that succumbs to the mere flow of time, to the ticking of the seconds that Benjamin criticized in Baudelaire, we must ask ourselves to what extent a certain forgetting and exclusion serves the interests of domination and what canon it constructs. However, we also need to be aware that such a forgetting can never be entirely overcome, that indeed the very insistence on a tradition of the oppressed and on the distinction between the oppressors and the oppressed, also amounts to an interpretive construction. Such a construction is not entirely without violence, but is invested with power in the conflictual field of history.

The merit of Derrida's insistence on originary loss further consists in guarding against the naive faith in the possibility of saving loss; it points at originary violence, the forgetting that is part of finitude itself, and a condition of life, as Nietzsche argued. The suggestion is that it is better to acquiesce to it than to believe in its ultimate overcoming—a faith that, as Derrida argued against Marx, is always in danger of forgetting the spirits of the dead in the attempt to rid us of all ideologies. Aiming at the 'end of the spectral' might confuse it with the 'end of the political' as the end of violence, where what is at issue is precisely the (re)politicization of specters as well as the past violence they stand for and the politically necessary distinctions among them. Moreover, as we have seen, the thought of originary loss points out the impossibility of singling out a unique subject of memory, the privileged receiver of the messianic call, in whose interiority the dead are enclosed. It guards us against the belief in a good conscience, in the nonviolent memory of the 'victims' in their purity. Benjamin's subject on the receiving end of the messianic claim must always worry about (ab)using the claim, and the suffering of the oppressed, for its own purposes.

Furthermore, one might wonder whether the unrepresentability of the singular self, and the unreadability of violence on which Derrida insists, does not register a sense of absolute loss that might be downplayed in Benjamin's preoccupation with rescuing the voice of the nameless and the successful and responsible reception of the messianic claim or address of the dead. If the oppressed are nameless, does not their very namelessness indicate an impossibility of remembering them, at least in their singularity? We saw in chapter three that Benjamin indeed criticizes law, and by extension a history of law-imposing power, not only to allow for the proletarian strike, but also in the name of singularity. Especially if we do not commit ourselves without reservation to a new historical epoch devoid of enforceable law, must we then not admit that Derrida's absolute victim also points out the danger of losing or forgetting nameless singularity in the very act of naming it? Would the tradition of the oppressed not also be in danger of forgetting the nameless in the very act of representing them? And is the debt the present owes to the past not always excessive, ultimately beyond return or adequate response?

It is in the recognition of absolute loss, the deferral of justice to a future to come, and the consequent negation of a good conscience that Derrida's quasi-transcendental open-endedness of the future, in its link to the originary violence of the promise of repetition, appears necessary to Benjamin's strategies. If it is important to these strategies, as we saw in the first chapter, that history, in its richness of layers, remain interpretable against overly scientific attempts to represent it the way it really was, the open-ended future of repetition demonstrates the ineluctability of such infinite reinterpretability and recontextualizability. But the future to come then also shows that distinctions between originary and redressable violence as well as between the oppressed and the victors must remain renegotiable. As Derrida's call for a 'democracy to come' indicates, the insistence on originary violence and the openness of the future *can* support a space in which differing accounts of history are permitted to democratically contest one another, so as to reject the idea of a final closure of the past: History will not finally crystallize into the one true account, but will remain open to different interpretations, thus allowing the challenge of dominant conceptions of history in favor of the tradition of the oppressed.

At the same time, it is necessary to remember that the usual means of democratic negotiation, from institutionalized, parliamentary law-making to voting, are constrained by the history of past violence, especially what I called the instituting violence of capitalism. The so-called primitive accumulation, in which modern state apparatuses, as Marx recounts, played a crucial role, leads from the initial physically direct and state-organized violence to the "silent compulsion of economic relations" (*Capital* 899). Due to the resulting unequal distribution of productive assets up to this day, this compulsion severely circumscribes the choices democratic law-makers and citizens faced with capital flight have. Articulating originary responsiveness with the claim of history's oppressed thus also suggests that Derrida's *"la democratie à venir"* be supplemented with democratic projections that take into account the workings of economic violence, and thus help us to remember the victims of its institution—for example, the various models of market socialism, as versions of the Kantian Marxism whose compatibility with Derrida's messianic future we emphasized in chapter two.

The double strategy or productive oscillation I am sketching here, then, broaches the same difficulty that I treated at the end of the second chapter, only this time—if it may be permitted to distinguish what the promise of memory presents as intimately connected—from the side of the past, rather than the future. There, I argued that Derrida's memory of specters, the attempt to learn to live with ghosts, requires always renegotiable distinctions between good and bad specters. For this reason, I distinguished between the postutopian future of the promise of repetition and the projection of non-teleological, nonprogressivist horizons of social change, and argued for the possibility and desirability of the combination of both perspectives. While the former prevents the dogmatism of the latter and keeps it open for demo-cratic criticism, emancipatory horizons give concretion to the desire for change and allow us to forsake some specters in favor of others. Here, with regard to the origin of responsibility and the question of violence, the same productive oscillation asks us to recognize, on the one hand, the revisability and criticizability of definitions of violence as well as the originary forgetting in all memory, and, on the other, to insist on politically salient distinctions among the dead between the oppressed and the victors in order to remember and reinterpret the exclusions, epics, and constructions that fortify and jus-tify present and future injustice. The struggle against such injustice—despite Benjamin's opposition to Kantian ideals or utopias (unless they be wildly speculative), an opposition I have exposed, in chapter three, as too radical—cannot dispense with futural horizons, while such horizons need to be aware of their own exclusions and recontextualizability.

If the future to come, then, exposes the violence and fragility of pro-jected horizons, originary violence deconstructs the exclusivity and good conscience of the subject inheriting the messianic claim. Derrida's thought of originary loss places the 'memory of the nameless' in a double bind according to which the inheritance of the promise of the future also signals the absoluteness of the victim ab-solving herself from memory. The contradiction in the contradictory injunction would consist in the fact that we both have to attempt to faithfully remember the oppressed, and be open to the differ-ential repetition from a future that cannot help reconstituting the oppressed in light of present concerns. This is the contradiction that no latecomer can avoid and, due to the delay of time itself, we are all latecomers, coming after a history of violence. As we have seen, for Benjamin, this essential belated-ness of the present means that the "spark of hope can only be fanned," that is, the promise of the past accepted, with the awareness that "the dead will not be safe from the enemy if he wins" (Thesis VI). But this lateness is also productive of a true gift, generating an unanticipatable promise out of itself.

For the paradox of repetition, as an originary violence, implies that there is indeed a true gift in every heritage. What Derrida names the excessive remainder or *restance* of a tradition, what remains incalculable or "irreceivable" (*irrecevable*; *Points* 17/24) in the past, is precisely what cannot be given by the past, for it does not possess it: Those rereadings, interpretations, and uses of what is handed down that could not be anticipated or foreseen, slipping through the blind spot in the future of a tradition. *Restance* names what in a tradition is open to the promise of the future beyond anticipation. As a judge also has to be unfaithful to the letter of the law in order to be just, so inheritors have to be unfaithful to the past in order to truly receive its gift, and hence be faithful to it. In a certain sense, the unfaithfulness of the inheritors and latecomers, the very violence they cannot but help commit against a tradition, makes the gift possible. This is why Derrida could write that a tradition "will always keep its secret" (SM 93/153), a secret exposed to the *indirection destinerrante* of an open future.[53] It is this nonpositive, indeterminate secret that names the promise of memory and, as the fourth "Thesis" tells us, allows us to "challenge every victory, past and present."

Notes

EXORDIUM

1. Celan, *Poems*, 140ff. For a detailed commentary upon "Engführung," see Szondi.

2. See Hatley. For Levinas's affirmation of Celan, reading his poetry as exemplary for a "saying without a said," see Emmanuel Levinas, "Paul Celan: From Being to the Other."

3. Jacques Derrida, "Shibboleth. For Paul Celan" 50, 38, and passim.

4. Dennis Schmidt has pointed out that Celan had to invent his own calendar. See his "Black Milk and Blue."

5. See Benjamin, Thesis XIV. Celan almost certainly knew this text, as he refers to Benjamin on a number of occasions. His "In One" presents precisely the constellation that Benjamin had called for in the "Theses."

6. Celan, *Poems*, 210ff. A few words on the historical references in the poem are in order. "February 13," written in Austrian dialect ("Feber"), recalls the general strike of the Viennese workers against the Austro-fascist regime on that date in 1934. "Peuple de Paris" was the headline of the calls of the Paris communards to the people of Paris in 1871. *"No pasaràn,"* literally "They will not pass," the battle cry of the largely anarchist Republicans in the Spanish Civil War of 1936 against Franco's fascist troops, fighting a crucial battle near Huesco. "Abadias" names an old Spanish revolutionary who lived in French exile and whom Celan knew personally. In 1917, shots from the cruiser *Aurora* on the Tsarist palace in St. Petersburg opened the October Revolution.

7. Celan, "Der Meridian," 135.

INTRODUCTION

1. In their detailed study of U.S. media in particular, Edward S. Herman and Noam Chomsky note that the distinction between "worthy" and "unworthy" victims

contributes to the formation of propaganda in favor of class inequalities and the political and economic elites in Western countries. See their *Manufacturing Consent*, xixff.; 37ff.

2. See, for example, the classic study of postwar Germany from the late 1960s, Mitscherlich, *Die Unfähigkeit zu Trauern*; for more recent claims along similar lines, see Nassehi, Weber, *Tod, Modernität und Gesellschaft*.

3. For an overview, see Kevin Avruch and Beatriz Vejarano, "Truth and Reconciliation Commissions: A Review Essay and Annotated Bibliography."

4. See, for example, Louis Pojman, "The Moral Status of Affirmative Action," 183, and Thomas Hill, "The Message of Affirmative Action." Hill argues that both deontological backward-looking arguments and utilitarian forward-looking arguments send the wrong message, so that a different conception of the relation between normative value and time is required. He finds these different values in cross-time wholes, such as Alasdair MacIntyre's value of the narrative unity of a life instead of valuing different moments in isolation. While I agree that the opposition between the past and the future needs to be overcome, I will put into question the temporal unity and unified national identity on the basis of which Hill makes his case. Both of these contribute to the notion of moral progress and the exclusion of voices of suffering from a national past that precisely stands in need of challenge.

5. See, for example, Hans Blumenberg's investigation into the logic of epochality arising with modernity. Blumenberg argues that modernity is the first epoch to understand itself as an epoch, thereby depriving itself of the possibility to legitimize itself by recourse to tradition. "Modernity [*Neuzeit*] was the first and only age that understood itself as an epoch and, in so doing, simultaneously created the other epochs." He continues to note that the problem of legitimacy lies in modernity's "claim to carry out a radical break with tradition, and in the incongruity between this claim and the reality of history, which can never begin entirely anew." Hans Blumenberg, *The Legitimacy of the Modern Age*, 116.

6. Courtois (ed.), *Livre Noir du Communisme*. With its central claim that communism ravaged Europe more than fascism because it produced more victims, this book created quite a stir in European countries faced with the aftermath of a century of totalitarian violence. The subsequent popularity of 'black books'—whose most important claims come in numbers—confirms the trend to quantify and compare. One might here also think of the debate between historians about the number of the victims of the British slave trade, figured variously between eight and twenty million.

7. See Przeworski, "Material Bases of Consent" in his *Capitalism and Social Democracy*. See also Przeworski and Wallerstein, "Structural Dependence of the State on Capital"; Dryzek, *Democracy in Capitalist Times*, 24ff.

8. Of course, one might always worry that images of past oppression lead to a melancholic or even cynical failure of nerve, rather than to a motivation for struggle. In my experience, however, one should not underestimate the role of such images in cultivating sensibilities for oppression and motivating resistance. Where normative arguments regarding, for example, the crucial question of property rights, fail—partly because such arguments abstract from history, or, as in the case of Nozick, greatly

underestimate the extent of past oppression—recounting the largely neglected history of oppression is often radically effective. Social science can provide us with some empirical confirmation of this view: in the United States, for example, white people generally do not connect their personal biography and family genealogy with 'history' at large, whereas nonwhites do, thereby building a community in connecting with a history of oppression, turning it into what Roy Rosenzweig and David Thelen have called a microcosm of history reminiscent of Benjamin's "monad" (Thesis XVII). Their reasonably extensive survey of 'popular uses of history' in the United States revealed the following: "White respondents rarely spoke about their family history as a microcosm of the history of the nation, their region, their local community, or their ethnic group, but black respondents often described their family history as an exemplar of the black experience in America. The black Americans we interviewed tended to blur the 'I' and the 'we.'" Rosenzweig, Thelen, *Presence of the Past*, 150. See also the review of this book and related literature in Michael Kammen, "Carl Becker Redivivus."

9. In his publication of the "Theses on Feuerbach" after Marx's death, Engels added the "but" to the eleventh thesis that opposes interpretation and change. In Marx's manuscript version, it reads: "The philosophers have only interpreted the world in various ways; the point is to change it" (Marx and Engels, *The German Ideology*, 617).

CHAPTER ONE. BENJAMIN'S READING OF MARX

1. See Löwith, *Weltgeschichte*. Löwith sees it as his task to "detect the root of the *Communist Manifesto* in Jewish messianism and propheticism" (*Weltgeschichte*, 49). Perhaps unwittingly, he thus inaugurated a tendency, especially prevalent in a postwar West Germany that had to establish its identity vis-à-vis communist East Germany, to dismiss communism as the attempt to realize a religious, transcendent idea. Ernst Nolte, primary "revisionist" participant in the German *Historikerstreit* of the 1980s, can be seen as a late offshoot of a tendency that ends up using the reference to an institutionalized messianism to explain—and justify—fascist violence in Germany and Italy. This background might help us to assess what I called the opportunity provided by the events of 1989: They sever the link between institutionalization and messianic inspiration, giving us the chance to reread and inherit the messianic promise anew. It is for this reason that one might suggest a return to those "Western Marxists" who, according to Michael Theunissen, became aware of "the affinity between radical eschatology and theory becoming practice" (Theunissen, 356). Theunissen mentions Bloch, Benjamin, Adorno, Horkheimer, Marcuse, and Lukács in this context. Derrida, apart from his more detailed readings of Benjamin, has tried to read this "tradition" under the sign of a "Jewish Kant" by focusing on Rosenzweig and Cohen. See "Interpretations at War."

2. See the discussion of the question "Materialism or Messianism" in Bulthaupt (ed.); see also the discussions following the 'leftist' critique of Adorno's interpretation of Benjamin in *Alternative* (1967/1968), and in Unseld (ed.).

3. See de Man, "Conclusions" and Derrida's reading of Benjamin in "Des Tours de Babel."

4. Perhaps the best case in point is Anselm Haverkamp's interpretation of Benjamin's concept of the dialectical image, an interpretation that attempts to submerge the image into a deconstructive theory of language in order then to explicitly denounce the political import of the image ("Notes on the 'Dialectical Image").

5. See, for example, Eagleton, *Walter Benjamin*, and the response by Bennington, "Demanding History." See also the special issues and special sections on Walter Benjamin in *New German Critique* 34 (Winter 1985) and 39 (Fall 1986). In my view, neither the defensive Marxist strategy nor the postmodern appropriation, basing itself on Benjamin's literary strategies (ironic detotalization, allegorical destruction, quotation and allusion, etc.) championed by the so-called postmodern turn, contribute to an understanding of Benjamin's relation to Marx, and they do not help to bring about the necessary complications of the opposition between modernity and postmodernity.

6. Following Derrida's negotiation of Marx (see chapter two), this apparent ambivalence on Benjamin's part toward Marx could be seen as his attempt to maintain the critical spirit of Marx and uncover more fruitful ways of reading his texts. Nonetheless, the ambivalence frustrates commentators like Rolf Tiedemann, in an essay whose very title announces an opposition that is in question here. He writes in response to "Thesis XIV," which speaks of the dialectical "leap under the open sky of history as which Marx understood the revolution": "*this* was not how Marx imagined the conclusion to the pre-history of human society. . . . But this leap is not dialectical, nor is it how Marx understood the revolution" (Tiedemann, "Historical Materialism," 200f.).

7. Marx, *Contribution*, 22.

8. Koselleck has shown that 'history' comes to be seen as available (*verfügbar*) to human action at the moment, which he situates around 1780, that it assumes the form of the collective singular. See Koselleck, 264ff.

9. Marx, "The Eighteenth Brumaire," 146.

10. Marx, "The Eighteenth Brumaire," 149.

11. Marx, *Marx–Engels Reader*, 15. The reference to a 'cheerful' (*heiter*) parting with the past is from the *Contribution to the Critique of Hegel's* Philosophy of Right, written in the same year (1843), in a passage that anticipates the later and more famous opening of the "Eighteenth Brumaire": "The modern *ancien régime* is the comedian of a world order whose *real heroes* are dead. History is thorough, and it goes through many stages when it conducts an ancient formation to the grave. [. . .] Why should history proceed in this way? So that mankind shall separate itself *gladly* [heiter] from its past" (*Marx–Engels Reader*, 57). Today, this sense of cheerfulness seems more reminiscent of Nietzsche (see *The Gay Science*, section 343) than of Marx, but it is by way of the latter that it has left a strong imprint on Benjamin's relation to the past (see V 583).

12. Marx, "The Eighteenth Brumaire," 146. This is why Ricoeur, in his analysis of the Enlightenment theme of the 'mastery of history,' can refer to Marx as the critic of the idea of humanity as the agent of its own history, insofar as he, perhaps most explicitly in the sentences preceding the ones previously quoted, insists on the circumstantial and thus thoroughly historical nature of human action. See Ricoeur, 213.

13. Rancière, "Archaeomo dern Turn," 30. Rancière's work over the last thirty years not only agrees with Benjamin's critique of Marxism's neglect of history's oppressed, but also with the concern for the 'voice of the nameless' as those who, in the past as well as in the present, are hindered in their symbolic enrollment in political representation. Consequently, politics is said to consist in the inexorable struggle of the speechless for speech (see his *Disagreement* as well as *The Nights of Labor* and *The Names of History*).

14. In times when many are competing for victim status, it is significant that Benjamin refuses to use the language of victims, despite the fact that he speaks of what might be its antonym, namely the "victors" of history (see Thesis VII). Indeed, Benjamin seems to go to great lengths to avoid this language, and instead speaks of those who engaged in "nameless toil" (Thesis VII), "the oppressed" (VIII), "enslaved [*geknechteten*] ancestors" (XII), "generations of the defeated [*Geschlagener*]" (XII), and, at one point in the "Theses," simply of "past generations" (II). This might not be so surprising if we keep in mind Benjamin's overall strategy, especially in the "Theses": memory of past violence is not motivated by the 'melancholy' that commentators, beginning with his friend Scholem, often attribute to him, but by the quite different attempt to draw strength for present and future struggles from it, to assume the promises of past struggles, and to avoid inflicting in historical presentation—for a second time, as it were—the oppression and oblivion of the downtrodden.

15. Indeed, Benjamin cites this passage from Marx without comment at V 887.

16. Marx, "Die Junirevolution," *Marx–Engels Werke*, 136. A translation of this article may be found in Marx, *On Revolution*, here: 150.

17. Marx, "Die Junirevolution," *Marx–Engels Werke*, 137.

18. "The discovery of gold and silver in America, the extirpation, enslavement and entombment in mines of the indigenous population of that continent, the beginnings of the conquest and plunder of India, and the conversion of Africa into a preserve for the commercial hunting of blackskins, are all things which characterize the dawn of the era of capitalist production" (*Capital* 915). For a more recent account of economic history confirming Marx's view, see Perelman.

19. *Capital* 920; see also Marx and Engels, MEGA, II:5, 604.

20. The interesting adjective "inextinguishable" [*unverlöschlichen*] does not appear in the English translation, but in MEGA, II:5, 577. It indicates a sense of unredeemable or absolute loss, and perhaps the despair of which Bloch speaks (see later), that is rare in Marx's work. See also *Capital* 925f.: "If money, according to Augier, 'comes into the world with a congenital blood-stain on one cheek,' capital comes dripping from head to toe, from every pore, with blood and dirt."

21. Bloch, *Geist der Utopie*, 325.

22. Compare the following passages: "At a certain stage of their development, the material productive forces of society come in conflict with the existing relations of production. . . . Then begins an epoch of social revolution." Marx, *Contribution*, 22. "At a certain stage of development, [a mode of production] brings into the world the material means of its own destruction. From that moment, new forces and *new pas-*

sions spring up in the bosom of society, forces and passions which feel themselves to be fettered by that society. It has to be annihilated; it is annihilated" (*Capital* 928; my emphasis). One has to wonder whether it is not the indignation at the violence Marx uncovers in Part 8 of *Capital* that forces him to grant the "most infamous, the most sordid, the most petty and the most odious of passions" (ibid.) a role in history comparable to that of the forces of production. This would indicate that, as I am arguing, a genuine sense of mourning for the victims of history requires a modification of the scientific, law-governed account of history in terms of anonymous forces, and that Marx experienced this in the writing of *Capital*. One could thus proffer a reading of Marx's magnum opus that plays off the emotional-polemical side against its scientific claims. Such a double attitude in Marx's text has often been noted with regard to the question whether or not Marx makes *moral* arguments against capitalism, as his language would often lead one to imply. Of course, Marx denies moral arguments at the level of theoretical statements about the course of history and the relegation of morality to the superstructure. See the debate in Cohen et al. (eds.), *Marx, Justice, and History*.

23. One question that imposes itself here is whether Marx transforms his indignation into what might deserve the name of revenge, a revenge for an irrecoverable loss in the past. It is clear that Benjamin read him this way: "The subject of historical insight [*Erkenntnis*] is the struggling, oppressed class itself. In Marx, it appears as the last enslaved class, as the avenging class [*rächende Klasse*] that leads to the end the work of liberation in the name of generations of the slain [defeated: *Geschlagener*]" (Thesis XII). This would have to be a notion of revenge that is not subject to Nietzsche's critique of the "spirit of revenge" as an "ill will against time" in *Thus Spoke Zarathustra*, 180. It should be noted, however, that Benjamin turns to the idea of revenge not in order to aim at an overcoming of the irreversibility and finitude of time, as Nietzsche wrote of the idea of redemption and the Last Judgment. For Benjamin, revenge is precisely not projected into the future in order to punish offenders in an imagined act of divine judgment, although his language in the "Theses on the Concept of History" is perilously ambiguous. Rather, the idea of revenge is introduced to allow a struggle to be motivated not by the certainty of progress, and not even by images of a liberated future, but by an 'inextinguishable' loss in the past. Notice also that an early fragment of Benjamin explicitly rejects the link between messianic "Judgment Day" and vengeance (*Vergeltung*), arguing that the former's significance can only be understood morally, in the concept of divine "forgiveness" (*Vergebung*, VI 98). Rebecca Comay has also argued that Benjamin's concept implicitly challenges Nietzsche's (and Heidegger's) critique of revenge in her "Redeeming Revenge." However, Comay does not seem to be aware of the passages in which Benjamin associates revenge merely with a rejection of the status quo, without thereby deferring action to the future (V 428).—Irving Wohlfahrt has also suggested that, in order to counter a Nietzschean critique of resentment, one might distinguish Benjaminian vengeance from resentment: "One might speak here of an opposition between vengeance . . . and *ressentiment*, between Judaic and Judaeo-Christian, Old and New Testament versions of socialism. It is because Nietzsche essentially equates socialism with the latter that he denounces it as a perpetuation of the 'slave revolt in morality'" (Wohlfahrt, "Resentment," 257).

24. Marx and Engels, *Collected Works*, volume 6, 174.

25. A recent historical analysis of the failure of Social Democracy in the Weimar period can be found in Mommsen, "Social Democracy."—It is of course irresistibly tempting to suppose that the dominant theological language in the "Theses" is also a response to the Hitler–Stalin alliance and to Benjamin's resulting political pessimism and despair (which would then also place his subsequent suicide in the context of this pessimism). Rolf Tiedemann, in an influential article, was the first to explain Benjamin's retranslation of Marxist language in the terms of Jewish mysticism and messianism, by these extrinsic circumstances, rather than by theoretical reasons (see his "Historical Materialism"). As I will argue, these latter reasons can be found in the connection between a theory of messianic interruption (of progress and linear time) and political resistance, a sense of resistance that is, I believe, not quite compatible with the melancholy and despair often attributed to the Benjamin of this period.

26. Marx, *Marx–Engels Reader*, 193.

27. See Laclau and Mouffe, chapters 1 and 2. On Lenin, see especially, 55ff.; on Kautsky, 19ff.

28. Perhaps the first one to point out this connection between economic determinism and political quietism was Georges Sorel (in 1903), as Laclau and Mouffe pointed out (44n29). For Sorel, especially in his *Réflexions sur la Violence*, the unforeseeability of the future, which essentially depends on action and will, is to be opposed to determinism and quietism alike. As we will see in chapter three, Benjamin was familiar with Sorel's writings, as his essay "On the Critique of Violence" demonstrates, and he might have inherited the idea of resisting communist goals by insisting on the goallessness of ethical action from Sorel. (To my knowledge, there is no study of the anarchist and syndicalist influence upon Benjamin's commitment to communist action.)

29. For an elaboration of Benjamin's revision of the base-superstructure hierarchy in his "The Work of Art in the Age of its Mechanical Reproducibility," see Garcia Düttmann, "Tradition and Destruction."

30. See Kittsteiner, "Historismus," 171: "The attacks on historicism in the "Theses" could prove to be a side show, and the critique of the philosophy of history and its concept of progress could emerge as the true theme." Kittsteiner, however, does not link this philosophy of history, especially in German idealism, to Social Democracy. My reference to Kittsteiner is not meant to support his thesis that Benjamin is "closer to historicism than he thought" (ibid.). For a direct response to, and critique of, Kittsteiner's thesis, see Osborne, 138ff.

31. See Mosè, *L'Ange de l'Histoire*, chapter 4.

32. For a philosophical analysis of the Historical School, reading it as a response to the Hegelian philosophy of history, see Schnädelbach.

33. The reference to Nietzsche here is not fortuitous. Although Benjamin did not present a detailed reading of Nietzsche's "On the Uses and Abuses of History for Life," he uses a citation from it as an epigraph in his "Theses" (I 700), and ends his essay "Über einige Motive bei Baudelaire" with a reference to this text (I 653). Benjamin's

critique of cultural history as a "triumphal march" of history's "victors" (Thesis VII), and its concept of labor (Thesis XI), is also reminiscent of Nietzsche: "[W]e may compare the splendid culture with a victor dripping with blood, a victor who in his triumphal march, drags along those he conquered as slaves enchained to his wagon. A beneficent power blinded the eyes of the slaves so that they—almost crushed by the wheels of the wagon—nonetheless shout: 'The dignity of labor!' 'The dignity of the human being!" (Nietzsche, *Der griechische Staat*, In *Kritische Studienausgabe*, vol. I, 768f.). A detailed study of Benjamin's many notes and allusions to Nietzsche is still outstanding. For a beginning of such an analysis, see Pfotenhauer, and Wohlfahrt, "Resentment."

34. To some extent, we might say that this emphasis on the retroactive constitution of history explains the resurgence of interest in Benjamin's understanding of history in contemporary discourses that emphasize linguistic perspectivism and the interpreted character of what is then problematically called the 'real.'

35. von Ranke, 8.

36. See the landmark study by Koselleck, 264ff.

37. Gadamer, especially Part 2.

38. Gadamer, 304.

39. Gadamer, 302.

40. Needless to say, this brief comparison of Benjamin and Gadamer, if illuminating, is hardly exhaustive. The most detailed reading of Benjamin as a hermeneutician is Kaulen's. In the secondary literature, however, the view of Benjamin as critical of the hermeneutic emphasis on understanding, of Benjamin as an "anti-hermeneutician," dominates (as is to be expected with the proliferation of 'postmodern' readings of Benjamin). See, e.g., Menke, *Sprachfiguren*, and Hörisch. In general, I would say that Benjamin shares with Derrida, and against Gadamer, a suspicion of the stability and authority of traditions, languages, and truth. Benjamin would want to point out the violent and exclusionary forces at work in the canonization of any tradition, the way in which its 'continuity' is constructed and suppresses the violent processes that gave rise to it. The task is then to interrupt these processes in order to expose their inherent instability and changeability.

41. Marx, *Marx–Engels Reader*, 172.

42. In Thomas Aquinas, *accidia* refers to the opposite of the joy that springs from love of God. He determines it as "tristitia de bono spirituali inquantum est bonum divinum" (*Summa Theologiae* II/II, 35), and considers it one of the cardinal sins.—See Benjamin's earlier treatment of *acedia* and melancholy in his study of the German *Trauerspiel*, I 332f. There, Benjamin predicates it of the irresolute character of the baroque tyrant who is doomed on account of *acedia*. This suggests a close link between the resolute political decision that Benjamin insists on, and the breaking up of victor-history in order to "appropriate the true historical image" (Thesis VII).

43. See also *Capital III*, where Marx writes: "It is one of the civilizing aspects of capital that it enforces this surplus labor in a manner and under conditions which are more advantageous to the development of the productive forces, social relations, and

the creation of the elements for a new and higher form than under the preceding forms of slavery, serfdom, etc." (*Capital III*, 249f.). See also the passages in the *Grundrisse* called "The Dynamics of Capitalism" (*Marx–Engels Reader* 249f.).

44. This thesis is, I believe, in no way invalidated, but certainly complicated, by the fact that Benjamin uses Marx's analysis of machinery in *Capital I*, most notably in section VIII of his "On Some Motifs in Baudelaire" (I 629ff.), in order to argue that technology today conditions human perception. For one can rely on Marx's argument that modern machinery reverses the role of the working conditions that now employ the worker as a tool—the thesis of alienation—without subscribing to the final dialectical overturning of this relationship through the revolution. Benjamin credits Marx only with showing the "ambiguity" of the capitalist economy, "very clearly visible, for example, in the machines which sharpen exploitation instead of relieving the human lot" (V 499).

45. Benjamin's treatment of the relationship between politics and technology is, to say the least, complex, and I cannot do justice to it here. One charge that, in this abstract form, Benjamin levels against both the Social Democratic Marxists and fascist theorists is that they remythologize technology by treating it in isolation from social organization and the very notion of experience in modernity (see Thesis XI and III 247ff., II 307f.). For Benjamin's critique of Jünger, see Steiner, "Säkularisierung."

46. Benjamin's vituperative attacks on what he called leftist melancholia is nowhere as explicit as in a short review of Kästner's poetry ("Linke Melancholie," III 279–283). His charge there is that leftist intellectuals in the Weimar period, while expressing moral indignation at social injustice, ultimately played into the hands of the ruling classes by avoiding political action that would have made its class alliances transparent. An analysis of this text can be found in Pensky, *Melancholy Dialectics*.

47. Benjamin, *Gesammelte Briefe*, vol. 3, 158f.

48. See also Wolin, 115.

49. See Adorno, "Fortschritt."

50. Lotze, 23.

51. Naturally, an exhaustive treatment of the concept of secularization in Benjamin is beyond the bounds of this study. Such a treatment would require a detailed examination of Benjamin's references to Carl Schmitt's political theology and his relationship to a Jewish tradition that, for him, was mostly mediated by Hermann Cohen, Frank Rosenzweig, and, of course, his friend Gershom Scholem. See the overview by Steiner, "Säkularisierung." The last few years also gave birth to a plethora of publications treating Benjamin's relation to Carl Schmitt. See Heil; Bolz; and Weber, "Taking Exception." On Benjamin's theology generally, see the study by Wunder. On Benjamin and Rosenzweig, see Mosès, "Benjamin and Rosenzweig."

52. See Kant, "Idee zu einer Allgemeinen Geschichte," 29f. See also Kant's "Über den Gemeinspruch: Das mag in der Theorie richtig sein, taugt aber nicht für die Praxis" in *Kants Gesammelte Schriften*, vol. VIII, 310ff. For Hegel's reference to the cunning of reason, see Hegel, *Die Vernunft*, 105; *Wissenschaft der Logik*, 398; *System der Philosophie*, § 209.

53. Schelling, 662.

54. Smith, 456. See Kittsteiner, *Naturabsicht*.

55. Speaking of the fetishization of commodities, Marx, for example, endows the law of value with the status of "a regulative law of nature": "It is just a law that rests on the lack of awareness [*Bewußtlosigkeit*] of the people who undergo it" (*Capital* 168fn30).

56. See in particular Kittsteiner, "Historismus." See also Rancière, "Archaeo-modern Turn."

57. See Benjamin's letters to Horkheimer and to Adorno (March 28, 1937, May 17, 1937), in which he asks for further support in order to investigate the conception of a collective unconscious.

58. Adorno, "Fortschritt," 33.

59. See Roberts, 126ff. Roberts relates Benjamin to Hermann Cohen's *Die Religion der Vernunft aus den Quellen des Judentums* and to Adolf von Harnack, the Lutheran church historian, whom Benjamin was studying at the time.

60. Benjamin refers in this short text to Max Weber (VI 100), whose *The Protestant Ethic and the Spirit of Capitalism*, as is well known, argues that the (Protestant) idea of 'justification by works' contributed to the emergence of capitalism and its work ethic. Benjamin, however, wishes·to go beyond Weber, who, according to Benjamin, saw capitalism as "religiously conditioned," whereas it has to be seen as "an essentially religious phenomenon" (VI 100). "Christianity at the time of the Reformation did not aid the emergence of capitalism, but it transformed itself into capitalism" (VI 102). In the "Theses," Benjamin argues against "vulgar Marxism" that it "resurrected, in secularized form, the old Protestant ethics of work among German workers" (Thesis XI). The *embourgeoisement* of the working classes would thus appear to be also a Christianizing in secular form.

61. See Kant, "Idee zu einer Allgemeinen Geschichte," 19.

62. Löwith, *Weltgeschichte*; Popper, *The Poverty of Historicism*.

63. In his review of Kafka, Borges put this point, familiar from Nietzsche, most succinctly by applying it to the event of authorship: "The fact is that each writer *creates* his precursors. His work modifies our conception of the past, as it will modify the future" (Borges, 243).

CHAPTER TWO. DERRIDA'S READING OF MARX

1. Marx, "The Eighteenth Brumaire," 149.

2. By "Western Marxism" I mean the strand of Marxism that developed in the 1920s as a reaction to Soviet Marxism, and which largely shifted the emphasis from political economy and the state to philosophy, culture, and art. This loose collection of individuals and trends would include Gramsci, Lukács, Korsch, the so-called Frankfurt School, and, after the war, Goldmann, Sartre, Merleau-Ponty, Lefebvre, and others. What unites this group is thus a geographical area and, perhaps, the defeat or absence of West European revolutions. See Anderson; Jacoby.

3. Horkheimer, Adorno, *Dialektik der Aufklärung*, 3.

4. The term "anamnestic solidarity" is taken from Christian Lenhardt's study of the Frankfurt School's revision of the 'Marxist' concept of universal brotherhood in terms of a memory of the dead, which yields the "aporia of redemptive solidarity." See Lenhardt, "Anamnestic Solidarity," 138. See also Baars.

5. Beginning with the 1984 analysis of the structure of the promise (in *Mémoires: For Paul de Man*, 153n10), Derrida regularly appeals to Benjamin for the messianic structure. Apart from *Specters*, Derrida also refers to the "Theses" in *Archive Fever* (AF 69/110), in an attempt to think the 'narrow door' of the future to-come that is not determined as a future present. See also Caputo, who claims that "by 1993, Derrida, like Levinas before him, had begun to associate himself with the word 'messianic'—almost always by way of a reference to Walter Benjamin" (Caputo, *Prayers and Tears*, 117). Further Derridian references to, and readings of, Benjamin can be found in: "Des Tours de Babel"; "+R (Into the Bargain)"; "Back from Moscow"; *Memoirs of the Blind*; *Points*; "Interpretations at War"; and, of course, "The Force of Law."

6. But see also Derrida's *Fichus*, the acceptance speech he delivered at receiving the Adorno Prize in 2001.

7. As early as the *German Ideology*, Marx, after having defined history as "nothing but the succession of the separate generations," writes that "this can be speculatively distorted so that later history is made the goal of earlier history" (*Marx–Engels Reader*, 172).

8. Heidegger, *Beiträge zur Philosophie*, 138.

9. Marx expressed this most clearly toward the end of *The Poverty of Philosophy*: "The working class, in the course of its development, will substitute for the old civil society an association which will exclude classes and their antagonism, and there will be no more political power properly so called, since political power is precisely the official expression of antagonism in civil society" (*Marx–Engels Reader*, 218f.).

10. Habermas in particular has criticized Marx for subsuming intersubjective relations under the "basic conceptual restraints of the philosophy of the subject" that alone would allow Marx to criticize all further social differentiation as alienation. See Habermas, *Der Philosophische Diskurs*, 79. See also his *Theorie des kommunikativen Handelns*, vol. 2, 489ff. (English trans. 332ff.). That we need to distinguish between a political community and the 'remainder' or excess of all forms of political organization is, of course, a commonplace in contemporary French political thought. For a lucid analysis, see, for example, Nancy, *The Inoperative Community*. Naturally, pointing to this convergence is not to deny fundamental disagreements concerning theoretical accounts of the social and political field.

11. For an account of the philosophical origins of the model of the self-realizing individual in German idealism and Romanticism, see Taylor, 3–50.

12. *Specters* is dedicated to Chris Hani who had been assassinated "as a communist" in South Africa (SM xvi/12).

13. See Freud, "Trauerarbeit und Melancholie."

14. Derrida, ". . . and pomegranates," 326.

15. See also Löwith's classic study *Meaning in History*.

16. Bloch, *Geist der Utopie*, 372. See also Bloch, *Das Prinzip Hoffnung*, 347, where Bloch quotes himself in a renewed reflection on the meaning of the future, a reflection that would merit discussion here.

17. ". . . the messianic structure is a universal structure. As soon as you address the other, as soon as you are open to the future, as soon as you have a temporal experience of waiting for the future, of waiting for someone to come: that is the opening of experience" (Derrida, "The Villanova Roundtable," 22).

18. Derrida, "Faith and Knowledge," 9. See also, 6, 15, 17f.

19. John D. Caputo considers the possibility that this distinction could solve the problem by viewing the messianic in general as the universal ground that, however, can only be known through the revelatory tradition of particular messianisms. Caputo continues to point out, however, that this cannot solve the aporia for Derrida: "The problem with all this, and I include here the way that Derrida himself tends to put the question, is that the whole discussion is framed within an assured set of distinctions— between fact and essence, example and exemplar, real and ideal, particular and universal—which it is the whole point of deconstruction to disturb" (Caputo, *Prayers and Tears*, 138).

20. I believe Derrida's formulations tend to conflate this question with another one, namely the question of whether only 'revelatory events' (from Abraham and Moses to Marx) or all events, as temporal experience, allow the 'unveiling' of messianicity. Given the universality of the conditions in question, he has to affirm the latter alternative, though some events, texts, or experiences may lend themselves more easily to the elaboration of a futural opening. (This would be confirmed by the observation that Derrida's messianic temporality is, via its debts to Heidegger, connected with the latter's reading of Pauline and Augustinian messianism. See Heidegger, *Phenomenology of Religious Life*.) I will return to some of the features of Marx's texts that suggest such distinctive readability.

21. Derrida, "The Villanova Roundtable," 23f.

22. Kant, *Kritik der reinen Vernunft*, 106 (B 89).

23. For the Marxist tradition, see the classic exposition by Lukács.

24. For the concept of praxis or production as a transcendental, world-constitutive concept, see Henry; see also Demmerling, 24ff. Habermas has analyzed Marx's concept of praxis as a normative category, especially with regard to the distinction between objectification and alienation. See his *Der philosophische Diskurs der Moderne*, 80ff., and his early critique of Marx's normative concept of labor as neglecting human interaction in "Arbeit und Interaktion."

25. See Bennington, "Derridabase," 281f.: "One can state as a general law that any attempt to explain transcendental effects by invoking history must presuppose the historicity of that same history as the very transcendental which this system of explanation will never be able to comprehend."

26. Derrida, "Deconstruction and Pragmatism," 81. See also OG 61/89ff.

27. For this and the following, see Gasché, *The Tain of the Mirror*, 212ff.

28. See de Saussure.

29. See Searle.

30. See in particular the section in OG called "Linguistics and Grammatology." More recently, see also *Aporias*, where the question of the relation to death and the future plays a particular role. For a good commentary on the former in terms of the "quasi-transcendental"—a commentary to which I owe some of the insights here—see Beardsworth, 6–25. This thought develops in Derrida, in both texts previously named, in a confrontation with Heidegger's "ontico-ontological difference," which is said to break with and repeat the "great ontologico-juridico-transcendental tradition" (Derrida, *Aporias*, 45; see also OG 19ff./31ff.). Derrida's use of the term "quasi-transcendental" has recently—with good reason, given its significance—come under increasing scrutiny. See Gasché, *The Tain of the Mirror*, 216ff., 316ff.; Caputo, "On not Circumventing," 267ff.; Bennington, "Derridabase," 267ff.; Hobson, chapter I: "History and Transcendentals"; Protevi; Thompson; Rorty, "Is Derrida a Transcendental Philosopher"; Rorty, "Derrida and the Philosophical Tradition."

31. Derrida, *Edmund Husserl's Origin of Geometry*, 141.

32. It is no accident that Derrida used the phrase "quasi-transcendental" first in *Glas*, to indicate the necessity that constrains Hegel's system to include, as its condition of possibility, that which it must also exclude: the figure of the sister, specifically Antigone. For a clarifying analysis of this point in *Glas*, see Caputo "On not Circumventing." Another example of this complication of inside-outside distinctions would be Derrida's reading of Searle's system of types of speech acts in *Limited Inc.*: In order to arrive at a systematic taxonomy of speech acts, the system has to exclude 'nonserious' uses of speech, such as citations, fake promises, literary or theatrical stagings of speech acts, and so forth. Derrida essentially responds by saying that a sufficiently general theory of language and its pragmatic uses should not simply exclude that which does not fit its taxonomy. Rather, it should be able to account for these nonserious uses and their possibility to contaminate a theory of speech acts. Looking at these nonserious uses shows that already the 'normal' speech acts, those grasped by the taxonomy, are inhabited by iterability as their condition to be recontextualized in ways that are not controlled or anticipated by the system. What the theoretical system excludes is thus shown to be its condition of possibility, and yet its condition of impossibility.

33. Gasché, *Tain of the Mirror*, 146f.

34. For an attempt to avoid this conclusion in a pragmatist, roughly Habermasian manner, see Menke, *Die Souveränität*, 217ff. I cannot here treat this important matter in any detail. Suffice it to say that the inescapability of contradictions and aporias plays a large role in Derrida's ethics of responsibility and the politics of a democracy to come. In *Of Hospitality*, for example, Derrida writes that an "ethics of hospitality" is "limited and contradictory *a priori*" (Dufourmantelle, Derrida, *Of Hospitality*, 65). In *Specters of Marx*, Derrida appears to extend this claim to all obligations and injunctions, claiming that they are always contradictory and inevitably lead us into a double bind (SM 16/40). The inevitability of thinking difference and identity together is

also behind Derrida's claim that Marx is not to be faulted for not beginning with the nonpresent beginning of the messianic promise, the one that introduces haunting ghosts into every conceptual order (SM 175/278).

35. Derrida has at times presented such historical accounts of his own approach to philosophical questions. *De la grammatologie* in particular contains numerous reflections on the reasons for the emergence of what is now known as the linguistic turn, and of the opposition between writing and speech as central to Western philosophy, condensing the oppositions between the sensible and intelligible, nature and culture, passion and reason, body and mind, present and absent, and so on. This history of ideas does not invalidate transcendental reflection. Further, this history could be, in a more materialist vein, supplemented by an account of socioeconomic history.

36. Laplanche, Pontalis, 112. Obviously, in this citation Derrida would challenge the opposition between 'meaningful incorporation' predicated of 'lived experience in general' and 'unassimilated experience' with its characteristic 'deferred revision.' The point would be, once again, to generalize traumatic experience (as, e.g., in the account of Levinas's originary call to responsibility as traumatic to an equally generalized narcisissm) while nonetheless taking Western modernity's traumatic structure, as condensed in the experience of Stalinism, in all its specificity.

37. Derrida has reverted to Freud's notion of the *coup* of the *après coup* on many occasions. The task is always to radicalize the notion of the unconscious—"that metaphysical name" (Derrida, *Margins*, 20)—in order to have it designate "unconscious structures of temporality" (OG 67/98), a process of presentation that is itself not thinkable on the basis of presence, an originary 'woof' that is a non-origin "outside any teleological and eschatological horizons" (WD 203/303), an alterity whose anteriority cannot be limited to the past, but bears an essential relation to the future (see Derrida, *Margins*, 21).

38. See Derrida, *Margins*, 21.

39. What would deserve further consideration in this context is Derrida's thesis that the great totalitarianisms of this century need to be understood together. Without qualification, this thesis might lend itself to a quick assimilation to the extraordinary claim of the 'revisionist' participants in the German *Historikerstreit* (historian's debate), Ernst Nolte in particular: namely, the thesis that fascism, its crimes and its 'racist' ideology, need to be understood as a response to communism and its 'classist ideology.' Derrida, however, claims that "there is nothing 'revisionist' about interpreting the genesis of totalitarianisms as reciprocal reactions to the fear of the ghost that communism inspired beginning in the last century" (SM 105/173).

40. Derrida, *Glas*, 79.

41. Derrida, *Points* 276/290. We will return to the question of the originary otherness as both crime and responsibility in chapter four.

42. Derrida refers to Levinas's definition of justice at this point: *"La relation avec autrui—c'est-à-dire la justice"* (SM 23/48). One would thus have to show how Derrida reads Benjamin's messianic time in history together with Levinas's understanding of ethical time, the temporality of our relation to the other extracted from what Levinas calls "the heritage of dead wills," a historiography recounting "the way the survivors

appropriate the works of the dead to themselves," "forgetting the life that struggles against slavery" (Levinas, *Totality and Infinity*, 228). See my comments in chapter four.

43. See OG 106ff./155ff. In his reading of Levi-Strauss, Derrida distinguishes the concept of originary violence from empirical violence as the transgression of the system of a moral law (OG 112/164).

44. Critchley has therefore called this double reading a *clôtural* reading. See his *Ethics of Deconstruction*.

45. See Derrida, "Plato's Pharmacy."

46. Critchley questioned Derrida on the use of the term "ontological" in relation to Marx (in his "On Derrida's 'Specters of Marx'," 5). However, the early Marx himself employed the word in the *1844 Manuscripts* to refer to the self-creation of humanity through labor as the "truly ontological affirmation of essence" (qtd. in Marcuse, "Neue Quellen," 17).

47. On the distinction between objectification and alienation, and between essence and existence, see again Marcuse's 1932 commentary on the *Manuscripts*, "Neue Quellen."

48. Whereas Marx described in some detail a communist society in the so-called *1844 Manuscripts* (see the Third Manuscript), and elsewhere, he claims in the *German Ideology*: "Communism is for us not a *state of affairs* which is to be established, an *ideal* to which reality has to adjust itself. We call communism the *real* movement which abolishes the present state of things" (*Marx–Engels Reader*, 162). We have seen that Benjamin tends to focus on the Marx who is supposed to have said in 1869 that "whoever drafts programs for the future is a reactionary" (qtd. in Sorel, *Reflections on Violence*, 150; see Benjamin's reference to Sorel in "Zur Kritik der Gewalt," II 194.)

49. *Marx–Engels Reader*, 87.

50. Derrida, *Margins*, 19ff. See also Derrida, "From Restricted to General Economy. A Hegelianism without Reserve" (in WD). In the context of the discussion of the quasi-transcendental, a reference to Hegel cannot be accidental. Already Hegel's *Phenomenology of Spirit* questions Kant's distinction between the transcendental and the empirical, all the while maintaining transcendental arguments. Hegel tried to show that all apparently logical determinations are already informed by political, social, and cultural patterns of recognition. That is why the *Phenomenology* mobilizes such a bewildering combination of philosophical, historical, scientific, and aesthetic conceptual and cultural phenomena. But Derrida's argument is still more radical in exposing the ultimate impossibility of this 'empirical' material coming into its own in pure reflection. This impossibility, we might say schematically, is one of memory, for no reflecting consciousness or *Geist* will be able to recall its conditions, but will be drawn in an infinite process of reflection that loses even when it gains. This, we might say, is why Derrida's insistence on the infinity of play, on the infinity of substitutability (see WD 289/423) appears as a "bad" or "spurious infinite" from Hegel's standpoint, one that does not reach the heights of philosophical thinking. For a detailed treatment of this issue, see Gasché, "Nontotalization," 3.

51. Habermas, "Arbeit und Interaktion." See also Apel, "Can 'Liberation Ethics' be Assimilated?"

52. *Marx–Engels Reader*, 193.

53. See Osborne, 37ff. For a list of references to this 'school,' see ibid., 212n40.

54. For an analysis of this logic of incarnation, see Laclau, 20ff.

55. Marx, "The Eighteenth Brumaire," 146.

56. Derrida, ". . . and pomegranates," 326.

57. Marx, *The German Ideology*, 193.

58. Derrida analyzes this elsewhere as a "half-mourning [*demi-deuil*]" or an "impossible mourning," according to which the interiorization of the dead other in mourning is both demanded and, if we wish to respect otherness, prohibited. See in particular *The Postcard*, 355, and *Mémoires—for Paul de Man*. Derrida himself gives further references to the theme of mourning in his work on Marx (at SM 178n3/24n1).

59. In chapter four, we will briefly return to Marx's critique of fetishism to argue that it remains necessary for a memory of suffering in history, despite Derrida's deconstruction of the ultimate possibility of overcoming all spectral alienation. For fetishism not only blocks an understanding of the social and exploitative relations behind exchange value, but also suppresses a memory of the violent origins of capitalism, a memory that, I will suggest, is precisely necessary for the inheritance of Marx's promise.

60. Marx, "The Eighteenth Brumaire," 146.

61. Marx, "The Eighteenth Brumaire," 149. Toward the end of his book on Marx, Derrida argues that this "impossible" and yet possible call to let 'the dead bury the dead,' insofar as it is a call in the name of "absolute life," constitutes an "absolute evil" (SM, 175/278). It is perhaps significant—and in the Marx book, Derrida does not seem to be aware of this—that this call is itself inherited, an unacknowledged quotation from the Bible whereby Marx slips into the role of Jesus. In Matthew 8:22, Jesus replies to one of his followers who wished to bury his father before leaving with him: "Follow me, let the dead bury the dead." Derrida later recognized the quotation as taken from "Christ, the spectre of spectres" (*The Politics of Friendship*, 266).

62. There are of course those who think that Derrida's suggestions for such a community—which he calls the New International—fail to deliver adequate political strength. See, for instance, Rose, *Mourning Becomes the Law*, 12: "Derrida's 'return' to Marx in the name of 'Spirit' amounts to another nail in the coffin of Marxism . . . the notion he presents of 'the New International' reveals the anarchy and utopianism at the heart of the postmodern endeavour."

63. See, for example, Fletcher, 33, where he writes of Derrida: "The historically specific effects of capitalist production are collapsed into sociality as such. As a result, the Marxist project of eliminating the ghost-effects of bourgeois political economy and its categories through working to eliminate capitalism as a mode of production—with all its brutal and unprecedented effects of mass immiseration that Derrida so eloquently deplores—comes under the suspicion and the accusation of seeking to eliminate the other, historicity, and the relation to the future themselves." In a similar vein, Byung-Chul Han accuses the art of living with ghosts of a blindness that is not essen-

tial, but detrimental to justice: "Derrida's unacknowledged dilemma is that not every ghost is a guest whom one has to greet with a 'welcome.' . . . In one breath, he demands and prohibits the selection of ghosts" (Han, 165).

64. Derrida, *Margins*, 19.

65. See Gasché, *The Tain of the Mirror*, 317: "Nor are quasi-transcendentals finite, as one could prove by pointing to Derrida's persistent critique of the notion of finitude . . . the quasitranscendentals are situated at the margin of the distinction between the transcendental and the empirical." See also Gasché's "Nontotalization," 3.

66. Discussing the problem of the two 'messianic spaces,' Caputo makes this point and argues that: "After all, the Derridean messianic does have *certain* determinable features. . . . For Derrida's messianic is through and through an ethico-political idea. . . . Derrida's messianic has emerged under determinate historical conditions and takes a determinate form" (Caputo, *Prayers and Tears*, 142).

67. See also Bennington, "Deconstruction," 93: "This quasi-transcendental [arche-writing] ensures that *all* transcendentals are 'only' quasi-transcendentals, being originarily contaminated by what they transcend. This is the decapitation again, the radical empiricism, the impossibility of abstraction from context, of having a true starting-point, of determining Derrida's terms as concepts."

68. See, in particular, the interview Derrida gave the German weekly *DIE ZEIT* ("Ich mißtraue der Utopie, ich will das Un-Mögliche," March 5, 1998). Derrida says there of the Left (I translate from the German) "in which I would decisively find myself": "On the Left one finds the desire to affirm the future, to change [things]. To change things in view of the greatest possible justice. [. . .] To be on the right wing consists in being conservative, to retain something" (p. 48).

69. See Fritsch, "Derrida's Democracy to Come."

70. See, for example, Lefort, *L'invention democratique*, 173: "Democracy inaugurates the experience of a society which cannot be apprehended or controlled, in which the people will be proclaimed sovereign, but in which its identity will never be definitively given, but will remain latent." For Lefort, this democratic revolution first of all made possible the emergence of totalitarianism as an attempt to reestablish, on the social "organic" level, the unity of the loci of power, law, and knowledge, a unity that democracy has broken.

71. Derrida, "Ich mißtraue der Utopie, ich will das Un-Mögliche," *DIE ZEIT*, 49f.

72. See Kant's "Idee zu einer Allgemeinen Geschichte" in which Kant, just after specifying the *"Idee des Menschen"* required by progressive history as its goal (19), wonders that, while nothing is simply given to humans by nature except for the potential of reason to make itself "worthy of life and well-being," one generation receives a gift from the preceding one, a debt never repaid. "What will always seem strange [*befremdend*] about this," Kant writes, "is that earlier generations appear to carry out their laborious tasks only for the sake of later ones [. . .] without being able themselves to partake of the prosperity they prepared the way for. But no matter how puzzling this

is, it is nonetheless equally necessary once one assumes that one species of animal should have reason and that as a class of rational beings [. . .] it is destined to develop its capacities to perfection" (20/31). My claim here is that at the end of the twentieth century and the beginning of the twenty-first, we are called upon to take up and elaborate the strangeness that inhabits this promise, without adding the conjunction "but" that quickly overcomes this strangeness by opposing it to the necessity of a development. For an account of Derrida's deconstruction of the Kantian regulative idea, see Beardsworth, 61–70. See also Derrida's "The Ends of Man."

73. The constraints in question concern the "structural dependence of the state [and its citizens] on capital" (Przeworski, Wallerstein, "Structural Dependence") that resulted from the separation of producers from productive assets in the process we recounted, with Marx, in the previous chapter. Today, the most promising alternatives to this kind of unequal capital relation, politico-economic alternatives that are not teleological and seem feasible in taking the market's functional advantages (though usually not the memory of primitive accumulation) into account, are probably developed around what has come to be called market socialism. For some work on this model, see Roemer; Schweickart; and Kambartel.

74. It is, of course, Heidegger's *Sein und Zeit*, which attempted a thinking of finitude as the exposure to the constituting work of a future that, as such, never comes, remaining the impossible possibility of human existence: namely, death. To analyze Derrida's debt to Heidegger's trajectory would obviously explode the bounds of this work. It might suffice to point out that one can find in Heidegger's *Beiträge zur Philosophie*, 138ff., and elsewhere, an attempt to think the 'goal-lessness' (*Ziel-losigkeit*) of the present, at the moment of metaphysics' exhaustion, as the condition for recognizing a genuine finitude, one that would also see metaphysics as 'nihilism.' Furthermore, one would have to take into account Heidegger's references to Marx by name, in particular in "Brief über den Humanismus," which already suggest that the category of alienation needs to be thought on the basis of a more originary 'oblivion of Being.'

CHAPTER THREE. THE CRITIQUE OF VIOLENCE

1. In English, this immediate association of a legal order with violence might seem surprising. Hence, a terminological clarification is in order. Benjamin's German term *Gewalt*, as has often been pointed out (especially by Derrida—see FL 927), does not exclusively refer to acts of brutality, of violation, and to illegitimate violence, though the word may refer to these and always carry their connotations. It also refers to the legitimate and authorized use of force and institutionalized power. Thus, *Staatsgewalt* is state power. Despite this ambiguity, many commentators-cum-translators think that the perils of euphemizing the problems in question are too great not to use "violence" in all contexts. While these dangers are not negligible, I think that "power" is the better translation—with the exceptions of "divine violence" (*göttliche Gewalt*) and, perhaps, "mythic violence" (*mythische Gewalt*). For, in speaking of *Gewalt*, Benjamin mostly concerns himself with phenomena and processes of legal institutionalization. Still, consistency with existing and now standardized translations and discussions of the text, as well as the dangers mentioned, render the exclusive use of power inadvisable. For this reason, in my

translations as well as my exegesis, I will most often speak of violence or power, or use the terms individually if the context allows it.

2. Indeed, Habermas makes this claim of Durkheim's a centerpiece of his critical social theory in the tradition of Western Marxism and the Frankfurt School, of which Benjamin may be considered a fellow traveler. See Habermas, *Theorie des kommunikativen Handelns*, 175f. (English trans. 116f.). If any stable social system and legal order needs to claim to be, and appear to its subjects as, just and legitimate, and if such legitimacy can, in the last analysis, only be generated by what Habermas calls communicative action, then a critical social theory concerned to account for its critical standards can proceed from the ineluctability of an orientation to mutual understanding. It then has found its basis on which to criticize 'systematically distorted communication' and systemically induced disturbances (e.g., by a late capitalist economy) of the everyday lifeworld in which communicative action is at home. Benjamin's comments in "Critique of Violence" on language, "the proper sphere of 'understanding'" (II 192/CV 144), as a medium allowing the nonviolent resolution of conflicts, may perhaps be seen as an anticipation of Habermas's approach to critical theory after the linguistic turn. However, Benjamin would be much more suspicious of the power of ideology and the state apparatus to, as Habermas puts it at one point, "engineer mass loyalty" (*Theorie* 480/325; see also 509/346), especially when it concerns the relation to the past. For despite such engineering, and despite his insight into the instituting violence Marx recalled as necessary to create an economically subjected proletariat, once the capitalist mode of production is firmly established, Habermas claims legitimacy for primitive accumulation on account of the relative absence of sustained resistance to it: "In spite of the destructive side effects of the violent processes of capital accumulation and state formation, the new organizational forms gained wide acceptance and considerable permanency on the strength of their greater effectiveness and superior level of integration. The capitalist mode of production and bureaucratic-legal domination can better fulfill the tasks of materially reproducing the lifeworld [. . .] than could the institutions of the feudal order that preceded them" (ibid., 474/321). One is bound to ask here how such 'acceptance' and 'superiority' is to be measured and what explains the necessity for the transition to a new level of societal integration in the first place. Apparently, even Habermas's self-proclaimed abandonment of the philosophy of history does not prevent a progressivistic justification (even if only in perhaps a weak sense of the word) of past violence and injustice. A more detailed discussion of Habermas's account of social evolution, and his attempt to incorporate Benjamin's concern for the oppressed and their dead, under the rubric of 'anamnestic solidarity,' in his concept of justice (see Habermas, *Vorstudien und Ergänzungen*, 516f.; Habermas, *Der philosophische Diskurs*, 25f.), exceeds the bounds of the present concerns.

3. Benjamin refers to Spinoza's *Tractatus Theologico-Politicus* (see, in particular, its chapter 16). The relationship between Benjamin and Spinoza has recently attracted the attention of scholars; see Dobbs-Weinstein; also Erwin.

4. The history of secularization in natural law theory is well researched, especially the place of individual representatives in this tradition. With regard to John Locke, for instance, James Tully—partly by drawing on Michel Foucault's analysis of the modern concept of power—has attempted to show the theological origins and the secularization of Locke's theory of natural law. See Tully.

5. Max Weber, "Politics as a Vocation," 78.

6. See Hamacher, "Afformative, Strike," 113f. On the basis of Benjamin's essay, Hamacher develops a theory of the pure, preconventional performative, and what necessarily withdraws from this pure performative (the 'imperformative' or 'afformative'). My reading of Benjamin's notoriously recondite "Critique of Violence" is greatly indebted to Hamacher's essay, although I disagree with his direct identification of the afformative with revolutionary violence (ibid., 115).

7. Hannah Arendt's discussion of the link between revolutionary energies and the council system in "The Revolutionary Tradition and its Lost Treasure" (in On Revolution) would be most relevant here. She begins her account of this link by deploring the "failure of thought and remembrance" and the resulting loss of the "revolutionary spirit" in both European and American revolutions. She goes on to blame for this loss (in the U.S. case) the false identification of 'freedom' with 'freedom of enterprise' and the concomitant degradation of political freedom "to be a participator in government" to merely passive civil liberties (Arendt, 223, 219, 221). She continues to elaborate the paradox of every revolution, the one that Benjamin also wrestles with: the conflict between "the concern with stability [of founded institutions] and the spirit of the new" (Arendt, 225), that is, the task of achieving the freedom of the people while founding a durable set of institutions where it can be exercised again and again. She notes that in most revolutions, local and small council systems emerged spontaneously as a new form of government: the townships and townhall meetings of the American Revolution, the sociétés révolutionaires or sociétés populaires of the French Revolution and the Paris Commune, the soviets of the Russian Revolution, the Räte of the German revolution of 1918/1919. The preservation of the political freedom expressed in revolutions is to be sought, in her view, in these councils as a form of radical democracy in the spirit of Rousseau. Benjamin's early essay attempts to elaborate the logic according to which their power is usurped by a monopolistic state power that, however, also 'decays' by losing connection with the councils and their revolutionary spirit. His essay also attempts to provide for freedom apart from the institutional structure of the centralized nation state and its monopolization of the legitimate use of force.—References to Thomas Jefferson's opposition to the Constitution and his predilection for what he called the ward system are discussed by Arendt, 234–242, 252–259.

8. For Marx's endorsement of the dictatorship of the proletariat, see Marx–Engels Reader, 538 (see also 490, 505). In their rejection of this conception as leading to totalitarian oppression, Sorel and Benjamin follow Bakunin's 'anarchist' critique of Marx at the First International (see Bakunin, Statehood and Anarchy, 1873, and Marx's critical notes collected in Marx, The First International and After). Following Sorel (Sorel, Reflections on Violence, 191ff.), Benjamin may be said to determine the doctrine of the dictatorship of the proletariat as the point at which the Marxist theory of history translates into a fatefully oblivious politics of victory. This doctrine views the legal and political apparatuses of bourgeois class domination as to be taken over and utilized by the victorious proletariat in favor of the ultimate 'withering away' of the state. Benjamin sees this appropriation as forgetful of the oppressed of history in that it justifies further victimization of the new enemies of the state and as leading to discourses of legitimation that suppress the call of the victims. So even before the

Leninist and Stalinist perversions of the Marxist promise occurred or became known, Benjamin, like Bakunin and Sorel, may be said to seek to redefine the emancipatory promise in light of the victimization it will inflict. (For an argument exposing Lenin's and Stalin's use—and misuse—of Marx's conception of the dictatorship of the proletariat, see Draper, *The 'Dictatorship of the Proletariat' from Marx to Lenin*.) Furthermore, for Benjamin, the allegedly revolutionary use of state power forgets that it is a power imposing its law in order to maintain itself, such that the Marxist doctrine of the quasi-automatic withering away of the state is an illusion. Instead, we need to think what I call the finitude of power itself as making possible the resistance to oppressive legal and political institutions. It should be noted that Benjamin is quite aware of the difference between Marxists and anarchists on the use of state power. This is confirmed by his characterization of Sorel's proletarian strike, in opposition to the "law-positing" political strike, as "anarchist" (II 194/146). In his 1926 essay on French surrealism, an essay that deals with the question of how the (anarchist) revolt *(Revolte)* can contribute to the revolution, Benjamin writes of Bakunin: "Since Bakunin there has not been a 100% concept of freedom in Europe: the Surrealists have it" (II 306).

9. Despite the relative obviousness of linking the notion of political history (in "On the Critique of Violence") to the concept of a history of victors (in "Theses on the Concept of History"), this link has, to my knowledge, never been discussed explicitly or in any detail in the secondary literature on Walter Benjamin. Perhaps Irving Wohlfahrt, next to Marcuse, comes closest to this link when he writes: "His [Benjamin's] own 'Critique of Violence' was a theory of the 'divine' counter-violence capable of arresting the continuity of 'mythical' violence." (Wohlfahrt, "No-Man's Land," 164). The phrase "arresting continuity" echoes the language of the "Theses" (XV, XVI, XVII), but Wohlfahrt does not elaborate the link at which he gestures. Herbert Marcuse was perhaps the first to point out the connection between the study on violence and the later writings on history, focusing on the concept of the state of emergency. See Marcuse, "Nachwort," 99f.: "The violence criticized by Benjamin is the violence of the status quo, which has preserved in that status quo itself the monopoly of legality, of truth, of law, and in which the violent character of the law had disappeared so as to come to light with a vengeance in the so-called 'states-of-emergency' (which are, de facto, nothing of the sort). Such a state of emergency is, in regard to the oppressed, the rule; the task is, however, according to the *Theses on the Concept of History*, to 'bring about a true state of emergency,' one capable of exploding the historical continuum of violence." While Giorgio Agamben's recent investigation into the Schmittian concept of the state of emergency, and Benjamin's treatment thereof, can be seen as the best exploration of Marcuse's suggestions here (without mentioning his name), he does not discuss the true state of emergency as a resistance to a history of violent victories (see Agamben, *Homer Sacer* and *État d'exception*).

10. Rebecca Comay has addressed the opposition between the calendar and the clock in her "Benjamin's Endgame," 267f. She does not, however, discuss the connection to Benjamin's earlier account of political history and the imposition of violence.—That the Benjamin of the "Theses" is willing to use the French Revolution as an example of the discontinuous 'explosion' of history, and that he implicitly suggests it as a model for a future revolution, might be taken to imply that he now allows the

possibility that such a revolution will be a violent imposition of law. As we will see, the "Critique of Violence" still attempts to specify a nonviolent revolution in the proletarian strike, which does not posit law. The text between 1921 and 1940 that might be taken to signal this possible shift in Benjamin's thought is the essay on surrealism (II 295ff.).

11. The nature of these distinctions and their significance for Benjamin's notion of critique has been discussed, in the wake of Derrida's essay, in particular by Gasché, "On Critique." Gasché is interested in cleanly distinguishing deconstruction from critique and hence argues that Benjamin's critique operates by radical distinctions which it understands as clean cuts. Deconstruction, on the other hand, would limit the efficacy of such distinctions. For a critique of Gasché's procedure, see Menke, "Benjamin vor dem Gesetz," 217ff.

12. Bettine Menke is most vocal in her claim that Derrida misrecognizes the conceptual difference between both oppositional pairs ("Benjamin vor dem Gesetz," 219). She refers also to Dominick LaCapra and Samuel Weber as reading the pairs other than in a binary fashion (ibid, 259n7). See LaCapra, 1071; Weber, "Deconstruction before the Name," 1183ff. See also Rose, "Of Derrida's Spirit," 84. Agamben (*Homo Sacer*, 64f.) suggests that Derrida's "peculiar misunderstanding" of divine violence consists in confusing it with Carl Schmitt's sovereign violence, a confusion that stems from Benjamin's lack of familiarity, in 1921, with Schmitt's *Political Theology*. To the list of critics of Derrida's reading, we might also add Hamacher's essay "Afformative, Strike," written before Derrida's "Force of Law." Only Rodolphe Gasché's reading (see previous note) agrees with Derrida's. It should be clear that, on this point, my interpretation concurs with Menke's and Hamacher's, an agreement that does not, however, disregard the problematic ambiguities Derrida detects in Benjamin's conception of pure and divine violence.

13. Since Benjamin seems to name God the subject of pure violence, one must conclude that 'God' is here not thought as a personal agent and the initiator of divine violence, but as the mediacy of pure means themselves—the gift or givenness of the medium of language, for example, to which we will return, however briefly.

14. My exposition of Benjamin's text here is not meant to endorse or glorify anger as violence devoid of positing, nor does Benjamin do so. Instead, he associates such an "im-mediate" manifestation of violence with (Greek) mythology (as in the legend of Niobe), and even, problematically, goes so far as to claim that the imposition of law is initially such a manifestation, until it falls into the circle of positing its own preservation as its end (II 198/149f.). This reference to anger as an intentionless violence not directed to a purpose corresponds to a number of (Kantian) themes in Benjamin that would be relevant here. Benjamin analyzes as moral phenomena especially certain kinds of artworks that problematize their character of beautiful appearance (*schöner Schein*) and which stage what he calls the "moral word" (I 181) due to their intentionlessness and their abrupt intervention. Menninghaus has shown that Benjamin's central category of 'intentionlessness' ("Truth is . . . an intentionless being," I 216), like the 'expressionless' (*das Ausdruckslose*; I 181) or the 'lack of semblance' (*das Scheinlose*) communicate with Kant's meditation on the sublime as the disruptive intervention of the moral law on beautiful appearance (see Menninghaus,

"Das Ausdruckslose"). It is Kant himself who associated the sublime with the Judaic prohibition of graven images (another variant of '—lessness': *Bilderlosigkeit*) in *The Critique of Judgement* (Kant, *Zur Kritik der Urteilskraft*, 122). Insofar as "imagelessness" (*Bilderlosigkeit*) implies an open, non-anticipated or unanticipatable future, it corresponds to Benjamin's discussion of 'pure violence' as devoid of posited ends whose possible realization would be in the future. For Benjamin and Kant on the sublime, see also Gasché, "Objective Diversions."

15. Benjamin's association of divine violence with an annihilating power may also refer to Franz Rosenzweig's connection between a concept of divinity and nothingness. In the *Star of Redemption* (p. 37), which Benjamin knew, God is described as that which exists in everything "so that the world can move around it . . . it is that which, by being 'nothing,' makes a something 'useful'; it is the unmoved mover of the movable. It is the non-deed as the original ground of the deed." See Hamacher, *Premises*, 333n36.

16. Benjamin provides no argument for this division between public and private realms, a discussion of which I will here forego. Problems with this distinction emerge even on Benjamin's own terms, for in aiming at an interruption or even abolition of modern state power, the public-private division would also have to be interrupted or disappear.

17. Hamacher, "Afformative, Strike," 116ff.

18. See Derrida, "Roundtable on Translation," 123f.: "Pure language, says Benjamin, is not one which has been purified of anything; rather, it is what makes a language a language, what makes for the fact that there is language. A translation puts us not in the presence, but in the presentiment of what 'pure language' is, that is, the fact that there is language, that language is language. . . . This is what Benjamin calls pure language, '*die reine Sprache*,' the being-language of language. The [messianic] promise of a translation is that which announces to us this being-language of language: there is language, and because there is something like language, one is both able and unable to translate." See my discussion in chapter four.

19. Hamacher and Menke have explored in greatest detail Benjamin's reference to language as a sphere of mediacy, and the implicit reference to the earlier essay on language. See Hamacher, "Afformative, Strike," 116–120, and Menke, "Benjamin vor dem Gesetz." See also Menke's voluminous study *Sprachfiguren*. Derrida's most extensive treatment of Benjamin's concept of language is presented in "Des Tours de Babel," but see also the preceding note. That Derrida, in the early 1980s—before the 'Heidegger affair,' the 'de Man affair,' and the widespread attacks on deconstruction for its alleged irresponsibility—reads Benjamin's treatment of language in a largely affirmative manner while, in the early 1990s, severely criticizes it as an antiliberal 'archeoeschatology' akin to Heidegger, might seem to suggest that the real target in these criticisms is indeed Heidegger in an attempt to free deconstruction from association with texts viewed as anti-democratic and contributing to the rise of Nazism.

20. See, for example, Luxemburg. For a general overview of the First International, see Braunthal.

21. See Rose, "Of Derrida's Spirit," 85f.

22. In the Marxist tradition, Althusser has emphasized the need of power, both of capital's power of production and of the state's legal power, to reproduce itself and the means of production before it can produce. See his "Ideology and Ideological State Apparatuses" in *Lenin and Philosophy*. A confrontation with Foucault's analysis of power, and his critique of the 'juridical' model of power, might prove very fruitful here, but explodes the bounds of the present study. See Foucault, *The History of Sexuality*, as well as "Two Lectures." Beatrice Hanssen, in a brief—too brief—confrontation of Benjamin's politics of pure means with Foucault's micropolitics of power, suggests that while Foucault's "historicizing analysis of force relations not only announces the end of all critiques of power, but, by implication, also of a (Benjaminian) 'critique of violence,'" Foucault nonetheless, "like Benjamin, rejected the conventional juridico-political model, which located legitimate power in the state apparatus" (Hanssen, "Politics of Pure Means," 250, 251). I cannot agree, however, with Hanssen's assimilation of Benjamin's notion of critique to a Kantian "transcendental critique" (ibid., 238f.). Rather, as I have argued, Benjamin's critique draws on the underlying and undermining finitude and oscillating self-alienation of power, and cannot simply be equated with the self-critical stance of a Kantian operation that relies on clear demarcations and limits. Her later book that takes its title from Benjamin's essay argues that the latter testifies "to the crisis of the critical project" in that "the critical project, in its most rigorous assumptions, proved untenable, as he was moved to acknowledge the persistence of force in liberal institutions" (Hanssen, *Critique of Violence*, 4). This seems to me to miss that, and in what way, Benjamin analyzes such force and its inherent complications with a view toward its transformation.

23. Hamacher, "Afformative, Strike," 121, 125. Agamben has investigated the modern rule of power over Benjamin's notion of bare life, linking it to Foucault's investigation into modern 'biopower.' See Agamben, *Homer Sacer*.

24. Among those commentators who notice the crucial link between the idea of depositing and the conception of divine violence at all, we find different accounts and different explanations of Benjamin's ambiguity. There seems to be agreement, however, that Benjamin cannot characterize divine violence as both inherent in the discontinuous self-alienation of power *and* as a determinate and localizable historical and political event intervening upon this power from without. Hamacher ("Afformative, Strike," 115) speaks of "an infinite series of difficulties" linked to the idea of depositing, beginning with the question of its historical eventness and its agency, but he also claims that these difficulties "belong to the structure of deposing itself" and thus "do not allow for resolution" (ibid, 116). Bettine Menke agrees with Derrida that Benjamin may not approach a stable definition of divine violence, but she thinks the "Critique of Violence" must be read alongside the "Theologico-Political Fragment" that overcomes this ambiguity. The latter text is clearer, she argues, because it rejects the "founding recourse to divine violence" in its rejection of theocracy (Menke, "Benjamin vor dem Gesetz," 249). Agamben points out, against Derrida's "peculiar misunderstanding" of Benjamin's essay, that Benjamin had not yet read Carl Schmitt's *Political Theology*, and thus could not distinguish divine violence from Schmitt's concept of "sovereign violence," which alone would, Agamben implies, allow Derrida's interpretative link of divine violence to the Holocaust (Agamben, *Homer Sacer*, 64f.).

25. In Kant, we find the dream of a justice without external institutions enforcing its demands, relying only on each individual's rational capacity to formulate laws in accordance with the autonomy of the categorical imperative, where this dream takes on the form of a regulative ideal. When first discussing 'transcendental ideas' in the *Critique of Pure Reason*, Kant defends Plato's utopianism, from which the very term "ideas" was derived. He then imputes to Plato the idea of a state of "the highest human freedom according to laws"—laws, however, that do not need the threat of punishment, and thus no enforceability: "The more the legislation and government were established in agreement with this idea, the less frequent punishments would become, and hence it is very rational (as Plato claims), that in a perfect order of the idea, no punishments at all would be necessary" (Kant, *Kritik der reinen Vernunft*, 352; A 316f./B 373). The ideal of a 'kingdom of ends' would thus imply a justice without enforcement by external institutions. Benjamin's essay may be regarded as an attempt to push Kant beyond himself, to radicalize Kant by Kantian means—for example, by holding on to Kant's dictum that justice, determined by the categorical imperative, stands higher than mere life (see Kant, *Metaphysics of Morals*, § 49, 138) while rejecting that persons be treated not only as ends but also as means. Given this radicalized Kantianism, it must seem puzzling that Derrida attributes to Benjamin an anti-Enlightenment strategy, even if we take into account that, as Derrida argues in "Interpretations at War," there is a 'Jewish' Kant, especially in the eyes of some German critical theorists.

26. For Kant, see, for example, *Kritik der reinen Vernunft*, 536 (A551/B 579, note): "Thus, the genuine morality of our actions (desert and guilt), even that of our own comportment, remains entirely concealed." Kant does not hesitate to draw the radical conclusion that nobody "can judge [*richten*] with complete justice." Not with regard to this analogy between the categorical imperative and the proletarian strike, but in general terms, Güter Figal has explored the similarities between Kant' s and Benjamin's ethics. See Figal; also Folkers, "Zum Begriff der Gewalt bei Kant und Benjamin," in the same volume as Figal's.

27. Derrida, *The Other Heading*, 78. Further references to democracy to come may be found in *Specters of Marx* and, above all, in *The Politics of Friendship*, 574–597.

28. Derrida, "Déclarations d'independance," 20, 22. Derrida himself refers to this text at the moment he elaborates the necessary disavowal of time (Derrida, "Force of Law," 35n8). An analysis of this text to which I am indebted is to be found in Beardsworth, 98ff. See also Honig.

29. For the notion of "counter-time" or "untimeliness" in Benjamin's "Theses," see Hamacher, "Des Contrées des Temps."

30. Citing this same passage as evidence, Christoph Menke has argued that it is only Derrida's Levinasian conception of justice as speaking to the other without any horizonal predetermination that supports the thesis of originary violence. Accordingly, the passage cited earlier conflates doing justice to the other in the form of a speaking free from all hermeneutic determining (which is indeed impossible) and a speaking that is oriented toward the singular perspective of the other (which is possible, as Nietzsche's and Adorno's—and, we might add beyond Menke's text, Benjamin's—critique of egalitarian universalism points out; Menke, *Spiegelungen der Gle-*

ichheit, 66f.). This would criticize the extension, beyond the rule of law, of the law of oscillation to the law of repetition as an originary violence. Menke has criticized the conception of originary violence, which seems to follow only if we postulate an ineradicable "desire for plenitude" or presence, also in his *Die Souveränität der Kunst*, 219ff. In response, Derrida could not only insist, with psychoanalysis, on the ineluctability of a desire for presence (which he does, e.g., in the "Afterword" to *Lim Inc abc.*), but argue also that the second sort of speaking, the supposedly nonviolent one, must be animated by a Levinasian conception of nonhorizonal justice to be truly oriented to singularity, and hence fail. I do not wish to resolve the important issue here, partly because it seems to me that in our context the most significant consequences regarding the disunity of victor-history follow regardless of the side we take, and partly because a fuller discussion would have to look closely at Derrida's early essay "Violence and Metaphysics" (in WD) and at a crucial passage in OG (112ff./164ff.), at which Derrida distinguishes 'originary violence' (at the level of language in general, understood as a system of differentiation) from two other levels of violence: while the second level attempts to contain originary violence by means of moral and customary law as well as legal institutions, the third is the level on which breaches of the second are located, what we ordinarily mean by violence. In chapter four, I will revisit the issue of originary violence in its link to responsibility and point to further reasons Derrida gives for accepting it.

31. One might continue to multiply these questions concerning the difference between certain dimensions of Benjamin's text, such as the one indicated by his *vouloir-dire*, as Derrida says (FL 1033), and what in the text itself exceeds and compromises this dimension. These questions concern what Derrida calls the "auto-hetero-deconstruction" (FL 981) of the text and the "quasi-logic of the phantom" that haunts it in advance and undermines all the distinctions elaborated therein (FL 973). Here, I do not wish to go into these questions other than to point out that the distinction between Benjamin's intentions or his 'meaning-to-say' and the deconstructive, self-questioning level of the text remains problematic, as Derrida is well aware (FL 1007, 1033). For deconstruction, as we argued in chapter two, is not a method, but is "at work, in full negotiation: in the 'things themselves' and in Benjamin's text" (FL 973f.). Attributing to Benjamin, however, intentions that can simply be summarized as "anti-Enlightenment," "anti-parliamentarian," as a Marxist messianism and a triadic, eschatological philosophy of history, and then assimilating these alleged dimensions of Benjamin's discourse to Heidegger, Carl Schmitt, and to the rise of Nazism, and ultimately finding in them a possible justification of the Holocaust (FL 1044), does not only disregard the necessity of detailed demonstration, but must be problematized.

32. Benjamin's critique of language as a system of representation is a complex issue, and doing it justice here would involve a detailed reading of Benjamin's various language-theoretical texts. Suffice it to say that Derrida certainly shares the view that presents language as an unsurpassable medium, and not as merely fallen from its original presence. Derrida himself uses Benjamin's critique of representation to think the 'final solution' as unrepresentable and to advocate a "memory of the name" against the "historiographic perversion" of a "positivist, comparatist, or relativist objectivism" (FL 1042). For a more detailed treatment of Benjamin's theory of language in the con-

text of Derrida's deconstruction, see, again, the very detailed but difficult *Sprachfiguren*, by Bettine Menke.

33. For more on such a deconstructive politics, see Beardsworth, 46ff., and Bennington, *Interrupting Derrida*, 28ff. See also Fritsch, "Derrida's Democracy To Come."

CHAPTER FOUR. THE CLAIM OF THE DEAD ON THE LIVING

1. See Kittsteiner, "Historismus," 165. See also Raulet, 110.

2. See Lyotard, *The Differend*, 56ff. See also Lyotard, *Heidegger and the 'jews,'* 25ff.

3. See Levinas, *Totality and Infinity*, 226ff., 55ff. A rapprochement between Benjamin and Levinas on the question of history was to my knowledge first suggested by Wiemer, 142–153. But see also Critchley, *The Ethics of Deconstruction*, 30, where Levinas's "ontological history" is identified as "always the history of victors, never of the victims, and thus a history of barbarity, against which Levinas speaks in tones very similar to those of Walter Benjamin." This straightforward identification simply presupposes, of course, that Benjamin's 'victors' are Levinas's 'survivors' (*Totality and Infinity*, 228) and that Benjamin's oppressed̶again, Benjamin never used the word 'victim' in this context̶are Levinas' s singularities, an identification that seems questionable. See also Osborne, 225fn43. None of these three authors takes a closer look at the differences between Benjamin and Levinas on this question, differences that, due to space constraints, I will only note in passing.

4. For this original alienation and its connection with what we will see appear in Derrida as an originary violence, see my "Levinas on Ethical Responsibility."

5. Benjamin criticizes the idea of *Einfühlung* in a variety of contexts. He refuses the idea of empathetically entering the beauty of an artwork, for that misses the secret at the heart of beauty that consists in its veil, not in lifting it (I 195). Perhaps more relevant here is the critique of Aristotelian catharsis as a release of affects and emotions by way of empathizing with the hero of a drama (II 515; 535). Benjamin opposes to this *Einfühlung* Brechtian astonishment, achieved by an estranging *(verfremdend)* interruption of the course of a drama, which triggers a reflection on the suspension of disbelief in drama. This means that Benjamin would be critical of viewing historical events according to tragic, dramatic models taken from Aristotle's poetic theory. Of course, Benjamin also criticizes as a fetishism of commodities the purchase of commodities for their exchange value rather than their use value in order to enhance one's subjectivity and personal self-worth̶a very common phenomenon, according to recent critics of consumer culture such as Baudrillard and Deleuze. Benjamin calls this fetishism the "empathizing with the soul of the commodity [*Einfühlung in die Warenseele*]" (V 637). He also notes that this fetishism is inextricably wedded to sexism, for example, the male desire for prostitutes for their very availability by way of money, that is, for their exchange value (*Käuflichkeit*; see V 422ff.; V 427; V 435ff.; V 455; V 1243). For an analysis of these references to fetishism and sexism, see Buci-Glucksmann.

6. Benjamin cites Baudelaire's *Fleurs du Mal*, and its notion of "spleen," for this melancholy (V 437; V 440; V 445): "Et le Temps m'engloutit minute par minute/Comme

la neige immense un corps pris de roideur" (cited at I 632). Benjamin sees this melancholy experience of time, the *taedium vitae* characteristic of modernity (V 444), as the origin of a goalless and indecisive rage, as well as the reason for modern people's loss of personal and historical experience (I 642). As suggested in chapter one, it is thus quite mistaken to attribute a melancholic attitude toward a history of suffering to Benjamin himself, as is so often done in the secondary literature, particularly in an attempt to explain his use of Jewish theological categories in the "Theses."

7. In *One-Way Street*, Benjamin determines a 'corporeal' presence of mind as the ability to "notice in detail, what is happening in a second" which is "more decisive than cognitively anticipating the most distant [future]" (IV 141). The concept implies that recognition of what appears in a second can only be known retrospectively: "Presence of mind as a political category is beautifully brought out in these words of Turgot: 'By the time we come to discover that things are at a given juncture, they have already changed several times. Hence, we always perceive events too late and politics must always foresee, as it were, the present'" (V 598). On the basis of his notion of the discontinuous present (what Derrida would call the spectrality or anachrony of time), Benjamin describes the task of a nonmelancholic historian as the famous "historian as a prophet turned backwards" whose "seer's gaze is illuminated by the peaks of earlier human generations which are disappearing deeper and deeper into the past" (I 1237). The anticipation of the present by the historian's prophetic gaze allows us to understand the political chances of the present much better than those contemporaries who "keep up with the present" (ibid.), that is, those submerged in empty, homogenous time. "It is especially this concept of the present which is the basis of the actuality of genuine historiography," Benjamin concludes (ibid.). Since the future is unknowable, but its unknowability is inscribed in the heart of a constantly changing present (whose meaning is thus determined by the future), the true prophet must be a historian illuminating the present. Benjamin also calls this the "now of recognizability" (ibid.).— An excellent treatment of Benjamin's political category of *Geistesgegenwart* is to be found in Menke's *Sprachfiguren*, 349ff.

8. Marx notes the double sense of 'bourgeois' freedom for the newly created proletarian, implicitly criticizing what Benjamin, in the "Critique of Violence," called the demonic ambiguity of laws, and here of the human right of freedom: "Free workers, in the double sense that they neither form part of the means of production themselves, as would be the case with slaves, serfs, etc., nor do they own the means of production, as would be the case with self-employed peasant proprietors" (*Capital* 874).

9. I am thinking here of Robert Nozick's famous libertarian credo, *Anarchy, State, and Utopia*. Nozick notes three principles justifying entitlement in holdings, where the first two (fair original acquisition and fair transfer of property) are complicated by the third principle, which disclaims entitlement on grounds other than the first two principles, and thus includes the issue of the rectification of past injustice: "The existence of past injustice (previous violations of the first two principles of justice in holdings) raises the third major topic under justice in holdings: the rectification of injustice in holdings. If past injustice has shaped present holdings in various ways, some identifiable and some not, what now, if anything, should be done to rectify these injustices? [. . .] How, if at all, do things change if the beneficiaries and those made worse off are not the direct parties in the act of injustice, but, for exam-

ple, their descendants? [. . .] How far back must one go in wiping clean the historical slate of injustices? What may victims of injustice permissibly do in order to rectify the injustice being done to them, including the many injustices done by persons acting through their government [i.e., Benjamin's state power]? I do not know of a thorough or theoretically sophisticated treatment of such issues" (Nozick 152). Given the enormity of past injustice, for example in the United States (where claims to legitimate original acquisition on the part of settlers must be seen as rather spurious, given the failure of Lockean arguments, and where slavery played such a large role in capital formation), I take Nozick's last sentence here to be an admission that this problem cannot be solved on the basis of the three principles he suggests. If anything, it questions the very idea of fair original acquisition. For a good refutation of Locke's arguments in the *Second Treatise of Government*, arguments that justify the expropriation of Native Americans by casting them in the 'state of nature,' see Tully, 137ff. Tully also summarizes the secondary literature on the topic. For a Kantian critique of Nozick's own (restrictively Kantian) grounds of exclusively negative rights and duties, see, e.g., van Wyk.

10. See Lukács.

11. Michael Ryan noted this long before *Specters of Marx*, but, generalizing to the extreme, he does not see any disagreement here between Derrida and Marx. See Ryan, 182ff.

12. For the thesis that the emergence of an objective linear time is inseparable from modern production processes, see, for example, Le Goff, "Labour-Time," and Zerubavel.—Osborne argues that Benjamin understood historicism as precisely a 'bad' response to capitalism's and modernity's 'logic of the new,' that is, as an unreflective response to the breakdown of tradition. See Osborne, 138ff. "More specifically, historicism regulates interruption as series by the generalized projection of the abstract temporality of the new onto history as a whole. On Benjamin's analysis, this creates a time in which historical events appear indifferently as 'mass-produced articles'" (ibid, 139f.).

13. Marx, *Theories of Surplus Value*, 455.

14. "On the one hand, Marx insists on respecting the originality and the proper efficacity, the autonomization and automatizations of ideality as finite-infinite processes of differance (phantomatic, fantastic, fetishistic, or ideological)—and of the simulacrum which is not simply imaginary in it" (SM 170/269). Of course, as we saw in chapter two, this admission is followed, according to Derrida's double reading, by the claim that Marx grounds the critique of fetishism in an ontology that wishes to dissipate the fetish (SM 170/269).

15. In line with the double reading outlined in chapter two, Derrida argues that the crucial distinction between use value and exchange value, a distinction on which Marx's notion of fetishism is based, may be retained if the former is understood as a "limit-concept," which, however, must be understood to be "promised to iterability" and hence to capitalization from the beginning. He then calls for a reinscription of the distinction in a "more general theory of capital" (SM 160/254).

16. See Kaulen, 121fn27. That Benjamin reads the objectivity of language and social praxis together may be seen from Benjamin's determination of the dialectical

image, for example, which is generated by historical processes but "encountered in language" (V 577).

17. See, for example, Pojman, 181–206.

18. Benjamin quotes Turgot: "politics must always foresee, as it were, the present" (V 598). See also the frequent references in the *Passagenwerk* to Bloch's concept of the "darkness of the lived moment" (V 491; II 1064) requiring not only retrospective interpretation but also an anticipation of the present as the future of the past by the historian.

19. See my "Levinas on Ethical Responsibility." Note that Derrida, who misses this difference between Benjamin and Levinas, reads both as illicitly opposing the totality of the Greek logos to Jewish categories of ethics and nonviolence (FL 973, 981).

20. For Adorno's critical comments on Benjamin's method, see his *Über Walter Benjamin*. For accounts of the Adorno–Benjamin dispute, see Buck-Morss, *Negative Dialectics*. See also her *Dialectics of Seeing* and Pensky, *Melancholy Dialectics*.

21. This practice of quoting without quotation marks, which Benjamin indeed practices often and analyzes in his essay on Karl Kraus (II 334–367), has been examined in some detail in the secondary literature. See Balfour; Konersmann; and Fänkä.

22. The connection between the 'rescue' of historical phenomena and their monadological structure goes back to Benjamin's historical theory of ideas in the Epistemo-critical Preface to the *Origin of the German Mourning-Play* (I 227ff.). I cannot go into the notoriously difficult preface here, but see Hanssen, "Philosophy at its Origin"; Kaulen, 118ff. The most comprehensive treatment of Benjamin's use of Leibniz's monad may be Nägele.

23. See Wohlfahrt, "Et cetera?" 63. Drucilla Cornell names Derrida a *chiffonier* in her *The Philosophy of the Limit*, 63.

24. Benjamin hopes to retrieve buried energies out of the lack of experience and the melancholic boredom he sees as typical of modernity. The rapid outmoding of objects in the modern, capitalist production of commodities, argues Benjamin, may release "energies which lie in what is dated [*das Veraltete*]" (II 1031). According to Benjamin, fashion is exemplary for this as it expresses the "monstrous conditions of tension in the collective" (ibid.). Thesis XIV also associates fashion with a sense of historical similarities, a "flair of the topical" that is needed in order to construct constellations of the past and the present, which, in turn, may contribute to political struggles. Benjamin sees it as surrealism's great achievement to have perceived the problem of how the misery of capitalism, not only its social misery but the misery and poverty of its architecture, interior design, the blandness of consumer culture, and so on, may contribute to a "radical revolutionary nihilism" (II 1032). Thus, in the essay on surrealism, Benjamin extends the idea of inheriting revolutionary energies from the past to the derivation of energy from the rapid outmoding and aging of consumer commodities.

25. See my "Levinas on Ethical Responsibility," 123–145.

26. Derrida, *Aporias*, 75.

27. Derrida, *Aporias*, 76.

28. In his more detailed analysis of Derrida's negotiation 'between' Levinas and Heidegger, Richard Beardsworth neglects this by misquoting Derrida, thus assimilating Derrida to Levinas's critique of the mineness of death (Beardsworth, 119).

29. Derrida, *Aporias*, 77.

30. I have demonstrated, in greater detail, this connection between violence and responsibility, as well as the fragile distinction between responsibility and responsiveness, in my "History, Violence, Responsibility."

31. Derrida, *Politics of Friendship*, 241. See also *Points* 275/289f. Heidegger discusses the 'voice of the friend' in his *Sein und Zeit*, 163.

32. See *Points*, 275/289f., and *Of Spirit*, 133.

33. Derrida, "Interview with Derrida," 198. The reference to the inhuman is at *Points* 276/290: "This said, in this regard it is perhaps more 'worthy' of humanity to maintain a certain inhumanity." See also Lyotard, *The Inhuman*. There is, however, a significant difference between Lyotard and Derrida on this thinking of an inhumanity. By contrast to Derrida, Lyotard notes the danger of confusing the "inhumanity of the system which is currently being consolidated under the name of development (among others)" with the inhumanity of time, the originary other keeping the "soul hostage": "To believe, as happened to me, that the first can take over from the second, give it expression, is a mistake. The system rather has the consequence of causing the forgetting of what escapes it" (Lyotard, *The Inhuman*, 2).

34. On Benjamin's pure language, see Derrida, "Roundtable on Translation," 123f. Regarding Heidegger, see his *Unterwegs zur Sprache*, 175 and Derrida, *Of Spirit*, 132f. This is the passage in which Derrida links this *Zuspruch* to the notion of "being-guilty" (*Schuldigsein*) and to the origin of responsibility. The clearest exposition of the link between the promise of language and responsibility is to be found in the following passage: "[B]efore determined promises, all language acts entail a certain structure of the promise, even if they do something else at the same time. All language is addressed to the other in order to promise him or her to speak to him or her in some way. . . . Before I even decide what I am going to say, I promise to speak to you, I respond to the promise to speak, I respond . . . language is there before me and, at the moment I commit myself in it, I say *yes to it and to you* in a certain manner. . . . And it is there that I am responsible before even choosing my responsibility" (*Points* 384/397f.).

35. The sentence on the 'echo' of past voices in present ones has been omitted in Zohn's translation in Walter Benjamin, *Illuminations*, 254. Citing Thesis II in *Specters of Marx*, Derrida also leaves out the sentence, but indicates the omission (SM 181/96).

36. "The affirmation of the future *to come*: this is not a positive thesis. It is nothing other than affirmation itself, the 'yes' insofar as it is the condition of all promises and of all hope, of all awaiting, of all performativity, of all opening toward the future, whatever it may be" (AF 68/109). Derrida continues to interpret this affirmation of

what I called the blind spot in the future in light of Benjamin's "Theses" that speak of the "strait gate" through which the Messiah might enter "every second" (AF 69/110). Derrida is not aware, however, that Benjamin even anticipated Derrida's specific understanding of the promise toward the messianic future, which links it back to repetition and memory, as we have seen. For in his notes to the "Theses," Benjamin writes that the "strait gait turns in the hinge called memory" (I 1252).

37. Derrida, *Aporias*, 61. For the reference to originary mourning, see also *Aporias*, 39.

38. While this otherness, as an absolute past in Derrida's sense, is not (only or primarily) manifested in the 'victims' of history for Derrida, he does link it to the spirits of the dead haunting every self as well as every political entity (Derrida, *Aporias*, 61). As we saw in the last chapter, political entities display a tendency to represent their borders as natural or pregiven due to their efforts at self-legitimation and the 'juridical fiction' covering up the spectrality of time itself. Benjamin and Derrida thus suggest that the recognition of the permeability of the border between the living and the dead helps prevent the forgetting of the nonnatural positing. 'Learning to live with specters,' in particular the specters of the past, is emblematic for the recognition of the violence that always lies in the imposition of borders and limits. In the *Politics of Friendship* and elsewhere, Derrida has articulated such awareness in the call for a hospitable democracy to come beyond supposedly 'natural' nationality and fraternity. In this way, the spirits of the dead would form a spectral alliance with women as well as with strangers, foreigners, asylum-seekers, stateless refugees, and immigrants.

39. Derrida, *Aporias*, 76 (emphasis added).

40. "The 'Thou shalt not kill'—with all its consequences, which are limitless—has never been understood within the Judeo-Christian tradition, nor apparently by Levinas, as a 'Thou shalt not put to death the living in general'" (*Points* 279/293).

41. See Derrida, *Given Time*, and Derrida, *The Gift of Death*.

42. See also Derrida, "Living On: Borderlines," 118 et passim.

43. For Derrida's elaboration of the notion of *restance*, the excessive remainder of any heritage, see "Notices (Warnings)" in *The Postcard*.

44. Derrida, "Interview with Derrida," 198.

45. See also Wetzel.

46. Derrida, "Shibboleth," 38. See also, for example, Lyotard on Adorno and on bearing "negative witness to the fact that both the 'prayer' and the history of prayer are impossible, and that to bear witness to this impossibility remains possible" (Lyotard, *Heidegger and the 'jews,'* 47).

47. See also Bennington, "Derridabase," 310: "to save the loss is to lose it as loss."

48. See Derrida, *Aporias*, 61ff.

49. "The illegitimate transition is to think that from the impossibility of a presence closed in itself, from an 'ontological' condition in which the openness to the event, to the heterogeneous, to the radically other is constitutive, some kind of ethical injunction to be responsible and to keep oneself open to the heterogeneity of the

other necessarily follows." Laclau continues that, while democracy may be defended from Derrida's perspective if "something more" is added to the argument, "a case for totalitarianism can be presented starting from deconstructionist premisses" (Laclau, *Emancipation(s)*, 77f.).

50. Fritsch, "Derrida's Democracy To Come." Bennington, who has most strongly insisted on this ethics of the lesser violence while also subscribing to the quasi-transcendental argument that relies on the logic of non-contradiction, even speaks of "something like the categorical imperative in terms of a 'lesser violence in an economy of violence,'" Bennington, *Interrupting Derrida*, 28, 201. See also Beardsworth, 46ff.

51. Comparing him with Adorno, Bernstein has tried to make this point against Derrida (Bernstein, 15f., 159).

52. Derrida, "Shibboleth," 50.

53. See Derrida's more extended treatment of the secret in "Passions," 30f.

Bibliography

Adorno, Theodor W. "Fortschritt," In *Stichworte*. Frankfurt: Suhrkamp, 1969.

————. *Negative Dialektik*. Frankfurt: Suhrkamp, 1988.

————. "Über Tradition." In *Gesammelte Schriften* 10.1. Frankfurt: Suhrkamp, 1972 ff.

————. *Über Walter Benjamin*. Frankfurt: Suhrkamp, 1990.

Agamben, Giorgio. *État d'exception: Homo sacer 2*. Paris: Seuil, 2003.

————. *Homer Sacer: Sovereign Power and Bare Life*. Translated by Daniel Heller-Roazen. Stanford: Stanford University Press, 1998.

————. *Infancy and History: Essays on the Destruction of Experience*. Translated by Liz Heron. London: Verso, 1993.

Ahmad, Aijaz. "Reconciling Derrida: 'Specters of Marx' and Deconstructive Politics." *new left review* 208 (Nov/Dec 1994).

Althusser, Louis. *Lenin and Philosophy and Other Essays*. Translated by Ben Brewster. New York: Monthly Review Press, 1971.

Anderson, Perry. *Considerations on Western Marxism*. London: New Left, 1976.

Apel, Karl-Otto. "Can 'Liberation Ethics' be Assimilated under 'Discourse Ethics'?" In *Thinking from the Underside of History: Enrique Dussel's Philosophy of Liberation*, edited by Linda Martin Alcoff and Eduardo Mendieta. New York: Rowman & Littlefield, 2000.

Arendt, Hannah. *On Revolution*. New York: Viking Press, 1963.

Avruch, Kevin, and Beatriz Vejarano, "Truth and Reconciliation Commissions: A Review Essay and Annotated Bibliography." *The Online Journal of Peace and Conflict Resolution* 4:2 (Spring 2002).

Baars, Jan, "Kritik als Anamnese: Die Komposition der *Dialektik der Aufklärung*." In *Die Aktualität der* Dialektik der Aufklärung: *Zwischen Moderne und Postmoderne*, edited by Harry Kunneman and Hent de Vries. Frankfurt: Campus Verlag, 1989.

Balfour, Ian. "Reversal, Quotation (Benjamin's History)." In *MLN* 106 (1991): 622–647.

Balibar, Etienne. *The Philosophy of Marx.* Translated by C. Turner. London: Verso, 1995.

Beardsworth, Richard. *Derrida and the Political.* London, New York: Routledge, 1996.

Benjamin, Andrew, ed. *The Problems of Modernity: Adorno and Benjamin.* London: Routledge, 1989.

Benjamin, Andrew, and Peter Osborne. *Walter Benjamin's Philosophy: Destruction and Experience.* London: Routledge, 1994.

Benjamin, Walter. *Gesammelte Briefe.* 6 volumes. Frankfurt: Suhrkamp: 1995–.

———. *Gesammelte Schriften*, volumes I–VII, edited by Rolf Tiedemann and Hermann Schweppenhäser . Frankfurt: Suhrkamp, 1972–.

Bennington, Geoffrey. "Deconstruction and the Philosophers (The Very Idea)." *Oxford Literary Review* 10 (1988).

———. "Demanding History." In *Poststructuralism and the Question of History*, edited by Derek Attridge, Geoff Bennington, and Robert Young. Cambridge: Cambridge University Press, 1987.

———. "Derridabase." In G. Bennington and J. Derrida, *Jacques Derrida.* Chicago: University of Chicago Press, 1993.

———. *Interrupting Derrida.* London: Routledge, 2000.

Bernstein, Jay M. *The Fate of Art: Aesthetic Alienation from Kant to Derrida and Adorno.* University Park: The Pennsylvania State University Press, 1992.

Blanchot, Maurice. *The Writing of the Disaster.* Translated by Ann Smock. Lincoln: University of Nebraska Press, 1995.

Bloch, Ernst. *Das Prinzip Hoffnung.* Frankfurt: Suhrkamp, 1985.

———. *Geist der Utopie: Erste Fassung.* Frankfurt: Suhrkamp, 1985.

Blumenberg, Hans. *The Legitimacy of the Modern Age.* Translated by Robert M. Wallace. Cambridge: MIT Press, 1983.

Bolz, Norbert W. *Auszug aus der entzauberten Welt: Philosophischer Extremismus zwischen den Weltkriegen.* Munich: Fink, 1989.

Borges, J. L. "Kafka and His Precursors." In *Borges: A Reader*, edited by E. R. Monegal and A. Reid. New York: Dutton, 1981.

Braunthal, Julius. *History of the Internationals*, vol. 1. London: Nelson, 1966.

Buchholz, René. "'Verschräkung von Natur und Geschichte' Zur Idee der 'Naturgeschichte' bei Benjamin und Adorno." In *"Magisches Hinzugezogensein oder schauderned Abwehr": Walter Benjamin 1892–1940*, edited by René Buchholz and A. Kruse. Stuttgart: Metzler, 1994.

Buci-Glucksmann, Christine. *Baroque Reason: The Aesthetics of Modernity.* London: Thousand Oaks, 1994.

Buck-Morss, Susan. *The Dialectics of Seeing: Walter Benjamin and the Arcades Project.* Cambridge: MIT Press, 1991.

———. *The Origin of Negative Dialectics: Theodor W. Adorno, Walter Benjamin, and the Frankfurt Institute*. New York: Free Press, 1979.

Bulthaupt, Peter, ed. *Materialien zu Benjamins Thesen "Über den Begriff der Geschichte."* Frankfurt: Suhrkamp, 1975.

Callinicos, Alex. "Messianic Ruminations." *Radical Philosophy* 75 (Jan/Feb 1996).

Caputo, John D. *Against Ethics: Contributions to a Poetics of Obligation with Constant Reference to Deconstruction*. Bloomington: Indiana University Press, 1993.

———. "On not Circumventing the Quasi-Transcendental: The Case of Rorty and Derrida." In *Working Through Derrida*, edited by Gary B. Madison. Evanston: Northwestern University Press, 1993.

———. *The Prayers and Tears of Jacques Derrida: Religion Without Religion*. Bloomington: Indiana University Press, 1997.

Celan, Paul. "Der Meridian." In *Ausgewählte Gedichte. Zwei Reden*. Frankfurt: Suhrkamp, 1996.

———. *Poems of Paul Celan*. Translated by Michael Hamburger. New York: Persea Books, 1995.

Cohen, Marshall, Thomas Nagel, and Thomas Scanlon. eds. *Marx, Justice, and History*. Princeton: Princeton University Press, 1980.

Comay, Rebecca, "Benjamin's Endgame." In *Walter Benjamin's Philosophy: Destruction and Experience*, edited by Andrew Benjamin and Peter Osborne. London: Routledge, 1994.

———. "Framing Redemption: Aura, Origin, Technology in Benjamin and Heidegger." In *Ethics and Danger: Essays on Heidegger and Continental Thought*, edited by A. Dallery and C. Scott. Albany: State University of New York Press, 1992.

———. "Redeeming Revenge: Nietzsche, Benjamin, Heidegger, and the Politics of Memory." In *Nietzsche as Postmodernist: Essays pro and contra*, edited by C. Koelb. Albany: State University of New York Press, 1990.

Cornell, Drucilla. *The Philosophy of the Limit*. New York: Routledge, 1992.

Courtois, Stéphane ed. *Le Livre Noir du Communisme: Crimes, Terreurs et Répression*. Paris: Laffont, 1997.

Critchley, Simon. "Deconstruction and Pragmatism—Is Derrida a Private Ironist or a Public Liberal?" In *Deconstruction and Pragmatism*, edited by Chantal Mouffe. London: Routledge, 1996.

———. *The Ethics of Deconstruction: Derrida and Levinas*. Oxford: Blackwell, 1992.

———. "On Derrida's 'Specters of Marx'." *Philosophy and Social Criticism* 21, no. 3 (1995).

De Man, Paul, *Allegories of Reading: Figural Language in Rousseau, Nietzsche, Rilke, and Proust*. New Haven: Yale University Press, 1979.

———. "'Conclusions': Walter Benjamin's 'The Task of the Translator'." In *The Resistance to Theory*. Minneapolis: University of Minnesota Press, 1986.

Deleuze, Gilles. *Difference and Repetition*. Translated by Paul Patton. New York: Columbia University Press, 1994.

Demmerling, Christoph. *Sprache und Verdinglichung: Wittgenstein, Adorno und das Projekt einer kritischen Theorie*. Frankfurt: Suhrkamp, 1994.

Derrida, Jacques. *Adieu à Emmanuel Lévinas*. Paris: Galilée, 1997.

———. ". . . and pomegranates." In *Violence, Identity and Self-Determination*, edited by Hent de Vries and Samuel Weber. Stanford: Stanford University Press, 1997.

———. *Aporias: Dying—Awaiting (one another at) the "limits of truth."* Translated by T. Dutoit. Stanford: Stanford University Press, 1993.

———. *Archive Fever: A Freudian Impression*. Translated by E. Prenowitz. Chicago: University of Chicago Press, 1996.

———. "At this very Moment in this Work Here I am." In *Re-Reading Levinas*, edited by Robert Bernasconi and Simon Critchley. Bloomington: Indiana University Press, 1991.

———. "Back from Moscow, in the USSR." In *Politics, Theory, and Contemporary Culture*, edited by Mark Poster. New York: Columbia University Press, 1993.

———. "Before the Law." In *Acts of Literature*, edited by Derek Attridge. London: Routledge, 1992.

———. "Déclarations d'independance." In *Otobiographies: L'enseignement de Nietzsche et la politique du nom propre*. Paris: Galilée, 1984. English translation: "Declarations of Independence" in *New Political Science* 15 (1993).

———. "The Deconstruction of Actuality." *Radical Philosophy* 68 (Autumn 1994).

———. "Des Tours de Babel." In *Difference in Translation*, edited by Joseph F. Graham. Ithaca: Cornell University Press, 1985.

———. *Edmund Husserl's Origin of Geometry: An Introduction*. Translated by J. P. Leavey. Stony Brook, NY: Nicolas Hays, 1978.

———. "Faith and Knowledge." In *Religion*, edited by Jacques Derrida and Gianni Vattimo. Stanford: Stanford University Press, 1998.

———. *Fichus. Discours de Francfort*. Paris: Gallimard, 2002.

———. "The Force of Law" In *Deconstruction and the Possibility of Justice*, edited by Drucilla Cornell et al. New York: Routledge, 1992.

———. *The Gift of Death*. Translated by D. Wells. Chicago: University of Chicago Press, 1995.

———. *Given Time: 1 Counterfeit Money*. Translated by P. Kamuf. Chicago: The University of Chicago Press,1981.

———. *Glas*. Translated by J. P. Leavey and R. Rand. Lincoln: University of Nebraska Press, 1986.

———. "Interpretations at War: Kant, the Jew, the German." *New Literary History*, 22 (1991): 39–95.

————. "Interview with Derrida." In *Logomachia: The Conflict of the Faculties*, edited by R. Rand. Lincoln: University of Nebraska Press, 1992.

————. *Limited Inc abc*. Translated by S. Weber, Evanston: Northwestern University Press, 1988.

————. "Living On: Borderlines." *Deconstruction and Criticism*, edited by Harold Bloom et al. New York: Seabury, 1979.

————. *Margins of Philosophy*. Translated by A. Bass. Chicago: University of Chicago Press, 1982.

————. *Memoirs of the Blind: The Self-Portrait and Other Ruins*. Translated by P. A. Brault and M. Naas. Chicago: University of Chicago Press, 1993.

————. *Mémoires: For Paul de Man*. Translated by C. Lindsay et al. New York: Columbia University Press, 1989.

————. *Of Grammatology*. Translated by G. Spivak. Baltimore: Johns Hopkins University Press, 1976.

————. *On the Name*. Translated by D. Wood et al. Stanford: Stanford University Press, 1995.

————. *Of Spirit*. Translated by G. Bennington and R. Bowlby. Chicago: University of Chicago Press, 1989.

————. *The Other Heading: Reflections on Today's Europe*. Translated by P. A. Brault and M. Naas. Bloomington: Indiana University Press.

————. "Plato's Pharmacy." In *Dissemination*. Translated by B. Johnson. Chicago: University of Chicago Press, 1981.

————. "+R (Into the Bargain)." In *The Truth in Painting*. Chicago: University of Chicago Press, 1981.

————. *Points . . . Interviews, 1974–94*. Edited by Elisabeth Weber. Translated by P. Kamuf et al. Stanford: Stanford University Press, 1995.

————. *The Politics of Friendship*. Translated by G. Collins. London: Verso, 1997.

————. *Positions*. Translated by A. Bass. Chicago: University of Chicago Press, 1981.

————. *The Postcard: From Socrates to Freud and Beyond*. Translated by A. Bass. Chicago: University of Chicago Press, 1981.

————. "Remarks on Deconstruction and Pragmatism." In *Deconstruction and Pragmatism*, edited by Chantal Mouffe. New York: Routledge, 1996.

————. "Roundtable on Translation." In *The Ear of the Other. Otobiography, Transference, Translation*. Translated by P. Kamuf et al. Lincoln: University of Nebraska Press, 1985.

————. "Shibboleth. For Paul Celan." In *Word Traces: Readings of Paul Celan*, edited by Aris Fioretos. Baltimore: Johns Hopkins University Press, 1994.

————. *Specters of Marx*. Translated by P. Kamuf. New York: Routledge, 1994.

————. *Writing and Difference*. Translated by A. Bass. Chicago: University of Chicago Press, 1978.

———. "The Villanova Roundtable." In *Deconstruction in a Nutshell*, edited by John D. Caputo. New York: Fordham University Press, 1997.

De Vries, Hent. *Theologie im Pianissimo & Zwischen Rationalität und Dekonstruktion: Die Aktualität der Denkfiguren Adornos und Levinas*. Kampen: J. H. Kok, 1989.

Dobbs-Weinstein, Idit. "Re-reading the *Tractatus Theologico-Politicus* in Light of Benjamin's 'Theologico-Political Fragment.'" In *Piety, Peace, and the Freedom to Philosophize*, edited by Paul Begley. Dordrecht: Kluwer, 1999.

Draper, Hal. *The 'Dictatorship of the Proletariat' from Marx to Lenin*. New York: Monthly Review Press, 1987.

Dryzek, John. *Democracy in Capitalist Times*. New York: Oxford University Press, 1996.

Dufourmantelle, A., and Jacques Derrida, *Of Hospitality*. Translated by R. Bowlby. Stanford: Stanford University Press, 2000.

Eagleton, Terry. "Marxism without Marxism: Jacques Derrida, *Specters of Marx*." *Radical Philosophy* 73 (Sept/Oct. 1995).

———. *Walter Benjamin, or: Towards a Revolutionary Criticism*. London: Verso, 1981.

Erwin, Sean. "The Political Efficacy of Prophetic Imagination in Spinoza's *Tractatus Theologico Politicus*." MS. (1999).

Ferris, David S. ed. *Walter Benjamin: Theoretical Questions*. Stanford: Stanford University Press, 1996.

Figal, Güter . "Die Ethik Walter Benjamins als Theorie der reinen Mittel." In *Zur Theorie der Gewalt und Gewaltlosigkeit bei Walter Benjamin*, edited by Güter Figal and Horst Folkers. Heidelberg: Forschungsstäte der Evangelischen Studiengemeinschaft, 1979.

Fletcher, John. "Marx the Uncanny?" *Radical Philosophy* 77 (Jan/Feb 1996).

Foucault, Michel. *The History of Sexuality*, vol. 1. Translated by Robert Hurley. New York: Vintage, 1990.

———. "Two Lectures." In *Power/Knowledge*, edited by C. Gordon. New York: Pantheon Books, 1980.

Freud, Sigmund. "Trauerarbeit und Melancholie." In *Das Ich und das Es*. Frankfurt: Fischer, 1992.

Fritsch, Matthias. "Derrida's Democracy To Come." *Constellations* 9:4 (2002): 574–597.

———. "The Enlightenment Promise and its Remains." *Human Studies* 25:3 (2002): 289–296.

———. "History, Violence, Responsibility: Some Theoretical Considerations." *Rethinking History: The Journal of Theory and Praxis*, 5:2 (2001): 285–304.

———. "Levinas on Ethical Responsibility After a History of Violence" *International Studies in Philosophy*, 32:1 (2000): 123–145. (Written under the name of Matthias Ltkehermle.)

Fünke, Josef. "Zitat und Zerstöung. Karl Kraus und W   alter Benjamin." In *Verabschiedung der (Post-)Moderne?*, edited by J. Le Rider and G. Raulet. Tübingen: Narr Verlag, 1987.

Gadamer, Hans-Georg. *Wahrheit und Methode: Grundzüge einer philosophischen Hermeneutik*. 6th ed. Tübingen: Mohr , 1990.

Gagnebin, Jeanne-Marie. *Zur Geschichtsphilosophie Walter Benjamins*. Erlangen: Palm & Enke, 1978.

Garcia Dütmann, Alexander . *Das Gedächtnis des Denkens: Versuch über Heidegger und Adorno*. Frankfurt: Suhrkamp, 1991.

———. "Tradition and Destruction: Walter Benjamin's Politics of Language." In *Walter Benjamin's Philosophy: Destruction and Experience*, edited by Andrew Benjamin and Peter Osborne. London: Routledge, 1994.

Gasché, Rodolphe. "Nontotalization without Spuriousness: Hegel and Derrida on the Infinite." *Journal for the British Society of Phenomenology* 17 (1986).

———. "On Critique, Hypercriticism, and Deconstruction: The Case of Benjamin." *Cardozo Law Review* 12 (1991): 1115–1132.

———. "Objective Diversions. On Some Kantian Themes in Benjamin's 'The Work of Art in the Age of Mechanical Reproduction'." In *Walter Benjamin's Philosophy: Destruction and Experience*, edited by Andrew Benjamin and Peter Osborne. New York: Routledge, 1994.

———. *The Tain of the Mirror: Derrida and the Philosophy of Reflection*. Cambridge: Harvard University Press, 1986.

Habermas, Jürgen. "Arbeit und Interaktion: Bemerkungen zu Hegels Jenenser Philosophie des Geistes." In *Natur und Geschichte*, edited by H. Braun and M. Riedel. Stuttgart: Kohlhammer, 1967.

———. *Der philosophische Diskurs der Moderne*. Frankfurt: Suhrkamp,1985.

———. *Theorie des kommunikativen Handelns*, vol. 2. Frankfurt: Suhrkamp, 1987. 4th ed. (Translated by Thomas McCarthy as: *Theory of Communicative Action*, vol. 2. Boston: Beacon Press, 1987.)

———. *Vorstudien und Ergänzungen zur Theorie des kommunikativen Handelns*. Frankfurt: Suhrkamp, 1984.

———. "Walter Benjamin: Bewußmachende o der Rettende Kritik." *Philosophisch-Politische Profile*. Frankfurt: Suhrkamp, 1987.

Hamacher, Werner. "Affirmative, Strike: Benjamin's 'Critique of Violence'." In *Walter Benjamin's Philosophy: Destruction and Experience*, edited by Andrew Benjamin and Peter Osborne. New York: Routledge, 1994.

———. "Des Contrées des Temps." In *Zeit-Zeichen: Aufschübe und Interferenzen zwischen Endzeit und Echtzeit*, edited by Georg C. Tholen and Michael O. Scholl. Weinheim: Acta Humaniora, 1990.

———. *Premises: Essays on Philosophy and Literature from Kant to Celan*. Translated by Peter Fenves. Cambridge: Harvard University Press, 1996.

Han, Byung-Chul. "Phänomenologie des Gespenstes." *Deutsche Zeitschrift für Philosophie*, 44 (1996).

Hanssen, Beatrice. *Critique of Violence: Between Poststructuralism and Critical Theory*. London: Routledge, 2000.

———. "On the Politics of Pure Means: Benjamin, Arendt, Foucault." In *Violence, Identity and Self-Determination*, edited by Hent De Vries and Samuel Weber. Stanford: Stanford University Press, 1997.

———. "Philosophy at its Origin: Walter Benjamin's Prologue to the *Ursprung des deutschen Trauerspiels*." *MLN*, vol. 110.4 (1995): 809–833.

———. *Walter Benjamin's Other History. Of Stones, Animals, Human Beings, and Angels*. Berkeley: University of California Press, 1998.

Hatley, James. "Celan's Poetics of Address: How the Dead Resist Their History." In *Signs of Change*, edited by Stephen Barker. Albany: State University of New York Press, 1996.

Haverkamp, Anselm. "Notes on the 'Dialectical Image' (How deconstructive is it?)." *Diacritics* 22 (Fall/Winter 1992).

Haverkamp, Anselm ed. *Gewalt und Gerechtigkeit: Derrida-Benjamin*. Frankfurt: Suhrkamp, 1994.

Hegel, Georg W. F. *Die Vernunft in der Geschichte*, edited by J. Hoffmeister. Hamburg: Meiner, 1955.

———. *System der Philosophie: Sämtliche Werke*, edited by Hermann Glockner. Stuttgart: 1927–30.

———. *Wissenschaft der Logik*, edited by G. Lasson. Hamburg: Meiner, 1952.

Heidegger, Martin. "Brief über den Humanismus." in *Wegmarken*. Frankfurt: Klostermann, 1967.

———. *Beiträge zur Philosophie (Vom Ereignis)*, *Gesamtausgabe*, vol. 65. Frankfurt: Klostermann, 1989.

———. *The Phenomenology of Religious Life*. Translated by M. Fritsch and J. A. Gosetti. Bloomington: Indiana University Press, 2004.

———. *Sein und Zeit*. Tübingen: Max Niemeyer V erlag, 1984.

———. "Vom Wesen der Sprache." In *Unterwegs zur Sprache*. Pfullingen: Neske, 1986.

Heil, Susanne. *"Gefährliche Beziehungen.": Walter Benjamin und Carl Schmitt*. Stuttgart: Metzler, 1996.

Henry, Michel. "The Concept of Being as Production." *Graduate Faculty Philosophy Journal*, 10:2.

Herman, Edward S., and Noam Chomsky. *Manufacturing Consent: The Political Economy of the Mass Media*. New York: Pantheon Books, 2002.

Hill, Thomas E. "The Message of Affirmative Action." *Social Philosophy and Policy*, 8:2 (1991).

Hobson, Marian. *Jacques Derrida: Opening Lines.* London: Routledge, 1998.

Honig, Bonnie. "Declarations of Independence: Arendt and Derrida on the Problem of Founding a Republic." *American Political Science Review* 85:1 (March 1991): 97–113.

Hörisch, Jochen. "Objektive Interpretation des Schönen Scheins." In *Walter Benjamin: Profane Erleuchtung und Rettende Kritik,* edited by Norbert W. Bolz and Richard Faber. Würzburg: Köighausen und Neumann, 1982.

Horkheimer, Max, and Theodor W. Adorno. *Dialektik der Aufklärung: Philosophische Fragmente.* Frankfurt: Fischer, 1969.

Jacoby, Russel. *Dialectic of Defeat: Contours of Western Marxism.* Cambridge: Cambridge University Press, 1981.

Jameson, Fredric. "Marx's Purloined Letter." *new left review* 209 (1995).

Jarvis, Simon. *Adorno: A Critical Introduction.* New York: Routledge, 1998.

John, Ottmar. "Fortschrittskritik und Erinnerung. Walter Benjamin als Zeuge der Gefahr." In *Erinnerung, Befreiung, Solidarität: Benjamin, Marcuse, Habermas und die Politische Theologie,* edited by Edmund Arens et al. Düsseldorf: Patmos V erlag, 1991.

Kambartel, Friedrich. *Philosophie und Politische Ökonomie.* Frankfurt: Wallstein, 1998.

Kammen, Michael. "Carl Becker Redivivus: Or, is Everyone Really a Historian?" *History and Theory* 39:2 (May 2000).

Kant, Immanuel, "Idee zu einer Allgemeinen Geschichte in Weltbürgerlicher Absicht." In *Kants Gesammelte Schriften,* edited by Königlich Preußche Akademie der Wissenschaften, Vol. VIII, Berlin: 1912–1923 (reprint by De Gryuter, Berlin: 1968).

———. *Metaphysics of Morals, Part One: Metaphysical Elements of Justice.* Translated by J. Ladd. Indianapolis: Hackett, 1999.

———. *Zur Kritik der reinen Vernunft.* Edited by Raymund Schmidt. Hamburg: Meiner, 1993.

———. *Zur Kritik der Urteilskraft.* Edited by Karl Vorländer . Hamburg: Meiner, 1993.

Kaulen, Hermann. *Rettung und Destruktion: Untersuchungen zur Hermeneutik Walter Benjamins.* Tübingen: Max Niemeyer V erlag, 1987.

Kittsteiner, Heinz Dietrich. *Naturabsicht und Unsichtbare Hand.* Frankfurt: 1980.

———. "Walter Benjamin's Historismus." In *Passagen: Walter Benjamins Urgeschichte des XIX. Jahrhunderts,* edited by Norbert Bolz and Bernd Witte. Munich: Fink Verlag, 1984.

Konersmann, Ralf. *Erstarrte Unruhe: Walter Benjamins Begriff der Geschichte.* Frankfurt: Fischer, 1991.

Korsch, Karl. *Karl Marx.* Frankfurt: Europäische V erlagsanstalt, 1967.

Koselleck, Rainer. *Vergangene Zukunft. Zur Semantik geschichtlicher Zeiten.* Frankfurt: Suhrkamp, 1979. (Translated by Keith Tribe as: *Futures Past: On the Semantics of Historical Time.* Cambridge: MIT Press, 1985.)

LaCapra, Dominick. "Violence, Justice, and the Force of Law." *Cardozo Law Review* 11 (1990).

Laclau, Ernesto. *Emancipation(s)*. London: Verso, 1996.

Laclau, Ernesto, and Chantal Mouffe. *Hegemony and Socialist Strategy: Toward a Radical Democratic Politics*. London: Verso, 1985.

Lacoue-Labarthe, Philippe. *Heidegger, Art and Politics: The Fiction of the Political*. Translated by Chris Turner. Oxford: Blackwell, 1990.

Laplanche, J., and J. B. Pontalis. *The Language of Psychoanalysis*. London: Hogarth, 1973.

Lefort, Claude. *Democracy and Political Theory*. Translated by D. Macey. Minneapolis: University of Minnesota Press, 1988.

——— . *L'invention démocratique*. Paris: Fayard, 1981.

Le Goff, Jacques. "Labour-Time in the 'Crisis' of the Fourteenth Century: From Medieval Time to Modern Time." In *Time, Work, and Culture in the Middle Ages*. Translated by A. Goldhammer. Chicago: University of Chicago Press, 1989.

Lenhardt, Christian. "Anamnestic Solidarity: The Proletariat and its *Manes*." *Telos* 25 (1975).

Levinas, Emmanuel. "Paul Celan: From Being to the Other." In *Proper Names*. Translated by Michael B. Smith. Stanford: Stanford University Press, 1996.

——— . *Otherwise than Being or Beyond Essence*. Translated by Alphonso Lingis. The Hague: Nijhoff, 1981.

——— . *Totality and Infinity*. Translated by A. Lingis. The Hague: Nijhoff, 1979.

Lindner, Burkhardt "'Natur-Geschichte'—Geschichtsphilosophie und Welterfahrung in Benjamins Schriften." *text und kritik*, vol. 31/32 (1971).

——— . *Walter Benjamin im Kontext*. Königstein: Athenäm, 1985.

Lotze, Hermann. *Mikrokosmos: Ideen zur Naturgeschichte und Geschichte der Menschheit. Versuch einer Anthropologie*, vol. III. Leipzig: Hirzel, 1909.

Löwith, Karl. *Meaning in History*. Chicago: University of Chicago Press, 1957.

——— . *Weltgeschichte und Heilsgeschehen* (1949), *Sämtliche Schriften*, vol. 6. Edited by Klaus Stichweh et al. Stuttgart: 1981–1988.

Lukács, Georg. *Geschichte und Klassenbewußtsein*. Darmstadt: Luchterhand, 1967.

Luxemburg, Rosa. *The Mass Strike*. London: Bookmarks, 1986.

Lyotard, Jean-Francois. *The Differend: Phrases in Dispute*. Translated by G. Van Den Abbeele. Minneapolis: University of Minnesota Press, 1988.

——— . *Heidegger and "the jews."* Translated by A. Michel and M. S. Roberts. Minneapolis: University of Minnesota Press, 1990.

——— . *The Inhuman: Reflections on Time*. Translated by G. Bennington and R. Bowlby. Stanford: Stanford University Press, 1991.

——— . *Political Writings*. Translated by B. Readings and K. P. Geiman. Minneapolis: University of Minnesota Press, 1993.

Macherey, Pierre. "Remarx: Derrida's Marx. Marx Dematerialized, or the Spirit of Derrida." *Rethinking Marxism*, vol. 8, no. 4 (Winter 1995).

Magnus, Bernd, and Stephen Cullenberg, eds. *Whither Marxism? Global Crises in International Perspective*. New York: Routledge, 1995.

Marcuse, Herbert. "Nachwort." In Walter Benjamin. *Zur Kritik der Gewalt und andere Aufsätze*. Frankfurt: Suhrkamp, 1965.

———. "Neue Quellen zur Grundlegung des Historischen Materialismus." In *Ideen zu einer Kritischen Theorie der Gesellschaft*. Frankfurt: Suhrkamp, 1969.

Marin, Louis. *Utopics: Spatial Play*. Atlantic Highlands: Humanities Press, 1984.

Marx, Karl. *Capital, Volume One*. Translated by B. Fowkes. New York: Vintage Books, 1977.

———. *Capital*, Volume III, edited by F. Engels. New York: International Publishers, 1967.

———. *A Contribution to the Critique of Political Economy*, edited by M. Dobb. New York: International Publishers, 1972.

———. "The Eighteenth Brumaire of Louis Bonaparte." In *Surveys from Exile*, edited by David Fernbach. New York: Vintage Books, 1974.

———. *The First International and After*. Harmondsworth: Penguin, 1974.

———. *On Revolution*. Translated by S. K. Padover. New York: McGraw-Hill, 1971.

———. *Theories of Surplus Value*. Moscow: Progress Publishers, 1971.

Marx, Karl, and Friedrich Engels. *Collected Works*. London: Lawrence and Wishart, 1975.

———. *The German Ideology*. Moscow: Progress Publishers, 1976.

———. *Marx–Engels Gesamtausgabe (MEGA)*. Berlin: Dietz Verlag, 1956.

———. *The Marx–Engels Reader*. Edited by Robert C. Tucker. New York: Norton, 1978.

———. *Marx–Engels Werke*. Berlin: Dietz Verlag, 1959.

McCole, John. *Walter Benjamin and the Antinomies of Tradition*. Ithaca: Cornell University Press, 1993.

Menke, Bettine. "Benjamin vor dem Gesetz: Die *Kritik der Gewalt* in der Lektüre Derridas." In *Gewalt und Gerechtigkeit. Derrida-Benjamin*, edited by Anselm Haverkamp. Frankfurt: Suhrkamp, 1994.

———. *Sprachfiguren: Name-Bild-Allegorie bei Walter Benjamin*. Müchen: Fink V erlag, 1989.

Menke, Christoph. *Die Souveränität der Kunst: Ästhetische Erfahrung nach Adorno und Derrida*. Frankfurt: Suhrkamp, 1991.

———. *Spiegelungen der Gleichheit*. Berlin: Akademie Verlag, 2000.

Menninghaus, Winfried. "Das Ausdruckslose: Walter Benjamins Kritik des Schönen durch das Erhabene." In *Walter Benjamin, 1892–1940, zum 100. Geburtstag*, edited by Uwe Steiner. Bern: Lang, 1992.

Missac, Pierre. *Passage de Walter Benjamin*. Paris: Éitions du Seuil, 1987.

Mitscherlich, Alexander, and Margarete. *Die Unfähigkeit zu Trauern: Grundlagen kollektiven Verhaltens*. Leipzig: Reclam, 1990.

Mommsen, Hans. "Social Democracy on the Defensive—The Immobility of the SPD and the Rise of National Socialism." In *From Weimar to Auschwitz*, translated by Philip O'Connor. Princeton: Princeton University Press, 1991.

Mosè, Stéphane. *L'Ange de l'Histoire: Franz Rosenzweig, Walter Benjamin, Gershom Scholem*. Paris: Éitions du Seuil, 1992.

———. "Emmanuel Levinas: Ethics as Primary Meaning." *Graduate Faculty Philosophy Journal* 20/21:2/1 (1998).

———. "Walter Benjamin and Franz Rosenzweig." In *Benjamin: Philosophy, Aesthetics, History*, edited by Gary Smith. Chicago: University of Chicago Press, 1989.

Nägele, Rainer. "Das Beben des Barock in der Moderne: Walter Benjamins Monadologie." *MLN* 106:3, 501–528.

Nancy, Jean-Luc. *The Inoperative Community*. Minneapolis: University of Minnesota Press, 1991.

Nassehi, Armin, and Georg Weber. *Tod, Modernität und Gesellschaft: Entwurf einer Theorie der Todesverdrängung*. Opladen: Westdeutscher Verlag, 1989.

Nietzsche, Friedrich. *Kritische Studienausgabe*, edited by Giorgio Colli and Mazzino Montinari. Berlin: de Gruyter, 1988.

———. *The Gay Science: With a Prelude in Rhymes and an Appendix of Songs*. Translated by Walter Kaufman. New York: Random House, 1974.

Nozick, Robert. *Anarchy, State, and Utopia*. New York: Basic Books, 1974.

Osborne, Peter. *The Politics of Time: Modernity and Avant-Garde*. London: Verso, 1995.

Pensky, Max. "Ghost Stories: Critical Remembrance and Justice in Derrida and Habermas." In *Phenomenology, Interpretation, and Community*, edited by Lenore Langsdorf et al. Albany: State University of New York Press, 1996.

———. *Melancholy Dialectics: Walter Benjamin and the Play of Mourning*. Amherst: University of Massachusetts Press, 1993.

———. "Tactics of Remembrance: Proust, Surrealism, and the Origin of the *Passagenwerk*." In *Walter Benjamin and the Demands of History*, edited by Michael P. Steinberg. Ithaca: Cornell University Press, 1996.

Perelman, Michael. *The Invention of Capitalism. Classical Political Economy and the Secret History of Primitive Accumulation*. Durham: Duke University Press, 2000

Peukert, Helmut. *Science, Action, and Fundamental Theology*. Translated by James Bohman. Cambridge: MIT Press, 1984.

Pfotenhauer, Helmut. "Nietzsche und Benjamin." In *Walter Benjamin im Kontext*, edited by Burkhardt Lindner. Köigstein: Athenäm, 1985.

Pojman, Louis. "The Moral Status of Affirmative Action." *Public Affairs Quarterly* 6:2 (1992).

Popper, Karl. *The Poverty of Historicism*. London: Routledge, 1960.

Protevi, John. "*Given Time* and the Gift of Life." *Man and World* 30 (1997): 65–82.

Przeworski, Adam. *Capitalism and Social Democracy*. Cambridge: Cambridge University Press, 1985.

Przeworski, Adam, and Michael Wallerstein. "Structural Dependence of the State on Capital." *American Political Science Review* 82:1 (March 1988): 11–29.

Rancière, Jacques. "The Archaeomo dern Turn." In *Walter Benjamin and the Demands of History*, edited by Michael P. Steinberg. Ithaca: Cornell University Press, 1996.

———. *Disagreement*. Translated by J. Rose. Minneapolis: University of Minnesota Press, 1999.

———. *The Names of History*. Translated by H. Melehy. Minneapolis: University of Minnesota Press, 1994.

———. *The Nights of Labor*. Translated by J. Drury. Philadelphia: Temple University Press, 1989.

Raulet, Gérard. "Benjamins Historismus-Kritik." In *Walter Benjamin, 1892–1940, zum 100. Geburtstag*, edited by Uwe Steiner. Bern: Lang, 1992.

Ricoeur, Paul. *Time and Narrative*, vol. 3. Translated by K. Blamey and D. Pellauer. Chicago: University of Chicago Press, 1988.

Roberts, Julian. *Walter Benjamin*. Atlantic Highlands: Humanities Press, 1983.

Roemer, John E. *A Future for Socialism*. Cambridge: Harvard University Press, 1994.

Rorty, Richard. "Derrida and the Philosophical Tradition." In *Truth and Progress*. Cambridge: Cambridge University Press, 1998.

———. "Is Derrida a Transcendental Philosopher." In *Essays on Heidegger and Others*. Cambridge: Cambridge University Press, 1991.

Rose, Gillian. *Mourning Becomes the Law*. Cambridge: Cambridge University Press, 1996.

———. "Of Derrida's Spirit." In *Judaism and Modernity: Philosophical Essays*. Oxford: Blackwell, 1993.

Rosenzweig, Franz. *Star of Redemption*. Translated by W. Halo. South Bend: University of Notre Dame Press, 1985.

Rosenzweig, Roy, and David Thelen. *The Presence of the Past: Popular Uses of History in American Life*. New York: Columbia University Press, 1998.

Ryan, Michael. *Marxism and Deconstruction: A Critical Articulation*. Baltimore: Johns Hopkins University Press, 1982.

de Saussure, Ferdinand. *Course in General Linguistics*. La Salle: Open Court, 1983.

Schelling, F. W. J. *System des transcendentalen Idealismus*. In *Ausgewählte Schriften*, vol. I., edited by Manfred Frank. Frankfurt: Suhrkamp, 1985.

Schmidt, Dennis J. "Black Milk and Blue." In *Word Traces: Readings of Paul Celan*, edited by Aris Fioretos. Baltimore: Johns Hopkins University Press, 1994.

Schmitt, Carl. *Political Theology: Four Chapters on the Concept of Sovereignty*, trans. G. Schwab. Cambridge: MIT Press, 1985.

Schndelbach, Herbert. *Geschichtsphilosophie nach Hegel: Die Probleme des Historismus*. Freiburg: Alber, 1974.

Scholem, Gershom. *The Messianic Idea in Judaism and Other Essays on Jewish Spirituality*. New York: Schocken, 1971.

Schweickart, David. *After Capitalism*. New York: Rowman and Littlefield, 2002.

———. *Against Capitalism*. Cambridge: Cambridge University Press, 1993.

Searle, J. R. *Expression and Meaning: Studies in the Theory of Speech Acts*. Cambridge: Cambridge University Press, 1979.

Smith, Adam. *An Inquiry into the Nature and Causes of the Wealth of Nations*. vol. 1. Indianapolis: Liberty Fund, 1981.

Sorel, Georges. *Reflections on Violence*, trans. T. E. Hulme. New York: Peter Smith, 1941.

Spinoza, Baruch. *Theological-Political Treatise*. Translated by S. Shirley. Indianapolis: Hackett, 1991.

Steiner, Uwe. "Skularisierung: Überlegungen zum Ursprung und zu einigen Implikationen des Begriffs bei Walter Benjamin." In *Walter Benjamin, 1892–1940, zum 100. Geburtstag*, edited by Uwe Steiner. Bern: Lang, 1992.

———. "'Zarte Empirie': Überlegungen zum Verhältnis von Urphänomen und Ursprung im Früh- und Spätwerk Walter Benjamins." *Antike und Moderne: zu Walter Benjamin*, edited by Norbert W. Bolz and Richard Faber. Würzburg: Königshausen und Neumann, 1986.

Szondi, Peter. "Durch die Enge geführt: Versuch über die Verständlichkeit des modernen Gedichts." In *Celan-Studien*. Franfurt: Suhrkamp, 1973.

Taylor, Charles. *Hegel*. Cambridge: Cambridge University Press, 1975.

Tiedemann, Rolf. "Historical Materialism or Political Messianism?" In *Benjamin: Philosophy, Aesthetics, History*, edited by Gary Smith. Chicago: University of Chicago Press, 1989.

Theunissen, Michael. *Hegels Lehre vom absoluten Geist als theologisch-politischer Traktat*. Berlin: De Gruyter, 1970.

Thompson, Kevin. "Hegelian Dialectic and the Quasi-Transcendental in *Glas*." In *Hegel after Derrida*, edited by Stuart Barnett. London: Routledge, 1998.

Tully, James. *An Approach to Political Philosophy: Locke in Contexts*. Cambridge: Cambridge University Press, 1993.

Unseld, Siegfried. ed. *Zur Aktualität Walter Benjamins*. Frankfurt: Suhrkamp, 1972.

van Wyk, Robert. "Perspectives on World Hunger and the Extent of our Positive Duties." *Public Affairs Quarterly* 2 (April 1988).

von Ranke, Leopold. *Über die Epochen der neueren Geschichte*. Darmstadt: Wissenschaftliche Buchgesellschaft, 1965.

Weber, Max. "Politics as a Vocation" *From Max Weber: Essays in Sociology*, translated by H. H. Gerth and C. Wright Mills. London: Routledge, 1967.

Weber, Samuel. "Deconstruction before the Name: Some Preliminary Remarks on Deconstruction and Violence." *Cardozo Law Review* 13 (1991).

——. "Genealogy of Modernity: History, Myth, and Allegory in Benjamin's *Origin of the German Mourning Play.*" *MLN* 106:3 (April 1991).

——. "Taking Exception to Decision. Walter Benjamin and Carl Schmitt." In *Enlightenments: Encounters between Critical Theory and Contemporary French Thought*, edited by Harry Kunnemann and Hent de Vries. Kampen: Kok Pharos, 1993.

Weigel, Sigrid. *Body- and Image-Space: Re-reading Walter Benjamin*. London: Routledge, 1996.

Wetzel, Michael. "Lebewohl Asche." In *Jacques Derrida, Feuer und Asche*, translated by M. Wetzel. Berlin: Brinkmann & Bose, 1988.

Wiemer, Thomas. *Die Passion des Sagens: Zur Deutung der Sprache bei Emmanuel Levinas und ihrer Realisierung im philosophischen Diskurs*. Müchen: Alber , 1988.

Willard, Dallas. "Predication as Originary Violence: A Phenomenological Critique of Derrida's View of Intentionality." In *Working Through Derrida*, edited by Gary B. Madison. Evanston: Northwestern University Press, 1993.

Wohlfahrt, Irving. "Et cetera? Der Historiker als Lumpensammler." In *Passagen: Walter Benjamins Urgeschichte des XIX. Jahrhunderts*, edited by Norbert Bolz and Bernd Witte. Munich: Fink Verlag, 1984.

——. "No-Man's Land. On Walter Benjamin's 'Destructive Character'." In *Walter Benjamin's Philosophy: Destruction and Experience*, edited by Andrew Benjamin and Peter Osborne. New York: Routledge, 1994.

——. "On the Messianic Structure of Walter Benjamin's Last Reflections." *Glyph* 3 (1978).

——. "Resentment begins at Home: Nietzsche, Benjamin, and the University." In *On Walter Benjamin: Critical Essays and Recollections*. Cambridge: MIT Press, 1988.

——. "Smashing the Kaleidoscope: Walter Benjamin's Critique of Cultural History." In *Walter Benjamin and the Demands of History*, edited by Michael P. Steinberg. Ithaca: Cornell University Press, 1996.

Wolin, Richard. *Walter Benjamin: An Aesthetic of Redemption*. Berkeley: University of California Press, 1994.

Wunder, Bernd. *Konstruktion und Rezeption der Theologie Walter Benjamins*. Wü zburg: Köigshausen & Neumann, 1997.

Zerubavel, Eviatar. "The Standardisation of Time: A Sociohistorical Perspective." *American Journal of Sociology* 88:1 (1982).

Index

247